Oil In Our Lamps

Oil In Our Lamps

The Journals of Mary Davis Brown

From the Beersheba Presbyterian Church Community
of York County, South Carolina
1854-1901

Published with permission of
The South Caroliniana Library
University of South Carolina
Columbia, SC

Printed by CreateSpace

ISBN: 1452812934
EAN: 9781452812939

FOREWORD:
The World of Mary Davis Brown

York County, South Carolina lies on the border with North Carolina in the area known as the Piedmont, the foothills of the Blue Ridge Mountains that cut across northern Georgia and the western Carolinas and Virginia. It was here, in 1822, that Mary Davis Brown was born, and it was here that she lived her entire life and where she died in 1903. During Mary's life, the Carolina Piedmont, and the South in general, underwent tremendous changes, not only in material lifestyle but in cultural, social and economic systems as well. When Mary was born, the French and Indian War, the Revolutionary War and the War of 1812 were still within living memory, and almost every family boasted at least one or two veterans of those conflicts. York County (or York District, as it was known from 1800 to 1868) was primarily a rural, agricultural area where the majority of the population grew their own food and made their own clothes. Cotton was beginning to take hold as a cash crop, but staple grains like corn, wheat and oats still dominated the landscape, and most rural families raised their own livestock on plantations of 100 to 400 acres. Slavery had been around since the earliest days of the colony, but the Carolina Piedmont had lagged behind the coastal regions in the development of large slave-owning plantations until Eli Whitney's invention of the cotton gin in 1793. After the 1820s, the number of slaves in York County and the rest of the Piedmont increased dramatically as cotton planting became more and more profitable. Mary and her husband Robert Jackson Brown were among York County's many slave owning families: in the 1850 census, they are listed as owning four slaves, and Mary frequently mentions these slaves by name in her diary.

For rural families like Mary's, the church was the center of life, and in York County that originally meant the Presbyterian Church, a legacy of the heavy settlement by Scotch-Irish Presbyterians during the last half of the eighteenth century. Mary attended Beersheba Presbyterian Church in northwestern York County, one of the four original churches established here in the 1760s. Known locally as "the four B's," these Presbyterian congregations—Bethel, Bethesda, Beersheba, and Bullock's Creek—comprised the bulk of the local Whig or Patriot militia during the American Revolution, and all four are still in existence today. If Mary Brown's diary does nothing else, it demonstrates for the modern reader just how important family and religion were for rural Southerners during the nineteenth century. Among Mary's many neighbors in the Beersheba congregation were my father's family, the Scoggins, whom she counted among her closest friends and relatives.

When Mary was ten years old, South Carolina plunged headlong into an economic and political crisis that was to have far-reaching ramifications, not only for the South but for the entire United States. The Nullification Crisis of 1832 laid the groundwork for the doctrine of secession in the South, and it solidified the growing strength of the pro-slavery political party. By the time Mary began her diary in 1854 at the age of 32, the rhetoric of secession and the preservation of slavery in the South was at the forefront of national politics. The growing abolition movement in the North forced the slave-owning South to go on the defensive, and for the second time in thirty years the talk turned to secession and war. Mary's diary occasionally highlights these national events—she mentions, for instance, the execution of the notorious abolitionist John Brown in 1859—but there is a gap between October 1860 and April 1861 covering the period of South Carolina's secession and the Battle of Fort Sumter, so we do not know how Mary felt about these events.

She does take note, however, as increasing numbers of men from her neighborhood join the state militia and then the Confederate army, including her fifty-year-old husband Robert and her sixteen-year-old son Lawson. On September 25, 1863, she writes, "this is the day my dear Husband, Robert Jackson Brown left his home and family at h[i]s countrys call to go to Charlston and was fifty the 15 of this month." In December 1864, we find an even more poignant entry: "my dear son, Lawson has left his home to go in his countryes defence the 5 of Dec 1864 on monday mornin. He is sixteen yeares one monthe and nineteen dayes ould. A wounderful thing to take such boyes out….Oh Heavenly Farther I now plead with thee and earnestily commend to thee my absent son, separited from the family circle by the call of duty to oure endangered country." Her prayers were answered, as both men survived the war and returned home. Mary also mentions important battles like Manassas, the Wilderness, and Union general William T. Sherman's march through the Carolinas, and she describes the many casualties and innumerable hardships that she and her neighbors endured during the four tragic years of the War Between the States.

Every family in the Piedmont was touched by the Civil War in some way, and York County suffered the highest per capita loss in Confederate soldiers of any county in the state. The conflict itself, however, was always far removed: the fighting raged in northern Virginia, eastern Tennessee, and Charleston, but not here. The same could not be said for the ten year period following the end of the war, the period known as the Reconstruction. Governor Robert Scott's disastrous decision in 1869 to create armed militia companies composed of former African-American slaves created a backlash among white Southerners, many of whom were veterans of the Confederate army, and by 1870 the Ku Klux Klan had begun its reign of terror in the Carolina Piedmont. What followed was a period of violence and anarchy reminiscent of the dark days of the American Revolution, culminating in President Ulysses Grant's declaration of martial law in South Carolina and the occupation of York and its neighboring counties by federal troops.

The violence peaked in 1871, affecting the lives of Mary Brown and her neighbors even more directly than the war ever had. "Oure men has been fighting the negroes down towards Chester," she notes in the entry for March 9 of that year. "Have killed some eight ore ten and taken about twenty to jaile." On October 15, she writes with trepidation, "Great excitement to day. It is reported that marshall law is declared and that the yankeyes will commence arresting the men at eney time." Two days later, we read, "Lawson, Eb & Wille Jonson, Harve Gunings, Gim Love left this morning at thre oclock fore parts unknown. …We don't know whether ever to return." Throughout these troubles she never lost her faith that God's will would prevail; eventually the men did return, and the violence did subside, but it took the election of former Confederate general Wade Hampton as South Carolina's governor in 1876 to finally end the civil strife and racial unrest that prevailed for much of the 1870s.

The year 1880 brought the dawn of a new era for York County; that year, construction began on two cotton mills, one on the Broad River at Cherokee Falls and one in nearby Rock Hill, a railroad town and cotton brokerage center that, thanks to the textile industry, was soon to become the largest city in the county. By the end of the decade, York County could boast six cotton mills and by 1910 that number had tripled, including mills in nearby York and Clover and the birth of the future Springs Industries in Fort Mill. This marked the beginning of the end for cotton farming as the dominant livelihood for York County's citizens, as the entire region embraced the rapidly expanding textile industry. Even so, many rural families like the Browns continued to rely on cotton as their major source of income until well into the twentieth century.

The textile industry supported, and was in turn supported by, the railroad industry, which during the 1850s became the dominant form of mass transportation in the South. By 1888, York County was crisscrossed by four different railroad lines, connecting it to markets and suppliers all over the Southeast. These rail systems brought prosperity and a new way of life to the nearby western York County towns of Smyrna, Hickory Grove and Sharon, as well as York, Clover, Bowling Green, Rock Hill and Fort Mill. In 1904, the year after Mary died, the Catawba Power Company completed work on the area's first hydroelectric power plant, which fueled the industrial growth and expansion of the entire Piedmont and laid the foundations for the energy giant Duke Power in the process.

Mary Davis Brown would live to see most of these developments in her lifetime, whether she commented on them or not: civil war and the destruction of the Old South, the demise of slavery and cotton farming, the rise of railroads and cotton mills, telephones, automobiles and even electricity. By the time of Mary's death, life for much of York County had undergone a major transformation, although for country folk like her and her family much remained the same: the change of the seasons, planting and harvesting, going to church, spending time with family and friends—these things endured. Fortunately for us, her diary survives as a rare and heartfelt window into the rural South of the nineteenth century, a time when faith in God and the good earth were still the pillars of family life.

Michael C. Scoggins
Historian
Culture & Heritage Museums
York County, SC
March 2009

INTRODUCTION
Barbara Courtney Thomas

What would Mary Davis Brown say to us, her descendants, if she were alive today? Would she be appalled that we are revealing the contents of her diaries, putting them in print for all to read? Or would she be honored and humble, saying that her simple efforts at penning her thoughts aren't worthy of so much attention?

But Mary Davis Brown has no say in this decision. We, her descendents, have assumed this responsibility because we realize that her words are more than worthy of being preserved and shared. We believe that we are not only honoring her but are helping make the history of her era richer, more complete.

Mary would not want to be called a saint. Her writings reflect her humility and faithful dependence on God for strength to face life's challenges. She led a simple life, but she was not a simple person. Amazing in her ability to express herself with her limited education, she remains a paragon of her time.

When Mary died in 1903, she was living with her youngest living son, William Given Brown, and his wife, Minnie in the Bersheba Presbyterian Church community outside of York, South Carolina. William, "Willie," as she called him, often read the diaries, usually on Sunday afternoons, and kept them in his mother's old trunk. William and Minnie moved to Liberty Street in York in approximately 1915, and the diaries went with them. William died in 1932 and Minnie in 1951, and the trunk containing the diaries, the old family photo albums, and other family mementos were entrusted to Rob, the oldest son of William and Minnie who lived outside of York. Rob stored the trunk in his well house. At Rob's death in 1958, his sister, Kate Thomas, moved the trunk to her home in Clover.

The family was aware of the delicate condition of the books, some over 100 years old. The writing had faded and some of the books had come apart. Dewey Gentry, one of Mary's many great grandchildren and a high school social studies teacher, realized the historical value of the books. He suggested that the diaries be donated to The South Caroliniana Library on the University of South Carolina campus. After investigating this possibility and conferring with the family, it was decided to do this. In the spring of 1966, the diaries were entrusted to Barbara Courtney Thomas, another great grandchild of Mary who lived in Columbia and was also a teacher. After she carefully catalogued and organized the nine volumes, she presented them to the library. They were immediately stored in a fireproof, humidity and temperature controlled vault. Eventually they were photographed on microfilm. Because of their delicate condition, the actual books are no longer available to researchers, but the microfilms can be viewed at the library. The South Caroliniana Library appreciates the opportunity of housing and protecting the diaries, realizing how much they enrich the primary sources available concerning the history of York County and the state of South Carolina.

It was the wish of the family that the diaries be published, and in 1990 steps were taken to begin the process. With permission by the family, Jerry West of Sharon, South Carolina and president of the Broad River Basin Historical Society began the work of transcribing the diaries from copies of the microfilm. At that time one important volume was missing, the one from the Civil War years. Fortunately it was located by Maurice Allsing, another descendent of Mary Davis Brown, who obtained a copy and gave it to the library. In 2004 the Mary Davis Brown Diaries Publication Committee was organized to finish the transcriptions and prepare the manuscript for publication. All members of the committee are descendents of Mary Davis Brown.

Kenneth Talley
Betty Talley Stevens
Esther Talley Dean
Barbara Courtney Thomas
Joy Courtney Brown
Catherine Brown Michael
Rebecca Thomas Chambers
Dorothy Thomas Berry

Several members of the committee helped with transcribing various portions of the diaries. Cathy Michael and Becky Chambers assumed the massive tasks of editing, researching people's names, providing extensive endnotes for clarification, and final typing of the manuscript. Since it was decided to leave spelling and grammar exactly as Mary wrote it, much proofreading was necessary.

As we see the culmination of this long-awaited project, we are relieved yet gratified that we had the opportunity to put into print a book that will not only be valuable to the hundreds of descendents of Mary Davis Brown, but will add enrichment to the history of South Carolina. We are honored and fortunate to have descended from this outstanding woman. If she were here, we believe she would smile on our efforts.

Barbara Courtney Thomas
Gr. Grandaughter of
Mary Davis Brown

Oil In Our Lamps

BACKGROUND
Catherine Brown Michael

In October, 1854, Mary Davis Brown began recording her thoughts, poetry, prayers and daily activities in a rural community of York County, South Carolina. She was thirty-two years old. She was a wife to Robert Jackson Brown, a mother to seven children, and a caretaker and teacher to the small family of five slaves who lived and worked alongside her on the family farm.

Mary was a constant, devoted member of her beloved Beersheba Presbyterian Church. Living next door to the church enabled her to attend nearly every service, missing only because of her own illness or that of a family member. Only rarely did the weather keep Mary away from church. For a short time she did not attend because her beliefs and convictions were in direct contrast with the minister. She constantly prayed for guidance during his one-year term of service.

Mary was a daughter of William and Dorcas Brown and a sister to seven siblings, all of whom lived in the area. Since she married her first cousin, she was a sister-in-law as well as a cousin to a larger, extended family, and their home was a frequent gathering place for that family, many neighbors, and visiting ministers.

As she put her pen to paper on that particular day in October, 1854, she was writing to express her pain and tremendous sadness at losing her young son, eight-year-old William Given Brown. We don't know the cause of his death but feel through her words the heartache of losing a precious child. We learn that her faith in the Lord provided the solace and strength needed to face another day. We have no record or knowledge that she kept a diary before this date, but from that day forward Mary shares with us her family and the people and events that make up the fabric of her life.

Mary Davis Brown was born in York County on March 21, 1822, to William and Dorcas Floyd Brown. William, known as "Uncle Billy" in the community, migrated with his mother and two brothers to York County in 1790. He was born in 1767 in Cecil County, Maryland to John and Jane Vance Brown. In 1759, the Browns, with one daughter, Jane, emigrated from Ireland, possibly County Antrim in Northern Ireland. Oral family history has it that John Brown, Jr. was born aboard ship, and Robert and William were later born in Maryland. Other children were Margaret, Sarah and Hannah, and we know very little about them.

When William was seven years old, the family moved west to the adjacent county, Hartford, where he lived until he was twenty-three. While in Maryland, William was a member of Bethel Presbyterian Church which is located near the Pennsylvania line in Madonna, Maryland. The church was founded in 1769, and its old graveyard contains many graves of York County ancestors, many unmarked.

William's father, John, died in March 1786, leaving one-half of his property, "Brown's Choice," to his wife, Jane, and son, Robert. The other half he left to sons John, Jr. and William. Daughter Jane had married John Black and had moved to York County with their children, John and Jane. Shortly after John Brown, Sr.'s death, the family had the property surveyed and leased it to Shadrack Rutledge.

The history of the Bethel Presbyterian Church states that in mid-1780, a large group of younger members migrated to South Carolina, most likely due to the poor soil and farming conditions in Maryland. Surnames such as Allison, Turner, Bell, Vance, Meek and Black are among those who migrated to York District and later intermarried with the Browns of York County. William, his mother Elizabeth Jane, and brothers John, Jr. and Robert were among those who migrated southward, eventually settling near Bullock Creek, a tributary of the Broad River in York County. Jane Brown lived to be ninety-five and is buried in the church yard of Bullock Creek Presbyterian Church.

In 1806 William Brown married Mary Davis. It is not known who her parents were. Mary bore seven children and five lived to adulthood. Elijah Davis

Brown died in October, 1817, at age eight months, and is buried alongside his grandmother, Jane Brown, in the Bullock Creek Churchyard.

In 1818 William purchased 200 acres on the headwaters of Fishing Creek, about three miles north of Yorkville, and moved his family there. The land is located in the present day community of Filbert. After the move, Mary became pregnant with their seventh child. In April, 1819 both died at the child's birth. By this time the family had joined Beersheba Presbyterian Church, and Mary and the child were buried in the Beersheba Churchyard.

William was left a widower with five young children. In those days, it was typical for a widower with young children to remarry soon after losing his wife. William followed this practice, and in 1820 married Dorcas Tabitha Floyd who was twenty-four years his junior.

Dorcas was the middle child of Andrew and Nancy Gordon Floyd. Andrew was a Revolutionary War veteran, having fought in many campaigns, most notably the Battle of Kings Mountain. He was a successful farmer and wheelwright and made his home on the west side of Henry's Knob at the present day border of Gaston County, NC and York County, SC. He was an elder at Bethel Presbyterian Church, having been one of the three men who chose the site for the church in 1786.

Less than a year after their marriage, a child was born to William and Dorcas Brown. They named her Mary Davis in memory and honor of his first wife. Two years later, another girl named Ann was born, but not before young Margaret, William's first born, was married at age sixteen to John Floyd, Dorcas Brown's brother. Two more girls, Harriet and Sarah, were born to William and Dorcas whose family now numbered eight children.

Oral family history says that Mary had a "third grade education." Clearly, her diary entries show that she had some type of formal education. She read the newspaper, the Bible, and books on the catechism. She may have attended one of the local academies that existed in the mid-1800's. Her mother, Dorcas, could not write, having signed an "x" to legal documents. All evidence shows that William Brown was literate. He was an elder in the church. Both of William's brothers were appointed constables for a year. When each died, books were listed among their possessions.

On November 14, 1839, Mary, at age seventeen, married her first cousin Robert Jackson Brown. He was twenty-four. Jackson or R. J. as he was often called was the youngest son of Robert Brown (William's brother), and Mary Given Brown. Robert must have been more affluent than his brother William to have acquired more property, built a larger home, and served his community in various appointed positions, but there is no record that he was ever elected elder at any church.

Robert Brown owned approximately 400 acres of land adjacent to Beersheba Presbyterian Church, between Bullock and Buck Horn Creeks, and about five miles west of the town of York. In 1820 he built a home on this land. The census for that year shows that he was a farmer with seven slaves. He listed his occupation as saw and grist mill owner. At his death in 1835 he left a comfortable estate to his wife, Mary Given Brown, and his children. He deeded 200 acres to his eldest son, William C. Brown. To his widow, he left a life estate in the home place. He left the balance of his land to his youngest son, Robert Jackson.

A year after his mother died in 1838, Robert Jackson and Mary Davis Brown were married and she moved to R. J.'s home where she lived for all but the last two years of her life. Her closest neighbors were her cousins who became upon her marriage also her in-laws. Living on land adjacent and just up the hill to the south of R. J. and Mary was brother William C. Brown and wife, Catherine Cain Brown. On the other side was sister Hannah Brown and husband George Franklin Ferguson. Dr. Good and Rev. William B. Davies dwelt on nearby properties. In the same community were other extended family members, the Turner and Burns families.

Marrying a first cousin makes it difficult to sort out the various connections. However, it's clear from the census records and Mary's diaries that her most common day to day interactions were with her husband's siblings. Brother William C. and his wife, Katherine Cain Brown were referred to as "Unckle" Billy and Aunt Caty. Emily Brown and husband, William Rooker Alexander were called Emily and yet another "Unckle" Billy. Sister Hannah Brown and her husband, George Franklin Ferguson are called Aunt Hannah and Frank.

In 1854 Mary and R. J.'s family included the following children: Emily, 12; Harriet, 10; Lawson, 6; Sallie, 4; and Maggie, 18 months. Mary is four months pregnant with daughter, Jaily Cate. Also living with the family is Mary Jane Brown, age 12, R. J.'s niece, the daughter of John Given and Sarah Good Brown, both of whom had died within months of each other in 1849.

R. J. Brown was a yeoman farmer who grew cotton and other crops. The 1850 census shows him as having an estate valued at $1,000 for real property and owning four slaves: a black male, age 28, a black female, age 26, a black female, age 15, and a black female, age 4.

When we first hear Mary's voice through her diary in 1854 she was typical of many women her age in York County. Most families lived on farms of varied sizes, typically ranging from 200 to 500 acres. Her life was lively and busy with many of the ups and downs we face today. Illness, unforeseen circumstances and political debate on the more pressing topics of the day, particularly slavery, were intermingled with the more joyous themes of daily life such as church singings, picnics, weddings and worship services.

It would be a mistake to see Mary as confined to the farm and wedded to the hard work of an agrarian life. She often traveled to Yorkville for shopping, visiting friends and picking up news and gossip. She read the local newspaper, "The Yorkville Enquirer." Frequently, she traveled and visited with family and friends. When she records a visit, she always says, "I went …" or "I visited …" We do not know whether she drove the wagon alone when she made her travels up to Crowder's Creek or Bethel or Yorkville.

The diary of Mary Davis Brown gives her descendants and anyone interested in the history of upstate South Carolina a unique snapshot as she matured from a young mother to a wise sage and observer of the world around her.

Catherine Brown Michael
Gr. Gr. Grandaughter of
Mary Davis Brown

OIL IN OUR LAMPS

The Journals of Mary Davis Brown

1854

Thou art gone to rest in a lonley bed
Sweet form of my lovely child
In the silent grave rests thy little head
And hushed is thy voice so mild
Asleep in Jesus blessed sleep
From which none ever wakes to weep.

William Given Brown departed this life Octoba the 6 on fryday evening
at 6 oclock 1854

So William lives but not whare time
Is measuread out by woes
Not whare cold winter chills the clime
Ore cancor eats the rose.

unknown

Thou art gone to the grave, I now longer behold thee
Nore tread the rough path by thy side
But the wide arms of mercy are spread to enfold thee
And siners may hope since the sinless has died.

Thou art gon to the grave but twase rong to deplore thee
When God was thy ransom, thy gurdan and guard
He gave thee and took the and soon will restore thee
Where death has no sting sence the saiviour has died.

[October 9, 1854 was a Monday] This day is tusday of court Oct the 9 1854. A calm and solem day it has been to me, thinking of my lovely son and in trying to prepare to meet my God and him in another and better wourld. Open the bars of my preson that my eager soul may spring forth to thee and cast itself at thy feet, at the feet of that Jesus whome having not seen, I love, and in whome thou now I see the not; yet beleving, I rejoice with joy unspeakabel and full of glory. Mary D Brown

When in thy lonley bed
Lovely William thou art lying
When joyful wings are spread
To Heaven thy joyful soul has fled
Would I to sin and pain
Call back that dear soul of thine again
No dearest Jesus no
To thee dear Saiviour let his free spirit go
Ransomed fore ever more.
unknown

[November 18, 1854-Saturday] November the 18 this is a cold, dark and stormy night reminds me of the long night of darkness that awaits the wicked siner. Oh my Lord, I pray thee that it may never be my case; oh, that I may allways have before my eyes that I am born to die and be prepard fore that change.

Oh by how weak and frail a thing
May the hearts deapth be stird
How close and long will memerry cling

To one light look ore word
Well he is happy now dear children
His ransomed soul has fled
He feels no more earths hollow joys
Or real misery
I strove indeed to breath thy will be done
But it was hard to say
Nature clings hard and fast
To such a child as dear William was

[December 6, 1854-Wednesday] Dec the 6 Too months this night since William left this wourld of sin and sorrow; as I humbly hope and trust to go that bllesed Saivour who, in his humain flesh, took little children in his arms and blessed them and said, "Of such is the kingdom of Heaven." He is landed on that peaceful shore where the stormes of trouble never blow; he is forever out of the reach of sorow, sin, temptation and snares. Now he is before the throne, singing the sweet songs of reediming love forever more.

[December 25, 1854–Monday] December the 25 this is christmas day. We are caled this morning to bhold thee exceeding riches of thy grace in thy kindness towards us by Christ Jesus. May we contemplate this matchless event with all those views and effections whitch its importance demands. Mary D Brown

[December 26, 1854-Tuesday] December the 26 this is the day that Elen and Hardy was married. Their has been too born, too married and one died in my family this year. But thou hast commanded us to remember all thy ways which thou hast led us in this wilderness. The seen of our journing has indeed been a wilderness. But the hand that has conducted us is divine. Thou hast corected us; but it is of the Lords mercies we are not consumed. I have had my afflictions, but how few have they been in number, how short in continuance, how alievi-ated in degree, how merciful in design, how instructive, and useful in their result. It is good fore me that I have been afflicted.

[December 29, 1854-Friday] December the 29 this is the day that James Vic-ers was hung fore stabing Daubson.[1] Great is our warefair, great is our work; and far greater than ever I expected it to bee, is my weekness, but my suffiency is of God.

[December 31, 1854-Sunday] Dec the 31 sabeth knight. My Heavenly Farther, I appear before thee this knight to close another of periods of my fleting existince, earnistingly praying that this seasen may not pass away without suitibel and serries refflections. O, let me not imagen, in spite of scripture and observation and reasin and feelings, that I have many of those perieds to notice. But may I say with Job of ould, "When a few years is come, I shall go the way whence I shall not return." It may bee only a few months ore weeks ore days ore hours, fore I know not at what hour the sone of man cometh. I have felt like this is the last year that I will bee a travler in this willderness of sin and sorrow and if so, I humbly trust and hope that I may be prepared to meet my God with the bright robe of Christ richeness. MDBrown

[1854 Births, Marriages and Deaths]
Mimays John was born Aprile the 6 1854
Betsey Cains Louisa was born May the 9
Toms ben died June the 16
Elens Martha was born July the 5
Elizabeth Cains Louisa died Sept the 1
Robbert Alexander and Mary J Brown was married Sept the 14 1854
The Reverent Mr Boles preached at Bershaba on the 19 of Nov
Jane Dickey died the 28 of Nov

1855

[January 1, 1855-Monday] January the 1 1855 As I have enterd new peried of life, may I faithfuly examen myself to see whats been amiss in my former temper or conduct; and in thy strenth may I resolve to corect it. And may I enquire fore the future with a full determination to render my knowledge to practice. Lord, what will Thou have me to doo? Prepare me fore the duties of thee ensuring year, all the wisdom and strenth nessary, fore the performance of them must come from thee. May I theirefore live a life of self distrest, of divine dependence and of prayer. May I ask and receive, that my joy may be full. May I live in the spirrit. If I am indulged with prospreity, O let not prosperity destroy me ore injure me. If I am affected with adversity, suffer me not to sink in the hour of trouble or sin against God. May i know how to be abased without despaire and to abound without pride. If my relatives com-forts are continued to me, may I love them without adrolitry and hold them at thy disposal, and if they are recold from me, may I be enabeled to say, "The Lord gave and the Lord hath taken, and blesed be the name of the Lord."

Newyears evening Cathern Brown is verry bad. They have Dr Alison and Dr Good both with her. Mr Syras Jonson died January the 25 1855.

[February 21, 1855-Wednesday] Feb the 21 Farther and Mother has come over to day and is gone down to see Mr Davis. [2]

[February 25, 1855-Sunday] Sunday 25 this is preachen day, but Mr Davis is not abel to preach to day.

[March 3, 1855-Saturday] March the 3 satturday morning This is the day Jaly Catharine was born.

[March 7, 1855-Wednesday] wensday the 7 Emily, Lawson and Sally is all bad with the new mony.

[March 9, 1855-Friday] friday 9 this is the day of the great wind and fire.[3]

[March 11, 1855-Sunday] Sunday the 11 this is the last day that Mr Davis preached. He preached his last sermon at bershaba, I was not theire. Mimmas John died wensday the 21 1855, nelly is verry bad at this time.

Mr Davis died March the 25 1855, Sunday night and was burried at bershaba church on tusday. Theire was a large congaration theire. Mr Samuel Watson preached his funeral sermon. Mr Monroe Anterson gave a prayer. Mr Watson red the 90 Psalm and then sung a funeral himn "Hark from the tomb." His tex was in Reverlations the 14 chapter and the 13 verse, these are the words. "And I heard a voice from Heaven saying unto me Write Blessed are the dead that die in the Lord from hnce forth yea saith the spirit that they may rest from theire laboures and theire works do follow them." Then a hymn on the death of a paster. " Now let our mourning hearts revive." Mary D Brown

[April 1, 1855-Sunday] Aprile the first. Lawson, Hannah and the baby is all sick.

[April 4, 1855-Wednesday] wensday the 4 the children is nearly all down with the scarlet fever. Mary Jane Alexander died Aprile the 9 on Monday 1855 and was buryed at bershaba grave yard. [4]

[April 12, 1855-Thursday] thursday the 12 we have all got better once more.

[April 13, 1855-Friday] friday 13 Lawson has relapts in the scarlet fever and is verry bad to day. I have been over to see Farther. He has been bad with a pain in his hench and foot but it is got better now.

[April 22, 1855-Sunday] Aprile sunday the 22 I have been at another com-

munion at bershaba to day. Mr Watson gave us fine preaching. I have witnessed many and solem sights sence I last was theire. On that ocasion the aged and the young have gone forth to meet the bridegroom to heare theire sentence. Whether preprard ore unprepaird, they must go. Oh Heavenly Farther I pray thee that thou will give me a pure and clean heart that I may be prepared fore that day and hour.

[April 26, 1855-Thursday] 26 we have all got abel once more to be up and about. We have had too months of wounderful sickness. Oh God, all of our times is in thy hand, all diseases come at thy call and go at thy bidding. Though redeemest oure life from distruction and crownest us with loving kindness and tender mercies. We bless the that thou hast heard our prayers and commanded delliverance to those that has been under thyne afflictive hand. Thou has chastened us; but not delliverd us over to death and may we ever remember that a recoverry is only a reprieve. That the sentence dooms us to the dust is only suspended; and that at most, when a few yeares are come, we shall go the way whence we shall not returne. May we theirefore secure the one thing needful, and live with eternity in view.

Nanny Cain died June the 1 a friday 1855.

[June 3, 1855-Sunday] June the 3 sabeth evening Mr James Adams preached at bershaba to day and I was theire. He gave us great preachen. His morning tex was in Psalms 119 chapter and 126 verse, these are the words: "Thy testimonies are wounderful, theire fore doth my soul keep them." His evening tex was in Ezekiel 33 chapter and the 11 verse: "Say unto them as I live, saith the Lord God, I have no pleashure in the death of the wicked, but that the wicked turn from his way and live: turn ye, turn ye from your evil ways; fore why will ye die o house Isriel." Oh Lord, may not this holly sabeth day pass unimprooved; awaken, O Lord, in my concience the inquiry, how shall I escape if I neglect so great salvation. But Oh God, the effects I experrience while waiting uppon the, though delightful, are as often transitory and like the morning cloud and early dew beffore the laps of a singel day. I am compeled to complain. My Soul cleaveth unto the dust. Quicken Thou me according to thy word. Render theirefore the impression made upon me deep and durabel. Keep thees things forever in the imagination of my heart, and let thy word dwell in me richely and prepare me fore rest that remains fore thy people. Mary D Brown June 3

Child of man whose seed bllow
Must fulfil theire race of woe
Heir of want and dust and pain
Dose thy fainting heart complain

Oh in thought one night recall
The knight of griefe in Herrieds hall
Theire I bore the vengence due
Freely bore it all fore you.

When this you see rember me if you on earth no more i see.

[June 24, 1855-Sunday] June the 24 Mr Dougless has preached at bershaba to day. His morning tex was in seckond Timothy 2 chapter and 19 verse. "Nevertheless the foundation of the Lord standeth shure having this seal. The Lord knoweth them that are his, and let every one that nameth the name of Christ depart from iniquity."

[June 28, 1855-Thursday] June 28 I have been over on a visit at my Farthers. They are all well except himself. He says theires but one step between him and the grave. And it will be a glorrious change fore him, from pain and sickness to a place prepared fore him and that long and wait fore his coming.

[July 15, 1855-Sunday] July the 15 I have been to Center[5] to day at a Communion.[6] Mr Watson preached, tex 2 corrinthians 4 chapter and 5 verse. I saw Cousin Chambers Floyd and his wife and Margaret Floyd.

[July 21, 1855–Saturday] July 21 Asel Enloe preached at Mrs Cains. His tex was in luke the 13 chapter the 3 and 5 verses.

[July 22, 1855-Sunday] July the 22 1855 Asel Enloe preached at bershaba July 22 1855. His tex was in Romans 9 chapter and 32 verse. His evening tex was in Mathew 13 chapter and 4 5 6 7 8 verses. He done better than was expected by the people. Theire was none of Mrs Davis family theire. MD Brown

[July 31, 1855-Tuesday] tusday the 31 My dear ould Farther has been over to day. He has not been here in a long time before. Everry time he comes over i think it will be the last time; but theire hase been many a stout and hearty one gone sence then.

[August 3, 1855-Friday] August the 3 this is the day Sister Eliza Duff and James, came in from tenisee[7] on a visit to see all of theire friends in south carolina.

[August 9, 1855-Thursday] thursday the 9 i have been up on a visit at crowders creek to see Henry and Jane and took sister Eliza up theire and left her theire.

[August 17, 1855-Friday] August the 17 this is the day oure communion commencis at bershaba. Mr Alexander Banks preached to day. His tex was in Luke 16 chapter and 15 verse. Mr William Banks preached to day. Sister Eliza Duff and James and sister Jane Glenn here and theire is preachen at amis burnses to night.

[August 26, 1855-Sunday] August 26 Mr Dow preached at bershaba to day. He preached to the young people in the morning. His tex was in proverbs the 8 chapter and 17 verse. These are the words. "I love them that love me, and those that seek me early shall find me." He seems to bee a great preacher. The people is powerfully taken with him.

[September 13, 1855-Thursday] September 13 I have been over to Farthers to day to see sister Eliza and the rest of them and they are all well and sister Eliza is gone to start home in a few days

[September 15, 1855-Saturday] saturday the 15 this is the day that sister Eliza and James started home and we all met at york the night beffore. And theire was about 25 of us went on the car with her as fare as chester and took dinner in the depo and then we parted. It may be the last time that we will ever meet ore part in this wourld.

[September 28, 1855-Friday] 28 i have been over to see my Farther and Mother. They have not been well but is better now.

[September 30, 1855-Sunday] Sunday the 30 we have no preachen to day. We have not got a preacher yet but we are in hopes that we will have the revernt Mr Dow beffore long.

[October 4, 1855-Thursday] Oct the 4 Jackson is gone up to the great celabration at Kings mountain sence yesterday morning.[8]

[October 6, 1855-Saturday] saturday evening Oct the 6 this evenging twelve months sence my deare little William bid adiew to all the trials and troubels of this wourld.

[October 7, 1855-Sunday] Oct 7 this evening twelve months agoe sence my sone was laid in the cold and silent grave, theire to rest till the morning of the reserection when I hope and pray that we will all meet on Christs right hand, an unbroken family to part no more. And O God I pray through the interces-sion of Christ that it may not be in vain. I pray that though woulds aid and assist us all in fulfilling the part that though hast appointed us. While travling through this wourld of tears, be a wall on our right and left hand. The time is short, the seasen neare, when death will us remove.

[October 22, 1855-Monday] Oct 22 I have been over to see my Farther. He has been bad with the chills and fever. He cant stand them long if he cant git them stopped.

[October 28, 1855-Sunday] Oct 28 sabeth evening. Mr Adams preached at bershaba to day 1 Timithy 1 chapter and 15 verse. Our expatations has all been blasted about gitting Mr Dow to preach to us, but we will live in hopes that we will have one yet.

[November 1, 1855-Thursday] Nov the 1 this is the day Newton Vickers got out of jaile.

[November 2, 1855-Friday] Nov the 2 1855 Mr Wilsons negro girl was hung fore poising his child. Mary D Brown

[December 16, 1855-Sunday] Dec the 16 Mr Ervin preached at bershaba to day. He is a begging money fore to pay fore the female collage in yorkvill.[9] His tex was in John the 3 chapter and 16 verse. MD Brown

[December 17, 1855-Monday] Dec 17 Jackson and I have been up at Ould Mr Enloes to see Isiick Enloe. He has been in this cuntry on a visit. He is to start back in a few days.

[December 20, 1855-Thursday] Dec the 20 this is the day that Isic Enloe started fore the Missippi and Henry Duff and Jane Riddel came in from tenessee.

[December 24, 1855-Monday] Dec 24 Hiram, Harriet and the children came over and took christmust with us.

[December 29, 1855-Saturday] Dec 29 Jackson, me and the children has been over to Farthers.

[December 30, 1855-Sunday] Dec 30 Lawson and Jane and Henry Duff came home with us and stayd all night and John Cain from alabama was here the same night.

[December 31, 1855-Monday] Dec 31 this is the last day of 1855 and it is fast day too and I had a crowd fore dinner too. Franklin Cane was here too. This closes another of the fleetting time. Theire has been many an aking head, sick heart and broken spirriet sence this yeare came in and many a one gone to theire long home to give an acount of theire stewerd ship. Only think of the bodies that lies mouldring in the dust and be admonshed. Think how evalalel must be the immortal soul, sence the pitty of the emackulate son of God was so much concernd in its behalf. Think of the vanity of earthly things and of the shortness of life. Oh think of eternity and be wise. Mary D Brown Dec 31 1855

1856

[January 1, 1856-Tuesday] January the 1 day 1856 A new years day we are all weel and at home and have need to thank the Lord fore his goodness in tacken care of us throu all the chainging senes of the last year, and in bringing us saffley through all the trials and troubels that I have been caled to wade throu.

[January 4, 1856-Friday] friday night the 4 this is the night of the big snow.[10]

[January 9, 1856-Wednesday] wensday the 9 Jackson has gone over to stay with Duff to night. This is the last night he will be in this country.

[January 10, 1856-Thursday] he started home the 10 day. Jackson has gone up to Robert Alexanders to see John Alexander run out his land.

[January 12, 1856-Saturday] saturday the 12 we had another big snow last night.

[January 15, 1856-Tuesday] tusday night the 15 Marth Meek had a fine son.

[January 18, 1856-Friday] Friday the 18 we had the Rev Mr Grady with us last night and Jackson has gone with him to Mr Burns.

[January 20, 1856-Sunday] Sunday the 20 Mr Grady preached at bershaba to day.

[January 30, 1856-Wednesday] Ould Ammy Cain died the 30 day of this month.

[February 3, 1856-Sunday] Febuary the 3 this is another snowey morning and Hiram and Buttler was her last night and they have gone home in the snow. MD Brown

[February 8, 1856-Friday] Martha Coldwell died Febuary the 8 and was Friday.

[February 23, 1856-Friday] 23 we had a great singing[11] here last kight and we had plenty of company. Billy Gimison was here this morning fore the last time.

[February 24, 1856-Sunday] sunday evening the 24 I have just got home from billy Gimison. I have been down to see them fore the last time. They are all going to the Mississipia.

[February 28, 1856-Thursday] William Gimison and family started fore the Missippia Febuary the 28 1856.

[March 16, 1856-Sunday] March the 16 I have been to heare the Revern Mr Boles. The Revernt Mr James A Davis preached his first sermon that he preached at Bershaba March the 16 1856. His tex was in Philipans 1 chapter and the 27 verse, this is the words: "Only let your conversation be as it becomith the Gospel of Christ: that whether I come and see you or else be absent, I may heare of youre affairs, that ye stand fast with one spirrit, with one mind striving together fore the faith of the gospel." I was verry hilly pleased with him and all the congration too. Mary D Brown

Mr Jeramiah Dawson was burried at bershaba sattuarday the 12 of Aprile. He was brought from Collumbia the same day he was burried. Catherin Enlo died Monday the 22 of Aprile. Mr Kurkendall died Monday the 28 of Aprile and was burried at Bershaba grave yard and Mr Lester, the Methidist preacher, preached a funeral sermon. His tex was in Job, "The Lord gave and the Lord taketh away and blesed be the name of the Lord." Mary D Brown

Elens baby was born the 25 of Aprile. It was dead born, a fine looking boy.

[June 1, 1856-Sunday] June the 1 I have been over to see Farther today. He is as well as common.

[June 8, 1856-Sunday] 8 I have been at preachen at bershaba to day and billy and Emily came home with me.

[June 10, 1856-Tuesday] Midays, Harriet Amanda was born June the 10 1856 and Mother ad Harriet was over to night.

[June 12, 1856-Thursday] 12 I had a good company of people last night.

[June 13, 1856-Friday] friday the 13 ant Emily is gone home to day and I have had a throw of company fore the last 3 weeks. It is a busy time fore harvist has come at last their. Mary D Brown

> Robert Alexander Margaret E Alison was married May the 22 day 1856
> Rasmus Alison and Mary Ann Chambers was married May the 21 1856
> Jseys Dick was born June the 14 1856

[June 16, 1856-Monday] June the 16 I have been verry bad with the cold and sore throat. I am some better this evening and I hope I feel as if these afflictions ware sent fore something.

[June 22, 1856-Sunday] June the 22 Lawson has been sick to day and I did not go to preachen to day but he is better.

[June 30, 1856-Monday] Tusday the 30 I have just got home from Farthers. He has not been well but he is better and all the rest is well at this time.

[July 2, 1856-Wednesday] July the 2 this is the day of the great commencement at the female college at yorkvill.[12] Theire is a great crowd of people a getherid theire and Eliza Ann and Emily Jane is gone.

[July 5, 1856-Saturday] July 5 we are all well to night and I have been to york to day.

[July 13, 1856-Sunday] July the 13 I have been to preachen to day and yesterday was the day of the sining at bershaba. I had company, John Alexander from alabamia was here.

[July 14, 1856-Monday] monday the 14 I had Mr James Davis and his Mother to day.

[July 17, 1856-Thursday] Thursday the 17 I had Mrs Sarah good down to see me to day.

[July 20, 1856-Sunday] Sunday the 20 this is the day of the communion at Center. I did not go, the children was not well. Mary D Brown

[July 23, 1856-Wednesday] wensday the 23 well i had a big quilting yesterday and Farther and Mother hapend over to it and they put the quilt out before night. Farther and Mother has gone home. Paw said he thought it might be the last time that he ever would be here. It makes me feel verry sober ever time he gose home from here.

[July 27, 1856-Sunday] Sunday eveng the 26 I have been at bershaba at preachen to day. We had a new preacher, a methodist preacher. His tex was in Mathew the 23 chapter and 1 2 3 verses. Our preacher, Mr James Davis preached in the evening. His tex was "But the path of the richous shineth more and more unto the perfict day." They both made verry fine sermins if we would doo as well as they tell us how, we need not fear what man can doo unto us, but serve the Lord.

[August 1, 1856-Friday] August the 1 Jaily and Jane Alexander is a staying out here and they are all gone to the mineral spring[13] and Franklin Furgison and Susan is gone up to shelba to see theire kin.

[August 10, 1856-Sunday] August the 10 well I have had the privilage of being to preachen once more and have heard great and solem truthes proclaimed from the pulpit that I have sat under the sound of from an infant. I humbly trust that it has not been in vaine. I have heard so many solem warnings theire and what I have heard to day was enough to awaken the carless siner. Mr Ervin preached too great sermins to day. His tex was in Luke the 24 chapter 26 verse, this is the words. "Ought not Christ to have sufferd these things and to enter into his glory." His evening tex was in Mark the 8 chapter and 36 verse. "Fore what shall it proffit a man if he gaines the whole wourld and loose his own Soule." He gave the people some solem warning concerning the great importance of the never dying soul. He also said he would drather die in hotten tot than in Bershaba with out the salvation of his soule. Mary D Brown

Green Gullet and Ammanda Floyd was married on tusday
the 12 of Aug 1856.
Andrew Quinn and Jane Thomison was married at 12 oclock on
Thursday the 14.
William Quin and Mary S Brown was married the same day at 4 in the
evening. I was at Mary Browns wedding and infare.[14]
Thomisons company met at John Browns and both companyes went home
to gether. They had a great dinner and then I left.

Cousin Eliza Thomison baby was born, Aug the 21 and died the 22
and was burried at Bershaba. I was at the burrieng.
Cousin Psalm and Margaret was at our house to day and children,
i was verry glad to see them.

[August 25, 1856-Monday] 25 yesterday and last night was the day of the great wind and rain. It has destroyd a great deal of corn.[15]

[September 6, 1856-Saturday] Sept the 6 i was down at Mrs Davises to day, i had a fine visit. They are so kind.

[September 7, 1856-Sunday] Sunday morning 7 we have no preachen to day. Jackson has gone over to see my ould Farther to day to spend the day in reading and talking on the scripture. Mary D Brown

[September 14, 1856-Sunday] September the 14 i have been at preachen to day at bershaba. Our young preacher dose well.

[September 15, 1856-Monday] monday th 15 Mr Umphry has got a singing at bershaba. He sung theire to day, his first day. Cinties wister was born august the 23 1856.

[September 17, 1856-Wednesday] Sept 17 i have been to york to-day and left Eliza Ann their to prepare fore the great wedding.

[September 21, 1856-Sunday] sabeth the 21 Jackson has gone over to enen to hear the baptist.

[September 24, 1856-Wednesday] wensday the 24 unckle billy Alexander has brought lida home to day and spent part of the day.

[September 26, 1856-Friday] Friday the 26 I have been to preachen today. It is the beginning of our sacrament. We expected Mr Leroy Davis but he did not come. Mr James Davis preached. His tex was in Ephesians the 3 chapter and 17 18 19 verses. He mad a verry fine sermon and Lawson and Jane Brown and Ann Neely and Ginny Mcarter came home with me to stay all night.

[September 27, 1856-Saturday] Saturday evening I have been to preachen today and we had Mr Leroy Davis. He done all the preachen. His tex was in Ephesians the 6 chapter and 10 verse. These are the words, "Finaly my bretheren be strong in the Lord, and in the power of his might." He preached 2 sermins on that text and Hiram and Harriet and Alunza Brown came home with us.

[September 28, 1856-Sunday] sabeth evening well I have been to another great communion at bershaba. Mr Leroy Davis preached.

Sister Harriet has gone home and took Lawson and Sally and Hannah home with her to stay till the weden is over.

[September 29, 1856-Monday] Monday evening I have had Mary and Jane and Susan and William Davis and little willey all up to see me to day.

[September 30, 1856-Tuesday] tusday evening the 30 this is the day of umphrey singing and John Alexander has been out and has took Eliza Ann home with him and Henry Glenn came here to night. They are all well but Jane. She has bad health.

[October 2, 1856-Thursday] Young Furguson and Jane Alexander was married, October the 2 day at 2 oclock in the evening and the Rev Mr James Adams married them and they had 2 waters apice, John Bierd and Hannah Alexander, Dick Palmer and Eliza Ann Brown. They had a large crowd and a verry fine supper and every thing that was nice and good, And then all went up to Mrs Furguson and took dinner and all was nice and good. So ends it.

[October 3, 1856-Friday] Billy Floyds baby died the 3 day of October and he is verry porrly.

[October 5, 1856-Sunday] Sabeth evening the 5 well i have just got all of my family home once more and is all well. I was over to see Farther yesterday.

He is not verry well and looks bad. Then i went to Hirams and stayd all night and got the children and went on to york to preachen and heard the Rev Mr Richerdson preach. His tex was, "Come fore all things are now ready." He is a great speaker indeed.

[October 7, 1856-Tuesday] tusday morning the 7 well i had Young and Jane and Mary Ann with us last night and theire gone home again and i have gone to the loom.

[October 13, 1856-Monday] Monday Oct the 13 well i have been a great trip up to crowders creek. Mother and I went up theire last satterday morning and stayd unto Sunday evening. I had a fine visit, seen a great many of my ould friends that i hant seen in a long time, Robert James and his wife and child. His wifes name is Mary and his daughters name is Margaret. He is a verry fine looking man and a great Dr too. He was to start home this morning for franklin town in north carolina. And this is court week and the election fore several offices. Theire is a great stir which will be elected, Witherspoon or Mccaw.

[October 17, 1856-Friday] Oct Friday night the 17 well this great election is over, Robert G. Mccaw was elected seniter. Robert G McCaw got 1389 votes, I D Witherspoon got 984 votes.

Well this is a wourld of cares and sorows but what of that the verry traveler never dreams of rest unto he lands at his journeys end and why should I expect enjoyment here while travling in this willdreness of sin, pain and sorow. It was once askt in Heaven who are those. Thes are they which have come through great tribulation which have washed theire robes and made them white in the blood of the Lamb. Oh my God i pray through the intercession of that dear Jesus that I may bee one of that who have washed theire robes and made them white in the blood of the Lamb and thy holly word says none shall plead in vain, none that asks shall be sent empty away. Well it is now verry late and i must close. Every thing is now hushed in silence but the ould clock. Every tick it gives brings me that much nearer death and eternity.

Forgive me Lord fore thy dear son
The ills that I this day have done
That with the wourld myselfe and thee
I ere, I seep at peace may bee
Teach me to live that i may dread

The grave as little as my bed
Teach me to die, that so I may
Rise glouries in that awful day
Oh let my soule on thee repose
And may sweet sleep, my eylids close
Sleep that shall me more vigerous make
To serve my God when I awake
If in the night I sleepless lie
My soule with heavenly thoughts employ
Lest no ill dreams disturb my rest
No powers of darkness me molest
Oh when shall I in endless day
Forever chase dark sleep away
And himns divine with angels sing
Glory to thee eternal King.

unknown

[October 19, 1856-Sunday] Sunday the 19 well Jackson and Eliza Ann and Emily Jane and Lawson went up to see Robert and Betsy Alexander last night and went up to bettehany to day. Theire is a sacrament theire to day and I have been at home with the little children today, have been reading in ould Burchet to day. I have been redding Christs sermins on the mount, an explanation. Theire is great promises and preceipts and examples contain in them three chapters.

Am I cold, I dare not stay. May not, must not disobey
Here I lay me at thy feet, Clinging to they mercy seat.
Thine I am and thine alone, Lord with me thy will be don.
Am I cold, what shall i bring As an offring to my King
Poor and bind and naked I Trimbling at they footstool
Not but sin I call my own. Nor fore sin can I attone
Am I called an haire of God Redeemed by precious blood.

[October 21, 1856-Tuesday] tusday evening 21 well Hannah Alexander is here sick and her Farther and Mother came out to day and Alexander has gone back home.

[October 22, 1856-Wednesday] 22 theire has been singing at the churche to day and Hannah is no beetter. Dr Alison has been to see her to day and John

Cain has started home this evening. Theire is a singing at Cains to night.

[October 24, 1856-Friday] 24 well Hannah is some better this morning ad she has concluded to go home ad Jackson has gone home with them.

[October 31, 1856-Friday] Oct the 31 Hugh love has been verry bad but has got better.

[November 7, 1856-Friday] November the 7 well I was at york yesterday an bought some dresses. Hiram and Harriet is over and Hiram and Leffayet and Jackson has gone a turkey hunting. Harriet and me was over to see Hannah.

[November 8, 1856-Saturday] satturday the 8 this is a wet day and Hiram and Harriet is gone home.

[November 9, 1856-Sunday] Mr McLeece, the man that preached Nov the 9, the young mans name was Mr McLece. A sabeth night well I have been to preachen to ould bershaba again and great preachen it was. It is the time of Sinod. It met in Chester and theire was a young man came up with Gimmy Davis and preached. He was from Saulsberry. His tex was in Judges the 3 chapter, 20 verse, These are the words. "I have a message from God to you." And I do think he preached as great a sermin as I ever heard. The mesage he gave the people of bershaba was verry solome indeed. His mesage to the christian was to that Christ had done great things fore him and to persavere on and fight the good fight of faith and they would win the prize. He had a mesage fore the luke warm proffesser. "He that is not fore me is against me." A mesage fore the worldly that if they gaind the whole world and loost their own soule it was a poore pitiance. At last he had mesages fore all that was theire and gave thim solem warning of death.

[November 20, 1856-Thursday] Nov the 20 this is fast day. We have no preachen. It is the time of the Methedist confference at yorkvill.

[November 21, 1856-Friday] Thursday the 21 Eliza Ann is gone down to see Hannah Alexander. She dose not seem to git well.

[November 23, 1856-Sunday] Sabeth evening I was not at preachen to day. I have not been well. I have had a verry bad cold and paine in my side. John Alexander brought lida home last evening and Hannah is some better.

[December 1, 1856-Monday] Dec the 1 i had ould Mrs cain up to see me to day and Betsy too. I was verry bad with a pain in my side last night but it is better.

[December 3, 1856-Wednesday] wednsday the 3 theire has been singing at the church today and theire is a great singing at Amos Burnses to night. Jackson ad lida and Emily is gone to it.

[December 4, 1856-Thursday] Thursday the 4 well Lawson and Jane has gone and left the ould people. They have moved in Peggys ould house and i have been up at Billeys to day to see Mrs Cain and Caty.

[December 5, 1856-Friday] Friday night the 5 I have been over to see Farther and Mother to day. They are well, but it looks lonsome to see them by themselves, left without a child. Once a large family of children, nine in number and now none. But I think theire is no danger of them lacking eney thing, theire children will never see them want. I wont while I can doo eney thing fore them. Franklin has a shucken to night and they are all gone to it.

[December 7, 1856-Sunday] Sabeth morning 7 Jackson and Emily Jane and Harriet is gone over to Farthers last night and has not come home yet and Eliza Ann is sick. She had a chill last night and is in bed to day. It is the cold i think.

[December 13, 1856-Saturday] Dec the 13 I have been down to york to day and Frances came home with us.

[December 14, 1856-Sunday] 14 Emily Jane has come home to day from her grand Farthers. She has been staying a week with them.

[December 19, 1856-Friday] Friday 19 this is the day that Docia Coldwell fell at the school house and cut her head verry bad. The Dr Good sewed it up and then they brought her here and stayd all night and Lorena and Rachel and Robert Coldwell. They have tacken her home the next day.

[December 22, 1856- Monday] Monday the 22 this is the day that Wesley Gimason came here to see us from the missippia on a visit to this country. He says he left them all well.

[December 25, 1856-Thursday] well this is Christmus day and it is a verry quiet one to me. i have had no company to day.

[December 26, 1856-Friday] 26 well i had some company last night. Wesly Jimason bot Brown and Susin and Eliza. Well I expect company to day and night.

[December 27, 1856-Saturday] Saturday 27 well I had a big croud last night. We had a singing here last night and the hous was as full as it could hold. And plenty of company last night, Hiram and Harriet, Jane and Hatty Jackson, Emi Hudson, Andrew Floyd, Billy Davis. They are all gone to the singing to day and Hiram and Harriet is gone home.

[December 29, 1856-Monday] Monday 29 I have been up to see Mrs Good to day.

[December 31, 1856-Wednesday] well this is the last of another year gone, gone, gone, yes, gone from time but fast recorded in eternity yet. What momentous events have taken place, how many importent changes have marked the histry of this year. Another yeare gone with all its trials and duties with all its joys and sorrows gone to give its account. Alas, how many wasted hour, how many wasted moments must I recall, how many sinful thoughts, how many acts of transgression. Who of us but have ocation to confess that we have sined. Let us go to God with sincere penitence and humbily ask forgiveness through Jesus Christ. Another year of probation is past and I am so much nearer my eternal home. Oh what a solem thought is this, and how it should stimulate me to prepare to meet my God. Safe in him I will feare no evil. Guided by his spirit I will pass through and when summioned away from earth I will enter a pun, a life where theire shall be no rolling years and changeful seasens but an unceasing round of worship and joy in the presence of God and the Lamb. Dec 31 1856 Mary D Brown

Bee this my one great business heare
With holy trembling, holy fear
To make my calling sure
Then Saviour, then my soul receive
Transported from this vale to live
And reign with thee above.

unknown

1857

[*January 1, 1857-Thursday*] January the 1 1857 this is newyears evening i have just got home from Farthers. I have been over on a visit to see them all and they are all well.

[*January 2, 1857-Friday*] 2 John Alexander has bough lida home to day and took Fanny home. Ant Hannah was here to day.

[*January 4, 1857-Sunday*] Sunday 4 we have no preach to day and Wesly was here to day.

[*January 5, 1857-Monday*] 5 this is sale day and Jackson is gone to york and he bought a fine mare. He gave a hundred dollars fore her. She is a fine young nag.

[*January 7, 1857-Wednesday*] 7 this is the day ant Hannahs, Mary baby, davis was born.

[*January 8, 1857-Thursday*] 8 well, Jackson and Lawson is gone up to unckle John Janses to the mill. John Thomison and Emiline Quinn was married to day. Hiram and Harriet was at the wedding.

[*January 10, 1857-Saturday*] 10 Wesly Jimison is gone down to york to day.

[January 11, 1857-Sunday] Sabeth 11 I have been at preachen to day. Jemes dose make som fine sermons.

[January 13, 1857-Tuesday] Tuesday 13 I have been down at york to day. I did not by much of enney.

[January 14, 1857-Wednesday] Wensday 14 Andrew Gladden and William Baty came here this morning to build a chimbly.

[January 15, 1857-Thursday] Young Furgison and Jane mooved out here the 15 of January to Alexanders ould place.

[January 16, 1857-Friday] 16 this is Umphries last days singing.

[January 18, 1857-Sunday] 18 well this is a dreddful morning. It is a snow-ing and blowing most dreadfully and Mr Umphriey has started home in it. He cant stand it i dont think. Mary Ann Alexander and Ann Furgison and Robert Brown and little bob Brown and Umphries was all here last kight and they are all gone and it is dreadful cold and is still a snowing and blewing.

[January 20, 1857-Tuesday] tusday the 20 it has been as cold weather as ever i have felt. It has been a close time. Mr Davis was here last knight.

[January 21, 1857-Wednesday] Wensday 21 this is a cold night. It has been a snowing some to night. It has blew of cleer and cold tonight. Jackson is gone over to stay with him to night and it is a blewing now.

[January 25, 1857-Sunday] Sunday the 25 I have been over to see brother Lawson. His horse threw him and fell on him the night of the big snow and hurt him verry bad but he is gitting better now. Farther is not so well to day when I left their.

[February 4, 1857-Wednesday] Febuary the 4 i was over to see cousin Eliza burns yesterday. She has had a verry bad spell and Mary and Susan Davis was here last night. They and lida and emi is gone up to see ant Caty to day. Andy Gladden has finished the chimbley.

[February 6, 1857-Friday] Friday the 6 Mrs Cain and Mr Hasting Alaxander was up to see me to day and spent the day. Eliza Ann and Emily Jane was gone

to union to a sining to day and to morrow. Mr Hill has a singing at the school house to day.

[February 8, 1857-Sunday] Sabeth evening 8 i have been to preachen to day.

[February 9, 1857-Monday] Monday 9 Wesly Gimason has got up here to day again. He is set in with his unckle Billy to work. John Alaxander and Margaret watson was married January the 15 day 1857 ad started fore the alibamia .

[February 11, 1857-Wednesday] feb 11 on wensday i saw them pass by my house.

[February 12, 1857-Thursday] Thursday the 12 i have been over to see Jane this evening and took supper with her. Jackson sold his Jack mule the 12 day of Feb to Mr John Davs. Jackson bought doll from David Scogings, January the 5 1857, she is five years old.

[February 15, 1857-Sunday] 15 Eliza Ann is gone over to see her grand Farther.

[February 16, 1857-Monday] 16 we have Mr Billy Davis with us to night.

[February 20, 1857-Friday] 20 Eliza Ann is gone up to Mrs Hudsons to night and to the singing.

[February 22, 1857-Sunday] 22 we have all been to preachen to day and Hiram and Harriet was over with us last night and all was at preachen to day.

[February 23, 1857-Monday] 23 i was over to see Farther and Mother last night and paw had a chill yesterday and was not verry well.

[February 24, 1857-Tuesday] 24 i have been down to york to day. I did not buye much of eny thing and Jaily came home with us. Mary D Brown

[February 26, 1857-Thursday] Thursday 26 I was bad with the cold yester and took a dose of blew pills. Jaly Alexander was here last night.

[February 27, 1857-Friday] 27 I have been down to see Mrs Mary Coldwell to day. She has an other son, it was born Febuary 26 1857. This is the night of the sining at Young Ferguson.

[February 28, 1857-Saturday] 28 I have had Billy and Mary Quinn to see us to day and Hannah. They are all gone home and Jackson is working on the road to day. Mary D Brown

[March 1, 1857-Sunday] March the 1 it is the sabeth day and we have no preachen to day and it is a very lon. Ould unckle Psalmy Turner departed this life March the 18 1857, 98 years old. Ould Sally Turner died March the 21 1857.

[April 1, 1857-Wednesday] Aprile the 1 pige colted the 6 of March. Ould Mrs Dickey was buried at bershaba April the 15 1857. Ould Mrs Linn the same day.

[April 17, 1857-Friday] Friday the 17 i have been down to york to day and they are all well as comen.

[April 19, 1857-Sunday] Sunday the 19 this is the sabeth day and we have no preachen to day. Jackson is gone over to see Farther. He is verry fraile and porly at this time. This is a cold backword spring.

[April 20, 1857-Monday] ould aunt Polly Burns died Aprile the 20 1857.

[April 24, 1857-Friday] Friday the 24 this is the commencement of our communion and Mr James Davis is to be oredaind at this time. Bethel Presbetary is to meet here now. We had Mr White with us last night and is still here now. Well i have been to preachen this morning and saw Presbatary opend by prayer by Mr White of chester and then Mr James Davis preached his trial sermon. His tex was in rommans the 5 chapter and the 1 vers. They ware examing him on one thing.

[April 25, 1857-Saturday] Saturday 25 we had Mr Watson with us last night and i have been at preachen to day and saw what i never saw beffore. I saw Mr James Davis ordain. It was a solim sight to see and heare. Mr Salmuel Watson preached his ordination sermon saturday morning. His tex was in Psalm the 127 chapter and the 1 verse. These are the words, "Except the Lord build the house the wokmen work in vain that build it." I tell you he preached a great sermon to the people and then he was ordain and then Mr Leroy Davis gave him his charge. MDB

Mr Say preached in the eveng and his tex was in Psalms the 42 chapter and the

11 verse. These are the words. "Why art thou cast down O my Soule and why art thou disquieted within me. Hope thou in God fore I shall yet praise him who is the health of my countenance and my God." It was another good sermon. Mr Say said it was a great day fore Bershaba. A day that God had gave them a minister to break unto them the bread of life and to be with them in prosperity and in adversity to be with them in sickness and death. And a day he said that would be talked of when we are all dead and gone. And oh my God, may it not be in vain that I have been witness of so many solom sights and so many solomn sermons, so many fervent prayers fore our young preacher and our own dying souls that we must all give an acount fore at death. M Davis Brown

[April 26, 1857-Sunday] Sabeth evening Aprile 26 well this has been another holy communion sabeth day. Mr Leroy Davis preached this morning. Mr Say got up and read a chapter and fenced[16] the table and he done it in a verry solem way and told the people what it was to remember him in that ordinance. Mr Say preached in the eveng. His tex was first Corinthians 1 chapter and 30 verse. These are the words. "But of him are ye in Christ Jesus who of God is made unto us wisdom and righteousness and sanctification and redemption." That closed the solem services of this ocation fore time but not fore eternity. And oh if we have not been made better, it will be fare worse fore in the great day than if we ware in heathen lands. But i hope and trust it is not so with me. Mary D Brown

[May 1, 1857-Friday] William Floyd died Aprile the 21 1857. May the 1 I have been up to see ant Caty to day and theire has been a fine rain to day.

[May 2, 1857-Saturday] the 2 Jackson has been at muster to day and it has been a wet day. And Jackson and Eliza Ann and Emily Jane has gone over to see theire Grand Farther and Mother to night.

[May 3, 1857-Sunday] Sabeth evening May the 3 well Jackson and Emily has come home and they are all well and left lida to stay a week with them.

[May 7, 1857-Thursday] the 7 last knight was a dreadful knights rain and i have heard that theire was a dreadful storme down below york and own to chester. It was dreadful indeed.

[May 9, 1857-Saturday] May 9 we are all well this morning and it is begining to apear a little like Spring had come at last. I have had some company yester-

day and last knight. Emily Alison and Martha Alexander was here yesterday and Young and Jane here last knight and now I am alone.

[May 11, 1857-Monday] May 11 I was at preachen yesterday. Mr Davis tex was in Luke the 16 chapter, verse 31. In the evening his tex was in 2 Corinthians 5 chapter and 14 15 verses. He mad 2 good sermons and theire was a great turn out of people. Eliza Ann and Emily Jane is gone down to Mr Cains to day to spend the day with Martha Alexander beffore she starts back to alibama. Lafayet Thomison is verry bad at this time. They don't think he can live many days. He hase a dreadful leg and i doo expect it will kill him yet. Ould Mrs Enloe is bad with the new mony.

[May 16, 1857-Saturday] May 16 I have just got home from a trip over to Farthers. I was to see them all and they ware all well. Paw is quit piert at times and then again he is very porly. Laffayet is still bad. They have a great fishing party to day and my children is gone too.

[May 18, 1857-Monday] Monday 18 theire has been a great deal of rain and severe storms of hail and wind. It has destroyed the wheet in some parts and is cold anough fore frost, the cotten looks like theire was.

[May 21, 1857-Thursday] May 21 this is the day of Billy Floyds sale and Jackson is gone up to it. He started yesterday morning and hant got back yet. I dont look fore him till tomor. Lida and Emily and Lawson and Jaly is gone over to stay all knight with theire ant Hannah to night and I and the little children is by our selves and i can stay well sattesfied. Mary D Brown

[May 25, 1857-Monday] Jane Browns John Franklin was born May 25 1857 and Jackson and i was over to see them. They ware a dooing well.

[May 27, 1857-Wednesday] 27 Eliza Ann and Emily, Jane and Jaily is gone down to coldwells to day.

[May 31, 1857-Sunday] 31 this is the sackrament at Bethany and Jackson and lida, emily and Jaily is gone up to it.

[June 2, 1857-Tuesday] June 2 Jackson has been up at unckle John Janses to mill.[17] Unckle John is verry bad with a bealen on his neck. James Thomison is here to night.

[June 5, 1857-Friday] friday evening 5 I have been at york to day. They ware all well but Mary Ann has not good health.

[June 7, 1857-Sunday] Sabeth evening 7 I have been at preachen to day. Mr Davis is improving verry fast. I think he is a verry fine young preacher. Mr Rufus Whitesides was here last knight.

[June 8, 1857-Monday] monday evening 8 Martha Meek, Betsy Cain, Caty Brown was all here to day on a visit.

[June 9, 1857-Tuesday] Tusday evening 9 i have been over to see Farther and Mother to day and Sister Harriet came over theire and they are all well. Mother has been up to see unckle John. He is some better. That bealen has broke and runs much.

[June 12, 1857-Friday] friday evening 12 we are all well this evening. MDB

[June 14, 1857-Sunday] Sabeth evening 14 Eliza Ann and her paw is gone down to york this evening and she is a going to stay a week or too.

[June 15, 1857-Monday] 15 Mrs Davis and Mrs Johnson has been up to spend the day.

[June 16, 1857-Tuesday] 16 this is the day it is prophiside that the comet is to fall and I have seen it this morning.[18]

[June 18, 1857-Thursday] 18 I dont know what has become of the comet. I have not seen it these too days. This is the day of the examination of the female colage at yorkvill.

[June 23, 1857-Tuesday] tusday 23 Emily and her Farther is gone down to york this evening to see the shows and bring lida home.

[June 24, 1857-Wednesday] 24 they have come home and brought Mary Ann home with them.

[June 27, 1857-Saturday] Saturday evening 27 Mr Hill had a singing at bershaba to day and the yongsters has all been theire and Mary Ann is gone over to Youngs to night. Unckle Hiram and Harriet and children is here to knight.

[June 28, 1857-Sunday] Sabeth evening I have been at bershaba to day and heard fine preachen and saw Mr Jeams Davis baptisse his first. Mr Jemes Mule-maxs child and Mr Ervins, also anterson and diseys child, Martha. He dose well. I dont think he can bee beet fore his practice. I have been over to see Jane and Young to day. Mary Davis Brown

[July 3, 1857-Friday] July 3 i have been over to see Farther to day. He is verry porly now fore some time. He says he is a wareing away verry fast this while.

[July 6, 1857-Monday] monday 6 Jackson and I have been down at york to day. I had 15 bags fore which I got 75 cents each.

[July 7, 1857-Tuesday] 7 ant Caty is verry bad with the flux[19] and Bolever Thomison wife is verry bad. They dont think she can live.

[July 12, 1857-Sunday] Sunday evening 12 Franklin had a little negro to die verry sudently. It took sick yesterday and died this eveng. It was Mary Anns oldest.

[July 15, 1857-Wednesday] 15 John Alexander and Mary Ann has been out to see us to day and they are all gone down to the mineral spring. Mary Ann is a going to stay here and tend the spring a while.

[July 18, 1857-Saturday] saturday the 18 Mr Hill has a singing at bershaba to day. They are all gone to it.

[July 23, 1857-Thursday] wensday 23 this is the day of the great temperance meeting at york. They expect it to be a great day. They are a going to have a picknick dinner. Jackson, Eliza Ann, Emily Jane and Lawson is all gone. Some people thinks theire was 3-4 thousand people theire. MD Brown

[July 29, 1857-Wednesday] wensday 29 we had a big quilting to day. I had Mrs Good and Betsy, Mary and Susan Davis, Mrs Jonson, William Davis, Hannah Alexander, Martha Alexander.

[July 30, 1857-Thursday] Martha Meeks James Ely was born July 30 1857.

[July 31, 1857-Friday] 31 I have had Jane and Lawson over with us last night and to day too. Hiram and Harriet too and they are all gone home now.

[August 2, 1857-Sunday] Elens John was born August the 2 1857 and she got along quick to what she generally dose.

[August 16, 1857-Sunday] Mimas Manda died August the 16 1857. Sister Jane Glenn died August the 16 1857. Jane Furgusons Mary Jane was born August 16 1857.

[August 20, 1857-Thursday] August the 20 this is the day of the great picknick at the mineral spring. Eliza Ann and Emily Jane is gone down to it.

[August 21, 1857-Friday] Friday 21 i have been over to see Jane and the babby to day.

[August 22, 1857-Saturday] saturday morning 22 i have been over to see Farther last night.

[August 23, 1857-Sunday] Sunday evening i have been to preachen to day.

[August 26, 1857-Wednesday] wensday 26 i have been up to unckle John Janses sale yesterday. Theire was a large gatheren of people. Theire was a heap of stuff sold. Theire was six negrose sold. They about foure thousand dollars and unckle John and ant Peggy Janes and Cousin James and Catharine all started for arkances the August the 31.

Mineyes _____ was born August 21 1857.

[September 5, 1857-Saturday] September the 5 Jane and the baby was over to see me to day.

[September 6, 1857-Sunday] the 6 Eliza Ann and Jaly is gone over to smerna to day and i have been over to see ant Hannah. She has been baad with the cold.

[September 7, 1857-Monday] Monday the 7 Jackson is gone up to henreys to the mill and lida is gone over to her Grandfathers.

[September 12, 1857-Saturday] Saturday 12 i have been over to see Hiram and Harriet last night and theire ould horse died this morning and then we came on and took dinner with Farther and Mother and then home.

[September 13, 1857-Sunday] Sunday the 13 we had Green and Ammand Gullet on a visit since yesterdy morning to this morning and theire sister who is attending the spring. Emily Jane and Wesley is gone over to heare the Baptest to day.

[September 15, 1857-Tuesday] tusday the 15 we are all well to night and all asleep. Mary D Brown   Rachel Cains was born Sept 15 1857.

[September 18, 1857-Friday] 18 Jackson, Eliza Ann and Emily Jane is gone to york to day.

[September 19, 1857-Saturday] 19 we had a great storm of wind and rain last evening and John and Hannah came home with them from york. Franklins horses run a way with the wagon. He was in the barn yard a putting up fodder and they got scared and run with him in the wagon and turned it over before they got out of the barn, throde him out, he did not git much hurt. They killed his grey mare.

[September 20, 1857-Sunday] Sabethe evening 20 we have no preachen to day and Jackson is gone up to see Andrew Turner. MDB

[September 27, 1857-Sunday] Sabeth the 27 i have been at Bershaba to day at a communion ocasion again. Mr Leroy Davis and his son was up to the meetting. His son, Psalm is a preacher too. I did not hear him preach, I was not well and was not theire yesterday.

[September 28, 1857-Monday] Monday 28 theire is a whole set of them gone to smerny to a singing to day and lida has Ruffes Whiteside home with her fore the last time. Soon he is going to start to arkases to morrow morning.

[September 30, 1857-Wednesday] wensday 30 this is the day of Leffayet Thomisons sale.[20] He is bown fore arkances too. I was over to see Farther to day. Hiram has bought his land. John Alexander is verry bad. They sent out fore his friends to day. They dont think he will git over it.

[October 3, 1857-Saturday] Oct 3 Jackson has been down to see John to day and bring Emily home. He is verry porly yet.

[October 4, 1857-Sunday] Sabeth 4 Eliza Ann has just come home from york and John is no better. Theire is preaching to day. Mother came by this morning

but I did not go. Young Mr Willson is to preach to day. Mary D Brown

[October 10, 1857-Saturday] Oct 10 Jackson and lada was down at york last knight and John is better.

[October 11, 1857-Sunday] the 11 sabeth evening Mr James Adams preached to day. I was not out.

[October 13, 1857-Tuesday] tusday the 13 this is court week. Jackson is gown.

[October 14, 1857-Wednesday] Oct the 14 on wensday this is the day Laffayet and Alves and Bolerver and Dr Thomison all started fore Arkances and Mrs Bogs family. Theire is a great stir in this country about going to arkances. Theire is land, opun land fore sale in this country fore sale.

[October 15, 1857-Thursday] Oct 15 this is the day Hiram and Harriet moved over to Laffayets house and Eliza Ann is over staying with her this week. Jackson is gone over to help them to day.

[October 17, 1857-Saturday] Saturday 17 Elida and Emmi is gone to the sining to day.

[October 19, 1857-Monday] Monday 19 I have not been well last night nore to day and Mother has been over to see me.

[October 28, 1857-Wednesday] Oct 28 on wensday my baby is a week ould to day. It was born October 21, on wensday.

Oh my God, I sinceraly thank thee fore thy great goodness to me and mine by supporting me in the houre of pain by making me the living mother of a living child, by strenthing me thus fare and by giving me the prospect of a speedy recovery and confirmed health. O thou whose goodness to them that feare thee knows no bounds to thee i owe myself and every blessing i posess. To thee I dedocate this infant. Lord take it fore thy own. On the soul of this dear child draw thine holy image and keep it fore ever from the pollutions of this wicked wourld. Give me and its Farther grace to set it a constant good exampel and may we bring it up in the nurture and admonation of the Lord. While we pray that its life may be spared, we also pray fore entire resignation to thy blessed will. but shouleas thou, as we hope, be pleased to allot to it the years of man, we earnestily beseech thee to make it a pillar in thy church, a blessing to the wourld and a lasting comfort to its parents. Mary D Brown

[*October 31, 1857-Saturday*] Oct 31 this is the day Tom Bell shot ould Mr Alen. He met him in the street and orderd him to lay down some circulars he had printed concerning a dispute between Bell and him.[21]

[*November 2, 1857-Monday*] Nov 2 Emily has been over to see her grandfarther and Mother. They are as well as common. Hiram is sick, the rest is well but colds. John Coldwell and the widow Good was married Nov the 5 1857. Mary D Brown

[*November 6, 1857-Friday*] 6 Friday night they have all been to sining to day and they are all gown down to Mrs Davis to a singing to night and John Alexander too.

[*November 8, 1857-Sunday*] Sabeth 8 this is preachen day and they are all gone to preachen today. Mary D Brown 1857

[*November 18, 1857-Wednesday*] Nov 18 Eliza Ann and Emily Jane is gone on a visit down to Mrs Davis to day.

[*November 19, 1857-Thursday*] 19 this is fast day and they are gone to preachen. It is a dreadful day of wind and i did allow to go over to see my Farther this evening but it is a blowing so I am afraid I cant go.

[*November 23, 1857-Monday*] 23 I have been over to see Farther and the rest. He has not been so well but he is better now. I seen Henry Glenn and Margaret and the boys was down on a visit to paws. They was all well and a doing well.

[*November 26, 1857-Thursday*] 26 Farther has hired mima fore a year and she is gone to day.

Betsy Alexanders William was born Dec 5 1857. Hiram and Butler was over here to day the 5.

[*December 8, 1857-Tuesday*] tusday 8 i have been up to spend the day with ant Caty.

[December 9, 1857-Wednesday] 9 i have been over to see Hannah to day. She has been sick.

[December 11, 1857-Friday] Friday 11 i had cousin Eliza and Eugenia Brown with us last. The girls was gone over to theire unckle Johns to a singing but they have got home and they are all gone over to see Jane and Young to day and to Franklins to night. Mary D Brown

[December 13, 1857-Sunday] Dec 13 sabeth evening well i have been per-mited[22] to go to churche again and heard a fine sermon by Mr James Davis. His tex was in luke the 2 chapter and 10 verse.

[December 15, 1857-Tuesday] 15 lida and emi is gone down to york to day.

[December 18, 1857-Friday] Friday 18 i had sister Harriet over yesterday and Jaily and Jane and it was a dreadful wet day.

[December 25, 1857-Friday] 25 another christmus day and it is a snowin down good fashion this morning.

[December 27, 1857-Sunday] sabeth evenging 27 we have had a crowd yes-terday and last knight. They was up at Gim Alisons at a candy stell a Friday night and a patridge hunting yesterday. William Coldwell, Robert Whiteside and Robert Brown and Susan Furguson stayd all knight and they are all gone to preachen to day.

[December 30, 1857-Wednesday] wensday 30 well we have had a big quilting yesterday. Theire was near fifty people here and they put out my quilt and had a big singing that night and they are all gone home and it is a good thing fore this is a wet day.

[December 31, 1857-Thursday] 31 it is now neare the close of another yeare. One houre more and 1857 is gone from man, gone from time but stands fast in eternity. MDB

1858

[January 1, 1858-Friday] New Year 1858 Another year is come. On the heels of the departing twelve months treads another of the daughters of time. With a countanance as yet unclowded an eye radiant of hope and arms ladend with blessings, the new born year comes to beare us company fore a little seasen on oure journy to eternity. How she pitties oure past short comings, how she invokes us to penitence, how she invites us to a better future, how she seems to say, "Now let us seal up the gloomy records of the years gone by wich affords so little food fore pleasentness, contemplation or let us remember them only to learn lessons of wisdom. Let us hope that all that is theire amiss will be washed away by the blood of the cross. Here is a new leafe of life as yet untarnished on its pure, pure page. Strive that theire may be writen records which you will not be ashamed to review from a dying bed or from the judgement bar." Whether eighteen fifty eigh shall be strewn with the seeds of immortal joy is humainly speaking, Fore each one now to determin as we begin it so most probaly we shall end it. How important that we should at the outset secure the guidance and blessings of God. Who can tell what this year may bring forth? Who knows whether it is to lead us over a comparitive smooth and beaten high way or over a rough and thorny path.

[January 4, 1858-Monday] Jan 4 this is sale day and Jackson is gone down to york. I have been over to stay with Farther while Mother and Harriet went up to see ant Polly. She has not been well. She has a sore leg. Holly had a daughter that knight they was theire and they are all dooing verry well.

[January 5, 1858-Tuesday] tusday 5 this has been a great day of rain.

[January 7, 1858-Thursday] Thursday 7 i have just got home from york, Harriet and me.

[January 10, 1858-Sunday] Sabeth 10 theire was a singing at the church yesterday and Hannah and rachel came home with them.

[January 12, 1858-Tuesday] 12 Jackson and I have been up to see bob and betsy and bill and Mary. They are all a dooing well. Theire has been a great election this week between John Enlo and Psalm More fore the clerks office and More beet over too hinderd votes.

[January 18, 1858-Monday] Monday 18 Jackson is down at Hirams a holowing shucks to york.

[January 20, 1858-Wednesday] 20 i have been down to see Mrs Cain to day. She is as helpless as ever. Mary Francis Burns and William Baty from North carolina was maried January the 21 1858.

[January 24, 1858-Sunday] Sabeth evening 24 Mother and Hiram was up here last knight and we have been at preachen to day and the words of his tex was, "And they all made light of it."

[January 27, 1858-Wednesday] wensday night i have had ant Hannah over to day. Jackson has been over helping Hiram to build a chimbly and lida went over to stay a week with them. Susan and Emily is gone a visiting down to Mr Coldwells to day.

Henrietta Hudson and Mr Mathis was married tusday the
12 of January 1858 by Mr Watson.

[February 1, 1858-Monday] Febuary 1 this has been a wet day. Theire is a singing at Hirams to knight and Emily and Harriet is gone over theire and Eliza is theire.

[February 7, 1858-Sunday] Sabeth 7 i have been on a visit over to see my Farther and Mother. He has not been so well. He is a failing but is still abel to go.

[February 9, 1858-Tuesday] 9 Jackson is gone down to york and took lida down theire to help Mary Ann to quilt this week. I have been over to spend the day with hannah.

[February 12, 1858-Friday] friday 12 this has been a severe day of rain and sleet and it is still a falling yet. This winter has been moderate so far but this has been a severe day.

[February 13, 1858-Saturday] Saturday the 13 it is still raining and freesing yet.

[February 14, 1858-Sunday] Sabeth 14 the like of ice i never have seen. It is a hanging so beautiful. Stems and twigs not larger than a straw is thicker than my thumb and three timber is poping like guns, faster than i can count. The timber is broke dreadful. Theire is more in the woods than would to burn fore years.

[February 16, 1858-Tuesday] Tusday 16 the ice is nearly all fell and the timber is lightend of its burden. Unckle Billy is gone down to york after lida.

[February 20, 1858-Saturday] Saturday 20 theire is to bee a big singing at center to day and Elida and Emile is gown up to heare them, and susen too.

[February 28, 1858-Sunday] Sabeth eveng 28 i have been at preachen to day. Mr Anterson preach to day. Oure preacher, Mr James Davis is gown a trip to see about little Wiley Johnsons estate. He has had bad lick in collecting it yet.

[March 1, 1858-Monday] March 1 monday night it has been snowing again and Mary Ann and Hannah is here to knight.

[March 2, 1858-Tuesday] Tusday night 2 i think this has been as cold a day as ever i have felt.

[March 6, 1858-Saturday] Saturday 6 this has been a verry cold week. This was a beautiful morning but it looks now like a storme was a coming. John Alexander and Wesly Gimison is here to day and i am going over to see Farther to night.

[March 7, 1858-Sunday] Sabeth evening 7 i have been over to see farther. He has had a sore foot but it is got better. It looks like another storme was on hands. The rest is well. MD Brown

[March 8, 1858-Monday] March monday the 8 this has been another stormy day and it ranned and blowd all night. It has been a sleeting and snowing all day and it will be, now the ground is froz. It is verr cold and still a snowing yet.

[March 10, 1858-Wednesday] March 10 these lines i hope to hear when i am dieing Mary D Brown 1858

> Oh sing to me of Heaven- When I am caled to die
> Sing songs of holy ecstasy, To waft my soul on high
>
> When cold and slugish drops, roll of my marbel brow
> Break forth in songs of joyfulness, Let Heaven begin below.
>
> When the last moment comes, O watch my dying face
> And etch the bright serapich gleam, That ore each feature plays
>
> Then to my ravished ear, Let one sweet song be given
> Let music me last on earth, And greet me first in Heaven
>
> Then close my sightless eyes, And lay me down to rest
> And fold my icey hands, upon my lifeless breast.
>
> *unknown*

March the 10, wensday night, ten oclock and all in bed asleep and all well. That is not the case with some. Some is sick and some is dead. Mrs Cain had a little negro died to day and theire has been a great stir down at Mrs Davis. This too or three days our preacher, Mr James Davis has been a trip out to tenisee and it is thought that he has caught the small pox as he was in the car with a man that was sick with the small pox and is now in sharlet bad with them. Mrs Davis and family is verry much alarmed at it. They have put James up stairs in a room and is trying to git nurses.

[March 11, 1858-Thursday] Thursday night i have been over to see Polly Burns to day.

[*March 14, 1858-Sunday*] Sabeth 14 we have no preachen to day. Theire is no appearance of Mr Davis taking the small pox yet and Jackson and Eliza and Emily is gone over to union to preachen to day as we have none. Mary D Brown March 14 1858

[*March 16, 1858-Tuesday*] Mr B Derer and Miss Sarintha Howel was maried in Union Destrict March the 4 1858. Mr B Derer was killed by Mr Tom Dickson in Yorkville March the 16 on tuseday. They was a disputing in Dicksons tailor shop and he strick him on the head and broke his scull with the pressboard. He lived too houres. They was cousins. Dickson was married about Christmas. Dickson is in Jail. Him and Tom Bell will be tried fore their lives next coart which is the 3 Monday in Aprile. A sad calamity to think theire is too in jail fore murder. It seems if people is a coming to a wounderful pass, both here and elese whare.[23]

[*March 19, 1858-Friday*] Friday night the 19 Mr Hill has a singing at thee school house to night and they are all gone to it. It was fore Wesley as he is a going to start home next tuseday fore the Missippi. MD Brown

[*March 21, 1858-Sunday*] March 21 sabeth evening I have been over to see farther and mother last night. He has not been so well fore a week or too. He spends the most of in studeyeng and talking about death and the realities of another and better world, wheire he soon expects to be. He sayes he thinks he wont be here long but he sayes he has Thought that fore some yeares but is still here. He is allways a giving us his views of that wourle of spirits whare the just are made perfict.

[*March 22, 1858-Monday*] March 22 Monday night Wesley is gown down to york to night to start home in the morning. His unckle Billy and Jackson and Robert and Eliza Ann is all gown to york with him. MD Brown

[*March 26, 1858-Friday*] 26 theire has been another scrape at york to day. Felix Mulinax hit Mr Tom Pagin with a rock and knocked him down and then jumped on him and beet his head bad with a rock. He is bad.

[*March 28, 1858-Sunday*] 28 the scare of the small pox is over. Mr Davis was out at the curch to day and preached fore us. Hiram and Harriet was over last knight.

[**March 30, 1858-Tuesday**] 30 John Alexander was out to day. He sayes the Dr have gave Mr Pagen out. They think he cant live yet they have put Mr Martin Mulenax and his son up in jaile to a wait theire trial.

[**April 1, 1858-Thursday**] Aprile 1 this has been a severe day of wind an raine and it is verry cold. Jackson is gone over to stay with the ould people and it is dark and stormey to night.

[**April 3, 1858-Saturday**] Aprile 3 I have been on a visit down at Mrs Davises today. They are all well and a doing well.

[**April 8, 1858-Thursday**] thursday 8 Jackson is gone over to help Hugh Love to role logs to day and ant Caty and John has been here.

[**April 9, 1858-Friday**] friday 9 I have been down at york to day. Ould unckle Roben Coldwell died Aprile the ninth on a Friday and was buried at bershaba.

[**April 10, 1858-Saturday**] the 10 oure people has got the measels. Sally , Nell, Martha, John has got them now. Sally is bad.

[**April 11, 1858-Sunday**] 11 this is preachen day and I have to stay with the measels peopel. Hiram was with us last night and Mother came by this morning. She says Paw was sick this morning and Harriet is staying with him to day.

[**April 18, 1858-Sunday**] Aprile 18 the res is down with the measels, Harriet, Lawson, Hannah, Jaily is got them now. Hiram and Harriet was over to day to see them. Farther is verry porely. He has a shortness of breath that he can scarsley git his breath.

[**April 19, 1858-Monday**] monday 19 I have been over to see farther this morning. He is verry porely.

[**April 20, 1858-Tuesday**] 20 Jackson is gone over to farthers and took Emily over to stay with them this week. This is court week and Jackson is going on to york. Farther is some better to day. M Brown

[**April 22, 1858-Thursday**] thursday 22 the children is bad with the measels.

[**April 23, 1858-Friday**] friday 23 this is the day of the commencement of oure meetting. Mr Leroy Davis was theire.

[April 24, 1858-Saturday] satturday 24 I have been at preachen this morning. Mr Leroy Davis preached a good sermon. His tex was in Ephesions the 4 chapter and 30 verse. "Grieve not the Holy spirit of God whereby ye are sealed unto the day of redemption."

[April 25, 1858-Sunday] Aprile 25 this has been the day of the communion at bershaba and I have been theire once more to comeremont the sufferings and death of oure dear Saviour and theire has severals joined the Church. Eliza Ann, has joined the church. I fondly hope that it is in reality and in sincerity. Oh though who sees the heart and knowest all things, give her a heart to love and serve the balence of the days thou hast apointed to her, and make her feel the great responcibility that she ows to love and serve the Lord.

William Davison and Sarah Alison was married Aprile the 22 1858.
MD Brown

[April 26, 1858-Monday] Monday 26 i was over to see Farther last night. He is verry week but can still go about. We have got perty well over the measels now. Little Willie has never tacken them yet. Court week is over and they have not hung Tom Bell ore Tom Dickson. They have fined Bell to a thousand dollars and a yeares imprisment. Dickson six months imprisment and pay too hundred ad fifty dollars fine.
Monday evening this has been a dreadful cold day and it has been a snowing a good deal to day. Theire will be a big frost to night.

[April 28, 1858-Wednesday] Aprile 28 theire was a big frost last night. It has done a great deal of injury. It has ruined the gardens. My beans is as dead as they can be and they was almost fit to bloom and every thing else is hurt and killed. I believe the peaches is all killed. Theire was plenty of ice too.

[April 29, 1858-Thursday] 29 Jackson is gone over to stay with Farther to night. He is verry bad. It seemes like he would not be here long. He has a difficulty about gitting his breath. Some times he seemes like he would smother up and then he gits better of it fore some time. MDBrown

[May 4, 1858-Tuesday] May the 4 tusday morning well I have just got home from staying with Farther sence last satturday. He is verry bad. He took a bad

spell yesterday about twelve oclock. We all thought the combat was at an end but he said it was only fore another. The friends was all sent fore. When ant Emily came she says, "Unckle, you are in a bad fix." "Oh no, I hope I will soon be in a good fix." He said it was nothing to live and it was nothing to die but he felt it was a great thing to be reddy to die. He longs to be gone and be with that dear saiviour he has loved and served so long. He is now in his nintieth first year and has been an elder of the Presbeterion church fore more than sixty years and theire has been few such men as he has been. O if i could but follow his exampel as far as he followed Christs exampel and only be as well prepared fore another wourld as he is, i need not care fore the things of this wourld. O my God, I humbily beseech thee to give me a heart to love and serve more and better than I ever have done from this verry solem day. MD Brown

[May 6, 1858-Thursday] May 6 Jackson has com from Farthers this morning. He is not so well as he was a day ore to ago. John Brown is verry bad with the mumps.

[May 8, 1858-Saturday] Satturday night the 8 Jackson and Emily is gone over to see Farther. Eliza Ann has been theire fore a week. One of them stayes all of the time with them sence Paw has been so porly.

[May 9, 1858-Sunday] May 9 Jackson has com home from Farthers. He is still bad.

[May 14, 1858-Friday] Friday 14 I have been over staying with paw sence last tusday. He was verry bad one night that i was theire. We did not think he would have seen morning but he has got better again. When i came home i found one of the little negroes sick with the flux. Ant Caty and Mrs Cain was here to day to help us to quilt.

[May 16, 1858-Sunday] Sunday 16 i have been over to farthers. He is better. Mima had a fine boy yesterday and they are both dooing verry well. I found John still bad with the flux. Mary Ann Alexander is bad with the flux. She is daingersly bad they say. We have not been to see her yet.

[May 18, 1858-Tuesday] tusday the 18 we have sent fore the Dr this morning fore the child is still bad yet.

[May 19, 1858-Wednesday] wensday the 20 Jackson and Eliza Ann is gown down to york to night. They think Mary Ann is a little better and John is still bad.

[May 21, 1858-Friday] friday night 21 I have been over to see Farther to day. He is abel to walk out in the yard with help but still has bad spells and cant sleep at night. I think John is a little better to day. Manda Gulic is bad with the fever and Hiram['s] vine is verry bad. It looks like an inflimation of the stomic. She throws up everry thing she takes and they cant git no pashish through her sence last tusday.

[May 22, 1858-Saturday] Saturday night John is better and vine is no better this morning. The Dr did not think she would see morning and Jackson is gone over theire to night. Billy Alexander is verry bad with the flux this too dayes.

[May 23, 1858-Sunday] Sunday morning 23 well we are all sent fore to go to see the last of Billy Alexander. They say he cant live without an alteration verry quick. They had 3 Dr with him last night. Jackson, Eliza and uncle Billy is gown down to see him. Emily has come home from her Grandfarthers this morning. She sayd he was verry bad a friday night but is better again. Vina is still alive but no better. This is preachen day but i cant go as Jackson is gone and this chile is not much better yet. Its bowels is still a runing of yet. Mary D Brown

[May 24, 1858-Monday] Monday night May 24 well I have been down at york this evening and I have seen the last of uncle Billy Alexander. He bid a diew to this world this evening at half past three oclock. Mary Ann is a little better. Vine is a living yet but no better. Farther was verry porly to day. Jackson and Lida is at york. Betsy is theire with her baby and it has the cough and none of the rest of the children could get to go to see him. Jane Willson baby died May 23 1858. Martha Falls baby died May 24 1858. John mends verry slow. Mary D Brown

[May 25, 1858-Tuesday] tusday 25 I have seen uncle Billy Alexander laid in the cold and silent grave to day. They opened the coffin at the graveyard. He did not look natureal. I thought he looked the wors gone fore the time that ever I saw. My ould Farther is verry porely and Eliza Ann is gown back to stay with him.

[May 28, 1858-Friday] friday 28 I have been over to see Jane this evening

and her baby is not well. John mends alittle.

[May 30, 1858-Sunday] Sabeth evening 30 I was over with my Farther last night and till this evening. He was quit lively last evening when i went and in a great gale of talking that night, talked till ten oclock before we could git him to quit. It was all on religion. John and Lawson was theire but he slep verry little all night and next day, sunday he was sick, bad sick all day and sick when i left him. Oure little negro was still sick and i had a bliged to come home. Eliza came home too and I bid him farewell that evening to meet no more in this world. He told me that it would not be long that I would have an earthly Farther but that he hoped that I had an Heavenly Farther that could do more fore me than he could do. Yes and ere another week closed I had no earthly Farther. I fondly hope that that Farther in Heaven is mine and i am his.

[May 31, 1858-Monday] Monday evening 31 Jane Furguson['s] baby is bad with the flux. Jaily came out yesterday and I have been home with her to day. Ant Emily came home with me. The chile is bad.

[June 1, 1858-Tuesday] June the 1 Jackson is gone to take ant Emily home this evening and he heard that Paw was no better. Janes baby is still bad.

My dear ould Farther died June the 3 1858. He was verry bad the night beffore. They thought it would not be long. Lawson and John and Harriet was all theire that night. John was gone home ad Harriet to send for the rest of us. Theire was none of us theire but Lawson fore all how long we had all been looking for it, theire was none of us theire at last. Harriet and John had not got home till the seen was over. He was up and walked to the dore, with help that morning and then they laid him down to rise no more. He died between six and seven in the morning of June 3 on wensday morning. A glourious change to him from pain to perffict happiness. MDB

[June 4, 1858-Friday] June the 4 friday evening Oh my God this solom day we have paid the last tribute of respect to my dear ould Farther. We have laid him in the grave, theire to remain unto the great reserection morning. Theire was a large company of people theire. Mr James Davis spoke a while and gave a prayer. Oh, but he did talk perty. He said, whare could the man be found that could fill his place. The church and all his friends have lost a great friend. Oh I never knew what it was to loss a Farther before but I must try and be resined to the will of God fore it is my loss but his gain, try and doo as he has tole us so often. When I was theire a few dayes before he died he tole me it would not be long that I would have an earthly Farther but he says you have an Heavenly Farther that can doo more fore you than I ever could. Pray to him, love and serve him, be shure that you deceive not youre self. Oh the warnings that he gave his children to prepare fore the houre of death, to search the scriptures day and night and serve God. MD Brown

[June 6, 1858-Sunday] June 6 I was over to see mother last night. She seemes to be a dooing verry well. Ann Neely is a going to stay with her this week. Hiram and Harriet was over. Mimay has had the mumps but has got well. Her and the chile is dooing verry well. Janes baby is better to day and Hannah is with her.

[June 10, 1858-Thursday] thursday morning 10 we have started Harriet to school this week to Miss Martha Love and she was home with her last night. Hannah was here last evening and i have been up to stay with ant Caty to day. Emily is gone home with Susen and Eliza Ann is gone over to youngs to stay with Jaily. Young took Hannah home to day and brought Jaily home with him. His mother is gone home this evening. She has been theire most too weeks. The chile is better and John is better.

[June 13, 1858-Sunday] Sunday evening 13 I have been at preachen to day but left the children at home. I am affraid of the cough. Mother and Sister Harriet was theire and we had good preachen too. MD Brown

[June 18, 1858-Friday] friday the 18 we had Miss Lorena and Rachel Coldwell on a visit to day.

[June 22, 1858-Tuesday] tusday the 22 I had a little quilting to day. Ant Emily was out and I had a few to help me to day. It is a beautiful quilt. It is the tulup. Mary D Brown

[June 26, 1858-Saturday] Saturday 26 Hiram and Butler came over this evening.

[June 27, 1858-Sunday] Sabeth evening 27 I have been at preachen to day. Mr Gimmy Davies is an excelent young man and a fine preacher.

[June 29, 1858-Tuesday] tusday morning 29 we had Mr Gimmy Davies with

us last night. The more i am with him the more i think of him.

[June 30, 1858-Wednesday] wensday evening 30 aunt Caty and me was up at Mr Turners on a visit to day. They are clover people.

[July 4, 1858-Sunday] July the 4 theire is a great celerabration at Bulix creek to day and a fine pick nick diner. The whole country was invited. None of oure pepol went, it was so fare.

[July 5, 1858-Monday] monday 5 I have been over to see Mother. Sister Harriet is bad with the tooth ach but it is a little better this morning. The rest is all well. John has got to walking again. He had a bad time of it.

[July 8, 1858-Thursday] July the 8 this has been a wet day. We had Robert Coldwell and Francis with us to day a helping the girls to quilt.

[July 10, 1858-Saturday] 10 Lida and i have been down to york last night.

[July 11, 1858-Sunday] Sabeth 11 I was not abel to go to preachin to day, i am bad with a pain in my shoulder. Sister Harriet came home with them from preachen.

[July 12, 1858-Monday] 12 Harriet and I have been over to see Hannah to day and we had a dreadful rain this evening.

[July 14, 1858-Wednesday] wensday 14 I have had company plenty to day. We had Mrs Johnson and Willie, Mary and Susan, William and Lilly and Sally Crenshaw all on a visit.

[July 18, 1858-Sunday] Sabeth evening 18 me and lida has been up to enen to day. Mr Mulenax held a sacrament theire to day. Theire was but few theire.

[July 20, 1858-Tuesday] tusday night Mrs Good has been down to day and spent the day with us and helpt us to quilt and ant Caty too.

[July 23, 1858-Friday] July friday night 23 I have put my quilt out this evening.

[July 28, 1858-Wednesday] 28 Hannah Alexander is staying here this week to attend the mineral spring. Her health is bad.

[July 30, 1858-Friday] friday 30 Mother has been over on a visit yesterday and last night. It is her first visit sence Farther did.

[August 5, 1858-Thursday] August 5 we have all been down at the Mineral spring to day at a great pick nick dinner. It was splended indeed. A tabel thirty feet long and heaped with every thing that was nice and good.

[August 7, 1858-Saturday] Satturday evening 7 I have just got home from Mothers. They are all well and in to the eyes a drying fruit.

[August 8, 1858-Sunday] 8 we have no preachen to day. Mr Davis has gone to assist Mr James at a proctred meeting.

[August 9, 1858-Monday] 9 Jackson has gone over to Mothers and took Lida, Emi, Lawson and Sally to dry fruit and make sider.

[August 11, 1858-Wednesday] 11 I have had strangers to day, Mr Cotheren and Rachel and the children and Lorena too. Also Mrs Caneda and aunt Caty, ant Hannah and now they are all gone. Mary D Brown

[August 14, 1858-Saturday] Agust the 14 friday this is the day of the general muster at york and Jackson is gone fore his last days muster and is gone by Mothers fore the girls this evenging.

[August 15, 1858-Sunday] Sabeth evenging 15 I was at preachen this morning and heard a great sermon indeed, as great a sermon as ever i heard Mr James Davis. His tex was, "What doo ye more than they that is, what doo ye the proffecers of Christ more than other men." It was good.

[August 16, 1858-Monday] monday morning 16 Lawson and Jane came home with us last evening and is gone home this morning. Andrew Thirner has come down to make a molases mill this week.

[August 18, 1858-Wednesday] wensday 18 I have been over at Franklins this morning. They have a little negro verry bad. Franklin and Hannah is gone to shelba on a visit.

[August 21, 1858-Saturday] Satturday evening 21 Hiram and Harriet has been over to day. They are done their molases mill and made some molases this evenging.

[August 30, 1858-Monday] 30 I have been up on a visit at dr goods to day.

[August 31, 1858-Tuesday] 31 we have been busy making molases to day and they are first rate. Jane and young is over here.

[September 5, 1858-Sunday] September 5 I have been at preachen to day. Mr Davis is a great young preacher. He did preach too as good sermons to day as ever i heard. His tex this morning was, "You must all stand before the judgement seat of Christ." In the evening, "Know ye not that ye are in Christ Jesus except ye be reprobates."

[September 7, 1858-Tuesday] 7 I was down at york, me and Emily. They are as well as common. I went down and took dinner with Peggy and Clementine, the first time in a good while.

[September 12, 1858-Sunday] Sabeth evening 12 Jackson is gone down to Bulix creek to the meeting and i look fore him home this evening.

[September 13, 1858-Monday] monday evening 13 I have had Mrs Martha Meek to see me to day and Jackson is gone after mima. The hooping is at Hirams and we are affraid that her chile gits it.

[September 14, 1858-Tuesday] 14 We have been making molases to day.

[September 15, 1858-Wednesday] 15 I have been over helping Jane to quilt to day and Mr McAlwee had a little negro to die last night with the hooping caugh. It is a verry bad cough. He hase some eigh bad with it. I am verry fraid of oure children gitting it.

[September 17, 1858-Friday] September 17 I have been down at Mrs Cains to day. Mrs Cain had a fine sone this morning, a big diner to day and a fine company of ould ladyes.

[September 18, 1858-Saturday] 18 I have been over to see Mother to day and have come home and sent fore mima this evening.

[September 19, 1858-Sunday] 19 Jackson, Eliza Ann and myself have all been over at smerna to day. Mr Castel had a sackarment theire to day.

[September 22, 1858-Wednesday] 22 we have been macking more molases today. We have made some eighteen galens.

Betsy Cains, Tomis Gibson was born September the 17 1858. MD Brown

[September 24, 1858-Friday] 24 friday night I have been to preachen to day. It is the comencement of oure sackrament. Mr Watson preached to day. His tex was in 2 Corinthians the thirteenth chapter and sixt verse. This is the words, "Examen your self whether you be in the faith ore no."

[September 25, 1858-Saturday] 25 a saterday night. we have some company to night, ant Emily and Mary Ann, ant Polly and Eliza and Ann Neely and little Ginny Macarter. Mr Leroy Davis preached this morning. His tex was in 2 Thessalonions 2 chapter and 16 verse. These are the words, "And hath given us everlasting conslation and good hope through grace." Mr Watson preached this evening. His tex was in Acts 11 chapter and the 20 and 21 verse.

[September 26, 1858-Sunday] Sabeth night another communion sabeth day. Mr Watson preached this morning. Psalm and Jackson and I came home at interval. John Alexander took a chill and we came home with him and he got better. Jackson is gone home with him. Mr Leroy Davis preached his farewell sermon this evening. He is going to Arkencis soon as he can git off this fall. John Enloe and Mary Ann Alexander was married September the 28 1858. Hannahs Marys baby, Dolf was born October the 1 1858.

[October 6, 1858-Wednesday] wensday the 6 I have been up at Andrew Turners to day to help them sow. They are busy gitting reddy to start to Arcances. They want to start next monday.

[October 9, 1858-Saturday] saturday 9 Jackson, Lawson and myself have been down at york to day. I had a web of janes cloth that come to 23 dollars and a half and Jackson had cotton down with him. It is selling at eleven and a half. MD Brown

[October 10, 1858-Sunday] Sabeth 10 Jackson, Eliza Ann and Emily Jane is gone to Caanan to preechin to day. We have none at Bershaba till the 4

of this month.

[October 12, 1858-Tuesday] 12 this is coart week and Jackson is gown down to day.

[October 14, 1858-Thursday] 14 I was over to see mother last night. Shee keeps well and hearty. Harriets children has the caugh perty bad.

[October 17, 1858-Sunday] 17 Jackson is gown up to Center to day and was going home with Mother to night.

[October 19, 1858-Tuesday] 19 Eliza Ann has put up her fine quilt to day. It will take lots of quiltten.

[October 20, 1858-Wednesday] 20 I have got my janes web out to day.

[October 22, 1858-Friday] 22 I have been down to see betsy Cains Baby to day. It has the cough and is bad. Oure children has got it too. Lawson and Jaily Cate is caughin bad.

[October 26, 1858-Tuesday] 26 Hiram has a big corn husking to night and Jackson, Eliza Ann and Emily and Lawson is all gone over to it to night. Myself and children is by oure selves and they are most all got the cough now.

[October 29, 1858-Friday] Friday 29 i have had John Enlo and Mary Ann fore diner to day and Rachel Coldwell this eveng.

[October 31, 1858-Sunday] 31 i have been over to see Mother to day. They are all well.

[November 1, 1858-Monday] Monday night Nov 1 well this has been the day of the sale at Alexanders. The negroes was all sole. John Bratten got Anesi at eleven hundred dollars. J Bollen Smith bot Milly at one thousand and seventeen dollars. Mr S A Mcelwee bot Margaret at nine hundred and eighty dollars. Mr Hugh Tate bought Ruff at eight hundred and sixty one dollars. Ant Emily Alexander bot liza and her chile, matha at three hundred dollars. She gave one dollar for ole Danel.

[November 2, 1858-Tuesday] the 2 this is the day of the sale over here at the plantation. I have had cousin Psalm Brown and Mr Summerford and cousin John Enloe and Mr Mcelhany fore dinner. The sale is over. Tom Bell got out of jaile last sunday evening. He has been in fore a year.

[November 3, 1858-Wednesday] wensday 3 Jackson ad Eliza Ann is gone over to Mothers and lide is a going to stay a while. We are all well but the hooping caugh. Oure family all has it now. That is to have it, there is ten got it now.

[November 7, 1858-Sunday] Sabeth evening 7 Hiram and Harriet was over last night. They hant been here in a long time with the children on the acount of the caugh. We all have it now and bettsy Cains baby is verry bad with it. They have to set up and watch it all night now fore the last to weeks.

[November 8, 1858-Monday] Monday the 8 this is election day and Jackson is gone down to york, election for Sheriff. Theire is thre candidates, Mr Love, Mr Stillwell and Mr Pagen. Jackson is a Love man.

[November 9, 1858-Tuesday] 9 we are caughing away.

[November 10, 1858-Wednesday] 10 Mr Stillwell is Sheriff. Pinkney Alison and Marth Meek was Married Nov 11 1858.

[November 14, 1858-Sunday] Sabeth 14 this is peachen day but i cant git to go. The children is so bad with the caugh that i cant leave them.

[November 16, 1858-Tuesday] 16 Billy Browns William has got his han badly mashed in the molases mill and Billy Brown has been up to see him to day. To of his fingers is off.

[November 17, 1858-Wednesday] 17 Jackson has been at york to day and Robert Brown came home with him.

[November 20, 1858-Saturday] 20 Robert Brown and Eliza Ann is gone to Waren Quinns to a big singing last night. It is verry cole.

[November 21, 1858-Sunday] 21 this is a sabeth morning and we have no preachen but we hav oure bibels and plenty of good books to read if we have the will to improve.

[November 24, 1858-Wednesday] 24 ant Caty, ant Hannah and Betsy good was all here to day to help us to quilt.

[November 25, 1858-Thursday] 25 this is thanks given day but the people is not keeping it.

[November 27, 1858-Saturday] 27 we have had Mrs Davis and Mother and Ann to see us to day. Little Willie is bad with the caugh.

[November 28, 1858-Sunday] Sabeth night Mr Davis preached to day but i did not git theire as Willie is still bad. I think about and long to git to preachen. Mother stayed and went to preachen. It is a wet evening. We had Dr Good to se Willie this eveng. The rest is all dooing verry well now.

[November 30, 1858-Tuesday] 30 Wille is no better yet and Mr James Davis and Susan is with us to night.

[December 3, 1858-Friday] December 3 Wille is still bad and the Dr thinks it is his teeth that makes him so bad. He cut his gums.

[December 4, 1858-Saturday] 4 Wille is a little [better] to day. We had ould Mr Coldwell with us to day on a visit and the Dr was here too.

[December 5, 1858-Sunday] Sabeth night 5 Wille is still better and Emily and Harriet was over with theire grand Mother last night. They are all well. We have had company to day. A bad way to spend the holy sabeth day. A day that God has gave us to prepare fore that Sabeth of rest that remains fore the children of God. If we sin we know that we have an advocate with the Farther, even Jesus Christ the richous. Hannah Alexander and Robert Brown and Peter Moses is all here to night. MD Brown

[December 15, 1858-Wednesday] wensday 15 Eliza Ann and Emily is gown down to york to day. Wille has got better and all the rest.

[December 19, 1858-Sunday] Sabeth night 19 I was over to see Mother and Sister Harriet last night. They was all well.

[December 22, 1858-Wednesday] 22 Jackson and myself has been down at york today.

[December 25, 1858-Saturday] 25 this is Christmas day and it is a still one. We have no company.

[December 26, 1858-Sunday] 26 I have been at preachen to day. I have not been theire much lately.

[December 28, 1858-Tuesday] 28 I have Juste got home from seeing sister Harriet. She has another fine daughter and there a dooing verry well.

[December 29, 1858-Wednesday] 29 Emily has gone over to see her ant Harriet and stay with her some dayes. We are all well. Lizas baby died 29 of the.

1859

[January 1, 1859-Saturday] New years morning we are all well, 1859.

[January 3, 1859-Monday] 3 this is sale day and Jackson has bought Alexanders ould place and gave ten dollars and fifteen cents per acor. It was a big price.

[January 8, 1859-Saturday] 8 Mother and Hiram has come up to day.

[January 11, 1859-Tuesday] tusday 11 we have Mr Ruffus Whiteside with us to night just from arcancis last week.

[January 12, 1859-Wednesday] 12 Eliza Ann and Ruffus and Emily and Harriet is gown over to help ant Hanah to quilt.

[January 16, 1859-Sunday] Sunday 16 i have been over to see Mother and Harriet to day. They are all well.

[January 23, 1859-Sunday] Sunday 23 we had Robert and Rachel Brown up

last night and it has turned dreadful cold. They are all gone to preachen. It is dreadful cold indeed. Ant Harriet has the pains and has sent fore Emily to go and stay with her a week.

[January 27, 1859-Thursday] 27 i was over with sister Harriet last night. She is bad with the pains cant walk a step.

[January 28, 1859-Friday] 28 Hiram has brough Emily home and i am a going over to stay a week with her. John Alexander and Mary Sutten was married January the 25. It was a runaway match but they have all got over it. Mary D Brown

[February 1, 1859-Tuesday] Febuary the 1 I have just come home from Hirams. Harriet is no better and i have to go back in the morning. She is verry bad.

[February 6, 1859-Sunday] Sunday 6 Jackson and lida came over to Hirams to day and i have just come home with them. The babby has taken verry bad this evening and i am now going to start in the night. MD Brown

[February 7, 1859-Monday] monday i have come back home thus morning. The babby is a little better. It was verry near gown. I did not think it could live one houre when i got theire. It was from the mopheen its mother had been tachen ore in giving it some oile in a spoon that the mopheen powdey had been tachen in. It was compleetly dead.

[February 10, 1859-Thursday] 10 Harriet and the baby is better and i have come home.

[February 20, 1859-Sunday] 20 I have been over to see Harriet. She mends slow but is abel to walk alittle. It is the sabeth and i am going to preachen.

[March 12, 1859-Saturday] March 12 Hiram and Harriet has come over to day, the first time she has been here sence last Oct, a long stay away.

[May 11, 1859-Wednesday] 11 Eliza Ann and Emily Jane is gone down to Betsy Cains, baby, C Thomis Gibson died May 11 on a wensday evening. It took sick a tusday night and died a wensday. MDB

[May 13, 1859-Friday] May 13 I have been at a great temperance meeting to day at bershaba. Mr Watson, Mr Baty and Mr Smith all spoke and theire a fine picknick diner and a great crowd. They gaind some members.

[May 14, 1859-Saturday] 14 I have been down at york to day and i seen Johns lady fore the first time.

[May 15, 1859-Sunday] 15 Jackson, Eliza Ann and Emily Jane is gown to smerny to day.

[May 16, 1859-Monday] 16 Hannah Alexander has been out staying a few days and Robert is gone to take her home. Theire was a dreadful storm down bulixcreek on last Sabeth night. Such a storm never has been in south carolina. It blew down one dwelling house and killed one woman and wounded another so bad she cant git over it. It rained, blowd and hailed. It is said that the hail is firteen feet deep whare it was banked up. It blew houses, wagons and corn cribs, with the corn in them cleen off.

[May 22, 1859-Sunday] 22 we have been at preachen to day and Mother was over with us last night.

Janes Furgisons Nancy Emily was born May 23 1859.

[May 25, 1859-Wednesday] 25 i have been down at the mineral spring to see ould Mrs Curckendall. She has been verry bad.

[May 30, 1859-Monday] 30 I have just cam from Mothers. They are all well. Ould Mr Wallace is a lying at John Brown verry bad.

[May 31, 1859-Tuesday] 31 I have been over to see hannah. She is verry porly at this time.

[June 11, 1859-Saturday] June 11 we have Mrs Betsy Cain and Miss Sally Curckendall up to see us this evening and Hiram and Harriet too.

[June 12, 1859-Sunday] Sabeth evening 12 Sally is gone home with her aunt Harriet.

[June 14, 1859-Tuesday] 14 I have been down at york to day and left Eliza

Ann to stay this week.

[June 16, 1859-Thursday] 16 this is the time of the examination at york. This is the big day.

[June 18, 1859-Saturday] 18 Robert is gown down after lide.

[June 20, 1859-Monday] 20 Robert Brown has started away to school to Tom McWee. Eliza Ann is verry sick, her bowels is working her.

[June 22, 1859-Wednesday] 22 i have been over to see Mother and Harriet to day. They had a good rain on yesterday and we are verry dry.

[June 26, 1859-Sunday] 26 we have all been at preachen to day and Ruffus was here last night. Mother and Hiram came home with us.

[June 29, 1859-Wednesday] 29 ant Hannah has been over to day. She has got better.

[July 3, 1859-Sunday] July 3 Eliza Ann and Emily Jane and William Coldwell has gown over to aunt Harriets last night and to the baptist preachen to day. Sabeth evening we have had a great rain this evening. We was verry dry, we had suffered bad.

[July 10, 1859-Sunday] sabeth 10 I have been at preachen to day. Mr Davis is improving fast. He has preached some great sermens lately.

[July 12, 1859-Tuesday] 12 Hanah Alexander is out staying a while and we had Mrs Mary Coldwell and Rachel to spend this day with us.

[July 14, 1859-Thursday] 14 Mother and sister Harriet has been over to day and i have not been well fore some time. I have often of the notion that my time on earth would be short but i have lived to see manny a day and many an up and down. I am now in my thirty seventh year and oh Lord God, if it be thy will i pray that though would spare my life fore the sake of the dear children that thou hast given me. And if not, into thy hands oh Lord I commend my motherless children. Keep them under thine own omnipitent eye. Oh be a God and Farther to them and oh my God, aid and support me in fulfilling the many duties encumbent on me as a mother. Oh will thou give me a praying heart and

a submissive will to all the troubles and trials of this wourld. Mary D Brown

[July 17, 1859-Sunday] 17 we have no preachen to day and all at home another sabeth day. Gods Holy day of rest.

[July 19, 1859-Tuesday] 19 Ant Harriet has been over to see us to day.

[July 21, 1859-Thursday] 21 we have had Ruffus up to spend the day with us.

[July 24, 1859-Sunday] 24 Jackson and Eliza has gown over to stay with Mother last night. It is the sabeth and i am not abel to go to preachen. A sabeth days journey i am to make, either fore the better ore the worse and oh my God, may it not be spent in vain.

[July 25, 1859-Monday] 25 well Jackson, Eliza Ann and Emily Jane is all gown to york to day. Lide is gown to git her wedding trimens.

[August 11, 1859-Thursday] Eliza Ann and Ruffus Whiteside was married August the eleventh on thursday evening at candel light by Mr James Davis. We did not have a big crowd, just a few of the kin.

[August 14, 1859-Sunday] 14 this is the sabeth and Ruf and lide has come up this morning to go to preachen and Mother has come by.

[August 15, 1859-Monday] 15 lide has gown home with him to stay this week.

[August 21, 1859-Sunday] 21 Emily and Harriet is gown to smerny to day and Ruff and lide has come home to night. M Brown

[September 2, 1859-Friday] Sept 2 Ruffus and Eliza Ann is gown over to see theire grandmother and ant Harriet. It is the time of the general muster.

[September 4, 1859-Sunday] Sabeth evening Emily and Harriet and Ruffus and Eliza is gown to union to hear the baptist and my health is bad.

[September 11, 1859-Sunday] Sabeth evening 11 Emily has com home from preachen with a chill on her. Theire is preachen down at Jeams Cains this evening by Mr Davis.

[September 12, 1859-Monday] monday evening Emily has had a hard chill to day.

[September 13, 1859-Tuesday] Meek Mcelwee and Margaret Ann Coldwell was married on tuseday evening, September the 13 1859 by Mr James A Davis.

[September 15, 1859-Thursday] 15 thursday Eliza Ann was up with us last night and Emily is got better.

[September 18, 1859-Sunday] 18 Sabeth Mother was over to see us last night and Jackson is gown home with her. Betsy Alexanders John Jemes was born the seventh of Agust 1859.

[September 19, 1859-Monday] monday 19 I have been verry unwell to day.

[September 22, 1859-Thursday] thursday 22 ould Mr Star More was burried at Bershaba to day and Jackson, Eliza and Emily was at the burrien.

[September 23, 1859-Friday] 23 this is the commencement of oure communion at Bershaba and i will not git out atall. MDB

[September 24, 1859-Saturday] 24 satturday evening Mother and Hiram and Harriet is here. They say they had great preachen. Mr James Adams was theire.

[September 25, 1859-Sunday] 25 Sabeth evening the meeting is over. Mr Anterson was out to day 25. I have had Mrs Davis and Mrs Cain to see me to day and Hannah Alexander and Susun and Emily is gown down to see lide.

[September 26, 1859-Monday] 26 Jackson is gown to take Hannah up to bobs.

[September 30, 1859-Friday] 30 friday Emily is down and the Dr says it is rumatism.

[October 2, 1859-Sunday] Oct 2 sabeth is no better and we had Gimmy Duff and Robert Brown last night.

[October 3, 1859-Monday] 3 Ruffus and Eliza has come home to night and Emily is verry bad with the pains.

[October 4, 1859-Tuesday] 4 Mother came up this evening.

[October 6, 1859-Thursday] 6 sister Harriet came over this evening. Emily is no better.

[October 9, 1859-Sunday] 9 this is preachen day but i cant go. Mother has come up to stay a while.

[October 12, 1859-Wednesday] 12 Mother has gone home and Emily is not much better. She has not walke a step in too weeks.

[October 14, 1859-Friday] My babby was born October the 14 on a friday morning at five oclock. I had Dr Good with me. The firs time i ever had a Dr. I got along verry. Oh how thankful i should be fore all things to doo so well, a living chile and living Mother.

[October 28, 1859-Friday] Oct 28 Harriet has been over to see us to day and I have got to feel perty well again. Emily has got abel to go again.

[October 30, 1859-Sunday] 30 Mother and Buttler was over last night and Lawson went home with them.

[November 10, 1859-Thursday] Nov 10 well we have had another sene. Elen had her babby this morning. It was dead born, a verry fine hearty looking boy. She was verry bad from tusday night unto thursday morning. We had Dr Good all the time and Dr Alison at last. She is still bad.

[November 12, 1859-Saturday] 12 Mother is staying with us and Elen is verry [bad] She cant move her legs nore turn herself in the bed.

[November 16, 1859-Wednesday] 16 Elen is some better and sister Harriet is staying with us now.

[November 20, 1859-Sunday] 20 Harriet is gone home and Ruffus and Eliza Ann was with us last night and they are gone to Smerny to preachen to day and Elen mends slow.

[November 25, 1859-Friday] 25 Mr McCaw has a singing at bershaba and he sung then to day. Theire is a singing at Franklins to night and all of our folks is gone. Ruffus and Eliza Ann is gone too and he sings to morrow too.

[November 27, 1859-Sunday] 27 Elen is verry bad to day. We have Dr Allison and Dr Good both with her to day. It is a dangures case. MD Brown

[December 2, 1859-Friday] Dec 2 Elen is verry bad yet. Dr Good is here twice every day. Hiram and Harriet was over last night. This is the day John Brown, the abalishenst is to be hung for the inserectionst at Harpers ferry.

[December 4, 1859-Sunday] 4 Sabeth night elen seems to be a little better to day. This year is drawing to a close and it has brought some troubles and triles with it, no more than i justley deserve and i hope that it will be all fore oure good. Thy promises are that all things shall work together fore good to them that love God.

[December 11, 1859-Sunday] 11 Sabeth I have been at preachen to day, the first time i have been at preachen in a long time.

[December 18, 1859-Sunday] 18 James Duff and Ruffus was here to day.

[December 21, 1859-Wednesday] 21 Harriet is gone over to see her Grand Mother to day and i have had a hard chill.

[December 25, 1859-Sunday] 25 this is christmas sabeth and i cant go to preachen to day. Elen is a little better. Lawson is gone home with Ruffus.

[December 27, 1859-Tuesday] 27 Ruffus and Eliza, Emily and Harriet is gone over to Hirams to a singing to night.

[December 29, 1859-Thursday] 29 there is a singing at the church to day and one here to night.

[December 31, 1859-Saturday] 31 theire is a big snow and we have a heap of company. MD Brown

1860

[January 1, 1860-Sunday] New Years day 1860 Theire was a big snow yesterday. The new year arose like a bride having on her weding dress adorend with pearls and dimonds. Little doo we know what another year will bring forth. The main thing fore us to know whether we are living with oil in oure lamps and reddy to go forth to meet the bridegroom, early ore late.

[January 22, 1860-Sunday] 22 I have been to preachen to day, the firs time I have been out in a long time. Heard a good sermon and saw too elderes ordained, Dr Good and Ruffus Meek and thre deacons, John Davis, Robert Alexander and Franklin Waker by Mr James Davies.

[February 4, 1860-Saturday] Feb 4 this is the day that elen started to Columbia to the Dr to operate on her. John Smith and Jane M F_____ married Feb 14 1860. MD Brown

William Coldwell and Sue Furgison was married Feb16 1860.
Robert and Sally Coldwell son, Feb 17 1860.

Robert Whitesides and Marg Shemphard was married Feb 21.
John and Polly Brown mooved to noth carolina 23 of Feb 1860. Ruffus and
Eliza mooved to theire own house 28 on clarks fork.
Sally Coldwell died March 7 1860.

[February 19, 1860-Sunday] 19 Elen has landed home safe and sound this
evening.

[April 3, 1860-Tuesday] April 3 James Duff left fore tenisee this morning.

[May 11, 1860-Friday] May the 11 this is the commencements of oure
communion ocasion. Mr Thommis Hall was theire. His tex was in Mathew
3 chapter, 3 verse, prepare ye the way of the Lord. Make his paths strait. He
preached a great sermon. He tole the people what it was to prepare the way
of the Lord and theire was 3 joined the church, Hiram C Thomison, James
McKnight and Emily Brown, My 2 daughter. I fondly trust and hope that
it will be fore theire own good and the glory of a God. Hiram and Harriet
got theire baby baptised. Its name was Ida Sharlet Amand and we got one
baptised, Fanny Vance. Vance is the maiden name of oure ould grand mother
Brown.

[May 13, 1860-Sunday] Sabeth evening another communion seasen over.
Mr Davies preached this morning and Mr Hall this evening. A fine meeting we
have had and oh my Heavenly Farther as I have set to my seal that I was on the
Lord side, I humbily pray thee that though woulds give me grace and strenth to
live that becomes a profoser of the gospel of Christ so live that I may not dread
the grave as little as my bed.

[June 16, 1860-Saturday] Mr Leroy Davies died at Mr Davies June 16 1860
and was buryed at Beeshaba.

[June 29, 1860-Friday] ould Mrs Cain died June 29 1860.

[July 8, 1860-Sunday] July 8 sabeth evening Mother was with us last night and
we have all been up to hear Mr Johnson preach to day. He is one of the nicest and
pertiest yong men that I did ever see and did preach the best sermons and make
the greatest prayers that I eve heard one of his age. His God has done great things
fore him.

[July 10, 1860-Tuesday] Andrew Quinn died July 10 1860.

[July 13, 1860-Friday] Henry Duff and Eliza came in on a visit July 13 1860.

[August 3, 1860-Friday] 3 Ruffus and Eliza has been up to day and we had a jolly crowd last night, Henry and Eliza Duff, Peggy Floyd, John Alexander and his wife, Billy and Jane Willson.

[August 20, 1860-Monday] 20 we have been at preachen to day to hear Mr Johnsen fore the last time. He is greatly beloved by the people.

[August 22, 1860-Wednesday] 22 Mother, Sister Eliza and myself have been down to see Ruffus and Eliza to day.

[September 10, 1860-Monday] Sept 10 this is the day that Henry and Eliza Duff and Peggy Floyd and Margaret Glenn.

[September 14, 1860-Friday] September friday the 14 ould M Davis and Mary Davis have been to see us to day and Jackson has started to Bethel to a Communion.

[September 15, 1860-Saturday] 15 Satterday night we are all well. One more week is nearly past and gone and oh my God have I made the improvment that I should have done. I know that I have come far short of what I should have done but I beleve that I have a great advocate with the Farther, even Jesus Christ who theire sets on Gods right hand pleading the cause of his chosen people and I hope and believe in his all sufficent grace to attone fore my sins. MD Brown

[October 28, 1860-Sunday] Margaret Ann Mcelwees Sally was born Oct. 28 1860. MD Brown

1861

[April 26, 1861-Friday] Aprile 26 1861 this is the commencing of oure meeting. We had Mr Beard with us.

[April 28, 1861-Sunday] 28 Mary Ann Enlo had twin babeyes to day and both dead.

[May 7, 1861-Tuesday] Little Sally Cain did May the 7 1861.

[May 12, 1861-Sunday] 12 Ruffus and Eliza and myself was on a visit up to see aunt Polly Floyd last night and went to Bethany to preachen to day.

[June 1, 1861-Saturday] June 1 I have been down to see Eliza to day. They are all well.

[June 9, 1861-Sunday] John Alexander, Robert died June the 9 1861. Aunt Harriets Dorcas Emily was born June 28 1861.

[July 5, 1861-Friday] July 5 Jackson and Mother is gone up to see aunt Polly. She is verry porley.

[July 11, 1861-Thursday] July the 11 1861 Eliza Ann came up last night and Hariet and Fanny Brown went home with her. Emily and Betsy Good is gone up to Mrs Hudsons.

[July 13, 1861-Saturday] 13 theire is a meeting of the people at the mineral spring to day to raise a company of volenteers to go to Virgina. Aunt Polly Floyd died July the 13 1861. Unikle John Janes died in arcances June the 11 1861. Cousin Gimmy Janes died in arcancis December 1806.

[July 15, 1861-Monday] 15 theire has been a series acksident happened to day. Mr William Whitesides of Noth carolina had to grown sons drowned to day. They was waidend in a mill dam when they got in the chanel and both got drownded.

[July 21, 1861-Sunday] 21 Jackson and myself was up at Center to day at a comunion to day. Mr Thomas Hall was theire. He preached this morning. His tex was in John 4 chapter and 21 verse. He preached a great sermon.

it was a solem day. News reached here this morning of a great battle in Richmon. the great Manasa battle. Mr Watson got up in the morning and beged the people to compose themselves and listen to the solem mesenger of God, as we stood in great need of help at this time and hoped it would be a day long to bee rememberd by many a one that was theire on this comunion ocasion. I humbaly hope that these seasones may not pass unimproved by me.

[August 11, 1861-Sunday] August 11 Robert Whitesides and Eliza was up last night. He is going to start to columbia tusday in Capt Millers company.

[August 15, 1861-Thursday] 15 Mother and I was up with aunt Sally Floyd last night and over at aunt Pollyes praisment of her estate.

[August 16, 1861-Friday] Franklin McElwee died august the 16 1861.

[August 18, 1861-Sunday] 18 Mr Davis preached to a good maney of the volenteeres to day fore the last time fore some of them.

[August 20, 1861-Tuesday] 20 Ruffus went down to day to join Capt Millers company.

[August 26, 1861-Monday] 26 Capten Mccorcale company left this morning fore camp of instruction.

[August 27, 1861-Tuesday] Meek McElwee died August 27 1861.

[September 1, 1861-Sunday] Emily J took the typhoud fever the 1 day of September.

[September 15, 1861-Sunday] 15 Emily is bad.

[September 28, 1861-Saturday] 28 Emily has taken a relaps in the fever and is verry bad.

[October 5, 1861-Saturday] Oct 5 Emily is verry low. It looks like that time with her would soon bee no longer.

[October 15, 1861-Tuesday] 15 Eliza is down too and Emily no better.

1862

[November 13, 1862-Thursday] Nelly died Nov the 13 on thursday night in 1862.

[November 23, 1862-Sunday] Elen died Nov the 23.

[November 24, 1862-Monday] Billeyes Jsey Nove 24.

[November 25, 1862-Tuesday] My dear chile Harriet died Nov the 25 1862. A solem time it has been to me but the Lord giveth, the Lord taketh away and blessed be the name of the Lord.

1863

[January 1, 1863-Thursday] Jan 1 1863 new years morning, all well. A great Blessing to enjoy good health.

[January 12, 1863-Monday] Hannas Alaxander died Jan the 12 1863.

[January 16, 1863-Friday] Johny Ruffus was born Jan the 16 on a friday morning 1863.

[January 31, 1863-Saturday] 31 Jackson started to Columbia this morning. He was sick and did not go with the company.

[February 6, 1863-Friday] Franklins Mary died the 6 of Feb 1863.

[April 9, 1863-Thursday] Mrs Isabella Enloe died April the 9 1863.

Emily took the typhorad fever the 1 day of september.
Hannah Alaxander died Jan the 12 1863

[September 25, 1863-Friday] September 25 this is the day my dear Husband, Robert Jackson Brown left his home and family at hs countrys call to go to Charlston and was fifty the 15 of this month.

[September 27, 1863-Sunday] 27 this is the close of another communion ocasion. We have had Mr Douglass and Mr Watson, fine young men and I have been spared to set to my seal that I am on the Lords side and I hope and pray that it may not be invane that such great preachen has been sounded in my eares while my deare Husband is fare away in the tented field. Oh my Heavenly Farther will though be pleased to give me a heart of submishion and resignation to thy Heavenly will, knowing and believing that whatsover thou dooest is right.

[October 16, 1863-Friday] Oct 16 Jackson is well and in a fine three story hous in Charlston and Mother was over to day.

[October 18, 1863-Sunday] Cateyes Rachels amey was born October 18.

[October 25, 1863-Sunday] Oct 25 Sister Harriets, Eliz Jane as born Oct 25.

[October 30, 1863-Friday] 30 Mother and Willey has been up to day.

[November 14, 1863-Saturday] Nov 14 I have been over to see Mother and got a letter from Jackson. He is now in Greenville.

[November 18, 1863-Wednesday] 18 they have left Greenvile and gone to Branchvile.

[November 29, 1863-Sunday] 29 Lawson has the mumps. The rest all well. Jackson is now home on furlow, hearty and well.

1864

[January 1, 1864-Friday] A newyears day 1864.

[January 9, 1864-Saturday] 9 Jackson has landed home to night with the mumps.

[January 11, 1864-Monday] Mrs Good died 1.11.1864.

[January 18, 1864-Monday] Brother Johns William was here to night 18. He was wounded and then taken prisener and now home.

[February 8, 1864-Monday] Feb 8 Jackson landed home this evening fore good. Theire company was disbanded.

[February 12, 1864-Friday] 12 Robert Whitesides came home from virging to day.

[February 14, 1864-Sunday] 14 Bob and Joe was up to day. He looks

hearty and well.

[February 23, 1864-Tuesday] 23 aunt Lersy Watson and Bob was up to day.

[February 24, 1864-Wednesday] ould Mrs Watson died Feb 24.

[March 22, 1864-Tuesday] Ebenezer P Castel and Emily J Brown was maried March 22 1864 by Mr Latham, a soseder preacher. He blongs to the twelfth regament, company B southcarolina troops.

[March 30, 1864-Wednesday] 30 E P Castel has left this morning fore his regament in virgina.

[April 5, 1864-Tuesday] Aprile 5 I have been over to see Mother and sister Harriet. All well. MD Brown

[May 7, 1864-Saturday] E P Castel has got a furlow and has landed back safe and sound this evening the 7 of May. Theire has been a big battle in virgina and Ruffus has telagraphed home that he was wounded in the thy. Robert Whitesides was killed the 6 of May. I was verry sorry to heare of it as Robert felt verry neare to me. He was killed in virging, the battle of the willderness.

[May 19, 1864-Thursday] Eliza Anns Hatty Lee was born May the 19 1864.

[May 23, 1864-Monday] 23 Mother was over to see Eliz and the Baby.

[October 23, 1864-Sunday] my dear ould Mother died Oct 23 on sabbeth night and was buried at Bershaba grave yard on monday. The last place she was from home was all night with me and went to preachen at Bershab. She bore her sickness with great patance and in the full asshurance of a glourious immortality beyond the grave. I stayed with her fore neare thre weeks, day and night and Oh my Heavenly Farther as i am now left without Farther ore Mother unto thee my Heavenly Farther I now commit myself and all thats mine into thine hands, relying on thy manifold promises those that put theire trust in thee. And now my heavenly Farther I doo humbily pray the in the name of my deare Jesus that I may never forgit the solem seens that I have been called to pass through and now deare Savioure I have been the chiled of manny prayers. Oh may I follow theire footsteps as fare as they followed thee and I doo beseech the my God that I may not bee deceving my never ding soule with a name to live by while I am dead in tresspasses and in sin. MDB

[October 26, 1864-Wednesday] 26 I have been back at the ould place and Sister Harriet and myself have devided her estate between us too with out a croose word.

[November 4, 1864-Friday] Nov 4 I have been back at the ould place but no Mother to meet me. Now it will soon be the case with us all. The places that now no us will soon know us no more.

[November 7, 1864-Monday] ould Eddy Chambers died Nov 7 1864. Mary Ann Enloes Eliza was born Nov 7 1864.

Marha Liles died Nov 9 1864. Eliza Ann mooved back to her own house thursday the 10 of Nov 1864. Lawson and Martha is gone to stay with her and now my heavenly Farther as I have left her without Farther, Mother ore Husband, I doo humbily pray the to bee Husband, Farther and Mother to her. Thou hast promised it to them that put their trust in thee and such, I fondily hope, she has done. Bless her in health and prosperity as far as though in thine own good judgement seese best fore her.

[December 5, 1864-Monday] my dear son, Lawson has left his home to go in his countryes defence the 5 of Dec 1864 on monday mornin. He is sixteen yeares one monthe and ninteen dayes ould. A wounderful thing to take such boyes out. He has been a fine study boy and I hope he will continue so. Oh Heavenly Farther I now plead with thee and earnestily commend to thee my absent son, separited from the family circle by the call of duty to oure endangered country. Be thou God, oure Heavenly Farther his guardien and comfortor, be thou instead of Farther and Mother unto him. Preserve his boddy in health and his mind in peace, Inspire him with such confidence in thee that he may commit to thy most powerful, wise and just providence, all his cares and burdens. Be thou the strenth of his heart and the anchore of his soule and keep him in peace and quietness and assurance. Deffend him from all danger. Help him in time of need. Comfort him in all timese of sickness, sorrow and paine. Perfect thy strenth in his weekness and may thy grace be sufficent fore him. Guide him in everry difficulty and heare him when he askes fore wisdom to direct, instruct and thourly furnish him fore everry duty involveng on him. Heare these my prayers most merciful God. MD Brown

[December 15, 1864-Thursday] Hew Nichles and Emma Hudson was married Dec the 15 1864.

[December 18, 1864-Sunday] 18 we have got a letter from Lawson. He has got to his company. They are at Grayems vill bellow Charlston. He has not got his box yet.

[December 20, 1864-Tuesday] William Davis and Eliza Brown was marred Dec 20 1864.

[December 22, 1864-Thursday] 22 another letter from Lawson. He has hard times. He dose not git enough to eat. He had to live one day and night on parched corn the cavelry horses left.

[December 27, 1864-Tuesday] Emily Jane Castel left home tusday morning fore Petersburg 27.

[December 28, 1864-Wednesday] 28 Lawson keeps well but has never got home. He has a hard time of it now in the camp, pinched fore something to eat and stand guard till he is nearly frozed to death.

1865

[January 1, 1865-Sunday] a new years day fore 1865 Let me begin this year with solem refflection and say with Job, "When a few more years are come I shall go the way whence I will not returen." Let me not only beleve this, but think of it and feel the importance of the sentiment. Yes, in a little time I shall be no more seen. How, Whare shall I be disposed of? The seasens will return as beffore, but the places that know me will know me no more fore ever. Will this be a curse ore a blessing? If I die in my sins I shall return no more to my posessions and enjoyments, to the calls of mercy, to the throne of grace to the house of prayer. If I die in the Lord, I shall, O Blessed imposibility, return no more to these thorns and briers to this vain and wicked world, to this aching head, to this throbing heart, to these temptations and troubles and sorrowes and sins. Mary D Brown

[February 5, 1865-Sunday] Feb 5 Jackson is gone down to stay with Eliza Ann to night. It may be fore the last time as he is orderd to the seet of ware this week. Hiram and Harriet is over to night.

[February 9, 1865-Thursday] Emily has landed home safe and sound to night Feb 9. She has been to Peetersburg since the 27 of Dec.

[February 11, 1865-Saturday] 11 this is the day my dear Husband has gone again to meet Sheermon and his invading foe. A great battle is expected about Collumbia soon. Oh that this cruel ware would end. God grant us peace once more. MDB

[February 15, 1865-Wednesday] 15 I have got a letter from my dear son Lawson. He is at Adams run near Charlston, nearly surouned by the yankeyes and has never got home yet.

[February 16, 1865-Thursday] 16 my Dear Husband has got home. He and Franklin has been sent home to gather up the rest of the men.

[February 18, 1865-Saturday] 18 I have been down to see Eliza to day and she has come home with me. Jackson expect to start back a monday to Collumbia. MDB

[February 21, 1865-Tuesday] 21 we have great excitment at this time. Shearmon has taken Collumbia and is marchen on this way as fast as he can. Jackson had never gone back. I don't know what has come of Hiram. He was left at Collumbia and I now not what has come of my poor chile, Lawson, when Charlston and Collumbia has booth fallen. He was at Adams run the last word but I trust that My God will protect him and bring him safe through.

[February 22, 1865-Wednesday] 22 we are looking fore the yankeyes every day. It is an awful time. Oure Husband and sons affraid to stay in theire houses and the people a running and tryin to hide something to eat and some of their close. I have hid nothing. I will trust in God and doo the best I can. Tom has gown down to bring Eliza home. She has run from the yanks.

[February 28, 1865-Tuesday] 28 the excitment has got over. The yanks has gone to the left. Emily is verry porly with the cronic rummatize. I doo feele verry humble and thankful that we have been spared from been over run by the cruel foe but oure time may come. They have made maney a destute family. They have nearly burnt up Collumbia and Hiram has got home.

[March 2, 1865-Thursday] March 2 Emily is verry bad. It has thrown her into spasms.

[March 4, 1865-Saturday] 4 aunt Harriet has been over last night and Emily is some better.

[March 6, 1865-Monday] March 6 Emily is some better and Mag Whiteside, Catty Castel, Drd Castel and his wife has all been here to day to see Emily and the Dr hors is verry sick.

[March 8, 1865-Wednesday] 8 I have once more got a letter from my dear son. He is Cheeraw. He is well but how he got theire he dose not say. MDBrown

1866

[April 22, 1866-Sunday] April 22 One more communion sabeth in the church Militent is over. Mr Davis preached a friday and Ebb and Emily had theire first son baptised. Its name is Leanerd Harris. Mr Robert Anitersan of York preached a satterday. A verry execlent man. William Davis wife, Eliza was baptized and joined the church and then had theire son baptised, Eda Clinton. Mr Porter preached a Sabeth day. Lawson Brown and Jane had theire son baptised. His name is Hew Jackson.

[April 29, 1866-Sunday] 29 Ebb and Lawson has gone down to Sharon to day to a sachrament.

[May 6, 1866-Sunday] May 6 I have been down to see Ruffus and Eliza to day and found them all well and took dinner with Mr tommy Whitesides. Lawson, Sally and Mag has gone over to Union to preachen today and the rest of us are at home in good health.

[May 18, 1866-Friday] 18 Lawson has gown down to see Ruffus and Eliza and

left Sally with them.

[May 25, 1866-Friday] Cattyes Coldwell was born May the 25.

[May 27, 1866-Sunday] 27 Lawson and John Brown is gone over to his unckle Hirams and gown down to Beth shilo to a sackrament and I have been at preachen at Bershaba to day and my little Ruffe is sick. The rest well.

[May 28, 1866-Monday] 28 my little son has got better and all the rest is well. Ruffus Whiteside was here this evening. They are all well.

[May 31, 1866-Thursday] 31 I was down with Eliza last night. Left Jaily and brought Sally home. They a all well and dooing well. MDB

[June 2, 1866-Saturday] June 2 sister Harriet was over to day. They are all well and we have had a fine rain.

[June 5, 1866-Tuesday] 5 Jackson and Billy has been down at york to day and we have had a great rain, some hail and wind. It was worse at york, blew down trees, unroofed houses and was verry severe.

[June 6, 1866-Wednesday] 6 Jackson and Emily was down to see Ruffus and Eliza to day. Eliza is not so well.

[June 7, 1866-Thursday] 7 Mrs Cain, Mary and Gimmy was up here to day on a visit.

[June 10, 1866-Sunday] Sabeth evening 10 I have been at preachen to day. I thought Mr Davis done better than common. His tex this morning was in Psalms 73 cha 25 verse. "Whome have I in Heaven but thee and theire is none on earth that I desire beside thee." This evening in 2 Corrinthians and 6 ch 1 verse, "We then as workers together with him, beseech you also that ye receive not the grace of God in vaine." He done his part but I feare he had many a slleepy hearer. Oure church seemes to bee on the decline. Our Zion is not in aflourishing state. We need more preaching people and more in the laws of Christ and cause. Oh God send thy holy spirit to enliven thees hearts of Bearshabo congaration.

[June 16, 1866-Saturday] June Eliza Ann Whitesides ___ was born June the

16 and satterday night in 1866. She is dooing verry well her self. The babe is not dooing so well. It has got an ugly ulcer on its back.

[June 21, 1866-Thursday] 21 I have now got home from Ruffes Whitesides. The babe is no better. Dr Barran was out to see it to day and Dr Dick is theire everry day but I fear they can doo but little fore it.

[June 23, 1866-Saturday] 23 I am now staying with Eliza and the babe.

[June 26, 1866-Tuesday] 26 I am at home once more and find them all well.

[July 1, 1866-Sunday] July the 1 I was down at Ruffs last night. The ulcer has broke and run a little. I see verry little change on it yet. I have been at Bershaba to day and I have brought little Hatty home with me.

[July 5, 1866-Thursday] 5 Ebb and Emily have been over with us last night and Lenny is not verry well. MDB

[July 6, 1866-Friday] 6 Ruffus has been up to day and took Hatty home.

[July 8, 1866-Sunday] 8 aunt Harriet and myself have been down at Ruffs last night. They are all dooing well.

[July 14, 1866-Saturday] 14 Jackson has been down to Ruffs last night, all well.

[July 15, 1866-Sunday] 15 Lawson and Sally have been to Center to day to a communion. Mr Watson preached. He had no help.

[July 17, 1866-Tuesday] 17 I have been on a visit over to Hirams to day.

[July 22, 1866-Sunday] 22 I have just landed home from Ruffs. Ruff and Eliza has come home with me fore to stay a week.

[July 24, 1866-Tuesday] 24 I and Eliza and little Ruff has been over with Eb, Emily to day.

[July 25, 1866-Wednesday] 25 Eliza and Emily and Sally has been over to Franklins to day.

[July 26, 1866-Thursday] 26 Jackson has gone to take Eliza home and I, Jaily and Willey have been over to Mrs Mulhollen to a picknick to day.

[July 31, 1866-Tuesday] 31 this morning my dear little Johny Ruffus was well and hearty and in all the bloom of health, but ear the clock had struck eleven, he was in the very aggoneyes of death. I was setting in the doore and he went in the room and came out with one hand ful of dryed beans he picked up of the bed and showed them to me and went out with them in his hand. In a few moments he gave a hollow. It is supposed that he put the beens in his mouth and one of the little negros hit him and then he sucked the bean down his wind pipe. He was struling fore breath when I got to him and was in great misary. His Farther was at Hew Loves. I sent fore him, fore Dr Whiteside and then for Dr Barren. They vomited him but theire could bee verry little done fore him, allthough we done a heap of things fore him but could do nothing to remove it. He had some spells that he was some lighter and would talk and want to be carried out. He was out in the yard the evening before he died. I supppose the bean slid in his wind pipe and then inflamation and chocked him up. Oh the paines and misary as that deare little Ruff. I never shall forget he closed his sweet little eyes in death to wake no more till the great reserection morning on a friday morning at half past five in the morning of the 3 of Augus 1866.

[August 4, 1866-Saturday] Satterday evening the 4 Great and adorable Farther in Heaven, one most sad and awful seen thou hast called me to pass through. Thou has taken my darling babe, Ruffe from the bosom of his Mother to live and dwell with thee in his saviours boosom. Oh my Heavenly Farther, I feel that it is a verry sore chastisment but oh may I submit with humble submision to thy heavenly will.

[August 5, 1866-Sunday] 5 Sabbeth morning Sue Coldwell and Emily stayed with us last night. Gods Holy sabbeth, no little Ruffe moans and groans I hear no more. His sweet lips lie closed in death. A solem warning fore us allwayes to be preapared fore to meet my God and oh my God may this solom warning that thou has afflicted me with make a solom and lasting imprection on my mind, never to be forgotten. Oh make me like thy servent of ould. Bless the day that I was afflicted.

[August 6, 1866-Monday] Cousin Rixeny Stepeson died August the 6 1866.

[August 8, 1866-Wednesday] 8 aunt Harriet was up to see us to day.

[August 9, 1866-Thursday] 9 Ruffe and Eliza was up to day and Emily was over.

[August 12, 1866-Sunday] 12 Sabbeth evening I have been at preachen to day, seen my dear little Ruffe grave and heard too fine sermon and seen too children baptised. Mr Schoghans, Mr Dicksons and hew Nickles was buried to day at Bershaba.

[August 20, 1866-Monday] 20 Mrs Cain was up to see me this evening.

[August 23, 1866-Thursday] 23 Jackson, Sue Coldwell and I was at york to day and this is the night he has left his home and Lawson and I was over with them to.

[August 26, 1866-Sunday] 26 Ruffers and Eliza, Hiram and Molly was with us last night and have all been at preachen to day.

[August 27, 1866-Monday] 27 Eliza Fulgason and I have been at york to day.

[August 31, 1866-Friday] 31 Jackson and Fanny has gown to see lide and bring Wilee home. Lawson, sally and Mag is gone over to theire aunt Harriets to night.

[September 2, 1866-Sunday] September 2 Lawson, Sally and Mag has got home and Emily is with us to night.

[September 3, 1866-Monday] 3 I have took supper with aunt Caty to night. Capt Glenn to candadate fore sherf is with us to night. Leney is sick and Emily has sent fore me to go over theire.

[September 4, 1866-Tuesday] 4 I have been over to see sue and Eliza. James Mason, the shereff, has been out theire to day and leveyed on Franklins property and he is gone.

[September 5, 1866-Wednesday] 5 Jane Furgason and the children was with us last night and I took supper with Mrs Cain this evenig.

[September 6, 1866-Thursday] 6 Jane Furgason, Sally and Mag has gone to Hew Loves to day.

[September 7, 1866-Friday] 7 Emily and Eb has gone down to Dr Castels to night and Ruffe and Eliza is with Sue and Eliza to night. Jackson has gone over to stay to bed time. MDB

[September 8, 1866-Saturday] 8 Ruff and Eliza came by this morning and stayed an houre. Lawson is gone to Union to a singing to day.

[September 9, 1866-Sunday] 9 Sept 1866 Sabbeth morning. Oh thou giver of all good, into thy hands I commend my self and all thats mine and thank the fore the mercies past. implore thy protecting hand to bee with me through this holy sabbeth day. Sabbeth evening Once more my God hast permited me to set under the sound of the gospel. Mr Davis tex was in Romans 8 21, "Delivered from the bondage of corruption into the glourious liberty of the gospel children of God." Under the sounds of such preachen I must either be made better ore worse. Oh my God may it not be in vane that I have enjoyed such privolages.

[September 10, 1866-Monday] 10 I have been up and took dinner with Aunt Caty to day. Aunt Sally Coldwell, Aunt Caty and Aunt Betsy Cain supper with me this evening.

[September 11, 1866-Tuesday] 11 I have spent part of the day with Emily to day and this evening with Sue and Eliz. My God foregive all that I have said ore done amiss. MD Brown

[September 16, 1866-Sunday] Sabbeth night 16 My family is all home once more and well. Jackson has got home and has been once more to a great communion at Bethel. Lawson and Sally has been over to Smerny to a meeten to day. My Heavenly Farther, I hope that this may not have been a mist spent sabbeth to those that have set under the sound of they Gospel this day. All that has been done ore said ammiss, Oh will thou freely forgive, fore the sake of thy dear son. I and the little Children have spent the day at home, no little Ruffe to keep us company. But while I view through faith the happiness he enjoyes, I Bless and magnify thy great and holy name.

[September 21, 1866-Friday] sept 21 this day is the commencement of oure communion ocasion. This day has been so wet that I did not git out but theire was preachen. Lawson was theire. Mr Porter and Mr Davis was theire. I hope the weather may change and we may have a fine meeting yet. Lawson is gone down to york fore Mr Wood.

[September 22, 1866-Saturday] satterday evening we have had fine preachen to day. Mr Porter this morning, Mr Wood this evening and theire is preachen to night. I have stayed at home and kept Eliza babby. Theire was several joined the church to day. Mrs Emma Nickles and had her son baptised. His name was Hew Joshua. Miss Susan Pursly also thre colerd members, Dina Davis, Emma Davis, Leroy Crosbey. On surtificate, Mr Davy Scoggins and his wife, Precious from shilo church.

[September 23, 1866-Sunday] Sabbeth night 23 oh mighty God and blessed Saiviour thou hast spared me to set to my seal that I am on the Lords side by proffesion. Oh Heavenly Farther grant that it may not be a name to live while I am dead in tresspasses and sins but grant that I may have oil in my lamp and stand watching to meet the Bride groom at eney watch of the night. I have been spared to heare great preachen to day, Mr Porter this morning and Mr Wood this evening. They are both great preachers. Theire was five more joined the church to day, Paten Wilkison, he was baptised this morning, Mr William Dackson, Miss Lar___ Dickson, Miss Cintha Dickson, Miss Ann Scoggins. I have been to preachen to night. Mr Porter preached. His tex was in Solomons song 8 chapter 5 verse, "Who is this that comes from the willderness leaning on the arm of her beloved?" It was a great sermon.

[September 24, 1866-Monday] monday night more fine preachen and more added to the church. Foure more joined to day, Miss Harriet McAphee and was baptised. Miss Mary Knox, Miss Jane Knox, Miss Margaret E Love. Mr Wood preached to night. He preached a great sermon. His tex was Mathew 8 chapter 22 verse, "But Jesus said unto him, follow me and let the dead bury theire dead." A sermon that will long be remembered.

[September 25, 1866-Tuesday] tusday night Sept 25 this preacious meeting and gloury revival is still going on and still more inquring the way to Jesus. Oh my Heavenly Farther, how can I praise and glowery thy goodness to thy people at this time of the outporning of thy holy spirit and the gracious manafestation of thy love to perishing sinners. Theire was thirteen joined the church to day, Mrs Polly Nickles, Miss Nancy Jane Wilkason, Mr Perry Watterson, those thre was baptised in the sesion house to day, also Miss Mary J Brown, Miss Sally D Brown, Miss Susan E Bell, Miss Sarah E Robison, Miss Mary McCarter, Miss Mary E Neely, Mr John G Brown, Mr Butler B Thomison, Mr Lawson R Brown, Mr Perry Watterson, Mr James Dover.

[September 26, 1866-Wednesday] wensday night the meeting is still going on. We have Mr Wood and his Wife and Mr Porter with us to night and a great deal of company [at] the time of the meeting. Theire was preachen to day and to night. M Wood preached to night. His sermon was on the last, the great day of judegment day. Theire was too more joined to day, Mr Joe Bell, Mr William Black. Mr Black was baptised to night.

[September 27, 1866-Thursday] thursday night Mr Porter preached to night. His tex was, "You must give an acount of the past, present and future." It was the last of oure great meeting but I have no dout this great sermon with the formore one, the past, the present and the future will ring in some poore sinner eare through all eternyty. And now oh Heavenly Farther, oh Blessed Saiviour, how shall I gloweryfy thy great and holy name fore the outporing of thy holy spirit on the people of oure church at this time. Such a revival amonst oure people as I have never seen before and Heavenly Farther thou hast manny promises to them that seek the early. Most of those that have joined the church was in the bloom of youth and the flower of health. Allmighty God fore the sake of thy dear son, keep those dear children in the hollow of thy hand unto such must we look fore the prsperity of oure church. Soon they shall take oure places and we be numbered with the dead. Oh Heavenly Farther as they have set to theire seal that they will serve the Lord, oh give them understanding hearts to read thy holy word. May the lay up theire treashures in Heave whare moth doth not corrupt nore theaves break through noire steal. My Heavenly Farther, I doo humbly plead in the behalf of those dear children. I hope that my dear Saiviour is now pleading in behalf of those dear children saying that they are mine. I will that none of them be lost, oh greant that I and all that have named the name of christ may have oile in oure lamps and be ready to go forth to meet the bride groom whene ever the summens comes. Mary D Brown

[September 30, 1866-Sunday] Sept 30 I have been over to heare the Methadose yesterday and last night and to day and stayed with Amos and Eliza Burns.

[October 4, 1866-Thursday] Oct the 4 I have been over to see sister Harriet to day.

[October 7, 1866-Sunday] 7 I have been down to see Ruff and Eliza. They had a house raisen and had a good manny of theire friends theire. Ebb and Emily went on to William Castels.

[October 11, 1866-Thursday] 11 Jackson has gown down to see Ruff and Eliza and rode Lawsons colt.

[October 13, 1866-Saturday] 13 Lawson, Sally, Mag and I and Ebb and Emily was all over at Hirams at a singing last night. Emily stayed with her aunt Harriet and theire was a singing at Bershaba to day.

[October 14, 1866-Sunday] 14 sabbeth evening I have been spared to set under the sound of the gospel once more. Mr Davis tex was in Colations 3 chapter 11 verse, "Christ is all in all." Theire was a fine turen out and theire seemes to be more of a liverly dispotion in the congaration. MD Brown

[October 18, 1866-Thursday] Oct 18 I have been down to spend the day with Betsy Cain to day. Mr Cain had a crib rasen. We are all well.

[October 19, 1866-Friday] Oct 19 Perry and Mary Patterson oldest son was born Oct 19 1866.

[October 22, 1866-Monday] Oct 22 I and Lawson have been on a great trip up to Bethel to a protracted meeting. Mr Watson, Mr Wood and Mr John Watson was up at Henry Glenns and stayed all night with George Patrick and Mary, his wife. They all seeme to be a gitting allong verry well as to the things of this life, but as to the thing on most importance i cant say. Theire was great preachen. Mr Wood, a satterday and Mr Watson on Sabbeth. He preached to the young people. His tex was in Psalms 144 chapt and 12 verse, "That our sones may grow up as plants grown up in theire youth that oure daughters may be as pollished corner stones, pollished after the similitude of a pillor ." A great congaration of people and the greates preachen and singing that I ever heard. Oh my God, what manner of life should we live that have such great blessings bestowed on us. Oh my God will thou be pleased to send thy holly spirit to enliven oure hearts to make a right improvement of such invalluabel blessings to the precious soule.

[November 1, 1866-Thursday] Nov 1 Jackson has gone over to stay with Hiram and Harriet to night and Lawson has gone to Mr Ginkences to a corne shucking.

[November 2, 1866-Friday] 2 Emily is over to day.

[November 4, 1866-Sunday] 4 we are all well this holy sabbeth morning. I have been at preachen to day. Mr Davis gave us a fine sermon. His text was in Hebrews 12 chapter, 25 verse, "See that ye refuse not him that speaketh; fore if they escaped not who reffusd him that spake on earth, much more shall we not escape, if we turen away from him that spaketh from Heaven." It was a great sermon. Gimmy Duff came home with us. Sister Eliza son from tenesee, brother Lawson and Hiram came by and took Dinner with us.

[November 6, 1866-Tuesday] Nov 6 I was down at R G last night. Theire little son, Ruffe Jackson is sick.

[November 7, 1866-Wednesday] 7 Lawson and E J Furgeson has gone up to crowders creek to theire cousen, Gim Duffs wedding & Lawson has got home. They had a nice time of it. Gimmy Duff and Jane Craig was married November 7 1866.

[November 9, 1866-Friday] 9 Emily was down with Eliza last night. She think body is some better.

[November 13, 1866-Tuesday] 13 I have come home from R G Little Jacky is verry bad. If he dont soon git a chang he cant last long. He dose suffer great pain. This is the day of the eliction. Jackson, Lawson and Willey has all gone to york and Emily is down with Eliza to day and night. MDBrown

[November 16, 1866-Friday] 16 I left Eliza and little body hooping once more to meet them soon but little Jackey died the next morning after i left. Eliza babe departed this life Nov 14 at five in the morning, a wensday 1866. In the provadence of God I have been called on to give up another of my friends. Three months and eleven dayes sence I laid my dear little Johny Ruffe in his narrow house of clay till little Jackson Ruffe was laid theire too. Theire is some thing so crushing to the heart to see a dear chile die, life going out, quivering and flikering in its sokets, pressed frome its inner fountains and shudering allong the feeble and wasted boddy. The light dying in the eyes, the lips no more vocal with that rich music which poured a gladdneng flood through oure hearts. And then, life gone, the eyes closed, the lips sealed, the voice hushed, the spiret fled, naught left but the cold clay with its rigid lines and marbel features. O the desolation, the terror, the irresponcibility agany of Death. Now relegion is the only comfort to beleve in, the lord of life, the redeemer of sinners. It points to the wound in his boddy and the love wich saves His people in life and

in death. It cleares the eyes of faith from the mist of earth and directs it far away to the spirit land. It opens the doore of a blessed houshold, the fammily of God in heaven and reveales the loved ones theire. Theire in everlasting light. My loved one is not here. My loved one is not in the cold grave, Yonder, Yonder In glory among the blessed. Every facelty glowes with the noblest life, every feeling is awake. He lives in condition of glorified existence. The sleeping body shall awaken in imortal fresshness and beauty. Then i hope to meet him both soule and boddy to part no more. I will meet you, i will love you. In the far off Eden land, I will walk with you forever. I will hold you by the hand, I will talk to you my darling. I will heare youre sweet replys as we wander by the river that flowes through paradice. I know theire is a round you A circle of the blesst, But i know when i behold you I will know you from the rest. I will know you by youre voice And the love light in youre eyes. Oh ill know you and ill love you, When we meet in paradice.

[*November 18, 1866-Sunday*] 18 I have been blessed with life and health to attend Gods house of worship once more and heare Mr Davis preach. His tex was in first timothy first chapter and sixteenth verse, "Fore this cause I obtain mercy." A fine congration of people. Ruffe and Eliza came up last evening took supper with Emily and stayed with us all night and to preachen to day. They are verry much hurt about the death of theire babe but we beleve Gods word that every thing shall work together fore good to them that love god. It will try theire faith and I hope it will make them cling close to the cross of Christ. They are gone home and Fanny with them to stay a while. Sister Harriet and Buttler came by but they are gone home. Mary D Brown

[*November 20, 1866-Tuesday*] 20 tusday the children is all gone to the singing school to day. Mr William Willson has a school at Bershaba. Yesterday was his first day. Mr Willson and Dosha Coldwell was with us last night.

[*November 21, 1866-Wednesday*] wensday 21 Mary Ann Enloe baby was buried at Bershaba to day. It was dead born. MDBrown

[*November 26, 1866-Monday*] 26 Jackson and I was down at york last night to stay with aunt Emily. She is verry poorly.

[*December 2, 1866-Sunday*] Dec 2 sabbeth evening one more holly sabbeth day spent. Mr Davis gave us fine preachen to day. His tex was, "Let youre light so shine beffore men that they may gloaryfy youre Farther in Heaven." Ruffes and Eliza and aunt Harriet was with us last night and all went to preachen to day and then home.

[December 4, 1866-Tuesday] 4 this is the day that Franklin Furguson was sole out by the sheriff. The girls bought the most of the property that was sole for a meare mention, one horse afore ten dollars, waggen too, buggy six and so on.

[December 5, 1866-Wednesday] 5 theire was a singing to day and the children is gone down to a singing at Mrs Davis to night. Emily and Ebb is with us. Emily and Salley was down at Mrs Davis last monday the 3.

[December 8, 1866-Saturday] Liney is not dooing well last night and to day. Ebb went down to york last night and brought Dr Jackson out to see him. Dr Baren was out to day.

[December 10, 1866-Monday] 10 we are all well. We have killed oure hogs to day. We have a fine chance of meat.

[December 13, 1866-Thursday] 13 Ebb, Emily and I have been down to york to day. Leney is no better. Dr Bratten examined him. He thinks he is ruptured but not serten. MD Brown

[December 15, 1866-Saturday] 15 this has been singin yesterday and to day. Addy and Laurey Brown was with us last night and this is a cold, stormy, sleety day.

[December 20, 1866-Thursday] 20 we are all at home and all well and it is a great blesing to enjoy good health. Mr McCarter and Dealy Packerd was married to night by Mr Davis. Leney has got better.

[December 22, 1866-Saturday] 22 Rufus and Eliza has been up to day and Mr and Mrs Porter called on us this evening on his road from Yorkvill. He has been down assisting Mr Wood, he has a communion on tomorow. He is going to leave them, he is going to Georgia to take care of his parents. The people of York and Bershaba is verry loath to give him up. He is such a great preacher and so much bloved but duty to his aged parents calls him and we must be resined.

[December 23, 1866-Sunday] 23 Mr Porter preached at Bershaba to day. His tex was in Mica 6 chapt 8 v. "He hath shown the, oh man, what is good and

what doth the Lord require of thee but to doo justly and to love mercy and to walk humbily with thy God." He is another great preacher. He is talking of leaving us too. I am mighty sorry to part with Mr Porter and Mr Wood but i must be resined to my lot beleving that all things shall work to gether fore my good if I am a chile of God.

[December 25, 1866-Tuesday] 25 this is christmas day. Mag and her Paw has gone to york. Ebb and Emily has gone over to Meek Whitesides. Lawson and Sally has gone down to Ruff Whitesides. I and the little children is at home and little Leney.

[December 27, 1866-Thursday] 27 Jackson and Ebb and Wille have gone over to Hirams.

[December 29, 1866-Saturday] 29 we have had another singing yesterday at the church and one here last night. A dreadful cold night and every room was full. We had Mr Willson, Charly Wat, Rachel Quinn, Molly Thomison, Wille Thomeson to stay all night with us. Harvey Gunings took supper with us fore the last time. He is going home with Ruff Meek. He is to start next monday fore Arcances. MD Brown

1867

[January 1, 1867-Tuesday] A new years morning, tusday 1867 what is man that though takes notace of him. Great allmighty god that though has brought me to see the light of another new years mornning, myself and family enjoying good health and plenty of earth. How shall i praise and magnify thee as i ought, a poore week, hell deserving sinner that i am. Naught but Christ, naught but Christ. Can i rely on the great attoning sackrafice fore such sinners as i that i have been spared through another year. I have had many and great mercies bestowed on me and mine through the cloosing yeare and thoug hast called me to pass through many sore triales and through many temptations. I have had many a thorn in my flesh but as thou hast said to thy servent of ould, "My grace shall be sufficent fore thee." Oh my Heavenly Farther as thou has brought me saffely through the cloosing year, i now beseech the to continue thy loving kindness and thy tender mercies to wards me and mine. Oh my Heavenly Farther, now renew my dedacation of myself and all thats mine to thee. Heavenly Farther, Bessed Saviour will thou axcept this offring in thy strenth and not in my own weakness? Great God send thy holy spirit to enliven this cold, dull and stupid heart of mine to love and serve thee as i ought. Be this the perpuse of

my soule, my solem, my determind choice dayes, months and yeares must have an end. Eternity has none. New yeares night – Ebb and Emily has been with us to day. Mr Massabough and Jaily is with us tonight and they have a fine hearty son, William Agustus.

[January 2, 1867-Wednesday] 2 this is the day Ebb and Emily has mooved over to theire unckle Lawsons ould house on the big road.

[January 3, 1867-Thursday] Ruff has been up to day. They are all well and he has got Martha. Mr Massabough and Jaily has started home this evening to Spartningburg.

[January 5, 1867-Saturday] 5 this is oure preachen day. The weather is so bad that Mr Davis did not come. I have been over to see Emily last night. They are very well moved and plenty of help and I spent the day with aunt Harriet. I have been at Bershaba to day. Mr Davis tex was in Job 19 25. These are the words, "I know that my Reedeemer lives," a good sermon and oh may i remember that this is not the last of these great sermones. If they are not rightly emproved theire will be a solom account to give of theme. Oh my Heavenly Farther, may i make a right improovement of these great privalegese though has blessed me with.

[January 17, 1867-Thursday] 17 just from Ruffe. They are all well and hearty.

[January 21, 1867-Monday] 21 Sister Peggy has spent the day with us to day. She is staying with Mrs Davis.

[January 23, 1867-Wednesday] 23 this is the day that Franklen Fuguson mooved down in the Coldwell house and Mr Davy Scoggins mooved in his.

[January 24, 1867-Thursday] 24 I have been down to help Mrs Cain to quilt to day.

[January 25, 1867-Friday] Eliza Ann has been up to day and her and Sally are gone over to see her aunt Harriet and her sister Emily.

[January 27, 1867-Sunday] 27 Ruff and Eliza, Ebb and Emily was with us last night.

[January 29, 1867-Tuesday] 29 I have been over to see Mr and Mrs Davis, sister Peggy and Mrs Black this evening.

[January 30, 1867-Wednesday] 30 i have been down to see Mr James Cold-well this evening. He looks like he would not be here long. Mrs Mary Davis babby was born Jan 31-1867. MDBrown

[January 31, 1867-Thursday] 31 Ebb and Emily gave the yong people a party last night.

[February 1, 1867-Friday] Feb 1 Mrs Cain has spent the day with us to day. MDB

[February 9, 1867-Saturday] 9 this is the last day of their singing and they had a fine dinner and a great crowd.

[February 11, 1867-Monday] 11 Mrs Cain and I have been on a visit to Mr Ginkenes to day and was well pleased with my visit.

[February 14, 1867-Thursday] 14 Sally has gone to see Ruff and Eliza and to a singing at the ould Man Whitesides.

[February 16, 1867-Saturday] 16 Sister Harriet has been up and spent the day with me today.

[February 17, 1867-Sunday] 17 Jackson was with Ebb and Em last night and Lawson has gone to Smerny to day.

[February 24, 1867-Sunday] 24 Ebb and Emily was with us last night. We are all well. Theire is no preachen to day. Mr Davis is sick.

[February 25, 1867-Monday] 25 I have spent this day with Mrs Scoggins. My first visit, well pleasd. Jackson was down at Ruff to day. They are all well.

[February 26, 1867-Tuesday] 26 Eliza Furguson and Ann Scoggins with us last night. 26 I have been down to see Mr Davis to day. He is verry porly with a pain in his side, something like pneumonia.

[March 3, 1867-Sunday] March 3 Gods holly sabbeth day. We are all at home

and all well. A cold and stormy day and no preachen. Oure deare pastore is laid on a bed of sickness and pain. He is thought to be a little better. Oh Heavenly Farther I pray the, if it be agreable to thy Heavenly will to restore him to the bosom of his family and to the bosom of his church once more, but if thou hast ordered other wayes, may we submit to thy holy will. I pray thee Heavenly Farther that my last end may be like his and be prepared fore death. Let it come when it may welcome the sweet messenger of death. To Jesus, the crown of my hope, my soule is in haste to be gone. Oh beare me ye cherubims up and wart me a way to his throne. Thou savioure whome absent i love, whome not having seen i adore, whose name is exalted above all Glory dominion and power, disolve thou the bands that detain my soule from her portion in thee. Oh break off these adament chaines and make me eternaly free. For the happy erea begins when arraid in thy glory i shine and no longer pierced with my sins, the bosom on which i recline. Mary D Brown

[March 6, 1867-Wednesday] 6 I have been over to see Emily to day. They are all well, the greatest earthly blessing that is bestowed on dying sinners and called to see Mrs Mullholland.

[March 7, 1867-Thursday] 7 Hiram, Jackson, and unckle Lawson has been over to see Mr Davis. He is thought to bee some better.

[March 9, 1867-Saturday] 9 I was down with Mr Davis last night and set up with him all night. He rested tolerable well and seemes as if he might be better. I have spent this day with Mr and Mrs Hill, verry fine neighbores. Ebb and Emily and Jaily have gone down to see Ruff and Eliza.

[March 10, 1867-Sunday] 10 Lawson has been to see Mr Davis to day. He is no better. Ruff and Eliza, Ebb and Emily has spent the night with us.

[March 12, 1867-Tuesday] 12 Mr Davis is worse. Mrs Ginkens has spent the day with me, it has been verry cold.

[March 16, 1867-Saturday] 16 cold and a big snow.

[March 17, 1867-Sunday] 17 I have been over to see Mr Davis this morning. He is verry bad. I fear that our good shepherd will soon be taken away and we will be left like sheep without a sheperd, no one to feed the sheep and none to feed my lames. 17 I have been over to Mrs Mullhollen school house to heare the baptist preacher, Mr Gaines. His tex was in first Timatha first chapter and eleventh verse. This is the words, "According to the glourious gospel of the blessed God which was committed to my trust."

[March 19, 1867-Tuesday] 19 I now have a most sollom scene to record. I have seen my beloved preacher laid in the cold and silent grave. He died March 18 1867, on monday evening at too and was buryed a wensday at in Bershaba grave yard at thre in the evening. Mr Dickson preached a funneral sermon. He red the 15 chapter of first Corrinthens and made a verry nice descorce and then sung the five hundered and eleventh him commence at thee fourth verse. The eternal shepperd still survives and soon great and allmighty and ever to be exalted lord God allmighty though hast sorley afflicted this thy church miletent by taken oure bloved Minister from the boosom of his family and his churce. His toils are past, his work is done, he fought the fight, the victory won. God has recalled his own. He has preached fore us eleven years. He preached his first sermon at Bershaba March 16 1857. Oh heavenly Farther i feel that though hast soorly afflected me by taken my bloved Gimmy Davis from me. Though hast but recalled thy own, oh may i still feel that the etternal shepherd still survives. That sweet voice that has so often warned me of sin and pointed me to a bleding saiviour now lies cold and silent in the grave. Oh my mercaf heavenly farther, may he not rise up in judgement aganst at that great day. Oh myghty God may I hold fast to the doctrins that he preached and be prepared to meet hm in that great when though shall come to make up thy jewles. This solom seen i think will mak a lasting impresshion on my mind and i pray the on my life and conversation.

[March 20, 1867-Wednesday] 02 this is a cold and stormy night. Jackson has gone over to see Emily. She is sick. He has taken Mag over to stay with her a week. MDBrown

[March 23, 1867-Saturday] saturday 23 Eliza has been up to day and Lawson and Sally went home with her.

[March 26, 1867-Tuesday] 26 I have had some company to day, Margaret and Ann Enloe, Bell Enloe, Mrs Scoggens, Mrs Johnson, Mary Davis, Aunt Caty and Jane White.

[March 28, 1867-Thursday] 28 I have been over to see Mr Amos Burns to beg of him not to bring Mr Ratchferd here to preach and I have been over to see Mrs Mcelwee this evening.

[March 31, 1867-Sunday] 31 this day is the commencement of oure sabbeth school.

[April 4, 1867-Thursday] Aprile 4 I have spent this night with Mrs Black and the too Mrs Davis at ould Mrs Davis.

[April 8, 1867-Monday] 8 Eliza came up this evening and brought Sally home and I have Mrs Marth Meek from arkances with us to night.

[April 9, 1867-Tuesday] 9 Eliza, Sally and I have been to york today.

[April 14, 1867-Sunday] 14 Lawson was over with Ebb and Em last night and we have Sabbeth school to day.

[April 20, 1867-Saturday] 20 Leney is not well and Ebb came over fore me this evening.

[April 21, 1867-Sunday] 21 I was at york to day and heard Mr Dickson preach a good sermon. His tex was that Christ had died, yea rather risen.

[April 28, 1867-Sunday] 28 Mr Ratchferd is to preach here to day. Ebb and Emily was up last night and Ruff and Eliza to night.

[April 29, 1867-Monday] 29 I have been at york to day. Ebb and Em had Leney opperated on to day fore the hydroseal. Dr Baren, Dr Bratten and Dr Castel was all present. They put him under the influence of moofephen.

[May 1, 1867-Wednesday] May 1 Lawson and Sally has been up to Center to day at a great May day party, had a fine diner and Leney is worse.

[May 3, 1867-Friday] 3 I was over to see Em and Leney last night. He is better. Lawson and his paw are gone to Smerny. I and the children has been to sabbeth school.

John Coldwell and Fanny Ginkens was married Aprile the 9 1867.

[May 12, 1867-Sunday] 12 Sabbeth evening, another sackrament over. We

have had some good preachen. Mr Cothers is a good man and a fine preacher. The words of his tex was, "Wich things the angels desired to look into." I dont like Mr Ratchford and I dont want to hear him peach.

[*May 14, 1867-Tuesday*] 14 aunt Caty, Mary Cain and I have been down to see Franklin and his daughters to day. Mr Mcelwee died May 14 1867.

[*May 17, 1867-Friday*] 17 I was down at Ruff last night, all well. Mrs Black and Mrs Gimmy Davis was here to day.

[*May 19, 1867-Sunday*] 19 I have been to sabbeth school today. I fear poore ould Bershaba is gone, sabbeth school and all. Sue Caldwell was with us last night and Lawson has gone to bethany.

[*May 20, 1867-Monday*] 20 I have been over with Mrs Schggins to day. She has had a bealed brest. Dr Hill lanced it this evening.

[*May 22, 1867-Wednesday*] 22 Jackson has been down to see Ruff and Eliza to day, all well.

[*May 25, 1867-Saturday*] 25 this is the day that the people of Bershaba was to meet to hold an election fore Ratchford to see whether he will preach theire ore no, but it was a wet day and there was no meeting.

[*May 26, 1867-Sunday*] 26 we are all well in boddy but I am sorely trubled in mind fore the sake of my beloved churche, Bersha. I believe the dye is cast, her doom is certian with out the aid of an allmighty power.

[*May 27, 1867-Monday*] 27 Mag, Jaily, Fanny has started to school to Mrs Mullhollen to day.

[*July 4, 1867-Thursday*] July 4 1867 I have spent the day with Hew Love and family.

[*July 7, 1867-Sunday*] 7 I have been to heare Ratchford preach one sermon to day. His preachen dose me no good.

[*July 14, 1867-Sunday*] 14 I have been over to heare Mr Gaines preach to day. He is the best Baptist preacher that I have heard in some time, stayed all night with Emily. Ould aunt Polly Byers was buried to day the 20, the last of My Mothers kin.

[July 16, 1867-Tuesday] 16 Ebb and Emily and myself have been down on a visit to see Ruff and Eliza. They are all well and a fine prospect of a good crop. MDB

[July 21, 1867-Sunday] 21 Gods Holy sabbath day. I have been sparred to spend one more sabbeth at home. I seldome go to preachen. Dear ould Bershaba, a name that has ever been deare to me, whare I have been borne and raised and was baptised and have had eleven children baptised theire and have spent manny a happy day and I hope through the grace of God it has not been in vaine that I have spent so manny houres theire. I have three children buried within the walls of Bershaba grave wall. William Given, my ouldest son was buried theire Oct the 7 1854, Mary Harriet was buried theire Nov 26 1862, Johny Ruffe, my youngest son was buried theire August 4 1866. Alas, Alas fore ould Bershaba without the interposition of All Mighty God, I fear we are a devided congration, a Laommi in thy sight, that is, ye will not be my people and I will not be youre God. My God thou hast prommised to bee with me in six troubles, yea in seven though will not leave me nore forsake me. Verryfy thy promis to mee now in this houre of trouble. Lawson has gown to heare Mr Lory Sutten preach to day. Sally and Mag has gone over to the school house to heare Mr Gaines preach.

[July 24, 1867-Wednesday] 24 Eliza Furguson has been up on a visit to day.

[July 25, 1867-Thursday] 25 Mrs Cain, aunt Caty, Ann Scoggins and Mag has been on a visit to day.

[July 28, 1867-Sunday] 28 Wille has been sick to day.

[July 30, 1867-Tuesday] 30 Ruff and Eliza and Joe Whiteside has been up on a visit last night and Wille has gone home with them.

[July 31, 1867-Wednesday] 31 Mag and I have been down to york on a visit to day.

[August 1, 1867-Thursday] 1 Mrs Hill and her sister Unity Whiseenth was on a visit here to day.

[August 2, 1867-Friday] 2 Jaily and her Paw has been down at Ruffes White-sides to day, all well and the young people have had a picknick at the mineral spring to day. We have had a fine rain last night and it is greatly needed. Oure corn is burnt up.

[August 4, 1867-Sunday] Aug 4 this is the day of the communion at Center. I wanted to go but could not git leave to go but Heavenly Farther though has promised to bee with me in six troubles, yea in seven though wilt not forsak them that put theire trust in thee and such oh my God, I fondly hope I have done but if it is possable that I am deceiving my never dying soul, I know that it may be posable the heart is deceatful above all things and desperately wicked. Oh thou searcher of the hearts and tryer of the reighns of the children of man, try me oh my God, search my heart. Though hast promised to give thy Holy Spirit to them that askes it of thee in spirit and truth. Mary D Brown

[August 8, 1867-Thursday] 8 Jackson and I have been down at Franklin Furgusons. I have been down to help Eliza to fix fore her wedding.

[August 10, 1867-Saturday] 10 Ruffus Whiteside and Eliza, Eb and Emily Castel both happend on a visit here to day and went home to night. I have been sick this week with this disease of mine, the worst spell that I ever have had. I feel that I have need to have oil in my lamp to be reddy to go forth to meet the Bridegroom at eny watch of the night. I feel as if lief was verry frail, short and unceartin.

[August 14, 1867-Wednesday] Jackson and Hiram Thomison started this 14 of Aug up to north Carrolina to see Brother John Brown and family.

[August 15, 1867-Thursday] Joe Willson and Eliza Furguson was married Aug 15 1867 on a thursday at thre in the evening by ould Mr Watson. She mad but little wedding, my Lawson and John Brown, M and F Doubson and R Coldwell was all she asked.

[August 16, 1867-Friday] 16 Mary and Isabella Love has been on a visit to day and we have had a fine rain.

[August 17, 1867-Saturday] 17 Jackson has got home to night. He has been all the rounds, was to see them all. Robert wife has a son about too weeks ould an Mary has a daughter about a month ould. He was at Henry Glenns and was

at Mr Willsons to se Henry Duff from teenesee. He is verry porly. He looks like he would never git home.

[August 18, 1867-Sunday] 18 Mr Ratcheord preaches to day at Bershaba. I have never got my mind recenciled to go to heare him preach. It has been a sore trouble to me, a place that has been ever deare to me. I hope that God in his all wise providence will order all things right. Theire is some dark misteries to short sighted man. But oh my God, though in time will try all things as Gamiliel of ould said, "If his works be of man it will come to naught, but if be of God it cannot be over throded." I will leave the event with God trusting to his all wise care and preservation. Eb has tacken Mag home with him to stay a week.

[August 19, 1867-Monday] 19 this is the morning that Lawson has started to school to Mr Barron. He bords at Ruffes Whitesides. The other children has started to Mrs Mullholand.

[August 23, 1867-Friday] 23 Lawson came home last night and Sally has gone down to stay with Eliza a while.

William and Eliza Davis William Bufard was born August the 23 1867.

[August 24, 1867-Saturday] 24 this is the day that they have been working on the grave yard and Hiram, Harriet and Buttler has been up to day and took dinner with us, also ould Mr McCall and uncke Billey.

[August 25, 1867-Sunday] 25 this is the day of thee meeting at Smerny. Lawson has gone over and Sally was to go with Eliza. This is blustery, wet evening. MDBrown

[August 26, 1867-Monday] 26 I have spent this day with aunt Caty.

[August 29, 1867-Thursday] 29 aunt Caty and I have been to spend this evening with cousin Eliza Davis.

[September 1, 1867-Sunday] September 1 we had the Rev Mr Wratchford with us last night and I have been to hear him preach to day.

[September 2, 1867-Monday] 2 Ruff and Eliz, Ebb and Emily was with us last night.

William Burns and Margaret Robison was married Sept 5 1867.

[September 7, 1867-Saturday] Sept 7 I have been over to hear the Baptist preacher, Mr Ganes on yesterday. He gave the Baptist a good raken. I was on a visit to see aunt Hat and Em Castel. They are all well.

[September 14, 1867-Saturday] 14 theis is the time of oure meeting and I am sick and did not go.

[September 15, 1867-Sunday] 15 I have been at Bershaba to once more to set to my seal that I am on the Lords side and now my Heavenly Farther as I have proffesed to be on thy side, oh give me faith, strenth and love to battle fore thy cause. Oh wilt thoug assist me in living the life of meek and lowely follower of the meek and lowely. Jesus prepare me fore death and the final Judgement. MD Brown

[September 17, 1867-Tuesday] 17 oure meeting is over and I have been sick. I have not been out much.

[September 22, 1867-Sunday] 22 Lawson and Sally is gone over to theire unckle Hirams to attend a meeting at Bethshilo. They have had a fine meeting and a good manny joind.

[September 23, 1867-Monday] 23 Mrs Gimmy Davis and Children spent this day with us. She is an amiable woman. I love her and the children fore Christs sake and fore my once beloved pastore sake, who is no more.

[September 24, 1867-Tuesday] 24 I have been down at Ruff to day. Eliza is not well. She and Hatty came home with me.

[September 25, 1867-Wednesday] 25 Eliza and I have been over to see Emily to day. They are all well. Ebb is teaching school.

[September 26, 1867-Thursday] 26 Eliza and Sally is gone up to stay with aunt Caty to night.

[September 27, 1867-Friday] 27 Eliza and I have been down to spend the day with Mrs Cain. Ruffus has came up fore her and they are gone home.

[September 29, 1867-Sunday] 29 Lawson was over with Emily last night and at Union to day.

[October 4, 1867-Friday] Oct the 4 Bethel Presbatary meets at Bullexcreek church to day. R J Brown is gone down in company with Wratchford. I think so little of him that it makes me feel more lik a buryen than a Presbatary meeting. Oh God though in thy providence has so permited and though has said in thy reveled word that all things shall work together fore good to them that love thee. It has been one of thy dark mysteries to me that though has permitted it to be so. Oh Heavenly Farther, all hearts are bare and open to thy all searchen eye. Thou knowest that I love him not as I awlawase have loved thy professed desiples. Oh my God if I have had rong views of thy proffesed deciple I doo pray the to forgive all that I have said ore done amiss to thee, to thy professed deciple and myself. I know that I am a poore worm of the dust but it has been a heart rendering scene to me to think that my once beloved Bershaba had come to have such a minister to break unto us the bread of eternal life. I will submit and pray the that in thy own good time thou would work some way of deliverance. Heavenly Farther, I feel that we need thy chasting hand. We have not done oure duty to oure preachers, oure duty to oure Church and to oure Families. Awaken oure peple to theire duty. Send thy spirit with power on thy proffesed followers that we may have praying Farthers and praying Mothers, prayind sons and prayind Daughters till theire will be a shaking amonst the dry bones of Bershaba. MDB

[October 6, 1867-Sunday] 6 Bethel Presbetary has ajurned and R J has got home and Ratchford is here to night.

[October 12, 1867-Saturday] Oct 12 R J and I went down to york to night to see Mary Enloe. She is verry porly at this time, also down to Mr Dicksons meeting. I heard the Rev Dr Plummer preach. He is from the semenary in Collumbia. He is a great preacher. He is an ould gray headed man. His tex was in John the 21 chapter 17 verse. These are the words, "Lord thou knowest all things, thou knowest that I love the." It was a great sermon.

[October 13, 1867-Sunday] 13 Sabbath night I have heard the Dr Plummer preach to day. His tex was in Galations 3 chapter verse 13. The words, "Christ hath redeemed us from the curse of the law, being made a curse fore us," and then administered the Lords supper. Theire was a great manny theire in both of his sermons. He dwelt particularly on the love of Christ and the love we should have fore him and his cause, what great things he had done fore us. Oh thou Lamb of God, who bled and died on Calvaryes mount, I hope that theire though did bare my sins in thyne own boddy on that Cursed cross and now is seated on thy Farthers own right hand, theire pleeding the merriets of thy own blood. Oh blessed saiviour may I not be like the stonny ground hearers, go away from this great preachen and be so taken up with the cares of time and disonor thy cause and bring a curs on my soule.

Mr Dickson came to John Enloes this evening and administered the Lords supper to her. I never seen the like done beffore. He sung and prayed with her and gave her a nice talk. It was a solom sight to see. To all apperences it looks like it would be the last time.

[October 15, 1867-Tuesday] 15 I have been over with Em. Eb has been down to see his Farther. He is sick.

[October 16, 1867-Wednesday] 16 Mrs Schoggins spent the day with me.

[October 17, 1867-Thursday] 17 Eliza was up with us last night. All well. Mrs Cain and aunt Caty spent the day with me.

[October 20, 1867-Sunday] 20 Joe Willson and Eliza was with us last night and I have been to heare Mr Ratchford preach to day but I fear I have made a bad sabbeth dayes journey.

[October 22, 1867-Tuesday] 22 I have been down to see Mary Ann to day. I think her days are nearly numberd.

[October 26, 1867-Saturday] Mary Ann Enloe died Oct the 26 day at too in the evening of 1867 and was burried at Bershabah church. I have been spared to see another of my friends laid in the cold and silent toomb. One that in her dying houres gave sattasfaction that she was prepared and willing fore death, died in the full asurance of a glourious reserection. Blessed Jesus may these solom warnings not pass by unimproved. May they arrouse me from my stupidity to serve the Lord while health and life is given. Oh my God, give me grace to live by and I plaad with thee to give me dying grace through Jesus. MD Brown

[October 28, 1867-Monday] 28 Ruff and Eliza was with us last night, now gone home. Emilys, Mary Eliza was born Oct the 29 on tusday morning at eigh

oclock. A matter of great thankfullness, a living mother and a living child and all dooing well. Blessed Jesus to thy hand doo I commit. Thou hast said unto the parents, "Take this chile and rais it fore me."

[November 3, 1867-Sunday] Nov 3 Ruff and Eliza have come from Ebs this morning. They are all dooing well and Fanny is gone home with them. I have been at Bershaba to day to heare a Blind man preach. His name is Mr Canidy. He is from Norrh Carrolina. His tex was in Revelations the 3 chapter. These are the words, "Behold I stand at the door and knowck." He done past all expation.

[November 5, 1867-Tuesday] 5 Mr Canidy was with us last night. Him and I have been a visit down to Mr Burns to day and he is withe us to night.

[November 6, 1867-Wednesday] 6 I have Been down to see Mrs Gimmy Davis and ould Mrs Black is sick. She is som better.

[November 8, 1867-Friday] 8 Mr Canida was with us to day and him and the rest of my family is gone down to Mrs Davis to a singing to night.

[November 10, 1867-Sunday] 10 I was with Sister Harriet last night and have heard Mr Canida preach to day. His tex was in Hebrew 26 and 3 verse. "How shall we escape if we neglect so great salvation." He preached a verry good sermon and gave the congration a verry touching adress as a farewell.

[November 14, 1867-Thursday] 14 Mr Ginkens has come over this morning to work at oure screw [slough].

[November 17, 1867-Sunday] 17 I have been at preachen to day. I dont know that I can call it preachen. It was some of Ratchfords stuff without an alteration in my mind it will be the last. I have my Bibble and plenty of good Books that I will try through the help of God, to try and make the best improvement that I can. It is my daily prayer that my Dear Jesus will come and doo something fore oure bereved Church. Paten Wilkeson and Mat Black was married 21 of November 1867.

[November 22, 1867-Friday] 22 Mrs Black, Mrs Mary F Davis and family spent this day with me.

[November 23, 1867-Saturday] 23 this is the day of oure screw raising. They had plenty of help and got it up verry well. Eliza and Emily, Mrs Cain and aunt Caty, Molly Thomison was here. I had dinner today fore over fifty. MD Brown

[November 24, 1867-Sunday] 24 this is the sabbeth. We are all at home and all well. It has been calm and pleasent Sabbeth.

[November 25, 1867-Monday] 25 Mrs Macaphee and Hatty and Molly Smith was with [us] this evening. Sally, Mag, Hatty Mcaphee and Molly Smith is gone down to spend the day with Molly Cain.

[November 28, 1867-Thursday] 28 I have been verry unwell this week with my head and a pain in my side and shoulder. Oh my Heavenly Farther, if it be agrabele to thy holy will, remove these pains and diseses, but not my will but thine be done. Mary D Brown

[November 30, 1867-Saturday] 30 this is singing day. Mr Willson was with us last night.

[December 1, 1867-Sunday] Dec 1 this is Sabbeth, a verry cold day. I hope this has been a precious night to me with thanks to my Hevenly Farther fore the merceyes past. Imploring his aid and protection fore the future and renewing my vowes to give up myself and all thats mine, through thy grace strenthing me. MDB Witness ye saints who here me now, if I forsake my vow.

[December 6, 1867-Friday] 6 Sister Harriet has spent this day with me. I have been restored to some better health than I have had. Blessed Jesus, be all the glory to thy holy name be praise foreever more, amen.

[December 8, 1867-Sunday] 8 I was with Eb and Em last. They are all well except with colds. This is the sabbeth. We have no preachen to day.

[December 11, 1867-Wednesday] 11 I spent last night with Ruff and Eliza. They are all well. Mrs Nancy Whiteside is bad with the fever. Mrs Cain, Sue Coldwell, aunt Caty and Ann Scoggins have been here to day helping me to sow.

[December 14, 1867-Saturday] 14 theire was singing yesterday and last night and to day at the church and Chambers Brown and Laura was here.

[December 15, 1867-Sunday] 15 William Ginkens and Molly Thomeson was here last night. This has been Ratchford last day at Bershab. God in his works of provadence has so ordered it. He found the church all harmony and love, now he has had to leve it in discord and envy. Oh Heavenly Farther, will thoug over rule all these things fore the good of thy church and the benafit of thy people. Though has promised us when ye shall call upon me and ye shall go and pray unto me and I will hearken unto you and ye shall seek me and find me when ye shall search fore me with all yore heart. Oh blesed Jesus put it in the hearts of thy people to call upon thee with all theire heart, that though woulds send us a preacher of thy own choice to feed the sheep and to feed the lambs of thy flock. I dout not but it will be done. Blessed Jesus leave us not nore forsake us not in this oure houre of tryels and troubles but stand close by us and may love and harmony abound.

[December 16, 1867-Monday] 16 Jackson and I have been down to see Mrs Whitesides to day. She is verry bad, also called in to see Mrs Black. She is better.

[December 17, 1867-Tuesday] 17 R J and I was up at Dr Hills last night. He is going back to his ould home in the morning. Andrew Floyd and Sue mooved in the Good house the 19.

[December 21, 1867-Saturday] 21 Lawson, Sally and Mag was at a singing at theire unckle Hirams last night.

[December 25, 1867-Wednesday] 25 this is Christmas day. Spared by the mercy of God to behold another Christmas day and and all allone this morning. The children is all gone over to Mrs Mullholland school house to a Christmas tree and dinner but plenty of company to night, Eb and Em, Molly Thomison, Bob Coldwell, John Brown and unckle Bille.

[December 26, 1867-Thursday] 26 Lawson, Sally, Mag and Molly and Hatty Mcfee has gone down to Ruff Whitesides to night.

[December 27, 1867-Friday] 27 theire has been singing to day at the Church and to night at Mr Jacksons.

[December 30, 1867-Monday] Mrs Nancy Whitesides died monday, December the 30 1867. MDB

1868

[*January 1, 1868-Wednesday*] January 1 1868 a wensday the new year has come in, in a robe of white. Oh what an emblem of Christs robe of Richeness that he has prepared to clothe them with, that will come unto him. I have awoke this morning with simptoms of brest droppisy. Oh how erenest I should be to know if Christ has clothed this nacked soule of mine with that white robe of his richeness. Oh my Heavenly Farther as though has sparred me through the seenes of another year through danger, seen and unseen, though has taken care of me. Though manny has been the triels and crosses, though has brought me through in the death of my beloved paster, Mr Gimmy Davis. Then bringing in a man to stand in his place that I did esteem as I did him, was a thorne in the flesh. Oh blesed Jesus give me a heart of submission to thy heavenly will fore thou has said that all things shall work fore good to them that love thee. I thank the fore the manny blessings though has blessed both me and mine in the year past. Oh my God into thy hand I now commit myself, my Husband and Children and all that I have this new years morning. Through thy grace strenthing me, commit myself, my husband and my children unto thy Heavenly care and protection fore time and eternity. Thanks everlasting thanks be to thy ever blessed name and now oh blessed Jesus unto thy blesed hands I now commit myself, my Husband and Children and all that I have through thy grace strenthing me fore though has promised to give thy holy spirrit to hem that askes it of thee in spirrit and truth.

[January 2, 1868-Thursday] Lonny Hope and Ann Ferguson was married January the 2 1868.

[January 6, 1868-Monday] 6 Ruffe and Eliza has come up this morning and Ruff and Lawson is gone down to york.

[January 7, 1868-Tuesday] 7 Eliza, R J and I have taken supper with aunt Caty this evening.

[January 9, 1868-Thursday] ould Mr Newman McElwee was married to Mrs Crawford the 9 of January 1868. He is seventy three years ould. John Alexander little daughter, Anny died Jan the 9 1868. Mrs Gimmy Davis and Miss Eugenia Armstrong was on a visit to see me today.

[January 11, 1868-Saturday] 11 Sally has gone down to stay a week with Eliza and I have been down to stay a night with Franklin.

[January 15, 1868-Wednesday] 15 Franklin mooved down in Bethshilo neigh-berhood.

[January 16, 1868-Thursday] 16 I have been over to see Mrs Scoggins to day and R J has gone down to Ruff and left Wille and brought Sally home with him.

[January 19, 1868-Sunday] 19 Mr Beard was with us last night and preached to day, he done finely. His tex was, "How shall you escape if you neglect so great salvation?"

[January 20, 1868-Monday] 20 Emily and Lawson is gone down to see Eliza this morning and Sally is gone down to help Mary Cain to quilt to day and Nancy Coldwell, Mary Cain and Ann Scoggins came home with her and stayd all night.

[January 21, 1868-Tuesday] 21 we have a Mr Whisonthant with us to night, a brother of Mrs Hills.

[January 22, 1868-Wednesday] 22 Emily and Lawson has come home and her Paw has gone home with her.

[January 26, 1868-Sunday] 26 Mr Curethers preached at Bershaba to day; his tex was in Hebrews 12 3. He preached a fine sermon and had a fine congration.

[January 28, 1868-Tuesday] 28 Cousin Psalm Brown and Margaret, cousin William and Eliza Davis and Sister Harriett is all here to night. We had a merry time of it.

[February 3, 1868-Monday] Febuary 3 this is the day that Lawson has started to go to school to Ebb at Union and is bording theire. Leasley Burns and Miss McCelhany was married Feb the 14 1868.

[February 8, 1868-Saturday] 8 this is the day that they have met at the curch to see about having it covered. Mr Joe Ginkens is to cover it. He is to cover it fore one hunderd dollars. They have got the emount subscribed.

[February 9, 1868-Sunday] 9 we are all at home to day and grunting with the colds and sore throat. It is the sabbet and we have no preacher as yet, that is stated preacher, but I hope it will not be so long as we have the offer of Mr Corethers fore one fourth of his time. Also Mr Robert Anterson the half of his time and theire is a prostect of obtaining Mr Albert Jemes fore to preach and teach. The Lord of the vinyard bless us with his blessing i humbly pray. MDB

[February 11, 1868-Tuesday] 11 I have been down to see Ruff and Eliza, they are all well. I have spent this day with Mrs Jimmy Davis, quite a plesent visit.

[February 13, 1868-Thursday] 13 I was down at york with aunt Emily last night.

[February 15, 1868-Saturday] 15 this is the last day of the singing at Bershaba.

[February 16, 1868-Sunday] 16 we have all been to Bershaba to day to hear ould Mr Beard preach to day. Ruff and Eliza, Ebb and Emily was with us last night and all gone home.

[February 19, 1868-Wednesday] 19 I have been over to see aunt Harriet and

unckle Bille and aunt Caty was with me. We ware to see Lawson and Ebb and Emile.

[February 20, 1868-Thursday] 20 I have been down to help Mrs Cain to make a coat fore Mr Cain, also Mrs Scoggins, Mrs Land, Mrs Price and aunt Caty.

[February 21, 1868-Friday] 21 Mrs Scoggins, Mrs Cain and Sally and I have been up to uncle Billes to help aunt Caty to make a suit of close fore John.

[February 22, 1868-Saturday] 22 Sally was over with Emily last night. She is bad off with the toothach and bealed jaw. MD Brown

[March 29, 1868-Sunday] March 29 I have been to hear Mr Cothrethes at bershaba to day. Ebb and Em had theire little daughter baptised to day, her name is Mary Brown. Oh my God as they have gave up this theire chile to thee in Baptism doo though assist them in raising it up fore thee. If bee thy will spare its liff and may it be a comferet to its parents, an ornament to thy curch and sorciety.

[April 3, 1868-Friday] Aprile 3 Lawson was down at Ruffes last night, all well and brought Hatty home with him.

[April 5, 1868-Sunday] 5 Lawson and Sally is gone over to union to day.

[April 10, 1868-Friday] 10 Mrs Cain, Mary and Gimmy and aunt Caty spent this day with us.

[April 11, 1868-Saturday] 11 Sister Peggy Floyd and Macy Bell spent this day with us.

[April 12, 1868-Sunday] 12 this is the sabbeth day we have no preachen. A flock without a sheppard yet deare shepherd of oure church come speedly to oure relefe, send us a paster of thy own choice, one that shall break unto us the bread of eternal life. 12 Ruff Whitesides was up to day and took Jaily and Hatty home with him. They are all well.

[April 17, 1868-Friday] 17 Eliza A Whitesides, was born April the 17 day 1868 a Friday at ten in the morning.

[April 22, 1868-Wednesday] 22 I have just got home from Ruffs. Eliza and the babby is dooing well, a matter of grattude, a living mother and a living chile. Sally is gone down to stay with her a week.

[April 29, 1868-Wednesday] 29 aunt Harriet has spent this day with us and Ruff has brought Sally home, all well.

[May 3, 1868-Sunday] 3 I and R J has been down to see Ruff and Eliza. They are all dooing verry well.

[May 10, 1868-Sunday] 10 I have been over to see Em and aunt Harriet, they are all dooing well in one sence, whether in all i cannot say.

[May 14, 1868-Thursday] 14 Joe Neel and Miss Ema Jackson was married May the 14 1868. Lawson and Sally was at the wedding they had a large crowd and a fine supper.

[May 17, 1868-Sunday] 17 Jackson and Lawson is gone up to enen to preachen to day. MDB

[May 27, 1868-Wednesday] 27 Ruff and Eliza, Ebb and Emily was with us last night. We have all been to hear Mr Beard preach to day fore the last time. If providence permits he expects to start to Brazul in a few weeks. He preached to fine sermons. It was a solem thing to think I was hearring him fore the last time, never again to meet him till the moorning of the great reserection. The next meeting will be at the great judgement day. There I will have to give an account of the improvement that I have mad of the manny sermons that I have heard him preach. His morning tex was on Luke 17 chapter and 5 verse, "Increase our faith." His evening tex was I thessolonians first chapter and tenth verse, "Even Jesus who delivered us from the wrath to come."

[May 28, 1868-Thursday] 28 this day has been the commencement of oure meeting. Mr Coretherers preached to day. His tex was in Romans, 8 chapter and 14 verse. "Fore as manny as are led by the spirit of God, are the sones of God." He is a fine preacher.

[May 30, 1868-Saturday] 30 this is now satterday night. Eliza and Em and Jane Furgerson and families is with us and young Mr Hogue.

[May 31, 1868-Sunday] 31 Sabbeth evening Mr White preached Mr Davis memorial sermon this morning. His tex was in first Thesolonians 4 chapter and 13 14 verses. These are the words, "But I would not have you to be ignorant Bretheren concerning them that sleep, that ye sorrow not, even as others which have no hope. Fore if we beleive that Jesus died and rose again, even so them also which sleep in Jesus will God bring with him." He preached a great sermon on the happiness of the blessed. He gave deceased, beloved paster Mr Gimmy Davis a great name he said the blood roral runs in his veins. God saw he was too good and pure to live eney longer in this wicked world. In the evening the Lords supper was administered. It has been a precious time that we have spent in thy Church militent. Oh my Lord as though has spared this unproffatabel life of mine through an other sollom sene, a preffesed follower of the meek, but mighty Jesus oh that though would say to me as though did say to thy servent Paul, "My grace is suffiecent for thee." Mary D Brown

[June 1, 1868-Monday] June 1 Mrs Mary Coldwell, aunt Caty, Jane Furguson and Fanny Doubson has all been here on a visit to day.

[June 2, 1868-Tuesday] 2 Mrs Jane Jonson and Mary Davis on a visit to day.

[June 3, 1868-Wednesday] 3 aunt Caty, Fanny Daubson, Sally and I have been on a visit to ould Mrs Davis to day.

[June 5, 1868-Friday] 5 Mrs Preacher, Mrs Margaret Jonson and her sister in law, Miss Fanny Jonson, Fanny Dobsin, Mrs Cain has spent this day with us.

[June 9, 1868-Tuesday] 9 Mrs Black, Mrs Mary Davis and children has been on a visit to day.

[June 10, 1868-Wednesday] 10 Mrs Precious Scoggin, Newmen McElwee was born June 10 1868.

[June 14, 1868-Sunday] 14 Eb and Em was up with us last night and brought Mag home.

[June 15, 1868-Monday] 15 Sue Coldwell was with us last night and Sally is gone down to york to stay a week with her friends.

[June 16, 1868-Tuesday] 16 Mary and Isabbella Love has been to spend this

day with us.

[June 19, 1868-Friday] 19 I have been over to see Mrs Scoggins to day she and the babe is dooing well.

[June 21, 1868-Sunday] June 21 we had a Mr Cristy Strong to preach to day ore rather lecture from Psalms 32 Chapter, 2 verse. "Blessed is the man unto whome the Lord imputeth not iniquity and in whose spirit there is no guile." I am well pleased with him. He is a nooble youth. The first time I ever seen him he came by and took dinner with us. Mary D Brown

[June 22, 1868-Monday] 22 Mary Cain and Eliza Jackson spent this day.

[June 24, 1868-Wednesday] 24 Sister Harriet and Molly was over to day. MD Brown

[June 27, 1868-Saturday] 27 Joe Willison and Eliza is up with us to night.

[June 28, 1868-Sunday] 28 Joe, Eliza, Lawson and I have taken dinner with aunt Caty to day.

[June 30, 1868-Tuesday] 30 I have now got home from Ebbs. Little Mary Brown has been sick but is better.

[July 5, 1868-Sunday] July 5 Mr Cristy Strong has preached to day, his second day. He is greatly beloved as a stranger. He is preachen fore his brother, Mr Hew Strong. We have sent fore him to come and supply us to Christmas. He is engaged in a school in sumpter but will be up soon.

[July 8, 1868-Wednesday] 8 Mrs Scoggins and Jane Curry has spent the day with us.

[July 9, 1868-Thursday] 9 Sally and I have been on a visit at Mr Cains to day and we have Mr Cristy Strong with us to night.

[July 10, 1868-Friday] 10 Mr Strong has been back and is gone up to Bethel.

[July 12, 1868-Sunday] 12 R J, Sally, Jaily and I have been over to Hirams and to Union to hear the baptist preach to day. Mr Virge preached this morning. Sally is gone down to york to stay a week with her friends.

[July 18, 1868-Saturday] 18 theire is a singing at Bershaba to day. Emily is with us and Eb is gone to smerny to a meeting.

[July 20, 1868-Monday] 20 Lawson, Mag and I went down to R G Whitesides last satterday and went with them to Smerny to preachen on yesterday. It was theire communion. Mr Lathen preached Corrinthians 3.11. "For foundiations can no man lay than that which is laid which is Christ Jesus." Then administered the Lords supper. Theire was a fine congaration of people. It is very dry and dreadful hot, the hottest weather I think I have ever felt.

[July 25, 1868-Saturday] 25 we have all been down at the mineral spring to day at a picknick dinner, a large crowd and a fine dinner. Oure expected preacher was theire, Mr Hew Strong and he came home with us. We have had a wet day. Brother Lawson and his son, Bobby came home with us. Mary D Brown

[July 26, 1868-Sunday] Rev Mr Hew Strong preached at Bershaba to day, July 26 1868. His first sermon in the walls of ould Bershaba. His tex was, "Cast thy burden on the Lord." He has the apperance of beeing a man of God.

[July 30, 1868-Thursday] 30 this fast day Mr Hew Strong preached to us to day. Mrs Strong came up this week and Mr and Mrs Strong came home with us this evening, the first night they have spent with us.

[July 31, 1868-Friday] 31 Mr Strong and R J has gone over to Hiram Thomisons to night. Mrs Strong is gone down to Mrs Gimmy Davis and Dr Alisons to morow.

[August 2, 1868-Sunday] Aug 2 Lawson was down at Ruffs last night, all well. This is the sabbeth day, all well and at home except my babby, Fanny Vance. She is with her sister Eliza.

[August 4, 1868-Tuesday] 4 uncle Breathy Coldwell has spent this evening with us. He is failing fast.

[August 5, 1868-Wednesday] 5 Sally and I have been up to Mr Tom Bells on a visit to day. We had a pleasent visit. R G has brought Fanny home to day and Hatty with her. R G and Willie is gone to york.

[August 9, 1868-Sunday] 9 Mr Strong has preached here to day. His tex was in Zechariah 12 c 11 v. "In that day theire shall be a fountain opend in the house of David and to the inhabitants of Jerusalam fore sin and unclinass." He has all the apperances of a great man, strong by nature and Strong by name. I hope that God is about to send us a one of his own chois, a Minister that will unite oure people once more in the bonds of love and unity; one that will go in and out beffore this great congration, one that will act like a minister of the gospel, both in the pulpit and out of it. I hope that God by his grace and the prayers of this congration we will once more be a God fearing and a God serving people. Mr and Mrs Strong has come home with us this evening and is going to stay with us a while.

[August 11, 1868-Tuesday] 11 Mr and Mrs Strong, R J and Sally is gone up to spend the day with unckle Billy and aunt Caty.

[August 13, 1868-Thursday] 13 I have been on a pleasure trip with Mr and Mrs Strong, one night with Eb and Em, one day with Lawson and Jane Brown, one night at H C Thomisons and I left them theire to spend the ballance of the week. Mrs Matty Willkerson had twin babbyes, one boy and daughter Aug 11 1868.

[August 16, 1868-Sunday] 16 R J and Jaily was down at Ruff last night, all well.

[August 18, 1868-Tuesday] 18 I have had a crowd for dinner to day, Mrs and Mr Strong, Mr Cristy Strong, H C Thomison, Billey and Caty Brown and Brother John Brown from north caroliny. Mr Cristy Strong stayed all night. Mr and Mrs Strong went down to Mrs Davis.

[August 21, 1868-Friday] 21 Mr and Mrs Strong and Cristy is here to day. Mr Cristy Strong is gone over to Eb Castels to night. He is going to preach at Bethesda a sonday. A lady from sumpter has come up to attend the mineral spring. Her name is Mrs McBride, one daughter, Maud, one son Gil, one sister, Allace Warren. They are all here till they can obtain Board.

[August 22, 1868-Saturday] 22 theire is a singing at the church to day, the children is all gone, also Mr and Mrs Strong, Mrs McBride and children.

[August 23, 1868-Sunday] 23 this is the sabbeth it is a verry wet day. Mr Strong has preached, I did not git out. I stayed and minded Em and Eliza bab-

byes and they went. I had a crowd last night Mrs McBride and her family, Eb and family, R G Witeside and family, also Mag Whitesides, Ruff brother, Edward Whiteside from Arcancis. He is a fine looking man.

[August 24, 1868-Monday] 24 Mr and Mrs Strong is gone over to H C Thomisons to night him and his Brother is going a trip up in north carrolina.

[August 26, 1868-Wednesday] 26 Mrs Strong and I have been on a visit up to see Mrs Bell.

[August 27, 1868-Thursday] 27 Mr and Mrs Strong, Mrs Mcbride and I have had a plesent day at Mr Scoggins to day. Emily Castel, Lawson, Sally and Mag has gown to a quilting at ould Mr Thommis Whitesides they have made it fore Ed to see the friends and neighbores beffore he leaves and Mr and Mrs Strong has gone down to Mrs Davis this evening.

[August 30, 1868-Sunday] 30 Mr Strong preached to day. Eb and Em is gone home.

[September 1, 1868-Tuesday] Sep 1 I have been down at Mrs Davis we have been macking a suit of close fore Mr Strong and Sally and Mag is gone over to help Ann Scoggins to quilt to day.

[September 4, 1868-Friday] 4 Lawson and I have been down at york to day. Sister Polly Brown and her daughter, Mary, they are from north Carrolina, was at sister Peggeyes Floyd. We spent a plesent evening.

[September 6, 1868-Sunday] 6 Mr Strong preached to day, his tex was in luke 12. 20. "And God said unto him, thou fool, this night thy soule will be required of thee." He preached a great sermon. Mr and Mrs Strong came home with us, also H C Thomison, Edward and Joe Whiteside, Edes last visit. He leaves fore Arcancis in short time.

[September 7, 1868-Monday] 7 Mr and Mrs Strong has gone down to york to day to visit her relations.

[September 9, 1868-Wednesday] 9 this is the day the congaration has met to see what we can make up to pay Mr Strong to preach to us till Christmas. We done fine fore the turn out. Theire was near to hundird dollars raised. We want to mak thre hinderd fore the year and one half to bee paid at christmas. Mr and Mrs Strong is with us to night. MD Brown

[September 11, 1868-Friday] 11 this is the commencement of oure meeting. Mr Strong preached to day.

[September 13, 1868-Sunday] 13 Dr Mills from Georgia preached to day.

[September 14, 1868-Monday] 14 Mr and Mrs Strong has left to go to Sumpter this evening with the expectation of comming back to preach and teach fore us.

[September 15, 1868-Tuesday] 15 aunt Emily has come out to stay a week with us, the firs time she has been here in three years. Fanny Daubson is out.

[September 16, 1868-Wednesday] 16 aunt Harriet, Liza and Em, cousin Fanny Daubson, Billy and Caty Brown, aunt Emily, John Brown has all spent the day with us.

[September 17, 1868-Thursday] 17 aunt Emily, Fanny Daubson, Mrs Cain and I have spent this day with aunt Caty.

[September 18, 1868-Friday] 18 aunt Emily, Fanny Daubson, aunt Caty, Sally and I have spent this day at Hew Loves.

[September 19, 1868-Saturday] 19 Mr William Banks is with us to night and Eb and Em.

[September 20, 1868-Sunday] 20 Mr Bank preached at Bershaba to day. 2 Correnthians 8 9 verse in the evening 1 epistel of John 5 12 verse. He is a great preacher and a great man. He came back with us and took dinner and then Lawson took him down to york.

[September 23, 1868-Wednesday] 23 this is the day of the picknick at White-sides mill, a fine dinner, a large crowd and great speeking by Mr Simpson, Mr Hemphill and several others.

[September 24, 1868-Thursday] Eliza and Joe Willsons first son was born Sep 24 1868.

[September 25, 1868-Friday] Bethel Presbetry met at york church, Mr Dickson church, September 25 1868. Jaily and I have come down to attend it. Theire is a verry good turne out of ministers and elders. The ministers, Mr Watson, Mr Say, Mr Banks, Mr Carethers, Mr White, Mr Bogs, Mr Ervin, Mr Harrison, Mr Cooper, Mr Baily, Mr James, Mr Dickson, Mr Anterson, Mr Ratchford, Mr Bogs. Friday morning, Mathew 16 25 "What shall a man gain if he should gain the whole wourld and loose his own soul." Friday night Mr Ervin 2 Timithy 19, hymn, "Streched on the cross the Saviour hung." He preached a great sermon.

[September 27, 1868-Sunday] 27 Mr Cristy strong came out and preached at Bershaba to day from presbatary. His tex was "We doo all fade as a leaf." He preached a great sermon. He has the prospect of macking a great preacher if life and health is granted him. Mr Hew Strong did not git up in time fore presbatary. Mary D Brown

[December 29, 1868-Tuesday] 29 Nelson Thomison and Miss Hatty Mcaphee was married Dec 29 1868 by Mr Gaines. Lawson and Sally was at the wedding, had a fine supper.

[December 31, 1868-Thursday] 31 I have been over to see sister Harriet, and Lawson and Jaily was over at Mrs Thomison to a party.

1869

[January 1, 1869-Friday] new years morning of 1869. we are all at home living and a matter of great thankfullness, spared to see the light of another new years morning. Oh Lord, I thank thee fore all of these miracles that though has granted both me and mine. Oh my God, I pray that though wouldst continue thy loving kindness and thy many mercies, unworthie as I am. Theire was a singing at Mr David Scoggins to night and Molly Thomison, Rachel Turner and John is with us.

[January 3, 1869-Sunday] 3 sabbeth we have no preachen today at Bershaba. Lawson and Mag has gone over to Union today.

[January 4, 1869-Monday] 4 ___has got back, and was with us last night and the school has comenced again to day.

[January 5, 1869-Tuesday] 5 Joe Whiteside has taken dinner with us to day.

[January 6, 1869-Wednesday] 6 Mrs Jonson and Mary Davis was with us last night.

[January 10, 1869-Sunday] 10 Mr Strong has preached to day. His tex was in Mathew, v 2, "Why stand you here all the day idle." He did preach a powerfull sermon.

[January 11, 1869-Monday] 11 Sister Harriet and I have been over to see Em and took supper with her.

[January 12, 1869-Tuesday] 12 sister Harriet is gone and I have put in my web. Sally has been over to day and Hatty Thomison to quilt. Em and children was over.

[January 14, 1869-Thursday] 14 I have been to see Mrs Mary Davis to day. Mrs Black has got better.

[January 16, 1869-Saturday] 16 I have been down to see Ruff and Eliza. They are all well.

[January 18, 1869-Monday] 18 Mrs Cain has paid us a visit today.

[January 19, 1869-Tuesday] 19 Mrs Cain, Mrs Scoggins, aunt Caty and E A Whiteside have been helping Emily to sow to day. Lasleyes and Rachel Burns, Elizabeth was born Jan ___ 1869. Em and I have been over to see Lasly and theire new daughter to day.

[January 24, 1869-Sunday] 24 sabbeth all well and no preachen. Gimmy Davis, ould Mrs Black and Mrs Strong has spent this day with us. We have had a pleasent day.

[February 8, 1869-Monday] Feb 8 Dr Castel is verry sick, have sent up fore Eb.

[February 12, 1869-Friday] 12 Eb has been home. The Dr is no better.

[February 13, 1869-Saturday] 13 Dr Castle died Febuary 13 1869.

[February 14, 1869-Sunday] 14 sabbeth, all well. We have no preachin to day.

[February 15, 1869-Monday] 15 we have had ould Mr Bogs from Collumbia with us to day. He is a minister and Mr Strong took dinner with us to day.

[February 17, 1869-Wednesday] 17 wensday the seventeenth this is the day Mr and Mrs Strong has come to bord with us.

[February 20, 1869-Saturday] 20 Mr and Mrs Strong has gone down to york to day.

[February 21, 1869-Sunday] 21 ould Mr Boggs has preached to day. His tex was in Mark the tenth chapt, 21 verse, "Then Jesus beholding him loved him and said unto him, one thing lackes thou yet," and he came home with us and took dinner and then went back to york. We have voted fore the hymn book to day and he is going to send them on a short time.

[February 25, 1869-Thursday] 25 I have been over to see Sister Harriet and took Molly and Sally down to york to stay a few dayes with theire cousin, Fannie Daubson.

[February 26, 1869-Friday] 26 Mrs Strong is gone to the school house everry day to assist Mr Strong with his school. He has about thirty students, a verry good school.

[February 27, 1869-Saturday] 27 Mr and Mrs Strong has gone over to Amos Burnsis to night.

[February 28, 1869-Sunday] 28 Mr Strong is gone up to Hopewell to day and Butler has brought Sally home and it is verry cold.

[March 4, 1869-Thursday] March 4 Mr Strong has gone down to see his Mother to day.

[March 10, 1869-Wednesday] 10 I have been over to Hiram sence last sunday evening until this morning helping her to backe her cake.

[March 11, 1869-Thursday] 11 Eliza, Wille, Eb and Emily and aunt Caty was with us last night.

[March 14, 1869-Sunday] 14 Mr Strong is gone to Salem to day.

[March 16, 1869-Tuesday] 16 R J and Sally is gone over to see ____to night and Lawson and Eb is gone down to Ruffs to help him cover his house. Renus

Fewel and Molly Thomison was married March the 18, on thursday evening 1869 by Mr Curerthres. They had a right smart wedding, a fine supper, plenty of cake and every thing that was good to eat. They had no infare, theire was none went with them but Hiram and Butler.

[March 21, 1869-Sunday] 21 Lawson went over to his unckle Hirams last night. Him and Sally went to union to preachen and seen Renes and Molly show out and they have got home this evening. Mr Strong is gone to Shilo to a sackament to day, Mr Watson and him, sabbeth evening. MDBrown

[March 23, 1869-Tuesday] March 23 Mrs Strong and I have been down to see Mrs Black last night. She is verry sick, but some better this morning.

[March 24, 1869-Wednesday] 24 Mag and I have spent to day with Mrs Scoggins and Mr and Mrs Strong has gone over to arch Jacksons to night.

[March 26, 1869-Friday] 26 Mr Strong is verry sick to day & Ann & Mag Scoggins has helped me quilt to day.

[March 27, 1869-Saturday] 27 Mrs Strong has gone down to see Mrs Cain to day. Mr Strong has gone over this evening and they have been over to spend this evening with the Rev Mr Jonson.

[March 28, 1869-Sunday] 28 sabbeth evening Mr Strong has preached at Bershaba to day. I was not out, the firs day that I have missed sence the Rev Mr Cristy preached his firs sermon here last June. Oh Lord of host thou has greatly blessed me in giving me health and the oppertunity of attending thy house of worship and may I remember that to whome much is given, of them much will be required. We have our preacher boarding with us and he certanly is a man of God. He practies what he preaches to others.

[April 1, 1869-Thursday] Aprile 1 we are all well. Jaily, Wille and Fanny is going to school every day. They have fine teachers.

[April 2, 1869-Friday] 2 Mr & Mrs Strong took supper with Eb and Em this evening.

[April 3, 1869-Saturday] 3 Hiram is with us and Lenny is sick to night.

[April 4, 1869-Sunday] 4 Sabbeth evening Mr White preached fore us to day. His tex was in Psalms 37 chapt 5 6 verses. He came home with us and took dinner and then went back to york. Lenney is not much better.

[April 5, 1869-Monday] 5 a beautiful morning. We are all well. Mr & Mrs Strong, Jaily, Wille & Fanny is gone to school. Brindy has a fine heifer calf last wensday. I call it Lilly. MDBrown

[April 7, 1869-Wednesday] 7 Mr Strong and Mr Amos Burns has started to Presbetery this morning. It meets at unity Church over the cautaba river and Mrs Strong is tending to thee school and is gone to Mr Walkers to night.

[April 9, 1869-Friday] 9 Mrs Strong and Sally is gone to Amos Burnsis to night.

[April 10, 1869-Saturday] 10 Sister Harriet has been up to see us to day and a crowd besides.

[April 11, 1869-Sunday] 11 this is the sabbeth day, all well and all at home. Mr Strong was to go to Salem to day but it was too wet.

[April 14, 1869-Wednesday] 14 Sally has had a little quilten to day, did not git it out.

[April 17, 1869-Saturday] 17 I, Jaily and Fanny have been down to see Ruff and lide. They are all well. Maggie is a running every whare. Mr Strong is gone to Shilo to day.

[April 19, 1869-Monday] 19 Mr and Mrs Strong is gone to Mr Bells to night. We have all been sick with colds but is better. Theire has been so much frosts and colds that spring is verry backward fore this seasen. Mary D Brown

[April 23, 1869-Friday] 23 Eb and I have been down to york to day. Cousin Psalm Brown took dinner with us to day and took Mr & Mrs Strong home with him.

[April 27, 1869-Tuesday] 27 the rev Mr Boggs is with us to day and is going to stay all night and Mrs Strong is gone down to Mrs Gimmy Davis.

[April 30, 1869-Friday] 30 friday evening this is the commencement of oure meeting. Mr White is assisting Mr Strong. Mr White preached to day, his tex was in Psalms 81, verse 10, "Open thy mouth wide and I will fill it."

[May 1, 1869-Saturday] May 1 Mr White preached to day. His tex was in Psalms 42 chap 6 verse. These are the words, "Theirefore will I remember thee from the land of Jordan and of the Hermonites from the hill Mizar." He preached too fine sermones to day. He is a great man. The people was some what disapointed. We was expecting Dr Plumer from Collumbia, but if oure lives is all spared till the fall communion it may be that we will have him to preach fore us then.

[May 2, 1869-Sunday] 2 Sabbeth evening Mr White preached this morning. His tex was in Genesis 15. "Fear not Abraham, I am thy sheald and thy exceeding great reward," and then the Lords supper was administerd. Mr Boggs preached in the evening, his tex was, "How shall you escape if you neglect so great salvation." We had a fine meeting. The peeple paid good attention. Oh my Heavenly Farther, how pleasent it is to go to thy house and meet with thy blood bought curch of God, here in this vale of sin and sorrow and to look forward to the time when thy blood bought church shall meet to part no more. What I say unto you, I say unto all, watch, be reddy to go forth to meet the Bride groom in eney watch of the night that he may come, that we may have oil in oure lamps and be reddy when the summones may come. My farthers house, my own bright home though hast theire a place fore me, yet an exile frome that distant home by faith I see. MDB

[May 6, 1869-Thursday] 6 Emily and I have been over to see Sister Harriet. They are all well. Molly has mooved. They look sorty loansome.

[May 9, 1869-Sunday] Sabbath 9 Lawson and Mag is gone down to their cousin Psalm Browns last night and going to Sharan to day. Sally is down with Eliza. Sabbeth evening. When will my pilgramage be done, worlds long weeks be ore. The sabbath dawn that needs no sun that day that fades no more. MDBrown

[May 12, 1869-Wednesday] 12 Sally has come home to day and Mrs Strong has come home from her Motheren laws to day. Mrs Cain and aunt Caty took supper with us this evening.

[May 13, 1869-Thursday] 13 Eb and Emily, Sally and Mag has gone a visiting

down to cousin Will Davis. Ann Scoggins and I have got the supper. Lowrey and Lauro Walkers child was born May 1869.

[May 15, 1869-Saturday] 15 Mr and Mrs Strong has gone down to Bulix creek to the communion.

[May 19, 1869-Wednesday] 19 Mrs Black and Mrs Davis has spent the day with us, a pleasant visit.

[May 20, 1869-Thursday] 20 Mary & Isabella Love has paid us a visit to day.

[May 21, 1869-Friday] 21 Mrs Cain and I have been a visiting over to Mr Preacher Johnsons to day, quite a pleasant visit.

[May 22, 1869-Saturday] 22 Mr Strong has gone up to Hopewell to assist Mr Dickson at his meeting. Mrs Strong is down at Mrs Davis.

[May 23, 1869-Sunday] 23 Ruff and Eliza was up with us last night and Buttler Thomison. We have all been at preachen to day except Mag, she was housekeeper. Mr Strong preached a good sermon to day. His tex was in Haggia 2 c 7 verse. These are the words, "I will shake all nations and the desire of all nations shall come and I will fill this house with Glory saith the Lord of host." These are the hymns. "Though verry present aid" "Jesus lover of my soule." He preached a great sermon. Sally has gone home with Buttler to stay a week and help them quilt. Mr Strong is gone down to his Mothers to stay this week. Mag is gone over to help her cousin Molly quilt today.

[May 28, 1869-Friday] 28 Aunt Harriet has brought Sally home to day and spent this day with us. All well.

[May 29, 1869-Saturday] 29 Jackson and Wile has gone down to york fore Mr Strong.

[May 30, 1869-Sunday] 30 Mr & Mrs Strong, Lawson and Sally has gone to Smerny to day. Mr Strong preaches theire to day.

[June 3, 1869-Thursday] June 3 the neighborhood have all peaced a star and made a quilt fore Mrs Hill and we have all met at the mineral spring to day to quilt it and have had a fine picknick dinner and have got the quilt out and

bound beffore night. Mr Robbert Adams came home with us. He is the eldest son of the late rev James Adams. He has come on to take charg of the school as Mr Strong health is bad and he wants to quit teachen. Robert Alexander third wife was buried at Bershaba June 3 1869.

[June 5, 1869-Saturday] 5 Lawson has gone down to Whitesides mill to a fishing party to day.

[June 6, 1869-Sunday] 6 ould Mr Boggs preached fore us to day. His tex was in Mathew 28, "Goo ye into all the wourld and preach the gospel to every creature." He has come home with us to stay a week.

[June 8, 1869-Tuesday] 8 Mr Boggs, Mr Strong, Mrs Scoggins & I have spent the day with Eb and Em and taken dinner with them. Mr Boggs is with unckle Billey to night.

[June 9, 1869-Wednesday] 9 Mr & Mrs Strong, Mr Boggs is over at Mr Scoggins to night. Mr & Mrs Strong and Mr Boggs has gone down to ould Mrs Davisis to night, to Dr Alisons to morow, to Salam a sunday. They have left Mr Boggs over at Salam. Mr Robert Adams took charge of the school June 7 1869. MDB

[June 17, 1869-Thursday] 17 I was down with Ruffe and Eliza last night, all well and dooing well as to the things of the wourld and I hope of the one thing needfull too.

[June 19, 1869-Saturday] 19 the rev Mr Jonson and his wife, Margaret spent the day with us. They are fine company.

[June 20, 1869-Sunday] 20 Sabbeth evening the 20 Mr Strong has organised a Sabbeth School to day in the new__. Theire is foure classes, the Bibble class, Mr Strong attends to it, Mr Scoggins one class of Boys, scripturall questions, Mrs Davis, one class of girles in scripturle questions, I one class small children. Mr Strong preached to day. His tex was in Mathew 16 chap 24 , "Then said Jesus to his discipels, If eney man will come after me let him denye himself and take up his cross and follow me." He only preached one part of it to day. He is to preache the ballance in another sermon. He preached a great sermon, how we should denye oureselvs fore Christs sake.

[June 24, 1869-Thursday] 24 Mr & Mrs Strong is gone to Amos Burnses to night. Mr Strong is to preach at Zion tomorow fore the Methedist preacher, Mr Gatlin.

[June 27, 1869-Sunday] 27 Lawson, Sally, Mag is gone over to Zion to preachen to day. Mr Strong is gone to Shilo to preach. Mrs Strong at Zion.

[July 1, 1869-Thursday] July 1 I have taken aunt Caty down to ould Dr Allisons to day to stay a few dayes. She has been a complaining a good deal the last few weeks and to see if he can doo eney thing fore her. I was over to see Ruff and Eliza. They are all well, left Fanny with her to stay the vacation in her school.

[July 2, 1869-Friday] 2 all well, a nice shower this evening. Amos Burns has come over and mooved Mr & Mrs Strong over to theire house July 2. Em has a sowing to day. The girls are over a helping her.

[July 4, 1869-Sunday] 4 Mr Strong has preached to day. His tex was in thee same chapter of last Sabbeth, "You must take up youre cross and follow me," and he is to preach another sermon on the same verse.

[July 10, 1869-Saturday] 10 Emily has gone over to see Mag Whiteside and her sister, Eliza and I have Macy with me.

[July 12, 1869-Monday] 12 Em is sick and I have been over to see her, fear it is fever. Will is not well and Lawson is gone down to york to stay all night.

[July 13, 1869-Tuesday] 13 Lawson has brought Mr Burges home with him to day. He has improoved a good deal but looks bad. Mr Burgis and Sooe Bell is with us to night.

[July 14, 1869-Wednesday] 14 a merry crowd I have had to day, cousin Wille & Eliza Davis, Wille Jonson, Mary Cain, Sue Bell, Laura Brown and Mr Burgis. Mr Burgis has gone home with Wille Jonson to night. He is going to spend the summer with us.

[July 15, 1869-Thursday] 15 is some better this morning.

[July 17, 1869-Saturday] 17 Mag and I have been out on a trip. Took supper

with Lauson & Jane Brown last evening, went on over and stayed all night with Sister Harriet, went down to york and took dinner with aunt Emily. John Alexander is verry unwell.

[July 18, 1869-Sunday] 18 Mr Dickson has preached fore us to day.

[July 19, 1869-Monday] 19 Mrs Black and Mrs Strong has gone down to york to take the cars to go to see theire relations.

[July 24, 1869-Saturday] 24 we have had a nice picknick at the mineral spring to day. It was made fore Mr Burgis, a fine dinner and a nice crowd. Mary D Brown

[July 26, 1869-Monday] 26 I have been down to see little Eddy Davis. He has the fever, he is bad.

[July 30, 1869-Friday] 30 Mag has gone down to york and then going down to stay with her cousin Renes and Molly Fewel a week. Sally has gone down to stay a few dayes with Eliza and going to attend the meeting at Smerny.

[August 1, 1869-Sunday] August 1 Emily has gone over to stay with Mag Whiteside last night and Smerny to day. R J and Wille is gone over to Smerny too.

[August 3, 1869-Tuesday] 3 Lawson and Sally is down at ould unckle Tommy Whitesides to a quilting to day.

[August 5, 1869-Thursday] 5 Chambers, Adda and Laura Brown and cousin Lissa Thomison from chester was with us last night. Lawson and Sally and them all is gone over to unckle Hiram Thomisons and unckle Lawson Brown to day.

[August 7, 1869-Saturday] 7 I had a housefull of youngsters last night. Cousin Liza Thomison, cousin Ada Brown, cousin Lawra Brown, cousin Chambers Brown, cousin Molly Brown, cousin, John Brown, cousin Wille Thomison and they are all gone to a singing at Bershaba to day. August the 7 this is the day of the great eclips of the sun. The sun was entiraly coverd. It got so dark that the chickens went to rust and the stars was a shining, the greatest eclips that ever I have seen. It was about too hours from it comenced till it was over. Davis Brown was with us last night. R J Brown is gone down to Mr Hoods to see if

the Bulix Creek people will go in with us in macking out a call fore Mr Strong.

[*August 9, 1869-Monday*] 9 Mr Massabo is with us last night and to day. Jackson and Billey has been down to york and brought aunt Emily and Jaily Massabo out to day and Mrs Bell has spent this day with us too.

[*August 10, 1869-Tuesday*] 10 Mr Massabo and Jaily, aunt Emily, R J and I have spent this day at unckle Billeyes.

[*August 11, 1869-Wednesday*] 11 all of us at Ebs.

[*August 12, 1869-Thursday*] 12 all of us at Mr Cains.

[*August 14, 1869-Saturday*] August the 14 Jackson and I have been down to see cousin Wille Davis and Eliza to day. They have a stranger down theire, it is a daughter, Margaret Burgus. They are all dooing well.

[*August 15, 1869-Sunday*] 15 Ruffes and Eliza was with us last night and all at preachen to day. Mr strong has finished his great sermons. He has been preachen on one. His first sermon was, "If you will be my desipels deny thyself," his second was, "Take up thy cross," the third was, " Follow me," he done some great preachen.

[*August 16, 1869-Monday*] 16 Jackson has taken aunt Emily and Jaily up to Bob Alexanders to day.

[*August 17, 1869-Tuesday*] 17 theire is another picknick at the mineral spring to day. Lawson and Sally is gone.

[*August 18, 1869-Wednesday*] 18 Mr and Mrs Strong has got back. They called on us to day.

[*August 20, 1869-Friday*] 20 Emily and Mag is gone down to see Ruff and Eliza. R J and Jaily is gone over to H C Thomisons to night.

[*August 21, 1869-Saturday*] 21 Mr Burgus has spent this day with us. He dose not mend much. R J has come home and left Jaily to stay a week.

[*August 22, 1869-Sunday*] 22 Lawson and Eb is gone down to Sharan to day.

[August 24, 1869-Tuesday] 24 Wille Thomison has brought Jaily home, all well.

[August 25, 1869-Wednesday] 25 Mrs Scoggins has had a quilting to day. Em, Sally and I have been over to help her. Eb and Lawson came over and took dinner with us. We got it out and on the bed.

[August 29, 1869-Sunday] 29 Eb and Em and the children was with us last night, also Wille Thomison, Lawson and Sally. Wille and Eb is gone to enen to heare the Baptist preach to day. Jackson is gone over to Salem to the meeting. He started last friday. He intended to go to Ruff that night. Mary D Brown

[August 31, 1869-Tuesday] 31 Sally and Wille is gone down to Ruffs to help Eliza to git reddy fore her quilting.

[September 2, 1869-Thursday] Sept 2 aunt Harriet, Molly, Lawson, Mag and I have been down to Ruffs at a quilting to day. We did not git it out. Emily was down with us and we all came back home to night. Aunt Harriet and Molly stayd with Eb and Em.

[September 3, 1869-Friday] 3 aunt Harriet, Molly, Eb and Em has spent this day with us and all gone home.

[September 5, 1869-Sunday] 5 this is the sabbeth, the rest is all gone to preachen. I am at home by myself. Ruff and Eliza came by and took Fanny home with them.

[September 7, 1869-Tuesday] 7 Eliza Brown, Brother Johns daughter from north Carolina was here last night and Robert Coldwell and Docia Coldwell. We have had a fine picknick dinner at the mineral spring to day. It was made for Mr & Mrs Strong. Vilet Enlo, Ann & Mag Scoggins and John Brown staid all night.

[September 10, 1869-Friday] 10 Eb, Em, Sally & I have been down at york to day. Sally & I took dinner with Clem. Eb & Em took dinner with Fanny.

[September 11, 1869-Saturday] 11 Mrs Strong was here last night and Emily & the children. Mrs Strong, Jaily & I have been down and spent the day with Mrs Mary Davis and they helpt me to make my dress.

[September 13, 1869-Monday] 13 Lawson has gone down to help Ruff work at his house this week and Eb brought Fanny home with him.

[September 18, 1869-Saturday] 18 Jackson is gone up to Bethel to the communion and aunt Harriet and Emy was up to day.

[September 19, 1869-Sunday] 19 Harvy Gunings has landed here from Arcancis. He has spent this day with us. Mr Burns was over to day.

[September 24, 1869-Friday] September 24 this is the day oure communion comenced. Ould Mr Watson preached to us to day. His tex was in Rommans 8 30 "Moreover whome he did predestinate them he also called, and whome he called, them he also Justified, and whome he justified them he also glorified." He preached a good sermon. Theire was a small congration. Robbert Alexander and his too boyes, William and Joney, Jane Furguson and her three children, Mary, Emmy and Bobby has come down this evening to stay amongs us, the time of the meeting.

[September 25, 1869-Saturday] 25 satterday night Mr Strong is not with us at oure meeting. He is gone to the South Carrolina Presbatary. Mr Watson preached to day. His tex this morning was in st John 9 35, "Dost thou beleive on the son of God." Evening Acts 9 6, "Lord what wilt thou have me to doo." He preached to fine sermons. It brought back the rememberance of my sainted Farther. He allwayes thought he preached such plain and fine sermons. This is a wet night. I fear we will have a bad time. Ruffes and Eliza, Buttler and Robbert Alexander and his children is with us to night. Mary D Brown.

[September 26, 1869-Sunday] 26 Sabbeth evening verry wet morning we have had. It has rained so that the congration could not come out. In consquence of the wet morning oure communion was laid over unto the 4 of October. Mr Watson preached to them that did come out, a verry excelent sermon from Psalms 65 4, "Blessed is the man whome thou choosest, and causest to approche unto thee, that he may dwell in thy courts. We shall be sattesfied with the goodness of thy house, even of thy holly tempel." MDBrown
We have bid oure friends, Joe and Eliza and theire little son, Emmit farewell this evening. They are going to leave theire native home and going to seek a home in a distent land. Theyer going to Tennesse, going to start soon.

[September 30, 1869-Thursday] thursday 30 we had a congrational meeting

at the church to day. A bad turn out but them that was theire done well, 230, Ammos Burns, 25, Dr. Allison 25, Jackson Brown, 25, Frank Walker, 20, John Davis, 20, Mrs Mary Davis, 10, Mrs Eliza, 10, Mr William Davis, 8. I think we can make up foure hunderd at Bershaba if they will all do theire part.

[October 3, 1869-Sunday] Oct 3 Mr Strong has preached to day, theire was a small congration out. His tex was in John 11 35, "Jesus wept." He preached as good a sermon as ever I heard him preach and he took us all down this evening. He spoke as if he thought he might not preach for us eney more. He made no more appointments. MDB

[October 5, 1869-Tuesday] 5 oure deaces, John Davis and Mr Frank Walker met here this evening and brought in theire subscription papers. They have not got the foure hunderd yet. Some subscribed well and some don bad but I think they will make it yet. The congration made out a call on the satterday of oure meeting which was Sept 25 1869 fore Mr Hew Strong fore the half of his time. They put thre hunderd and seventy five in the call. I think we will mak out the foure hunderd yet and Salem is going in with us. She has mad out a call fore thre hunderd. We dont know what he will doo and wont know unto senod meets.

[October 6, 1869-Wednesday] 6 Jackson has started to presbetary this evening. Presbetry meets at Union Court house on tomorrow.

[October 7, 1869-Thursday] 7 Eliza has come up to day to stay with Emily a few dayes and help her sow. She is busy in preparing to start to Arcancis. Eb and Emily and Lawson is counting on starting in a few weeks to seek a home in the fare distant land.

[October 9, 1869-Saturday] Oct 9 Lawson and Sally is gone down to Sharan to preachen to day, Oct 9 and is going to stay with cousin Psalm Brown to night.

[October 10, 1869-Sunday] 10 Wille Thomison was with us last night and Wille, Eb and Em is all gone down to Sharon to day. It is the day of theire communion. Jackson has got home from Presbatary to night and brought Mr Henterson, the delagate from Union church home with him.

[October 11, 1869-Monday] 11 Lawson has gone down to help Ruff to cover his house and took Em and the children down to stay a few dayes with Eliza.

[October 13, 1869-Wednesday] 13 Ruff has brought Emily home and Eb has a shucking to night.

[October 14, 1869-Thursday] 14 Mrs Scoggins has been over to day to help me sow at Lawsons close.

[October 16, 1869-Saturday] 16 Lawson, Sally and Mag is gone down to Bethshilo to preachen to day.

[October 18, 1869-Monday] 18 the children has got home. They went home with Molly, took dinner a satterday evening, then Lawson and Sally went over and stayed with theire unckle Frank and cousin Sue and then to preachen a sunday, the communion at Bethshilo, then own to theire unckle Hirams that night and home this morning. I expect it will be Lawsons last visit fore this time and it may be fore life too. We know what is past but we know not what the future will be but I have gave them up to God. I put my trust in God that he will be with them and that he will take care of them and he will make all things well. Mary D Brown

[October 19, 1869-Tuesday] 19 Eb and Emily and the children, Fanny and I have been over to see unckle Hiram and family last night and then to york. Took dinner with aunt Emily and had the childrens pothographed and then home.

[October 20, 1869-Wednesday] 20 Hatty Thomison and Marrion McAphee and Ann Scoggins is here to night and unckle Bille and John Brown and had a fine singing. Mr Amos Burns, oure delegate from Bershaba is gone down to Chester to tend Senet and carry up the call fore Mr Strong, foure hunderd from Bershaba, thre hunderd from Salem.

[October 21, 1869-Thursday] 21 Mary Cain, Lawson, Mag and Sally, Harvy Guning, unckle Bille, aunt Caty, John and unckle Hugh Love and Mary and Isabella Love was all over with Emily to set to bedtime to night.

[October 23, 1869-Saturday] 23 Renes and Molly Fewel, Wille Thomison, Mon Thomison is all with us to night and Jackson is gone down to york to night to see if theire had come up a preacher to hold the communion at Bershaba to morrow.

[October 24, 1869-Sunday] 24 Jackson has brought Mr Dow out this morning to preach fore us to day. It is fourteen years the 26 day of last August sence he preached here last. His tex to day was in the Acts of the apostles 8 35 verse. These are the words of his tex, "Then Philip opend his mouth and began at the same scriptures and preached unto him Jesus." I tell you that Mr Dow opened his mouth and preached unto us, Jesus. He went back in immagination when Christ was in the bosom of the Farther beffore the world was made and preached Jesus on unto the present day, a great sermon. He did preach and preached it to some that may not, in the providance of God, ever meet theire again. My children was all theire on this memoriable day which in the course of providance I never expect to meet them all in the walls of that blessed church on earth again. Eb and Emily and the children, Lenard Harris and Mary Brown and my belloved son, Lawson will leave us in a short time to seek a home in a distant land. Whether we will ever meet again is only known to God who has prommised to take care of them that puts their trust in him. Eliza has come home with us to stay until the sale is over and my children and grand children, except Ruffes is all with us to night, the last night that they may ever spend under their Farthers roof. If we never meet together in an earthly Farthers house, I pray that we will meet an unbroken family in theire Heavenly Farthers house, in the manshion that Christ has gone to prepare fore all them that love and serve him in spirit and truth. MDBrown

[October 26, 1869-Tuesday] 26 Ebs sale is over, it looks like brackin up shore enough to see what little you have, all sold an gone. Things sold tollarable well, some things brought their value and some did not.

[October 27, 1869-Wednesday] 27 Eb and family has come over to stay with us till they leave. Mag Whitesides is her today and night. Lawson, his paw and Eb is gone to york to day.

[October 28, 1869-Thursday] 28 Lawson and Eb is gone down to stay all night with Ruff and Eliza. Emily and Sally is gone up to stay all night with unckle Bille.

[October 29, 1869-Friday] 29 Emily and I have been down at Mr Cains to day and took dinner with them. Eb has come home and Lawson has gone to a singing at Mount Vernon. Aunt Harriet has come up to stay with us to night.

[October 30, 1869-Saturday] 30 verry busy in fixing up things to day, back-

ing some and packing up their trunks. Their Paw has packed theire bedding and feather and varrious other things up in a bale. Mary Davis and Mrs Jonson is here this evening.

[October 31, 1869-Sunday] 31 A holly sabbeth morning. William Davis and Eliza was with us last night. So manny about and such a stir and so much excitement. We had to spend the day as we oughtnt to have done, it seems that it cant be helped.

[November 2, 1869-Tuesday] Nov the 2 a day long to be remembered by me if life is to be long. I have bid my children fair well this morning, the first scene of the kine that I have been called to witness. Oh my God, I have gave them up to thee in Baptism. They have gave themselves up to thee by proffession. My Lord and my God, I renew my vowes to give them up to thee both soul and boddy, both fore time and Eternity. Keep them by thy allmighty power from danger, seen and unseen. If agreeable to thy heavenly will, give them a speedy and safe journey, if not, not my will be done but thyne. Mary D Brown. Ruff and Eliza is gone home and we are left all allone. It feels both sollom and lonsome.

[November 4, 1869-Thursday] 4 we have got lines from Lawson this evening. It was wrote in Columbia. They ware gitting along fine. He said he was leaving South Carrolina in a hurry. MDBrown

[November 7, 1869-Sunday] 7 sister Harriet was up to day. She came up to preachen. Theire was none and she came over here a while. We miss oure children verry much but it will ware off after while.

[November 9, 1869-Tuesday] 9 we have got a letter this evening from Eb. They have got allong fine so far. They went to Memphis in too dayes, was in the steam boat a wensday night, eat breckfast their and would start at one a thursday. He said it would take them thre dayes to land at Des Arck. All had got allong fine, so far.

[November 11, 1869-Thursday] 11 Jackson and I was down with Ruff and Eliza last night, all well except colds.

[November 14, 1869-Sunday] 14 Sabbeth evening, all well and at home, no preachen. The children gone but theire is one friend that has prommised that he will never leave us nore never forsake us. If we live a life of prayer God is presenet with us.

[November 16, 1869-Tuesday] 16 we have got a letter. Oure children has arrived safe in Arcancis at their aunt Peggyes Janses. They was badly frightend on the Boat. It run against a snag and they was most all assleep and the Capt hollored for them all to git up, fore Gods sake, fore the boat was sinking. Theire was great excitement awhile till they found that the nose of the boat had struck and did not inger the hull. They had a fine trip except that and aunt Peggy and Cousin Bob well, his wife and daughter not so well. Aunt Peggy was so glad to see them she could not speak. Ruff and Eliza was up last night. They are all well. They have left Mag with us a week. We have got another letter from my children, not verry well pleased with Arcancis so far.

[November 25, 1869-Thursday] 25 Mrs Black and Mrs Davis and children has spent this day with us and Franklin to night.

[November 26, 1869-Friday] 26 we have received some more letters. Lawson and Cousin ___Janes has gone down to little Rock, the capital of the state. Lawson has been offerd seventy five dollars a month but has reffused to take it. Wille and I have been a big visit. We went down a satterday morning to unckle Hirams and took dinner, then Aunt Harriet, Buttler, Wille and I went down to see Renes and Molly. Found them all well and dooing well.

[November 28, 1869-Sunday] Sabbeth day went to Bethshilo to hear Mr Carthrethers preach. His tex was in Exadious about the children of Iseral. He cant preach like Mr Strong, then we went home with Franklin and Sue. They are all well. They are going to leave theire Sue theire. She was going to marry and then home to day.

[November 30, 1869-Tuesday] 30 Fanny and Mag was a visiting over to Mrs Scoggins to day.

[December 1, 1869-Wednesday] December 1 Ruffes came up to day and took Mag and his little Mag home with him.

[December 3, 1869-Friday] 3 Mr Mullholland has taken dinner with us today. He is to leave this neighborhood goin down on Dr Barrons place to make a crop, and then he expects to go to Arcancis. Mrs Cain has spent this evening with us.

[December 5, 1869-Sunday] Sabbeth evening 5 Mr Strong walked out from york in the rain this morning and took his breakfast with us and then went

to the church and preached fore us. his tex was in Isah the fifty fifth chapter and sixth verse, "Seek ye the Lord while he may be found, call ye apon him while he is near." He preached a fine sermon but he dose that all the time. It seems as he is going to leave us. He sayes he wants no one blamed and he wants no one to blame him. It is a strange thing the way that all things has turned around. I beleve it is the hand of God that has so overulled it. It may be fore oure good ore it may be that God has taken him away in anger from us. It seems that he has been visiting oure Church with strife after strife and God has said he that being often reprooved and hardenedth his neck shall suddenly be destroyed and that without rem_ he has also said that he will poure his furry out on all fammilies that call not on his name. He has delayed this judgement a long time but it seemes as if he is now visiting us with his judgements in taking oure paster and now causing us to be left as sheep without a shepherd.

[December 7, 1869-Tuesday] 7 Sally and I have been down to york to day and got no letter. I am verry axinious to hear from them.

[December 9, 1869-Thursday] 9 I have been down to help Mrs Cain to sow to day.

[December 10, 1869-Friday] 10 Mrs Scoggins has been over to day. Eliza and Mag has come up to day and Jaily is going home with her this morning.

[December 13, 1869-Monday] 13 Mary Cain has been up with us to night.

[December 17, 1869-Friday] 17 Sally and John Brown has gone over to Union to a singing to day and Mary Cain, and they are going to stay with Hatty Thomison to night.

[December 19, 1869-Sunday] 19 Jackson went down to Ruffs last night to bring Jaily home. This is Mr Strongs last day at Bersheba. I had a chill this morning and could not go.

[December 21, 1869-Tuesday] 21 R J has gone down to york for Mrs Strong. Mr Strong met her this evening and Mr and Mrs Strong and R J is gone down to Mrs Davis to the wedding. Allonza Brown and Sue Davis was married Dec 21 1869 by Mr Hew Strong. Mr Newton Glenn and Mrs Sue Coldwell was married Dec 21 1869 by Mr Watson.

[December 22, 1869-Wednesday] 22 this is a verry wet day and R J did not go to the infare.

[December 25, 1869-Saturday] 25 this is christmas day. Sally, Mag & Wille, John Brown, Ann Scoggins all of them went over to their unckle Hirams last night to a singing. Ruff & Eliza and the children came up last night to take Christmas with us and it is a verry wet day. We have had too letters from Eb and Emily. They have located in Yell near Dr Tom Whitesides. Eb is going to teach school. They are not verry well pleased with Arc. Also too from Lawson. He is Vanbran. He dont know what he will doo yet, is hearty and well. The children has come home this evening in the rain and Vilet Enloe & Ann Scoggins staid with them. Ruff has gone home and left Eliza and the children.

[December 26, 1869-Sunday] 26 Ruff has come back fore Eliza and Fanny is gone home with them.

[December 27, 1869-Monday] 27 still wet and raining, a bad time fore christmas spreeing.

[December 28, 1869-Tuesday] 28 R J has gone to york to day and out to Hirams to night. Mag & Jaily is gone down to Mr Cains to stay all night. Sally & Wille, Ann Scoggins and myself is all that is here. I have been verry unwell fore some time. I often think of the admonition given to the prophit. Set thine house in order fore thou shall die and not live. Heavenly Farther may I so live that I may be reddy to go forth to meet the Bride Groom in eney watch of the night. MDB

[December 29, 1869-Wednesday] 29 Wille and I have been down to see Mrs Mary Davis and Mrs Black to day. This has been a beautiful day. Some of the young people has gathered in here to night for a singing, Sue and Macy Bell, Mag Scoggins stayed all night.

[December 31, 1869-Friday] 31 Sally & Mag is patridge driving. R J was down at Ruff last night, all well. R J and Jaily and I have all been up and took dinner with aunt Caty to day. The children is all gone over to Mrs Mcaphee to a singing to night. We have got a letter from Lawson. He is not well pleased with Arcancis yet, sayes he may be home beffore long. Friday night, ten oclock, too houres more and 1869 will be gone. Manny, manny has been the changes sene this time twelve months. What this night twelve months will bring arround is known only to God and now the tex ocurs to me, "Arise ye and depart fore this is not your rest." Oh my God, a many a won thou has called to go but my unproffitabel life thou has still spared, unworthy as I am.

1870

[January 1, 1870-Saturday] a new years morning Jan the 1 1870 Eighteen hunderd and sixty nine is numbered with the past. It seemes but yesterday sence it commenced. How fast years fly away. How solem the thought that we are all haisting to an untried and unchaing eternity. One by one the teeming millions of the humman race are pooring into the ocian of another wourld. To look back and review the past is always proffatable, if not pleasant. It is the only means by wich we can accurately ascertain oure present standing in the sight of God. I feel verry unwell to day. I had a chill this morning. God has been bringing this poor frail boddy of mine through some of his chastismants.

[January 2, 1870-Sunday] Sabbeth evening dont feel much better. We have had no preachen to day.

[January 4, 1870-Tuesday] Tusday morning the 4 my dear son, Robbert Lawson Brown landed home last night at nine oclock in the night, walked from york and it a snowing. My God I thank the that thou hast watched over him. Thou has preserved him from dangers, seen and unseen and is now under his

Farthers roof. He has a verry bad cold and cough but I hope through care and attention he will soon be all right. He left Eb and Emily and the children all well, but not well sattesfied with their new home. He sayes that they may come back next fall if they are not better sattesfied.

[January 5, 1870-Wednesday] 5 we had a crowd of youngsters here last night, all gone this morning. R J has gone down to york fore Lawsons trunk and Lawson has gone up to take dinner with his Unckle Bille.

[January 7, 1870-Friday] 7 Lawson, Willie and I have been down to see Ruffe and Eliza, all well. Left Wille and brought Fanny home.

[January 8, 1870-Saturday] 8 Lawson has gone over to see his aunt Harriet to night.

[January 9, 1870-Sunday] 9 I have been at preachen to day. Mr Jonson, the methist, preached fore us to day. We are trying to git Mr Robbert Anterson to preach fore us the half of his time. This is a verry cold day. A poore turn out of the congratation.

[January 14, 1870-Friday] 14 Hiram, Wille, Ida and Liza was up last night.

[January 15, 1870-Saturday] 15 Mrs Cain and Franklin Furguson has spent this day with us. Lawson is gone down to cousin Psalms and Ruff a geny visit.

[January 18, 1870-Tuesday] 18 all well and at home. It has been a verry wet and warm spell of weather.

[January 23, 1870-Sunday] 23 Mr Robbert Anterson preached for us to day. He is going to preach fore us the half of his time this year ore as long as he stayes at york. His tex was in Hebrews the fourth chapter and too last verses.

[January 25, 1870-Tuesday] 25 Ruff and Eliza came up yesterday and I went with them to york and had a wet evening to come home and got a letter from Eb and Em, all well.

[January 26, 1870-Wednesday] 26 Eliza and Sue Jackson paid the girls a visit today. MDBrown

[January 27, 1870-Thursday] 27 Joe Bell and Harvy Gunings came down this evening fore Lawson, Sally and Maggy to go up to Bells to a conversation party. I have gave them theire suppers and all gone.

[January 29, 1870-Saturday] 29 cousin Sue Davis, cousin Ginny and Adda Brown, Wille jonson, Ann and Mag Scoggins Sue Bell was with us last night. All gone up to spend the day with aunt Caty.

[January 30, 1870-Sunday] 30 Sabbeth day, no preachen. I have been sick to day with a chill.

[January 31, 1870-Monday] 31 Lawson has been down to york this morning to git me some medison.

[February 3, 1870-Thursday] Feb 3 Jaily, Fanny and I took dinner with unckle Lawson on yesterday. Staid all night with aunt Harriet. Molly is up theire now to stay a while. Sally, Mag and I have been up helping aunt Caty to sow to day.

[February 4, 1870-Friday] 4 this has been a verry wet, cold, freezing day and I have been sick in bed.

[February 6, 1870-Sunday] 6 this is the sabbeth. Mr Anterson was to preach but it has rained so hard this morning that theire has been no preachen. Buttler was with us last night.

[February 10, 1870-Thursday] 10 Lawson has been down at Ruff. They are all well. We have got a letter from Emily. She has not been verry well and not sattesfied. A great deal of sickness. Jane Curry & Clorinda, Bud has spent this day with us.

[February 11, 1870-Friday] 11 aunt Harriett and Emmy has come up to see us to day. Aunt Harriet is gone home and left Emmy to stay unto sunday.

[February 12, 1870-Saturday] 12 Ruff and Eliza and the children has come up this morning.

[February 13, 1870-Sunday] 13 Mr Anterson has preached to day. I was not out. I have been sick and did not feel abel to go to church. Ruff and Eliza is gone home.

[February 16, 1870-Wednesday] 16 oure teacher, Mr John Carson is with us to night. Wille and Fanny is going to school to him. I think he is a good teacher.

[February 17, 1870-Thursday] 17 I have been over to Hirams. Molly has a fine daughter. It was born Feb the 17 at halft past one, a thursday evening, got allong fine, had her aunt Peggy with her. Her mother in law, Mrs Fewel, Jane Brown and I.

[February 20, 1870-Sunday] 20 we have a cold snowe day. Was to have preachen. Was to bad a day. Wille Thommison has brought Sally home and took Mag home with him to see Molly and the babby.

[February 21, 1870-Monday] 21 a verry cold day. It is reported that Eb and Em is on the road home but I dont beleve it.

[February 24, 1870-Thursday] 24 Lawson went over to his unckles Hirams last, and brought Mag home this morning. Molly is not gitting allong so well, she has had a chill. The babe is dooing fine. It is a cold day and a nice snow.

[March 2, 1870-Wednesday] March 2 Lawson and I was down at R G last night. They are all well. Mr McGills store was burned on yesterday morning by an incendiary. It was a great loss to him. Mr Carson is with us. He has a good school now and I think he is a good teacher.

[March 5, 1870-Saturday] 5 Mr Anterson preached to day. It is another wet day. Theire was a small congration.

[March 8, 1870-Tuesday] 8 this is court week but Lawson and his Paw has not been down. Mr Martin Hall is with us to night.

[March 9, 1870-Wednesday] 9 I have been down at Mr Cains to day helping them to quilt and Dr Hill is with us to night. I was glad to see him. He is a fine man.

[March 10, 1870-Thursday] 10 R J has gone down to york to night to stay all night and took Sally down to stay a week. Mag and Jaily is visiting at Tom Bells to day and they have caught too Berry boyes that has confessed that they burnt McGills store and put them in jaile.

[March 13, 1870-Sunday] 13 I have been spared to go to the house of God again and to heare a great sermon by Mr Anterson. His tex was in Mathew 26 chapter, "Lord is it I?" It was better fore that man he had never been born. He preached a great sermon. M J Brown and we have got another letter from EP Castel. They are all well as could be expected. Brown Whisenthunt has been sick, but better.

[March 14, 1870-Monday] 14 I have been visiting over to Scoggins to day.

[March 15, 1870-Tuesday] 15 Mag and Jaily is helping Mary Cain to quilt to day.

[March 20, 1870-Sunday] 20 Mr Anterson has preached to day. His tex was in Jobe. "If a man die shall he live again?" Ruff and Eliza was up last night and left little Mag with us this week.

[March 22, 1870-Tuesday] 22 we have got too letters from Eb this evening. Emmily has an other fine daughter. E P says it has black hair and blew eyes, the pertyest thing the sun ever shined on. It was born March the fifth on satterday evening at five oclock. Emily and the chiled is both dooing well. A matter of great thanksgiven and comfhert to me. MDBrown

[March 26, 1870-Saturday] 26 this is satterday of oure communion. It has been a wet day, rained so hard and studdy that none of us went up to the church but theire Paw. We thought theire would be no preachen to day but ould Mr Willson was at Mrs Davis. He came up and gave them that was theire, a lecture. Polly Burns came over last night to go to preachen and is still with us also HC & Butler Thomison.

[March 28, 1870-Monday] 28 oure communion was laid over until next Sabbeth on the account of the bad day and high watters. Mr Anterson preached. His tex was, "Rember the Sabbeth day." Cousin Daubson & Fanny, unckle Lawson, unckle Franklin, Butler, Daubson, Vilet Enloe came home with us last evening. Monday evening Ann, Mag Scoggins, Vilet has all been here to day. R J has gown to Ruff to take little Mag home and tak Sally down to stay with her sister a week. Vilet, Mag, Jaily is gone home with Ann to stay all night.

[March 29, 1870-Tuesday] 29 I had another chill last night and been in bed most all day. Mrs Scoggins has come over and staid with me to day. R J has come home, all well.

[March 30, 1870 - Wednesday] 30 all well, another wet evening. MDB

[April 2, 1870–Saturday] Aprile 2 we all have been to preachen to day. Mr Anterson preached one sermon. His tex was Isaah the first chapter, "Come now and let us reasen together saith the Lord. Though youre sins be as scarlet they shall be as white as snow. Though they be red like crimson they shall be as wool." Theire was thre children baptised, Mrs Bells Tommy, Loury and Laura Smith _____, Mr Robbert Love _____. He did not name the children, Child of the covenant, I baptise thee. Sally came up from Ruffs this morning and Mag Whiteside and Hatty come home with her. Them and Idah is all I have to night. Aunt Harriet came by and took dinner with us and then went home. A wet evening.

[April 3, 1870-Sunday] 3 Sabbeth evening we have had oure communion to day, a cold damp day. Mr Anterson preached a sermon. His tex was, "If you will be my desiple let him denny himself, take up his cross and follow me." It was a good searmon, then administerd the Lords supper. Theire was a small congration. I have been verry unwell to day, had a chill could hardily hold up to git home. I did not feel abble to go to church this morning but was axinious to go. It was oure communion and the last day Mr Anterson was to preach fore us. I felt that it might be the last time that I would ever be theire. Pain and disease is reducing both boddy and strenth but while the outward man is failing I hope that the inward man will grow in grace and in the knowledge of oure Saviour. Im but a stranger here. Heaven is my home, Earth is a desert drear. Heaven is my home. Dangers and sorrows stand Round me on every hand. Heaven is my Father-land. Heaven is my home what though the tempest rage. Heaven is my home. Short is my pilgrimage. Heaven is my home. And times wild wintry blast. Soon will be over past. I shall reach home at last. Heaven is my home. Therefore I murmer not. Heaven is my home. Whate ere my earthly lot. Heaven is my home. And I shall surely stand theire at my Lords right hand. Heaven is my Father land. Heaven is my home. Theire at my Saviours side, Heaven is my home. I shall be glorified. Heaven is my home. Theire are the good and Those I love most and best. Theire too I soon shall rest. Heaven is my home. MDB

[April 5, 1870-Tuesday] 5 Lawson, Sally, Jaily and Will is all at unckle Bill-eyes this evening. He had a log rolling and took supper with them.

[April 7, 1870-Thursday] 7 I feel some better this evening but must not complain. Ann Scoggins and ould aunt Susan Brown came over to see me this evening and Lawson is gone down to york to see Mr Falls. He is going to start back to Arcancis in the morning. He came home with Lawson when he was out theire. He lives in fifteen miles of Em. We sent some letters with him. Mary Cain was here to day to get Sally help her to make a pare of bag heddles. They got them done and Sue Bell is here to night.

[April 10, 1870-Sunday] 10 this is the Sabbeth day and I have reasen to thank God. I feel some better. The rest is all well and at home. Have no preachen and dont know when we will have eney more. We are left as sheep without a shepherd again. I have been readin Fisher and Burket on too questions today. They are these. What benefits will belevers receive from Christ at theire death. What benefits doo belevers receive from Christ at the reserection. I find great comphert and enceregement in them if I can only live a life to reap the benefits of them.

[April 11, 1870-Monday] 11 Lawson and his Paw has gone up to a Mr Mieres to git a bark mill to day. Theire is no shool fore too weeks as the measles has got in the school.

[April 13, 1870-Wednesday] 13 I have been down to york this morning and left Mag to stay a week with her Aunt Emily and cousin Fanny.

[April 14, 1870-Thursday] 14 Mary Cain is here to day helping Sally to make her dress.

[April 15, 1870-Friday] 15 I have been down to help Mrs Cain to put in a web of bags to day. This evening have been up at Bershaba to heare the Rev Mr Boice preach, a soceder. He preached fore the benaft of Miss Ann Enloe, a blind woman. His tex was in John 21 chapter 19 verse. He preached a fine sermon.

[April 17, 1870-Sunday] 17 Lauson is gone down to Sharon. It is the time of theire communion and presbatory. Sally wanted to go but it was a bad looking morning to go so far. Sally and her Paw went over to zion to heare the Methedist. Jaily went over to cousin Eliza Burnsis last night and to preachen to day and then back theire and stayed all night. This is easter Sunday, April 17, a cold, stormmy day. It was cloudy and raining this morning, then cleared off

then clowed up and had a good shower of hail and wind, then cleared off, then clouded up and rained and snowed and is verry cold and stormmy.

[April 18, 1870-Monday] 18 Lawson got home yesterday evening. He was at cousin Psalms a sunday night and went back to preachen yesterday. I had a chill yesterday but better this morning. Mag was down at Sharon a sunday and went back to york. She is going out to her aunt Harriets this week. She wants to go down to attend the meeting at Bethshilo next sunday. Sally is gone visiting over to see Eliza Jackson to day. We are all well. Measels is verry plenty. MDBrown

[April 24, 1870-Sunday] 24 R J went over to Hirams last night and going to preachen to day at Beth Shiloh. Lawson and Sally is gone. It has been verry warm today. I have enjoyed myself find to day, reading and studding and in trying to make a sabbeth dayes journey.

[April 27, 1870-Wednesday] 27 Mag has got home this eveng. She has had a big visit and enjoyed herself fine.

[April 29, 1870-Friday] Aprile 29 the ould D Allison was up to day. He had received a letter from Mr Anterson staitin to Bershaba Cession that theire was no chance a young minister from the Seminary. They had theire faces turned another way. Oh Heavenly Farther, remember this oure now destutete church, this vine of thy own planting, whare oure Farthers and Mothers worshiped thee and held sweet communion with thee with oure beloved pasters, Mr William B Davis and his son, Mr James A Davis, all gone home to Heaven, theire crown to weare within the last fifteen years. Oh Heavenly Farther deal not with us as oure sins deserve, but in thy loving kindness send us a paster of thy own choice. One that shall feed thy sheep and feed thy lambs. Oh that thou may say of us as of thy church of ould, the church of Philadelpha, "Behold I have set beffore thee an open doore and no man can shut it." Make haste oh God and come to oure relefe. Leave us no longer as sheep without a shepherd. MDBrown

[May 12, 1870-Thursday] May 12 I have got home from Ruffs this evening, found them all well. I have taken a big visit down theire since last satterday, near a week and left them as well as could be expected. Mag went home with R G to stay a while with her sister.

[May 15, 1870-Sunday] 15 all well this eveing. Lawson and Sally and Jaily is gone over to Zion to preachen this evening. Mag has not got home. Mary D Brown

[May 16, 1870-Monday] 16 aunt Harriet and Molly has been up and spent the day with us. I think Molly looks a good deal worsted. The babby is growing fine. Its name is Hatty Casort.

[May 18, 1870-Wednesday] 18 I and Fanny was over at Hirams last night. Found them all well.

[May 19, 1870-Thursday] 19 Mrs Cain and Mary Cain, Ann and Mag Scoggins and aunt Caty was all helping Sally to quilt to day.

[May 22, 1870-Sunday] 22 I have got home from Ruffs this morning. Eliza babby was born quarter past twelve, a wensday morning, May the 18 1870. She got allong fine. Dr Allison was with her. I have staid near a week. Her and the babe is dooing fine. Lawson came down fore me and brought Jaily down to stay a while with her sister.

[May 26, 1870-Thursday] 26 we have had a fine rain to day. We have been suffering very much from the drouth.

[May 29, 1870-Sunday] 29 Mr Baily preaches at Beershaba to day. I did not feele well enough to go out. I had a chill yesterday and was bad off, but better to day. Ruffes has come up to preachen to day and brought Jaily home and took Hatty home. Eliza and the babby is dooing well. We had a power rain on yesterday. Bullixcreek was fuller than it has been in years.

[June 2, 1870-Thursday] June the 2 unckle Bille and aunt Caty has taken dinner with us and Mary and Isabella Love supper with us.

[June 3, 1870-Friday] 3 Sally and Mag is gone a visiting over to Amos Burnses to day and Lawson has been appointed Capt of the road and he is working on the road to day fore the first time.

[June 4, 1870-Saturday] 4 Lawson and Sally has gone down to Ruffes to night, going to Smerny to preachen to morow.

[June 7, 1870-Tuesday] 7 Mrs Scoggins little Maggie and I have been up to spend the day with aunt Caty. Mun Thomison and Mr SeaPaw was here last night.

[June 12, 1870-Sunday] 12 H C Thomison, Joe Bell and Harvy has been here to day. They came to the church expecting preachen and was none.

[June 14, 1870-Tuesday] 14 I have had a verry bad spell but is better this morning.

[June 16, 1870-Thursday] 16 Ruffe and Eliza was up with us, the first time fore the little stranger. They are both gitting allong fine.

[June 19, 1870-Sunday] 19 we have been blessed with the privelage of going to ould Bershaba once more. God in his good provedence has sent us a young minister. His name is James H Douglass. He is to preach the half of his time fore us, one fourth fore Salem, one fourth fore Shilo. He preached but one sermon. He has been sick. His tex was in Mathew, the eighteenth cha., third verse, "And he said, verrly I say unto you, except ye be converted and become as a little child ye shall in no wise enter into the kingdom of Heaven." We all thought he done verry well. I have been told it was his second sermon. These are the hymns he sung, 349, "People of the living God," 228, "Hail ever blessed Jesus," 218, "Just as I am without one plea." I doo pray God that he may doo well and that the congration will doo theire part to a man. Ruffes was up at preachen to day and took Fanny home with him to stay a while.

[June 23, 1870-Thursday] 23 Mrs Cain, Mrs Bell, and aunt Caty has spent this day with us. It was perty much of a treat to hear Mrs Cain and Mrs Bell talk a day.

[July 3, 1870-Sunday] July 3 We have all been to preachen today. Had quite a company last night, Rufus and Eliza, Butlar Thomison, Davis Brown, Joe Whiteside and Brown Whisenthunt. Brown is just from Arcancis. I have heard all about Em and how she is gitting allong. They are dooing verry well but not sattesfied yet. Mr Douglass came home with us. He is verry weakly. He can scacerly stand to preach one sermon. He is going to stay with us a few dayes and drink some of the mineral water.

[July 5, 1870-Tuesday] 5 Mary and M Bell Love has been helping Sally to quilt to day and Mr Douglass is here. Aunt Harriet and Liza has been over to

day and have taken Sally home with her to stay a while.

[July 10, 1870-Sunday] 10 Lauson, Mag and theire paw is gone over to Smerny to preachen to day. They have a sacrament theire to day. Mag and Jaily is not well.

[July 14, 1870-Thursday] 14 R J is gone over to Hiram fore Sally.

[July 16, 1870-Saturday] 16 the youngsters has a fishing party at McElwees mill to day.

[July 17, 1870-Sunday] 17 Mr Douglass has preached to day. He is improving in health and I think he is improving in preachen. His tex was in Isah 45 22. "Look unto me all ye ends of the earth and be ye saved, fore I am God and besides me theire is none other."

[July 18, 1870-Monday] 18 Mary Cain has been helping Sally to quilt to day.

[July 20, 1870-Wednesday] 20 Mr Gimmy and Sally Coldwell, Mrs Cain, Jackson and I have taken dinner with aunt Caty and all come home with me and took supper. They are failing verry fast.

[July 24, 1870-Sunday] 24 all well Sabbeth evening and at home but Lawson. He is gone to Sharan to preachen to day and we have had a fine rain.

[July 27, 1870–Wednesday] 27 John Brown has thrashed oure wheat fore us to day. We fifty five Bushels, did not turn out well. Mr and Mrs Scoggins took dinner with us.

[July 28, 1870-Thursday] 28 Mag and I have been a visiting up to Tom Bells to day, had a fine visit.

[August 1, 1870-Monday] August 1 Wille and I went down to york last satterday and out to Hirams that night, down to Bethshilo on yesterday and heard Mr Catherees preach too fine sermons. His tex in the morning was in Psalms.

[August 6, 1870-Saturday] 6 we have had a fine picknick at the Mineral Spring today, had a crowd last night.

[August 12, 1870-Friday] August the 12 Eb and Emily and the children, Lenny, Mary and the little stranger, Sarah Francis all landed here last night harty and well and all looks hearty and well. Eb wayes over too hundred. Em is fleshy as ever I seen. Lenny had the chills before they left the state of Arcancis but looks well now. Oh my Heavenly Farther give me a heart of praise and thanksgiving fore thy manifestation of thy love and care to those dear children through dangers seen and unseen, both on watter and land, safe once more in theire Farthers house. Eliza and Joe Whitesides has been up to see them to day.

[August 17, 1870-Wednesday] 17 Jackson and I have been on a visit down to see cousin Psalm and Margarat Brown and to see Wille and Eliza Davis.

[August 18, 1870-Thursday] 18 we have had preachen at the church to day and an ellection fore Deacons. Lawson Brown was the highest candate, William Love next, Loury Smith next and subscription to see how much would make up fore Mr Douglass. The blind preacher, Mr Canidy preached fore us. Hiram and Harriet and Mr Canidy and Mr Douglass came home with us. Mr Douglas is gone home with Hiram.

[August 19, 1870-Friday] 19 Mr Canidy, Eb and Em, Jackson and I have been over to spend the day with Mr Scoggins to day and Mr Canidy has stayed all night.

[August 20, 1870-Saturday] 20 Mr Canidy, Eb, Em and theire Paw has gone down to Mr Cains to eat wattermillions.

[August 21, 1870-Sunday] 21 they have all been to preachen today but Fanny and I to heare the blind preacher and he went home with Mr Burns.

[August 23, 1870-Tuesday] 23 I have been down to see Eliza to day, have taken Eb and Em down to stay a few dayes.

[August 31, 1870-Wednesday] 31 Eb and Em and Mag is gone over to theire unckle Hirams to stay a few dayes.

[September 4, 1870-Sunday] September 4 we have had preachen to day. Ruff and Eliza came home with us. Mrs Scoggins baby was born September the 5 1870.

[September 5, 1870-Monday] 5 Em has had a chill to day.

[September 7, 1870-Wednesday] 7 Ginny Curry has been to se us to day and Em and Lenny has both had a chill.

[September 9, 1870-Friday] 9 Lawson and Mag is gone down to Ruff this morning.

[September 11, 1870-Sunday] 11 this is the Sabbeth. We have no preachen to day, but I hope we have tryed to spend it in a right way. Lawson has come home. Eliza and little Mary and Maggy has the chills and been perty bad off.

[September 14, 1870-Wednesday] 14 I have got to be very porly again. I was verry sick on yesterday. "This world is not my home I know. Fore sin and sorrow wound me. But mercy tempers every blow and goodness smiles arround me. Then let my lot be what it my be. Come gladness ore come sorrow. Im nearer to my home to day and may be theire tommorow." Jackson has been down to see Eliza. They have got some better.

[September 18, 1870-Sunday] 18 I feel verry unwell to day and Sister Harriet has been over to see me to day.

[September 23, 1870-Friday] September 23 this day is the commencement of oure communion. Mr Watson preached fore us to day. His tex was that the deciples was first called Christians at Antioch.

[September 24, 1870-Saturday] 24 Mr Watson preached to day. His tex was in Acts 16 chapt 30, "Sir, What must I doo to be saved?" Eb and Em had theire little daughter Sarah Francis baptised to day. William and his wife had one baptised. Its name was William Edward. Davis Burns and his wife joined the church and had theire child baptised. Bless the Lord and prais his holy name fore all his loving kindness to me and mine. Mag has joined the church to day and has acknowledged that she loves the Lord Jesus Christ. Oh my Heavenly Farther poure thy holy spirit out on her. May she addoren the gospel she has proffesed. May she be an ornament to thy church militant and made meet fore thy church tryumphant. Theire was too Deacons oredaind this evening, Loury Smith and my sone Lawson. Oh my God as he has been ordaind an officer in thy chrch poure thy holy spirit out on him. May he be a faithfull stwerd in thy house.

Oh my God thou hast greatly blessed me in giving me godly children. I have had six to join my bloved church Bershaba whare my Farther and Mother worshiped. My Farther was a rulling elder. My husband is one. My children has come out from the wourld and joined the churches as soon as they are capple of it. My Heavenly Farther thou dids love my little Wille eigh years ould, my little Ruffe, three years ould, loved and took them home to thyself. I have three more yet, Jaily Wille and Fanny. O my God may they not be wandring lambs but may they love theire Heavenly Farthers fold. I may never live to see it but I pray thee to gather us all in a bundle to meet an unbroken family in thy kingdom at last is the prayer of a poore mother.

[September 25, 1870-Sunday] Sabbeth evening oure meeting has closed and we have been blessed with a good meeting. Ould Mr Dr Plommer from collumbia was with us last night and preached fore us this morning. He is is a great and good man.

[September 27, 1870-Tuesday] 27 I have been verry bad off with a pain in my side sence sabbeth. Eliza staid with me until last evening. This is the day that Eb and Emily has mooved up on clarks fork. Eb is teachen school. John Brown and her Paw moved them.

[September 28, 1870-Wednesday] 28 Joe Bell and Eliza Jackson was married September the 28 1870.

[October 2, 1870-Sunday] Oct. 2 I have got some better and Eliza has been up to see me to day.

[October 9, 1870-Sunday] 9 we had Mr Douglass with us last night. His health is improoving. He preached a fine sermon to day and aunt Harriet and Butlar is with us to night.

[October 10, 1870-Monday] 10 Mr Scoggins and Ann and Sally is gone to the wool factery to git their wool carded.

[October 17, 1870-Monday] 17 I have been down to see Ruff and Eliza. They have been having some chills. Mrs Sue Jonson and Mrs Jane Jonson has spent the day with us and helped me to quilt and we have been down to see Mrs Cook who is boarding at Mr Cains. She is verry bad sick. R J has been up to see Em. They are gitting along fine.

[October 21, 1870-Friday] 21 Mrs Black, Mrs Porter from texes, Mrs Mary Davis has spent this day with us. A verry pleasant day we have enjoyed. Alonza and Sue Browns, Mary Edner, was born Oct the first 1870. Ould Mrs Cook died at Mr Cains on satterday of October 22 1870 of droppisy. She has suffered a great deal but it is belevd that she is gone to the reward of the richus.

[October 23, 1870-Sunday] 23 Sabbeth morning I have been down to Mr Cains, seen ould Mrs Cook laid in the coffin and Mr Jonson spok a few words and gave a prayer warning us all of the ceartenty of death and try to be prepared fore it. He told us fore aught we knew the Black winged angel was then hovering over us selecting his next victom and what an awful thing it was to die unprayerd fore. It is not all of life to live nore all of death to die. She has left foure orphan children, too sons, too daughters to mourn theire iretrevabel loss, but the Psalmist sayes I was wance young but now I am ould but I have never seen the richouse forcaken nore his seed begging bread. Sabbeth evening I have been blessed with the privalage of going to the house of God once more and Mr Douglass preached a fine sermon. His tex was in Hebrews the fourth chapter. Theire remaineth a rest fore the people of God. What great promises theire is to the weary travalar that he will soon be at home beyond the storms and troubles of this wourld of sin of sorrow and tears and death. MD Brown 1870

[October 25, 1870-Tuesday] 25 Wille and I was up to see Eb and Em at theire new home last night fore the first time. Em has not been well. They are well pleased with theire new home. Mrs Scoggins and children is here to day.

[October 27, 1870-Thursday] 27 Sally, Lauson and I have been down to york to day buying finry fore Lausons wedding.

[October 29, 1870-Saturday] 29 R J has gone down to see Eliza to night and Lauson to see his girl.

[October 30, 1870-Sunday] 30 Mr Douglass preached to day. It was a wet day but few out.

[November 1, 1870-Tuesday] Nov 1 Sister Harriet was over to day. All well and we are verry busy sowing.

[November 3, 1870-Thursday] 3 Ann Scoggins is helping the girls to sow to day.

[November 8, 1870-Tuesday] 8 Eliz went to york yesterday and stayed with us and is backing the cake to day, had fine luck, backed fifteen nice cakes.

[November 9, 1870-Wednesday] 9 Mary Cain and Ann Scoggins and Eliza is helping us to ice and trim the cakes to day.

[November 10, 1870-Thursday] 10 Eliza has got through and Wille is gone home with her.

[November 11, 1870-Friday] 11 Wille has got back. They all done fine while she was up here and we all gitting allong fine as to the things of the wourld. Oh my Heavenly Farther we are many Marthers now but in the midts of all oure buss and hurry may theire be manny Maryes in oure midts. MDB

[November 15, 1870-Tuesday] 15 Eb and Em and the children came down this evening.

[November 16, 1870-Wednesday] 16 Lawson and Eb is gone to york to day. Lawson is gone after his buggy.

[November 17, 1870-Thursday] 17 Lawson is now gone to git married. His Farther, Eb and Emily, his sisters Sally, Mag and Jaily his brother, Willie his brother in law, Ruffes Whitesides, his cousins Butler and Wille Thomison, his cousin John Brown was his company. Oh blessed Savior what honor thou hast put upon the ordancences of marriage thou has honored it with thy presence and first miracle whil here on earth. Now blessed Saviour I humbly beseech thee to bee spiritually present at my sons marrage this night. We need thy presence with us on this great ocasion. MDBrown

[November 19, 1870-Saturday] 19 We have this great seen over, another added to oure family. May God bless it to the comfert of us all, had the most of oure friends with us and neighbores. Theire was about seventy fore dinner. Plenty of every thing that was good to eat and got allong nice and smooth, all gone home. Lawson and Mag has gone down to her Farthers.

[November 22, 1870-Tuesday] 22 Wille Thomison came up last night and taken Sally home with him this morning to help to fix fore Buttler wedding.

[November 23, 1870-Wednesday] 23 Lawson and Maggy has come back to day to be reddy to start over to Hirams soon in the morning.

[*November 26, 1870-Saturday*] 26 we have got another big wedding over Buttler Thomison and Nanny Bryan was married Nov the 24 1870 by Mr Cotheres. We had a nice time of it. He took his Farther, Renes and Molly, Lawson and Mag, Sally and Mag, Davis Brown and Mary, his Brother Wille and Psalm wood was his crowd. They had a nice time of it. Jackson and I came home last night. The youngsters stayed till this morning. I had a chill this morning and not well.

[*November 27, 1870-Sunday*] 27 Mr Douglass preached to day but I don't feel well enough to church to day.

[*November 28, 1870-Monday*] 28 Lawson has come home and left Mag at her Farthers.

[*December 1, 1870-Thursday*] Dec the 1 William Coldwell and Matty Cambell was married Dec the 1 1870.

[*December 4, 1870-Sunday*] 4 Sally, Mag and Wille is gone up to Enen to preachen to day and I have been verry sick.

[*December 5, 1870-Monday*] 5 Lawson and Mag has come up this morning. She is going to stay with us this week.

[*December 8, 1870-Thursday*] 8 Eb and the preacher is gone down to see theire Farther. He is sick.

[*December 10, 1870-Saturday*] 10 this is the last day of theire singing and Buttler and Nanny came home with them. Will Thomison and Haullbrooks Good and R J is gone up to stay with Em tonight.

[*December 12, 1870-Monday*] 12 we was to have had preachen on yesterday but it was such a wet day and the creeks up that theire was none. Buttler and Nanny stayed with us from satterday till monday. Jackson has got home. Em is dooing fine. Lawson is gone to take Mag down home this morning.

[*December 13, 1870-Tuesday*] 13 Eb has got home. His Farther was dead and buried beffore he got theire.

[December 14, 1870-Wednesday] 14 I have seen Ruffes Meek to day, took dinner with him. He starts home in the morning. Nanny Coldwell has gone home with him ore rather started.

[December 15, 1870-Thursday] 15 Ruffes and Eliza was up to day. Eliza is having chills and not well. Some ones tryed to burn up the ould Mr Allison last night, set his shuck house affire and thought it would burn up the barn horses and all, burnt up his Gin house and seven bags of cotten and his saw mill.

[December 16, 1870-Friday] 16 the incendiaryes is coming nearer home. Lawsons meet house was burnt up last night but the house was providentialy saved. Theire was no one theire. The fire burnt with in a few steps of the house and died out. MDBrown 16 Mr Douglass, Amos and Eliza Burns has spent the day with us.

[December 18, 1870-Sunday] 18 this is the sabbeth and we are all at home. We have no preachen to day and all well.

[December 20, 1870-Tuesday] 20 Lawson, Mag and his sister Mag, is gone up to see Eb and Em to night and Mag is going to stay with her sister a while.

[December 24, 1870-Saturday] 24 I have had a chill this morning and it is verry cold.

[December 25, 1870-Sunday] 25 this is Christmas day and is on the sabbeth day and Mr Douglass preached to day. I was so unwell that I did not go and it is so cold it is said to bee the coldest weather that we have had in thirty years.

[December 26, 1870-Monday] 26 R J has gone up to Ebs fore Mag, verry cold yet.

[December 27, 1870-Tuesday] 27 Sally, Mag and Jaily is gone up to Tom Bells to take christmas.

[December 28, 1870-Wednesday] 28 R J has gone down to Ruffs to night and took Sally down to stay with her Sister a while and took little Maggie home and Ann Scoggins and Sue Bell was here last night.

[December 31, 1870-Saturday] 31 Wille Thomison was here last and I have had another chill and verry unwell and it dreadfull cold time.

1871

[January 1, 1871-Sunday] A new years a sabbeth morning of eighteen hundred and seventy one. Mr Douglass preached to day but it is so cold and I not well that I did not go. I should have been verry glad to have been in the house of the Lord on this memoriable day, not my will oh Lord but thine be done. Mary Davis Brown

[January 3, 1871-Tuesday] Jan 3 Eb and Emily and the children came down to day.

[January 5, 1871-Thursday] 5 Eb and Em, Lawson and Mag is all gone down to the Loves to night.

[January 8, 1871-Sunday] 8 Ruff and Eliza came up yesterday and brought Sally home and we have all been to preachen to day. Mr Douglass done well. His tex was "Allauya the Lord God omnpeent reigneth." It was a fine sermon.

[January 11, 1871-Wednesday] 11 Lawson and Mag has mooved to day.

[January 12, 1871-Thursday] 12 Eb and Em has mooved down to Mrs Mull-holans place to day.

[January 13, 1871-Friday] 13 I have spent this day down at Mr Cains with aunt Sally Coldwell and aunt Caty.

[January 14, 1871-Saturday] 14 Lawson, Mag and i have been down at York to day, seen cousin Sue Glenn and her babby. It is a fine boy of his age and I stayed all night with Em. She is fixed up verry well and R J is gone down to see the Bullix creek people about going in with us fore a preacher.

[January 18, 1871-Wednesday] 18 Sister Harriet was over to day.

[January 21, 1871-Saturday] 21 Butler and Nanny has come over this morn-ing to go down to see Ruff and Eliza and Mag, Lawson and Mag is all gone down to see them and Eb and Em is here to night.

[January 22, 1871-Sunday] 22 they have all been at preachen to day but Fanny and I. We stayed at home and kept little Sally Fanny.

[January 24, 1871-Tuesday] 24 Hiram Thomisons barn was burnt a tusday night the 24 and several other gin houses and mills. It was a great loss to him. Came near having his horses burnt up to in the flames but he got theire in time to save them.

[January 30, 1871-Monday] 30 monday night theire is great excitement to day. The negroes have threattend to burn York up to night and the men has most all gone to York and they are going to make the negroes give up the guns that Govener Scott gave them but General Anterson came up that night and said that he would have the guns all brought in the next day. They set one house a fire that night but it was soon put out and they had stirring times fore a while but they all got cooled down after a while and I set up till John and Lawson came home about one oclock in the night.

[February 3, 1871-Friday] Feb the 3 Wille and I was down at Ruff last night. All well. R G Is digging a well and Eliza has got a cook. All gitting along fine. Alis Castel and Mag and Jaily and Sally all been over to see Em to day and they have come home with them.

[February 6, 1871-Monday] 6 Jaily, Fanny and I have been over to see unckle Hirams people. Theire all well. Butler is busy working at his house. Martin Hall was here last night and they are all in a bustel a fixen to go up on Kings Mountain to morow.

[February 11, 1871-Saturday] 11 aunt Caty and John, Sue Jackson, Sally, Mag and Jaily and Martin Hall all started fore Kings Mountain this morning. Part of the crowd did not git to go.

[February 17, 1871-Friday] 17 Sally and Jaily is gone over to stay with Em to night. She is sick. Got the chills.

[February 18, 1871-Saturday] 18 Jaily has come home. Em is better. Mrs Scoggins & I have been up to see aunt Caty to day. John is not well.

[February 19, 1871-Sunday] Sabbeth evening 19 Wille Thomison, Eb and Em came over this morning and they have all gone over to Zion to preachen. Psalm McCarter and a company of men came here to day and took Peet, that is a darkey that is working here by the name of Pete, off on suspicion of burning his barn.

[February 20, 1871-Monday] 20 I have been over to see Mrs Scoggins this evening.

[February 21, 1871-Tuesday] 21 Mrs Cain and aunt Caty has spent this day with us and the too Mags was down at Mr Castels last night came by and took dinner with Eliza to day and brought Hatty home with them.

[February 23, 1871-Thursday] 23 Ann and Mag scoggins is here to night.

[February 26, 1871-Sunday] 26 I have been at preachen to day. Mr Douglass tex was "How shall you escape if you neglect so great salvation." Theire is a good deal of excitement to day. Anterson Brown was killed this morning and there is times of excitement in many places.

[February 27, 1871-Monday] 27 Mrs Mary Davis and John Davis was to see us this evening and a curerer has come with the news that the negroes has threatned to rise down below york to night and kill from the cradle to the grave and oure young men is all ordered to go and has gone. The boyes has

come back. Nothing searies was done. Theire has ninty yankeyes been sent up to york to day to try to keep peace. The negroes is still going up hanging and shooting allmost every day ore night.

[March 1, 1871-Wednesday] March 1 Eliza came up last night and her and I was over to see Em to day and Eb and Em came home with us and they are all gone over to Lawsons to night. Mr Martin Hall is here to night.

[March 2, 1871-Thursday] 2 Eliza is gone home and Jaily is gone home with her.

[March 5, 1871-Sunday] March 5 this is the sabbeth. I have been trying to spend it in a right and profitable way. These are trying times. A time when the people of God ought to be awake to theire duty that we be not as Sodom and Gomorrah that theire could not be ten richous persons found in it. Oh that we would imitate that citty Ninavah that repented at the preachen of Jonna and repent of oure wickedness and returen unto the Lord our God that he may have mercy on us and put an end to these dayes of fear and sorrow.

[March 6, 1871-Monday] 6 Lawson and Mag has come over to stay with us to night, the first night that they have been with us sence they left us.

[March 7, 1871-Tuesday] 7 Sally and Mag is gone up to a quilting at Bells to day and have not got home to night.

[March 8, 1871-Wednesday] 8 aunt Caty and I have been down to ould Mr Coldwells to day. Seen sister Polly Brown and her son Wille and his wife and little son, Jacob Franklin. Also heard Mr Ross preach a good sermon this evening. His tex was in the seventy first Psalm, "Fersake me not in ould age." It was preached fore the benafit of ould Mr Caldwell.

[March 9, 1871-Thursday] 9 we have stirring times to day. Oure men has been fighting the negroes down towards Chester. Have killed some eight ore ten and taken about twenty to jaile. Oure men has all gone on to see if they need reinforcement but some of them has come back, some gone on. They have got quiet again. Aunt Harriet and Butler, Bille and Caty, Lawson and Mag, Eb and Em, Ruffes Whitesides and Mrs Scoggins has all been here to day and Polly Brown and Wille and his wife was to be here to, but I think Polly got scarred at oure times here and left fore the ould North Carroliny state.

[March 10, 1871-Friday] 10 I have been up to the graveyard this morning and seen Mrs Huffman buried. Ruf has brought Jaily home and taken his little Mag home and R J and Fanny has gone home with him and Mag is over at her unckle Hirams to stay a week. Sally, Jaily, Wille and I am here by our selves. Friday night at ten oclock. M D Brown

[March 11, 1871-Saturday] March 11 Emily has the chills. Eb has come over fore Sally to go and stay with her.

[March 13, 1871-Monday] 13 Em is better and Sally has come home. Mag has got home too.

[March 15, 1871-Wednesday] 15 Sally and Mag was down at Mr Cains last night and Sue Bell and Ann Scoggins came home with them.

[March 16, 1871-Thursday] March 16 1871 we have bought a new cooking stove to day from Joe Bell, put it up and cooked supper on it. The children is hily pleased with it.

[March 19, 1871-Sunday] 19 this is the sabbeth and all well and all at home.

[March 25, 1871-Saturday] March 25 I have had a big visit. Went to York a thursday morning, took dinner with Fanny. Stayed all night with aunt Emily, took dinner with Sister Peggy and then out to Hirams, took supper with Butler and Nanny. Stayed all night with Sister Harriet and Hiram has brought me home this morning. We had a congrational meeting at the church to day for the purpus of macking out a call fore Mr Douglass to preach for us. He was unanimously elected.

[March 26, 1871-Sunday] 26 Eb and Em came over last night and to preachen to day. It has been a verry wet day and but few out.

[March 27, 1871-Monday] 27 we have had company to day, Cousin Wille & Eliza Davis and children, Chambers, Adda & Laura Brown. Wille Jonson, Miss Flora Jonson, Mr Douglass and aunt Caty. Quite a plesent day.

[April 1, 1871-Saturday] April the 1 I have come home from Ruffes to day, been down theire sence last Tusday. Eliza has had the chills, but better. I have had a fine visit, one day at Mr Whisenthunt at a big quilting. Put too quilts out

and left Sally down theire. Her and Ruff was expecting to go to Salem to the meeting. Bethel Presbatary met at Salem church this week. Dr Alison was the deligate from Bershaba.

[April 2, 1871-Sunday] 2 we had Mr Marten Hall with us last night.

[April 8, 1871-Saturday] 8 R J and I have been to York to day.

[April 9, 1871-Sunday] 9 been at church to day but few out.

[April 10, 1871-Monday] 10 been over to see Em and left Fanny with her. Im not well to day, had another chill, feel bad.

[April 16, 1871-Sunday] 16 Sabbeth evening all well and at home. A fine dayes reading without being mollested by company. Blessed sabbeth, sweet emblem of a eternal sabbeth in Heaven.

[April 23, 1871-Sunday] Sabbeth evening 23 Mr Willson preached this morning. His tex was in Psalms. He preached a great sermon. Mr Douglass administered the Lords supper and went through the evening services and then Mr Willson gave an adress and the solmon services was over. Oh my Heavenly Farther may we all make a right improvement of this ocation and be like thy servent of old that it was good fore us that we have been up to thy house of worship.

[April 24, 1871-Monday] 24 Mr Douglass, Mrs Scoggins and Ann, Sally and I have been up to Tom Bells to day.

[April 25, 1871-Tuesday] 25 I have been over and took dinner with Lawson and Mag to day.

[April 28, 1871-Friday] Aprile 28 a friday night. Bethel Presbatary a call presbatary met at Bershaba church this morning fore the purpes of ordaining Mr James H Douglass and enstolling him paster of oure church Bershaba. Minersters present Mr Dickson, Mr Douglass, M James, Mr Willson and oure preacher Mr James H Douglass and Ratchford. Mr James preached this morning. His tex was Leviticus the tenth chapter and first and second verses. He preached a great sermon but that is what he dose all the time. Then presbatary was called to order. Mr James, Modorator then Mr Douglass exammend by Mr

Haras, Mr Douglass and Mr Willson. His exmination was sustaind by presbatary then he was to preach his tryal sermon in the evening, recess fore thirty minets. A publick tabel, some twenty five feet long and it well filled from a boiled ham, a roast turkey and pound cake down and all envited to eat. All brought dinner and put it on the tabble. Dinner over. Mr James H Douglass preached his tryal sermon. His tex was in revelations, the nineteenth chapter the last claus of the sixth verse, "Alleluia fore the Lord God omnipotent reigneth." He done well and presbatary sustained it. The ordination to take place to morow. Ruffes and Eliza and the children all came up this morning and Ruff went home and Eliza is going to stay fore the meeting. Eb was theire. Em did not come. Lawson was theire and Mag at home. Saturday night Mr Jackson preached this morning. His tex was second Corrinthians, fourth chapter and seventh verse. "But we have this treasure in earthen vessels that the exelency of the power may be of God and not of us." Then Presbatary convened, was brought to order and the ordination servises commenced by Mr Douglass asking Mr James Douglass the ordination questions and then to the congration which they answer by holding up the right hand. Then he kneeled down in front of the pulpit and all of the preachers went up and laid theire right hand on his head and hell them theire while Mr James made a prayer, then prayer over, the ministers all went up and gave him the right hand of fellowship. Then the Elders, then the heads of families. Then Mr Wilson gave him his pasteral charge. Oh, it was a solom seen. He is quite yong. He told him he was only one year his seiniour. Then Mr Jackson gave a charge to the people. Then the solom ordination and installation was over. Farther, Son and Holy Gost was theire. Saints and sinners was theire, the devils looked on and trembeled. It is a day long to be remmemberd both in Heaven and in hell. My Heavenly Farther grant that it may be a day of rememberance to me. I thank the that thou hast spared this poore frail boddy of mine fore such a scene as this. Allila to thy all Glorious name that though has once more given us a paster. Heavenly Farther teach us oure duty especiously doo I pray the to teach us oure duty in prayer fore oure selves, fore oure paster, fore oure children and fore the whole world. I ask fore Jesus sake. Amen. I came home at interval. Emily had a chill and is verry unwell. I was sorry to leave as Mr Willson was to preach this evening. Duty required and I will submit, not my will, Lord but thyne be done. Cousin Urenas and Molly Fewell, Eb and Em, Wille and Ida Thomison, Martin Hall. Eliza is gone over to stay with Lawson and Mag to night. Presbatary adjourned this evening and the Ministers all left but Mr Willson.

[April 30, 1871-Sunday] Mr Scoggins house was burnd Aprile the 30 betweene the houres of ten and twelve. It is thought it was by ackcident. When they first discovered it was blazzing as high as brush heap in the top and was no chance to save it. They saved the most in the house.

[May 1, 1871-Monday] May 1 we have all of us been over to Scoggins to day to try to comfert them in theire sad loss. The neighbors has mos all been in to see them. Sue Bell is with us to night.

[May 3, 1871-Wednesday] 3 I have been down to see Hew Love to day. He is verry porly.

[May 4, 1871-Thursday] 4 I have been down to see ould Mrs Black to day. She is badly swelled. She can git out of the bed with help.

[May 7, 1871-Sunday] 7 Sally, Jaily, Wille and theire Paw is gone over to Smerny to day.

[May 10, 1871-Wednesday] 10 Mrs Scoggins and I have been up to see aunt Caty to day and it is verry cold. It will be verry much against the wheat and cottin and everry thing elce.

[May 12, 1871-Friday] 12 verry cold and wet. It seemes as if it is cold enough to freeze.

[May 14, 1871-Sunday] 14 Sabbeth evening. Sally and Mag, Lawson and Mag went over to theire unckle Hirams last night and going down to Beth-shilo to day to the communion. Eliza came up last night and we have all been at preachin to day. Mr Douglas preached a fine sermon. His morning tex was in Revelations, the first chapter and seventh verse. "Behold, he cometh with clowds and every eye shall see him and they also which pierced him and all kindreds of the earth shall wail because of him even so Amen." Mag has come home and her unckle Hiram had a chill this morning and was not abble to go to church to day.

[May 15, 1871-Monday] May 15 Ruff and Eliza has brought Hatty up to stay and go to scool to Eb. Fanny and her Hatty is here this morning the first day that Hatty has started to school. She is in a great glee about it. John and Mary, James Ross was born May 4 1871.

[May 18, 1871-Thursday] 18 Mag and I have been down at york to day to see Mary Alexander and her fine boy. The child is dooing fine. She is not so well.

[May 25, 1871-Thursday] 25 I have been down to see ould Mrs Black to day. I dont think she can live much longer. Her disease, the droposy has settled on the brain. She neither mooves nore speacks.

[May 27, 1871-Saturday] 27 I was down at Ruffes last night, Eliza and Mag and Mary has had the chills again and not well.

[May 28, 1871-Sunday] 28 I was with Mrs Black last night. She is still living. This is the sabbeth. I did not go to preachen to day after setting up last. I feel verry unwell to day. Mr Douglass baptised Mr and Mrs Scoggins baby to day. It's name is Mary Jessy. It is the first he ever baptised.

[May 29, 1871-Monday] 29 Sally was over with Mrs Black last night. She is still living but no better, never mooves, swalles nore mooves. Ould Mrs Sarah Black died May 29 half past eleven on monday night. She lay nearly too weeks without speaking ore eating.

[May 31, 1871-Wednesday] Wednesday evening May 31 we have committed her to her mother earth. She was taken into the church and Mr Douglass gave an address, a verry appropriate one and then sung the hymn, "Unveil thy bosom faithful toom, take this new treasure to thy trust." Theire was none of her friends ore children with her in her last houres but her daughter, Mrs Mary Davis, with whome she lived. Her daughter, Mrs Porter is in Arcancis. Her son, John Black, came just as they finished the grave. She was a good and great womman. A mother in Iseral gone to receive her reward. MDB

[June 2, 1871-Friday] June 2 this is harvest. Lawson and Mag is over to day. Lawson is helping them to cut wheat. Is verry trifling. The cold in the spring and the rust has ingired it so it is hardly worth cutting at all. Biscuit will be scarce this year.

[June 4, 1871-Sunday] 4 this is the sabbeth all at home and some company. We have been reading and singing and trying not to miss spend the holy sabbeth, sweet emblem of eternal rest.

[June 6, 1871-Tuesday] 6 Mr Scoggins and Ann, Sally and I have been over to see Eb and Em to day and git cherryes and a good dinner. They have got clear of the chills. All well.

[June 7, 1871-Wednesday] 7 I have been over to see Lawson & Mag to day. All well.

[June 9, 1871-Friday] 9 Mrs Freeman & Mary Cain has spent this day with us. Ruff Whiteside has come up for Hatty to take her home to stay a few dayes. Theire children is not well. Theire is a great manny children a dying with the flux and a good manny grown people has it but it dose not prove so fatel with them.

[June 11, 1871-Sunday] 11 I have been at preachen to day. Mr Douglass tex was in firs corinthians sixteenth chapter and tenth verse. "Now if Timothesis come unto you see that he may be with you without fear fore he worketh the work of the Lord, even as I doo." He preached a great sermon. He told the people the duty of a paster and the duties of the people to theire paster. His tex was in Luke in the evening tenth,"Rejoice not that the spirrits are subject to you but rejoice that youre names are wrote in Heaven." Mr Douglass came home with us this evening, Lawson & Mag, Eb & Em. Mr Douglass went home with Lawson and stayed all night.

[June 13, 1871-Tuesday] 13 I have been verry unwell to day. Had a chill yesterday and one to day and feel badly. Aunt Caty, Mrs Cain, Mrs Freemon has been to see me to day.

[June 14, 1871-Wednesday] 14 I feel a little better to day. Ruff & Eliza has come up to see me to day, Lawson & Mag & Alonzo Brown.

[June 15, 1871-Thursday] 15 I am better this morning. Em was with me last night. Mrs Castel & Mag has been over this evening & Lawson & Mag & Sally is gone down to york this evening.

[June 16, 1871-Friday] 16 Mrs Bell & Sue has been down this eveng to see me.

[June 18, 1871-Sunday] 18 I still feel better. Eliza came up this morning to see how I had got. Sally, Mag & Wille has gone over to the Methedist church to day to heare Mr Boyd.

[June 19, 1871-Monday] 19 I have been down to see ould Mrs Davis and family to day. All well.

[June 24, 1871-Saturday] 24 we had a dreadfull rain and storm of thunder and littning last evening. Theire was a young mister Ross Sutten killed last eveng by the lightning and his mule. Mr Hall was here last night and the girls and him is gone up to help aunt Caty quilt to day.

[June 25, 1871-Sunday] 25 Sabbeth eveng been to church to day. Have not improved it as well as I should have done. I mus try and doo better fore the time to come. Time, all important time may be verry short, fore this wourld is not my home I know.

[June 26, 1871-Monday] 26 Mr Huffman had a chile buried to day. The chollary-infantom is proualing amonxt the children and is prooving verry fatel among the children. Mr Preacher Jonsons child was born June 25 1871.

[June 29, 1871-Thursday] 29 Mag & I have taken supper with Mrs Scoggins this evening.

[June 30, 1871-Friday] 30 Wille & his paw has gone over to E P Castels school house this evening to an examination. Jackson has gone down to take Hatty home and Fanny went home with her to stay a few dayes.

[July 3, 1871-Monday] July 3 I was over at Ebs last night. Little Sally is not well. Mrs Wisters Allison was born June 3. I have been down at cousin Will Davis this evening to see little Burgis. She is verry bad with collary infanten.

[July 4, 1871-Tuesday] 4 Mag and Jaily was over with Em last night. Sally is no better. Have sent for the Dr.

[July 7, 1871-Friday] 7 been down at york and went out and staid all night with sister Harriet. All well. Came by to see little Sally. She is better. Came by to see little Psalmy Meek. He has the billious fever, is bad. Little Gim is sick too.

[July 9, 1871-Sunday] 9 Sabbeth eving Ruff came up this morning and brought Mag home. Eliza did not come up to preachen. The children is well. They think little Burges is better.

[July 11, 1871-Tuesday] 11 Mag & I was over to see Lasleyes Burnses babby to day. It is sick, but better, but little Burges has paid her last debt of nature. She died July the 10, on monday evening at six in the evening, 1871 and I have seen her laid in her mother earth this eveng, theire to rest till the arch Angel shall summons come to Judgment.

[July 15, 1871-Saturday] 15 Eb & Emily and the children came over last night. Eb & Em & Sally is gone down to see Eliza to day.

[July 16, 1871-Sunday] Sabbeth eveng 16 Eb & Em was with Lawson & Mag last night. Gone home this morning. Sally, Jaily & I have been over to hear the Methedist preacher, Mr Boyd. He preached a verry good sermon. His tex was on brotherly love and to be steadfast and unmovable.

[July 20, 1871-Thursday] 20 we have had a quilting to day. Ann & Mag Scoggins, Sue & Macy Bell, Mary Cain, Wille Thomison & John Brown.

[July 21, 1871-Friday] 21 Hatty is sick over at Ebs and Sally is gone over to see her. Mary & Bell Love came over to day and help us to put out oure quilt.

[July 22, 1871-Saturday] 22 Ann & Mag Scogins & Miss Origan Smith has taken supper with us this eveng.

[July 23, 1871-Sunday] 23 Sabbeth eveng been in the walls of my bloved church, Beershaba one more and heard the sweet actcents of reedeming love from the lips of oure loved paster. His tex in Luke, "Theire is joy in the presence of the Angels of God over one sinner that repenteth." Em staid and kept house. Wille nore hes is not well. Ruff & Eliza came by and took Hatty home to stay a week. M Hall is with us.

[July 24, 1871-Monday] 24 over at Lawsons this evening. Came home with a sad heart.

[July 25, 1871-Tuesday] 25 Lasly & his wife Rachel has spent this day with us.

[July 27, 1871-Thursday] 27 Jackson & I have been on a visit over to Amos Burnsis to see them and oure preacher Mr Douglass as he is boarding theire.

[July 28, 1871-Friday] 28 theire has been a meeting of the elders and deacons at the church to day to attend to the business of the church. Mr McCaw & Hiram came by and took dinner and eat wattermillions and peaches and then home.

[July 29, 1871-Saturday] 29 R J & I was invited over to Davy Scoggins to take dinner with them & his brother in law, Robert Howel and his wife, Jane and his son Vernon & daughter Adda.

[July 30, 1871-Sunday] 30 Sabbeth eveng no preaching to day. All well, all at home. No company. Calm and happy has this day been, sweet emblem of eternal rest, reading thy word & medating on thy precious promises to them that love & the awful denuncation against them that love the not. Heavenly Farther thou art now visiting with us with the rod of afflication. Thou has shortened oure wheat crop. Thou art now visiting us with a dearth. The Heavens has becom as brass above oure heads, the earth as steel. All vegatation is parched and burnt. Heavenly Father, we are a wicked and rebellious children, a wandering sheep. We did not love oure shepherds voice and loved afar to roam, but will thou draw us with the cords of thy love. May we foresake oure sins and turn unto thee with all oure heart. Thou has promised that all things shall work together fore good to them that love thee. This heart cheering promis, the Lord will provide.

Sabbeth Evening
Saviour breath an evening blessing
Ere repose my spirit seal
Sin and want I come confessing
Thou canst save and Thou canst heal
Thou destruction walk around me
Thou the arow near me fly
Angels guard from Thee surround me
I am safe when Thou art near.

Though thee night be dark and dreery
Darkness canot hide from Thee
Thou art He who never weary
Watches whare Thy people be
Should swift death this night oertake me
And my couch become my tomb

May the morn in Heaven awake me
Clad in light and deathless bloom
an other morn may never see

unknown

[August 3, 1871-Thursday] August 3 we have had a ould woman quilting to day, aunt Caty, Mrs Cain, Mrs Scoggins, Mrs Bell, Lawson & Mag, Emily, Unckle Bille & John. We have had a fine day eating watermillions & peaches, roast chicken, peach pie and everything els good. We did not git the quilt out. I looked fore Eliza up but she did not come. Eb and the children has come over to night. Quite a different day till this day five years ago. It was the day that my dear little Jonny Ruffe was laid in the lonly grave. That is the dear little boddy but the soule is, I dout not, singing the sweet songs of Zion with his blessed Saviour who said, "Suffer little children to come unto me and forebid them not fore of such is the kingdom of Heaven."

[August 5, 1871-Saturday] 5 Sally & Mag is gone over to Union to a singing to day and going to theire unckle Hirams to night. R J has gone down to see Ruffe and Eliza to day. No rain yet. Verry hot and dry. The corn is nearly ruined and everrything parched and burnt.

[August 10, 1871-Thursday] 10 I have been over to see Bell Love. She has the fever and is bad. Simpson is sick too. Eliza and the children has come up to day and we are going over to see her aunt Harriet. Lawson & Mag was over to day too.

[August 12, 1871-Saturday] 12 Eliza & I have had a fine visit Hirams thursday night. To york a friday and took dinner with aunt Emily on a friday night and stayed all night with Eb & Em and Ruffe came up last night to Ebs and they are all gone home. Theire is a big picknic at the mineral spring to day. Mag Whiteside was here last night and they are all gone down to it. Verry hot and dry and no rain yet. Dont look like macking picnic at this time. Look as if we could not make bread.

[August 13, 1871-Sunday] 13 I did not go to preachen to day. The res all went. Wille Thomison, Tom Wood and Press McAfee was here last night.

[August 14, 1871-Monday] 14 I have been over at Ebs to day cutting peaches. They have a fine chance.

[August 15, 1871-Tuesday] 15 Sally has been down to see Bell Love. She is some better.

[August 17, 1871-Thursday] 17 John Brown, Mary Cain, Sally & Jaily was over at Ebs last night. All well and at home. No rain yet. Verry hot and dry.

[August 22, 1871-Tuesday] 22 Jackson & I have been on a trip up to Crowders creek to see ould aunt Sally Floyd. She is verry ould, ninty seven past, not abble to go about and confined to her bed. Butler and Nanny Thomisons infand daughter born and died August 21 in Bethel, buried at Bershaba 22.

[August 25, 1871-Friday] 25 I have been over and brought little Sally Fanny home with me to wean her.

[August 26, 1871-Saturday] 26 theire was a singing at the curch to day and Mr Hall is with us to night.

[August 27, 1871-Sunday] 27 this has been a wet day but we have been at preachen. Eb & Em is gone home.

[August 28, 1871-Monday] 28 William & Eliza Davis & Eddy & Wille, Mrs Jane Jonson, Mrs Sue Brown & daughter Edner, Miss Mary Davis, Mr Will Jonson has spent to day with us.

[August 29, 1871-Tuesday] 29 Eliza Whiteside has come up to day and brought Hatty back to school.

[August 30, 1871-Wednesday] 30 I have been up to spend the day with aunt Caty and Sue Bell & Wille is here to night.

[September 1, 1871-Friday] September 1 Mrs Strong has been up on a visit this week. She took supper with us this evening. Also Mrs Sue Jonson, Mrs Mary F Davis & Wille, unckle Bille & Caty, Mrs Scoggins & Mary Cain. Mrs Strong is going to take the car in the morning fore home.

[September 4, 1871-Monday] 4 Fanny, Hatty & I have had a big trip to york a satterday to Lawsons that night, to Center a Sunday to hear ould Mr Watson, to Hirams that night and home to day. I did not see Nanny. She had not got home. When I came home, Newton & Sue Glenn was here. Had been on a

visit and I went with them over to see Mrs McAphee.

[September 8, 1871-Friday] 8 Hiram was over at the mill to day. Took dinner with us.

[September 10, 1871-Sunday] 10 Mr Douglass preached to day.

[September 11, 1871-Monday] 11 Butler Thomison is sick and Sally is gone over to see him.

[September 13, 1871-Wednesday] 13 I was over at Ebs last night. Mary has got her eye hurt. It is better. EP went over to see Butler last night. He is no better. Verry bad with the fever. They have sent fore Nanny.

[September 14, 1871-Thursday] 14 Jackson and I was over to see Buttler last night. He is verry bad yet. The Dr dont allow eney one to go in the room but the nurs. Mr Douglass went over with us but was not allowed to see him. This is the day that Mr Scoggins is raising his house. It is a log house and theire some forty hands.

[September 15, 1871-Friday] 15 Wille & I went down to Ruffs last night and took Hatty home as the school has stopped.

[September 16, 1871-Saturday] 16 I have been up helping Mrs Bell to quilt to day. Got the quilt out.

[September 17, 1871-Sunday] 17 Em sent fore her Paw & I to go over last night to see little Sally. She is sick. Dr Jackson was out last night to see her. She is better this morning but EP had a hard chill and is verry sick.

[September 18, 1871-Monday] 18 Lawson & I have been down at york to day, called by to see EP & Sally. They are some better. I heard from Buttler. He is mending.

[September 22, 1871-Friday] 22 this is the commencement of oure communion. Mr Dickson preached to day. His tex was "If the richous scarcely be saved whare shall the sinner and the ungodly appear." He preached a great sermon. Wille is gone down fore his cousin, Mary Alexander.

[September 23, 1871-Saturday] 23 Mr Dickson preached fore us to day. His tex this morning was, "He that bleveth not shall be damned." This evening, "Christ is oure passover" to as great sermons as ever I heard. Another member of oure family has come forth this day, has acknowledged her faith in Christ, enlisted under the banner of King Emmanual. Heavenly Farther I pray the cloth her with the whole armour of God that she may be abel to stand against the wiles of the devil. Mag Scoggins & Macy Bell joined at the same time. Lawsons Mag by sertifficate on friday, that is yesterday. Ginny Brown, Chambers Brown, Addy Brown & Laura Brown, children of cousin Psalm Brown joined and was Baptised by Mr Douglass. We have two strangers with us to night from Boolix Creek, Mr Hood & Mr Robbison. Eb & Em & children, cousin Mary Alexander and children, Wille Thomison.

[September 24, 1871-Sunday] 24 Sabbeth evening Mr Douglass preached to day. Had no one to assist him. He done verry well. Theire was a larg congration out. Eliza was up to day but Ruff was at home sick. They have hardly ever failed to bee with us at the meetings and her Farther is gone home with her to see him.

[September 25, 1871-Monday] 25 R J has come home and Ruff is better. Buttler has got well. Cousin Mary Alexander, cousin Fanny Daubson, aunt Caty & I have been over to spend the day with Lawson & Mag and they have come home with me to stay to night.

[September 26, 1871-Tuesday] 26 Mary, Fanny & Sally & I have been over to see Eb & Em to day & Mary Alexander has gone home & Fanny has come home with me.

[September 27, 1871-Wednesday] 27 Mr Daubson has come out fore Fanny this morning.

[October 1, 1871-Sunday] October 1 R J, Sally and I are going to Smerny to day. Mr Hall is here.

[October 2, 1871-Monday] 2 I went home with Ruffes last night from Smerny. Ruff and little Mag has had a spell of billious fever but they are better & I have come home & Sally is gone down to stay a week with them.

[October 7, 1871-Saturday] 7 Mag is gone to Bethany to a singing. M Hall

took her in a buggy. Jaily wanted to go but she had no way to go. Sally has come home and brought little Mag home with her.

[October 14, 1871-Saturday] 14 Sally & Jaily is gone over to see Eb & Em to night.

[October 15, 1871-Sunday] 15 we have no preachen to day. Great excitement to day. It is reported that marshall law is declared and that the yankeyes will commence arresting the men at eney time. Bille & Caty & John Lawson & Mag is here to night affraid to lie down to go to sleep. Eb was here this evening. He is gone down on clarks fork. Sally & Jaily is with Em yet and Wille is gone over to stay with them Monday morning.

[October 16, 1871-Monday] Monday morning 16 Lawson & John left this morning beffore day. Monday evening. I have been down at york to day to see what I could hear. They have made no arests yet, but great excitement. Theire is a good manny of the men left york. John Hunter & Wille Colcox & Cal Parish is all gone and cousin Daubson is badly down. He had laid in a great stock of new goods, his clerks all gone and such excitement that he is not selling. He is boxen up some of his goods and sending them back. I came by Ebs and brought Em and the children home with me. Marten Hall was here this evening and took supper with us & is now gone fore parts unknown. Whether we shall ever see him again God only knows. I have gave him up to his care and protection. John Brown has come back to day and got his close & him & Ruff Allison is gone. John came back while I was gone & is gone, yes gone & left a broken harted Farther & Mother. Lawson & Eb has come back this evening & Ruffe & Eliza has come home with them. Oure children & grand children is all under oure roof to night but it has the appearance that it may all never meet again.

[October 17, 1871-Tuesday] 17 Tuesday morning one of the mornings, one of the nights that has been a night to be remembered. I have not slept an hour in too nights, nore none of the family much. Lawson, Eb & Wille Jonson, Harve Gunings, Gim Love left this morning at thre oclock fore parts unknown. Heavenly Farther into thy hands I commend them. Thou art a God every whare present that will protect them that puts theire trust in thee. It was hard to see them leave. We don't know whether ever to return. Enabel me to say thy will be done. Ruff & Eliza is gone home, Tusday evening. Jaily & I have been over to Hirams to day. Hiram & Lawson put on theire hats this evening and steped off. Buttler & Wille left last week. I left sister with her three little girls and

Nanny. I dont know how they will git allong. Jane can do better. Mary is grown and Jacky is a fine boy. Ruff Whitesides was at york to day, cam by this evening. He sayes that the Yanks has commenced arresting this evening, has put up several. Jackson had his horse saddled to go over to sister Harriets to a shucking to night but when he heard that he did not go. The yankeyes went to sister Harriets that night of the shucking hunting for Buttler. They took Psalm Wood and to of the White boys that night. Emily & the children & Mag is with us.

[October 22, 1871-Sunday] 22 Mr Douglass preached to day but verry few out. Sister Harriet was theire. She said that the yankeyes was at her house last night and searched the house again but found no boddy. The yanks is going in everry direction gathering up and putting in jail. They have got William Coldwell.

[November 10, 1871-Friday] Nov 10 Fanny & I spent last night with unckle Bille & Caty a new visit fore to spend a night. It was a pleasant visit seen and heard what I never seen ore heard beffore. Seen & heard unckle Bille kneel in prayer beffore Allmighty God pleading with him fore his care & protection in these times of sorrow and trouble. I pray God that he will make him faithfull in his good work & that manny more will follow his exampell & that it can be said of Bershaba, they are a praying people.

[November 11, 1871-Saturday] 11 Cousin Nanny Thomison & her brother, Martin Bryan was here last night. The first time she has been here sence butler left. Sally & I have been down at york to day. Seen cousin Psalm Brown in jail from the road. I did not go up to see the prisoners. Dr Gim Allison second daughter died to day. Eb & Em was here when I came home.

[November 13, 1871-Monday] 13 Sally is gone over to stay a week with Em.

[November 15, 1871-Wednesday] 15 I have been down to see Mrs Cain to day. All well.

[November 16, 1871-Thursday] 16 Lawson is gone to york & Mag is here to day. Lawson has come home. He was at his aunt Jane Browns & took dinner with his aunt Harriet. All well. Theire has none of them come home yet.

[November 18, 1871-Saturday] 18 Miss Ann Scoggins is helping the girls to quilt to day. They have not got it out. Oure military authorities have seaced aresting so manny of oure men as at first. They have got the most of them now that they can git. Theire has a good manny gone and gave themselves up to the authirities & have been sent home till they call on them and a manny a one rather than be arrested and put in jail have left. They have arrested and put in jail thirteen this week. They arrrested one verry ould man, Mr Thomas Black and put him in jail but has sence let him out, also W W Cavany, Dr W Camp, J L Parker & J Pressly, negro. Ould unckle Gimmy Caldwell is verry poorly now, they don't think he can live long. William got out on a furlow to see his Farther but is gone back.

[November 20, 1871-Monday] 20 all well. Put out oure quilt to day. Times seem to be cooling down allittle at this time.

[November 22, 1871-Wednesday] 22 Mag is gone down to stay a while with Eliza & Lawson is gone down to Mr Castels as Mag is down there. Wille & his Paw is gone to york with cotton to day. It is selling at sixteen & a half. Nanny Coldwell & Mr Thompson from Arcancis was married by Mr Dickson, Nov 23 1871. Mr Douglass was gone to see his Farther. He is in bad health.

[November 24, 1871-Friday] ould unckle Gimmy Coldwell died Nov 24 1871 and was buried at Bershaba to day.

[November 25, 1871-Saturday] 25 a large burial, Mr G Jonson gave exertation, a verry suitable one. Bershaba has lost an other of its elders, a Farther in Iseral is gone. He has been an elder fore manny a long year. He was near his eightieth year. Amos & Eliza Burns, Eb & Em took dinner with us and then we all went to the buring. Em & Eb stayed all night. Lawson has brought Mag home this evening. Jaily & Wille went over to theire aunt Harriets last night. Jaily is going to stay a while. Wille is come back. He seen his unckle Lawson. He has come home. None of aunt Harriets has come.

[November 26, 1871-Sunday] 26 this is Sabbeth evening. No preachen. Mr Douglass is gone to see his Farther and not got home but I have been reading a good book, yea a blessed book fore it is all of Jesus Christ, the sweetest name that men ore angels ever heard. Flavel sayes, "Hear me, ye that labor fore the world as if heaven were in it. What will you do when at death you shall look back and see all that fore which you have spent youre time and strenth shrinking and vanshing away from you. When you shall look foreward and see vast eternity opning to swallow you up. Oh then what would you give fore a well grounded assurance of an eternal inheritance." Heavenly Farther, I pray thee to enable me to labor fore that meet that perishes not that I may be laying up my treashures in Heaven whare this would can never take it from me. MDB

[November 28, 1871-Tuesday] 28 Ruffe has brought Mag home this morning. She has been sick with the cold and sore throat.

[November 30, 1871-Thursday] 30 aunt Harriet came up last night & brought Jaily home. Hiram has come home. They are all well. I have been over at Lawsons to day. He killed too fine hogs waying three hunderd. It is verry cold and snowing.

[December 1, 1871-Friday] Dec 1 verry cold. A big snow. It is about six inches deep. Mag, Jaily & Fanny is gone over to Mrs Scoggins to day in the snow and brother Lawson, Mr Jonson & unckle Bille took dinner with us to day. The times is not so exciting as they have been. They are still arresting some yet. They have arrested six in the last week, have let out about fifty out of jail. Have sent twenty too to Columbia to the united states court. It conviened on last monday. Mr Stanberry, Reverdy Jonson & Judge Barnet of New York is all theire to see that the Klu Klux prisiners gits theire justice done them. Theire is still fifty one in jail yet.

[December 2, 1871-Saturday] 2 it is still verry cold but the snow is a melting. Eb was over and Wille is gone home with him.

[December 5, 1871-Tuesday] Dec 5 we have killed oure hogs to day. It is dreadfull cold.

[December 6, 1871-Wednesday] 6 Ann & Mag Scoggins has been here to day. Cold yet.

[December 10, 1871-Sunday] 10 Sabbeth evening have been at preachen to day. We have had a long rest from preachen. Mr Douglass preached us a fine sermon to day about the best that I ever heard him do. His tex was in second Corrinthians, fourt chapter, seventeenth & eighteenth verses. These are the words, "Foure oure light affiction which is but fore a moment worketh for us a far more exceeding and eternal weight of glory." While we look not at the things that are seen, but at the things that are not seen fore the things which are seen are temperal but the things which are not seen are eternal. A verry suitabel sermon fore the times and a perty good congration of people. Robbert Love was ordaed a deacon. Eliza & Hatty & little Mary was up last night. Ruffe came up to preachen to day and they are gone home.

[December 11, 1871-Monday] 11 all scattered about. RJ is gone to york. Sally is over at Lawson. Wille & Fanny with Em.

[December 17, 1871-Sunday] 17 Sister Harriet was over to day, all well.

[December 18, 1871-Monday] 18 R J is gone down to Ruffes to take him too cows.

[December 19, 1871-Tuesday] 19 R J and I have been at york to day. Nothing new. John Davis & Sally Allison was married December 21 1871 by Mr Douglass.

[December 24, 1871-Sunday] 24 this is the sabbeth. I did not go to preachen to day. Sister Harriet came hom with the children and took Fanny Vance home with her to take Christmas. Also cousin Davis Brown & Mr Collumbus Graham from fort mills.

[December 25, 1871-Monday] 25 Mag & Davis went over to Scoggins last night and has come back and Davis & Graham is gone home. Mr Scoggins came over and took dinner with us & Eb was over. A dull Christmas.

[December 26, 1871-Tuesday] 26 Sally, Mag, Jaily & Wille & Eb, Mag & Ann Scoggins, Davis Brown & Collumbus Graham is all gone to Ruff Whitesides to a singing & Emily & the children is with us.

[December 27, 1871-Wednesday] 27 the children has got home and is verry cold & Mr Douglass is with us to night.

[December 28, 1871-Thursday] 28 Mr Douglass is gone over to Brother Lawsons to day. Eb & Em is gone home. Jackson & I was invited over to Mr Scoggins to a big turkey dinner to day. R J did not go. I went. Had a fine dinner and plenty of company. Bob McElwee & his wife, Mrs Coldwell and several others. Sally, Mag, Jaily & Wille is gone over to theire unckle Lawsons to a singing to night. I have sent fore aunt Peggy Floyd to come out and stay a week. She is here now.

[December 29, 1871-Friday] 29 Sally & Jaily has come home. Mag & Wille is going to stay untill sunday.

[December 30, 1871-Saturday] 30 cold & wet. This is the day of the meeting at the church. Hiram came by this evening.

[December 31, 1871-Sunday] 31 Sister Peggy has been at preachen with us to day. The firs time she has been theire in a long time. Mag & Wille is got home. Mr Douglass preached to day. Mary Brown & Duffe & Mary Jeffery came home with us. This ends the year eighteen hunderd and seventy one with all the dire calemities it has been here too, one that will be long remeberd fore war, famin, disease and death and pain and tyrnical treatment but the God of justice will over rule it all right. 1871 adieu Mary D Brown

1872

[January 1, 1872-Monday] January the 1 1872 a monday morning all well & all at home. Kind & Heavenly Farther all praises to thy Glourious name thou hast spared these unproffitabel lives of oures through an other year to see the light of another new years day. I pray thee that though would santify these wicked harts of ours that we may love and serve thee fore thy time to come in a better manner than we have been doing. We have all been invited down to Mr Cains to day to a big turkey dinner, Sister Peggy, Mary Brown, Duffe Brown, Mary Jeffery, Sally Brown, Fanny Brown, & I have all taken dinner with Betsy, unckle Bille, aunt Caty & Ann Scoggins too.

[January 2, 1872-Tuesday] 2 they had a singing at Mr Scoggins last night. Joe Whitesides & Bob Whisenthunt came home with them last night. They are gone home this morning and Mary Brown & Duff & Mary Jeffery is all gone home. Sister Peggy and I have been over to see Mrs Jonson to day, she has a sore foot. She has not walked in some time with it. It is the aricipiliass in it.

[January 3, 1872-Wednesday] 3 Sister Peggy & I have been over to stay with

Lawson & Mag to day.

[January 5, 1872-Friday] 5 Lawsons, Gimmy Castel was born January the 5 1872, a friday morning before day. Sister Peggy, Dr Allison was both theire. She was bad but got allong all right at last. M D Brown

[January 5, 1872-Friday] 5 Eliza was up to day, Ruffes & the children is not well, she is gone home. Eb & Em was over to day, gone home. Lawson is gone to take his aunt Peggy home.

[January 6, 1872-Saturday] 6 Mrs Castel & I was with Lawson and Mag last night. Mag and the babe is dooing fine.

[January 10, 1872-Wednesday] 10 I have been down to see Eliza. They are all well. Seen Pinkney Allison from Arcancis. All well out their. Nanny & her ould man landed safe. Came home found Wille sick.

[January 11, 1872-Thursday] 11 over to see Mag & the babe, gitting allong fine. Her mother is gone home. Mag & Jaily is gone over to stay with them.

[January 14, 1872-Sunday] 14 I have been at preachen to day. Mr Douglass tex was in Isaih fifty fifth chapter, sixth verse. "Seek ye the Lord while he may be found, call ye upon him while he is near." He said that he intended to preach too more sermons on the same tex. Rufe & Eliza was up at preachen, left Maggie to stay a while. They are gone home, it is verry cold.

[January 17, 1872-Wednesday] 17 Mag & I have been down to york on a visit. Stayed all night with aunt Emily, took dinner with Fanny. Then Mag went and got her pothagraph taken. All tolerabel well.

[January 18, 1872-Thursday] 18 Mrs Scoggins & I have been up and stayed all day with aunt Caty. My Mag, Mag Scoggins & Jaily went down to Cains. Unckle Hiram & Lizzy came up to night.

[January 19, 1872-Friday] 19 Mrs Cain & Gimmy is here to day. Sally, Mary Cain, Alis Castle is gone to Scoggins on a visit. Verry cold and muddy.

[January 20, 1872-Saturday] 20 Mag, Jaily & little Mag is gone over to see Em.

[January 24, 1872-Wednesday] 24 they had a singing at Ebbs last night. Sue & Mace Bell & Alis Castel came home with them. Sally & Ann Scoggins stayd all night & Bob Whisenthunt & Joe Whitesides brought them home and it is verry cold, freezen weather.

[January 26, 1872-Friday] 26 I was over with Lawson last night and theire is a big snow this morning and dreadfull cold. Jackson & Bille is gone down to york to see aunt Emily. She is sick.

[January 28, 1872-Sunday] 28 been to preachen to day. Mr Douglass preached on his same tex, "Seek ye the Lord while he may be found, Call ye upon him while he is near." We will have no more preachen fore four weeks. M D BROWN

[January 30, 1872-Tuesday] 30 Mrs Cain had a big quilting to day, had too quilts up. Ruffe and Eliza came up to day and they have sent fore me to come home. They are gone over to stay with Lawson to night. Mag & Jaily is gone to bells. Unckle Bille is gone down to see aunt Emily. She is verry bad.

[February 1, 1872-Thursday] Feb. 1 Jackson, aunt Caty & I was down to see aunt Emily last night. She is some better.

[February 2, 1872-Friday] 2 we had a fine singing last night. Ebb & Em & the children & Caty Jackson & Joe Whiteside stayd all nght. Had a fine singing. This is a dreadfull day, sleeting raining, & freezing colld, cold fore good and they all have to stay on till theire is a change in the weather.

[February 3, 1872-Saturday] 3 Joe & Bob Whisenthunt is gone home. Eb is gone down to Ruffs. Em & cousin Cate is gone home. Lawson & Mag is gone home. They have been here since Thursday. The first time she has been over with the babe. It is dooin fine.

[February 5, 1872-Monday] Feb 5 Lawson & Eb is gone again. They have got bench warents fore a good manny men in the neighborhood and they thought it best to leave fore parts unknown. Em is here to night, Mag is at home.

[February 6, 1872-Tuesday] 6 Em is gone home & Fanny with her.

[February 7, 1872-Wednesday] 7 Sally & her paw is gone down to york to

day. Sally is gon down to have her potagraph taken. Aunt Emily is better. Jackson has brought Eb mare home with him to see if he can dr her up. She looks like she would die. Mag and her brother Gimmy, is here to night.

[February 8, 1872-Thursday] 8 another cold, freezin day. The timber is verry heavy with ice. I went home with Mag to help her to git fixed up to moove back to her farthers. We have got oure quilt out this evening.

[February 10, 1872-Saturday] 10 aunt Harriet & Em was over last night. We went over to see Mag this morning and she is gone home.

[February 11, 1872-Sunday] 11 I was over with Em last night. She looks desolate. William Castel has come up to day & brought Lawsons horse home. They have taken the car.

[February 12. 1872-Monday] 12 Wille is gone to take Mr Castel to york and it is raining.

[February 14, 1872-Wednesday] 14 Mr Castel has come up to day and mooved Mag back home & it is verry cold, the hardest winter I have seen in manny a year.

[February 15, 1872-Thursday] 15 Jackson has mooved Emily home in Lawson house to day. She is not well. The rest well. Ann Scoggins been here to day. Sheriff Glenn was out here to see R J this evening concerning Lawsons debts and he is gone down to york to night to see Daubson. Jaily is with Em to night, times of trouble, but if we are what we profess to be it shall be fore oure good. Heavenly Farther if it is thy will that we shall be refined in the furnice of afflicition, oh give grace & strenth, both of boddy & mind to bear up under these afflictions and say unto us as thou didst to thy servint of ould, "My Grace shall be sufficent fore the," not my will oh Lord, but thin be don on earth as it is in Heaven. M D Brown

[February 16, 1872-Friday] 16 Jackson & Bille is gone down to preacher Castels.

[February 17, 1872-Saturday] 17 Jackson has come home. He was at Ruffes last night & Mr Castels yesterday. Seen Mag & the babe, all well.

[February 18, 1872-Sunday] 18 it is the sabbeth day, no preachen. Em & the children is here. They are gitting allong as well as they can.

[February 19, 1872-Monday] 19 I have put in my web to day & Sue bell is here to day.

[February 20, 1872-Tuesday] 20 Mrs Mary Davis & children was here to day. We can allwayes spend a plesent day together.

[February 21, 1872-Wednesday] 21 R J & I have been at york to day. Got a letter from Eb. Lawson and him had landed safe in Tenisee at theire unckle Henry Duffs and well. Feels like they was at home with so manny of their kin, unckle Henry, James & his wife, unckle Frank, cousin Joe Willson & Eliza & Wille Thomison. Wille is going to school at the Collage at Mullberry.

[February 23, 1872-Friday] 23 I was with Emily last night she is not well.

[February 25, 1872-Sunday] 25 Sabbeth evening Mr Douglass preached to day on the same tex, "Seek ye the Lord while he may be found, call ye apon him while he is near." Their was a good congration of people out to day. I was not. I was house keeper to day. Butler & Nanny came home with them. Sally went with Joe down to Ruffes this evening to stay a week & Em & the children is here.

[February 26, 1872-Monday] 26 we have been macking garden to day. It looks like spring to day & cousin Wille Davis & Eliza & children is here to night. She has thre fine boyes, Eddy, Wille. & Psalm Brown.

[February 27, 1872-Tuesday] 27 Jackson & Wille is gone up to Tom Whisen-thunts to day, deepest snow that we have had this evening. Oh what a beauti-full sight my eyes have this day to see this earth of oures wrapt in such a mantel of purity. Blessed emblem of the robe of richeness that Christ died to procure fore all that love him and serve him in spirit and truth. Oh my Heavenly Far-ther, cloth this never dieng soule of mine with that spotless robe of Christs richeness. MDBrown

I have been over to Ames burns to day to see them & Mr Douglass. He has been sick, some better now.

[March 14, 1872-Thursday] 14 aunt Caty and Em is been helping us quilt to day.

[March 15, 1872-Friday] 15 Joe has brought Sally home this morning.

[March 19, 1872-Tuesday] 19 been over to see Sister. All well.

[March 22, 1872-Friday] 22 a cold snowey day & Star has a fine calf.

[March 23, 1872-Saturday] 23 this is the deepest snow that we have had.

[March 24, 1872-Sunday] 24 been at preachen to day. Mr Douglass has done the best to day that I have herd him. Em is not well.

[March 27, 1872-Wednesday] 27 I have had a big visit down to see Elliza & Mag & the babe, found them all well. I feel verry unwell to day. Beck has a fine heiffer calf.

[March 30, 1872-Saturday] 30 Wille Castles & Mag was up last night.

[March 31, 1872-Sunday] 31 Mr Douglas preached to day. It was a wet morning, not manny out.

[April 1, 1872-Monday] Aprile 1 I was with Em last night, she is verry unwell. Sally & Jaily is gone down to ould Mrs Davis, & cousin Wille Davis on a visit.

[April 3, 1872-Wednesday] 3 I have been at york to day, heard nothing new.

[April 4, 1872-Thursday] 4 Em & the children & I have been visiting over to Scoggins to day.

[April 5, 1872-Friday] 5 Jane & the children is here to day. She has hard work to make her living.

[April 7, 1872-Sunday] 7 Sally & Wille has been over to Zion to hear Mr Jonson preach to day & we have got a letter from Lawson to day. He has a notion of coming back soon.

[April 9, 1872-Tuesday] 9 all well. A fine rain to day and warm. Things is beggining to grow. MDB

Brother Johns Eliza & his little grand daughter, Maggy Jane Ramsy was to see us yesterday, she left. All well, also Mrs Cain, Doshy Coldwell, unckle Bille & aunt Caty, Emily & the children. R J is gone over to Hirams to night.

[April 14, 1872-Sunday] this is sabbeth morning. It is raining. I expect to go to the house of God today. God had proclaimed parden to all that beleve in the Lord Jesus Christ, both for now & eternity. Heavenly Farther, I humbly pray that thy parden has been granted to me, a dying worm of the dust & that ould sins are passed away, fore Jesus sake.

Wille Castel brought Maggie up to day to stay with us through the meeting.

[April 20, 1872-Saturday] Satterday evening we have had fine preachen to day. Mr Willson preached. His tex was in Hebrews, tenth chapter, thirty fist verse, "It is a fearful thing to fall into the hands of the living God." In the evening, Revelations twenty second chapter, the seventeenth verse, "And the Spirit and the bride say come." He preached too good sermons. He is a devoted servent. We was like the Ephesus was with Paul. We was sorowing he was going to leave us and not be with us tomorrow. Lawsons Mag & Lauraw Brown, Emmy Thomison, Jacky Brown is all we have to night.

[April 21, 1872-Sunday] Sabbeth Oure preacher, Mr Douglass preached this morning. His tex was in Philippians second chapter & eight verse, "And being found in fashion as a man humbeled himself and became obedient ento death, even the death of the cross." He preached a verry good sermon. Mr James Douglass of yorkville administered the Lords supper & then he preached a sermon. His tex was in Hebrews, fourth chapter, fourteenth verse, "Let us hold fast oure proffession." He done well. He told us whoes we had proffessed to be & how we should try to live & not to crucify the Lord affresh by oure wourldly walk & conversation, we was the salt of the earth. Theire was a great lack of my children & friends, Eliza, Emily, Lawson & Eb, was none of them. Often have we all met there but we may never all meet theire gain. They are wandering like lost sheep from place to place. A very good manny think he is improving verry few. Our tex was in St John c 3 verse 16, "Fore God so loved the would that he sent his only begotten son that whosoever beleveth on him should not perish but have everlasting life." Hymn 175, "I heard a voice that comes from far," 47 hymn "Rock of ages cleft fore me, let me hide." How thankfull I should feel that I am permitted to go to the house of God to heare the sweet songs of Zion, to heare the word preached & whare prayer is want to be made. Oh my God, poure thy holy spirit out on me that I may make a right improvement of these precious blessings that thou has blessed me with. Heavenly Farther, forgive the neglect of all passed oppertunities whether of omision ore comision. Remember them no more forever but may this unworthy name of mine be regersterd in thy Lambs faire book of life fore Jesus sake, amen. MDB

[April 26, 1872-Friday] friday night Aprile 26 oure communion services commenced to day. Young Mr Willson was with us to day. His tex was in second Corinthians, fifth chapter, seventheenth verse. "Theire fore if any man be in Christ he is a new creature, old things are passed away, behold all things are becom new," & his hymns

      15 "Praise to Thee Thou great creator"
      227 "Oh How divine, how sweet the joy."
      226 "Who can describe the joyes that rise."

He is a great man. He must be a chosen vesel like the desciple John, beloved of the Lord. He preached a great sermon and but few out to hear it. A beautifull day but the farmers is so busy they would not spend the day to go to hear it. The time may soon come when they may wish they had gone but we must all stand fore oure selves to oure own master. We stand ore fall. We was all verry much lifted up to day with the Tellagram from Charleston that President Grant had proclaimed a general forgiveness to all the cu clux. Wille is gone home & all the rest. Emily came and kept house fore me & we all went to preachen. We have had fine weather & a good many out today.

[April 30, 1872-Tuesday] 30 I have been Hew Loves to a quilting to day. Had a nice quilting of ould ladies. We did not git it out.

[May 3, 1872-Friday] Cousin Laura Brown was here to day and Sally went home with her to stay a few dayes.

[May 4, 1872-Saturday] 4 I, Lenny & Macy was down to see Ruff and Eliza last night. Eliza is not verry well. It is verry & cold.

[May 5, 1872-Sunday] 5 Mag, Jaly and Wille is gone over to Union to preachen to day.

[May 6, 1872-Monday] 6 cousin Addy has brought Sally here this evening, all well.

[May 8, 1872-Wednesday] 8 we are all well. Em was over to day she is not well. Fanny is gone home with her. Verry warm & dry. My garden is badly burnt.

[May 12, 1872-Sunday] Mr Douglas preached to day. His tex was in rommans the eight chapter. "Fore as manny as are led by the spirit of God, they are the sons of God." Bob & Joe Whiteside came home with us. R G came up & took Fanny home with him to stay with her sister a while.

[May 17, 1872-Friday] 17 I have been down to see Eliza to day. She is dooing perty well.

[May 18, 1872-Saturday] 18 I was with Em last night she is not well, verry poorly. Sally is gone to Smerny to a sackrament to day. Joe came home with her. Em is no better.

[May 20, 1872-Monday] 20 this is a day of note with me Emilys _____ was born five minets after twelve. Dr did not git theire in time. Mrs Cain, aunt Caty, and I had it all to our selves. She is gitting along fine. Lawson & Wille Thomison came home the other day from Tenesee & left Eb.

Emily & the babe both getting along fine. Heavenly Farther, I humbly thank the for the great mercy thou hast showed to me & living Mothers & living children, all right & dooing well. I pray the that thy choicest mercies may rest on them fore time and Eternity. MD Brown

[May 23, 1872-Thursday] 23 Mary & Bell Love, Macy Bell & Sally Hall has been here to day to help the girls to quilt to day & Lawson & Mag has come up this evening. The baby is growing fine.

[May 24, 1872-Friday] 24 unckle Bille & aunt Caty, Lawson, Mag has been here to day. All gone now.

[May 25, 1872-Saturday] 25 I have been with Em to day. Mag Whitesides has been to see her to day. All well.

[May 28, 1872-Tuesday] 28 I have been down to see Eliza this evening. Her & the babe is dooing well & brought Mag home with me.

[May 30, 1872-Thursday] 30 the girls is all gone up to Bells to a quilting to day. Aunt Harriet & Mag was over yesterday. Wille had a chill, looks bad.

[June 1, 1872-Saturday] June 1 Sally, Mag, Jaily has all been to McElwees mill pon a fishing. Had a fishing party theire this evening & theire was a negroe drowned in the pon while they was theire. He jumped in a deep place and could not swim. It was near too hours before they could git him out. His name was ___ Lach. Scared the girls purty near to death. Theire were several young men theire. Sylvanus and Joe Whitesides came home with them.

[June 2, 1872-Sunday] 2 Sally, Jaily & Wille & I is gone over to Zion to preachen. Mr Jonson has a communion their to day.

[June 4, 1872-Tuesday] 4 Lawson & Mag come up this morning & Sue & Mace Bell is here to night.

[June 9, 1872-Sunday] 9 Mr Douglass preached. We have had a fine rain this evening. Butler & Nanny, Ida & Wille Thomison came home with us and D___Brown & Collumbus Graham from fort Mill. Nanny & Butler & Ida went home and we have gone to the hoe. R G Whitesides is here to night. Em & the children has come over to day. The first time fore the little stranger.

[June 13, 1872-Thursday] 13 I was with Mrs Scoggins last night she sent out yesterday fore Dr Allison. Mrs Cain & aunt Caty & I stayed till this morning & it did not come off, we all went home. Back at Mr Scoggins the same evening in a hurry all over in half an hour no one there but Mrs Cain and I. They had started fore the Dr, called him back, all done well, a fine, big daughter. Wille was down to see Eliza last night they are all dooing well, expects to be up a Satterday. M D Brown

Amus Burns, George Davis was baptised by Mr Douglas June the 9 1872. Mrs Scoggins, Nanny Catherine was born June 13, a thursday 1872.

[June 23, 1872-Sunday] 23 Eliza & her babe, Em & her babe, Mag & her babe was to day at Bershaba to here Mr Douglass preach. Lawson & Mag had theire son baptised to day. His name was James Castel. William & Matty Coldwell, Hew Cammel, Albert & Cate Coldwells daughter, Betty Cain. Ruffe & Eliza came up yesterday morning, took dinner with Em & then came over here & stayed all night. They had a singing at the church yesterday. Not many there.

Came home with Sally. Had a fine rain this evening. Butler & Nanny came by.

[July 4, 1872-Thursday] July 4 Ruff has been at york to day, came by & took Em & the children home with him to stay a, took little Mary home with him. She has been up here a week, the first week that she has stayed with me.

Mary Cain has been taken sick to day. Gim & Betsy is sick & little Gimmy has the hooping cough. Mary was taken verry bad with a conjestive chill. I have been there all day. She did not think she would live eneytime. She has got better.

[July 15, 1872-Monday] 15 Ann & Mag Scoggins & Em is helping Sally quilt to day. Em, Ann & Mag went to see Mary Cain this eveing. She is very Porly yet. Mag stayed all night with her.

[July 22, 1872-Monday] 22 Mrs Scoggins has been over to day with the little stranger the first time Em and I have had a big visit over to Hirams to night with Renes Fewell and Molly. They are gitting allong fine. Took dinner with Butler & Nanny & stayed all night with Lawson & Jane, & home this morning.

[July 28, 1872-Sunday] 28 Ida Thomison & the girls is all gone to a singing up at the church to day. Molly & Duff Brown & Wille Thomison came home with them.

[July 30, 1872-Tuesday] 30 Ruff & Eliza has come up to day Mag gone to york with Ruff. Mary Cain has taken worse this morning.

[July 31, 1872-Wednesday] 31 all gone home.

[August 2, 1872-Friday] August 2 Gimmy Castle is here to day. I have been down to see Mary, no better. Lawson is gone down fore Mag & Joe Whiteside & Gim Summeford is here.

[August 3, 1872-Saturday] 3 Lawson & Mag, Joe & Sally & Gim & Mag, Gim & Jaily is all gone to the exabition to day.

[August 4, 1872-Sunday] 4 Gim Castel is gone this morning. Mary Cain is no better.

[August 6, 1872-Tuesday] 6 Lawson & Mag is gone on a visit over to their unckle Hirams to night & I have been down to see Mary, still porly, the Dr is theire every day.

[August 8, 1872-Thursday] 8 I was with Miss Mary last night. I cosidder her verry bad.

[August 10, 1872-Saturday] 10 Sally & Jaily was with Mary last night. She is verry near gon. Her dayes are about to end. Too Dr but they cant save life. Mary F Cain departed this life August the tenth ten oclock, a Satterday morning 1872. I was theire to witness the last strugle, to close the sightless eyes & close the icy lips in the sleep of death. To see a lovely youth in the bloom of life and her to be called a way is a solom warning to both old & young, but we morn not as those without hope fore give us great sattesfaction, both in health and sickness that all was well. Oh that I may live in readeness fore death & be prepared fore it. Let it come when it may.

[August 11, 1872-Sunday] 11 Mr Douglass was down their last night at eleven when Jackson and him came home. Mr Douglass preached a funeral sermon this morning, gave a verry nice address in deed. The hymns, "O land of rest fore thee I sigh," "Step by step my Farther leads" and now we have laid her away in the lonly grave theire to be till the reaserection morn. MDBrown

[August 14, 1872-Wednesday] 14 I have been down to see Mr & Mrs Cain. They seem to be gitting allon as well as I could expect. Miss Betsy Black is theire.

[August 17, 1872-Saturday] 17 the girls went up to the singing to day but it is a failure. They have gave it out. Joe & Gim came home with them. Caty Jackson & Eliza Stincen too supper with us & went over to stay all night with Em.

I have been down to see cousin Wille Davis. He & Wille are perty bad off with the fever & Eddy is sick too.

[August 23, 1872-Friday] 23 this is the day of cleening off the grave yard & Mr Douglass preached to day. His tex was in Psams 145, "Thy kingdom is an everlasting kingdom." Theire is to be an election of too elders but theire was such small congration that it was laid over till the fourth saterday in september. Hirram & Harriet, cousin Molly Fewel & her too little children, Hatty & Eddy came home

with us on a visit, Lawson & Mag, Em & her children. We had as many as fifteen & now the bad news has reached us that cousin Wille Davis little Wille is dead, that he died in a congestive chille to day, bout too this evening, & Hiram & Lawson is gone down.

[August 24, 1872-Saturday] 24 Sally & Mag & Hirram & Jackson is gone down to cousin Willes. Hiram & Harriet & Molle is gone home & little Wille buried this evening.

[August 25, 1872-Sunday] 25 Mr Douglass preached to day. He preached a great sermon to a small congration. We had a great rain last night. The creeks was all too full to cross. His tex was in Mark the sixteenth chapter & sixteen verse, "He that beleveth & is baptised shall be saved but he that beleveth not shall be damnd." Lawson & Joe is gone home.

[September 1, 1872-Sunday] September 1 Jackson, Sally & Jaily is gone on a trip to Union to preachen to day.

[September 2, 1872-Monday] 2 Sally and Jaily has come home, the meeting is going on yet.

[September 5, 1872-Thursday] 5 Fanny & I have been down to see Eliza, stayed too dayes, all well.

[September 6, 1872-Friday] 6 Em & I have been at york to day. Em got fifty seven dollars that Eb sent her. She spent about twenty five of it on buyin dressen fore her & the children to go to Tenesee to see him. He has bought land and expects to make Tenesee his home. He has a fine school, fifty schollars, dooing well.

[September 8, 1872-Sunday] 8 I have been at preachen to day Mr Douglas gave us a fine sermon. His tex was in Mark sixteenth chapter sixteenth verse, "He that belevith and is baptised shall be saved but he that beleveth not shall be damnd." He preached a fine sermon. John Opharell & Breathy Daubson was here last night. Ruffe & Eliza came to stay with us & Eliza is gone over to stay with Em to night.

[September 10, 1872-Tuesday] 10 Ruff & Eliza is gone home, left little Mag with us. Eliza has been busy helping Em to sow fore too days.

[September 11, 1872-Wednesday] 11 cousin Daubson and Fanny was out and stayed all night with us & Em & the children all gone home.

[September 13, 1872-Friday] 13 Lawson & Joe was here this evening. Ould Miss Sally Neel was buried to day.

[September 14, 1872-Saturday] 14 Joe Whitesides & Sally & Mag is gone down to york to go to Philadelpha to the camp meeting.

[September 19, 1872-Thursday] 19 Em & the children was here last night.

[September 20, 1872-Friday] 20 this is the comencement of oure communion. Mr Douglass preached to day. His tex was in Mathew eleventh chapter, "Blessed is he that shall not be offended in me."

[September 21, 1872-Saturday] Satterday Mr Jonson preached this morning, his tex was in Psalms one hunderd & twenty secon chapter. "Pray fore the peace of Jerusalem: they shall prosper that love thee." He preached a good sermon. I came home at interval. Ruff & Eliza & the children, Em & children, Wille & Ida & Liza Thomison is all with us to night. May be the las time that Eliza & Em may ever stay another nite to gether in this wourld as Em expects to start to tenesee next tusday.

[September 22, 1872-Sunday] 22 Sabbeth evening Mr Douglass preached this morning. He preached a good sermon. His tex was, "But seek ye first the kingdom of God and his rightoness, and all these things shall be added unto you." We have had a nice meeting, good preaching, good weather, and a good turn out of people. It has been a solom meeting, the faces that I have meet theire this day, I have no dout in saying, I shall never meet them all theire again. Some of them I shall never meet again untill the reserection morn. One by one oure dayes are fleein, one by one oure friends are leeving, some to Tenesee some to Arcancis, some to Heaven, some to hell. Oh what a solom thought is this. Oh my soule prepare to meet thy God, to meet thy God in Heaven.

[September 25, 1872-Wednesday] September 25 1872 a wensday morning I have bid Em and the children fare well this morning. They have started fore Tenesee. My second daughter Emily Jane Castel, her son Lenard Haris, Mary Brown, Sally Fanny, Netty Catherine. Foure fine harty children. Oh my God, I commend to thy care and keeping both soule & body fore time & Eternity is

the prayer of theire devoted Mother.

[September 29, 1872-Sunday] 29 R J & Jaily went down to Ruffes last night to go to Smerny to day. It is an unfaverable morning. Sally, Fanny and I are her by oure selves to day. Gods holy sabbeth and may we make a right improvement of it. MD Brown

[October 1, 1872-Tuesday] Oct 1 cousin Daubson has brought Mag home to day & we have got a letter from Eb. Emily & the children has landed safe. She left York a wensday morning and landed at unckle Henries a friday night. A matter of great thankfulness to God fore their safe journie.

[October 3, 1872-Thursday] 3 Lawson & his Paw was at york to day. Sold a bale of cotton fore sixteen and ___ dollars a hundred. Lawson is gone down to Mr Castels to night.

[October 8, 1872-Tuesday] 8 I have been down to see Mrs Mary Davis to day. Her son has been bad with the dipthera, some better now.

[October 9, 1872-Wednesday] 9 R J Brown and Mr Douglass started to Presbatary this morning in Union county. The churchs name Eneree, about forty three miles.

[October 13, 1872-Sunday] 13 Wille, Fanny and I have been to Zion to preachen. Mr Jonson had a communion to day.

1873

[January 1, 1873-Wednesday] New Years night of eighteen hundered & seventy three. Oh my Heavenly Farther none but a God who mooves in a mysterias way his mighty works to performe, can comprehend what another year will bring forth. Thy fruites will ripen fast unfolding every houre. We know something of the parts of the present. Oh Heavenly Farther prepare us fore the future oh my God. This is a cold, dark, and stormy night without & I have a verry heavey heart within this bosom of mine this new year night. Why it is, I cant tell. My children is all gone to Bells to a singing to night. I feel as if some of them would be killed ore cripled before they ever git home. Oh God my great comfort is that thou rulest all things & thou has promised that all things shall work to gether fore good to them that love God. Oh that I may remember theire is no promises to the wicked but a fearfull looking fore of judgement & firy indignation. Oh Heavenly Farther, send thy holy spirit to assist me in renewing the dedacation of myself, my Husband & children to thy service & to thy care, both fore time & eternity.

[January 2, 1873-Thursday] 2 this is a verry wet day. The Children all got

home safe & several come home with them. Joe Whitesides, Marten Hall, Gim Wood, Wille & Ida Thomison, Lawson & Mag was here too. All gone but Wille & Joe & Ida.

[January 4, 1873-Saturday] 4 Jackson & I have been at york to day to see Jaily Masabo. She has three fine, harty children. They are going down toward Charlston this year.

[January 5, 1873-Sunday] 5 I have been at preachen to day. M Hall is here to night.

[January 12, 1873-Sunday] 12 Joe Whitesides was here last night. All gone to preachen to day.

[January 13, 1873-Monday] 13 Mag & Jaily is gone over to Mr Scoggins to night.

[January 16, 1873-Thursday] 16 oure friend & neighbor, Mr David Scoggins hung himself this evening in the straw house at the barn & was found about dark. He laid his coat & hat in the barn dore. What came over him no one knowes. His mind has been a little wavering at times. I have often heard of such a thing but never witness it beffore. My God grant i never may witness such a heart rendaring scene again. Joe Whitesides was here that night. He went fore the coraner. We had a dreadfull rain that evening & the creeks was up. He was buried at Bershaba, a Friday. The word flew like lightning. The house and yard was full.

[January 20 1873-Monday] 20 Mag & Cate is gone over to stay with Mrs Scoggins to night. Joe is here.

[January 28, 1873-Tuesday] 28 Mag & I was at york to day & I went out & stayed with Harriet that night, buying trimmings fore Sallies wedding. Eliza is up with us to day. R J is gone to take Sally down to york to make her wedding dress.

[February 6, 1873-Thursday] Feb 6 Jackson has went down to york & brought Sally home & Fanny has come home with her to help her backe the cake.

[February 8, 1873-Saturday] 8 aunt Harriet has been up to help us. We had

fine luck in backing & trimming them & they are all gone home. Joe White-sides & Sally Brown was married by Mr Douglass

[February 13, 1873-Thursday] Feb the 13 1873 Had a nice supper and perty big crowd. Theire was about fifty. Every thing went on smooth & nice.

[February 14, 1873-Friday] 14 Mart & Mag & Wille came home to night. Jaily stayed with Sally.

[February 16, 1873-Sunday] 16 Daubson & Fanny has been with us sence yesterday morning. It has been raining ever sence yesterday morning, has cleared of this evening & they are gone home.

[February 18, 1873-Tuesday] 18 Joe & Sally has came up this evening & brought Jaily home, all well.

[February 23, 1873-Sunday] 23 we was all at preachen to day, Joe & Sally for the firs time. Aunt Hariet & Wille came by with us. Sally went home with Joe.

[March 2, 1873-Sunday] March 2 Joe & Sally has come up this evening & Sally is going to stay awhile.

[March 3, 1873-Monday] 3 this is one dreadfull cold night & windy & M Hall is here.

[March 5, 1873-Wednesday] 5 Mag & I went down to york on yesterday to git her wedding dooings. Left her with her cousin Fanny to git her help to make her things. Eliza has been up fore too dayes helping us to bake her cake. We have had fine luck. Got all well backed & nice trimmed & R G has came up fore her & she is gone home.

[March 8, 1873-Saturday] 8 brother Lawson Brown died the 8 of March 1873, a verry sudden death, took sick a friday & died a satterday. Mary was in Chester with her aunt. Duff in Spartinburg, going to school. They telagraphed fore Mary. She started about nine in the night, rode all night, got home about sunup. Oure friends is fast leaving us. They are numberd with the dead. A warning fore us all, prepare to meet thy God. He leaves a wife, too daughters & five sons to mourn their loss. He tole them to prepare to meet him in Heaven. He was buried in Bershaba grave yard a sabbeth evening after preachen, ocupied his seat that day too weeks ago, now lying in his grave. Wille went down & brought Mag home this evening. R J & I went over to Lawsons. M Hall was here this evening. The yankies is after him. He is in a fret.

[March 12, 1873-Wednesday] 12 M Hall is here to day. The yankies sayes they will have him dead ore alive. This is wensday. Mag & M Hall was to be married to morrow & everry thing ready & now he has to run again, not in a good humour, I can tell you, but these are some of oure crosses that we have to bear. Let us ask God to give us grace to beare those crosses, patience & meekness & say, not my will Oh Lord, but thine be done. Thou will direct all things are right & Sally is gone home with Joe.

[March 13, 1873-Thursday] 13 this is the day that M Hall & Mag was to be married. She is taken it verry hard. She has her crosses to bear in that line but i hope it will all be right in time. M D Brown I have been down to see ould unckle Breathy to day. He is still lying on his back, don't look lik he could last much longer.

[March 14, 1873-Friday] 14 I have been over helping Ann Scoggins to bake her wedding cake to day. Had fine luck. Got it nicely baked.

[March 16, 1873-Sunday] 16 Jaily & Wille has been over to Smerny to day.

[March 17, 1873-Monday] 17 Eliza has been up to day. Came up a horse back, now gone home & Sally is over helping Ann to ice her cake and trim them.

[March 20, 1873-Thursday] 20 Davis Brown & Miss Ann Scoggins was married March the Twentieth, a thursday night by Mr Douglass. They did not have a big wedding owing to the death of both Farthers so lately. R J was theire, Joe & Sally, Mag & Jaily. They had a nice little wedding. The boyes all came over here & slep, then went back fore breakfast. R J and I went over & took dinner with them the next day. They had a fine dinner. Mag & Fanny stayed at home & kept house, the rest of us all went. It was cold & windy. Joe & Sally went home with aunt Harriet on a visit.

[March 23, 1873-Sunday] 23 Joe & Sally came back last evening, had a fine visit. Joe went down to york, got Sally a fine dress & some other things. Miss Polly Burns was here yesterday on a visit. M Hall slipped in last night, would not go to preachen. Mag & him & I kept house. Joe & Sally is gone home & M

Hall has left again. I don't know when he will be back, not till the united states court is over & our civil court. That will be the first of next month.

[March 27, 1873-Thursday] 27 Shereff Glenn has sent out after Lawson to day. Harkness wants to make a witness of him. He dont want to be made a witness fore him.

[March 31, 1873-Monday] 31 I have been over to see Mrs McAphee to day. She has been sick, she is better.

[April 5, 1873-Saturday] Aprile 5 Lawson & I was down to see cousin Psalm people last night. All well but cousin Laura has a verry sore mouth from salavation. They are in great hopes that cousin Psalm will be pardened and git home soon. Lawson has went down & gave himself up to Glenn & went his own bale.

[April 7, 1873-Monday] 7 Lawson has been to court to day, nothing done yet.

[April 9, 1873-Wednesday] 9 the tryal came on to day. They could doo nothing with it. Lawson is set free. Joe brought Sally up to day & taken Mag down to stay a few dayes with Eliza. This has been a dreadfull dayes wind.

[April 11, 1873-Friday] 11 Sally & Jaily is gone down to see Mrs Cain to day M Hall has come back.

[April 12, 1873-Saturday] 12 I was down with Eliza last night, all well. Stopped & staid all day with Mrs Davis, all well.

[April 13, 1873-Sunday] 13 Sabbeth evening Joe, Mart & Denem Bell was here last night. Mart sayes he wont run no more. Aunt Harriet came home with us. Joe & Sally & Mart is all gone.

[April 18 1873-Friday] 18 Jaily & I have been at york to day.

[April 20 1873-Sunday] 20 Jackson & the children is all gone over to Zien to preachen to day.

[April 25, 1873-Friday] 25 this is the commencement of oure communion. I went this morning with the expectation of enjoying a fine communion meeting but I heard to day that Mr Douglass & Harriet Enloe was going to marry & it hurt me so that I fear that the preachen will not doo me much good. I did not think my preacher would have stooped so low. Sally & Jaily was down to se ould Mr Coldwell last night, he is no better.

[April 26, 1873-Saturday] 26 we had an election fore elders to day. John Davis & William Davis was both elected. Mr Jonson preached to day. Butler & Nanny, Wille & Ida came home with us.

[April 27, 1873-Sunday] 27 oure meeting is over but it has been a poore meeting to me. Oh my God forgive i praye thee to forgive all thy pure & holy eyes has seen amiss in me. Through this holly comunion sabbeth thou hast said the spirit indeed is willing but the flesh is week, poor frail & perishing creatures that we are. They are all gone home but M Hall.

[May 1, 1873-Thursday] 1 Marten Hall & Mag H Brown was married the first day of May by Mr Jonson as Mag did not want Mr Douglass to marrie her. It rained the whole day but the company all came but too. Theire was a large crowd, over fifty. All things carried on fine.

[May 2, 1873-Friday] 2 all gone to the infare, R J, Fannie & I am left by oure selves. Eliza did not git up. The children had the hooping cough & it rained so that Ruffes did not git here. Mr Douglass and Harriet Enloe was maried at Mr Burnses April 29 by Mr Douglass from york. Theire is a great deal of talk about it. The people of Bershaba is not pleased to have Harriet Enlo fore theire preachers wife.

[May 3, 1873-Saturday] 3 Jaily & Wille, Bob & Mag Whitesides came home this morning, had a fine time, a large crowd & plenty to eat.

[May 5, 1873-Monday] 5 Mart & Mag has come home this morning. Mart has left Mag & gone home.

[May 7, 1873-Wednesday] 7 Jackson has brought aunt Emily out to stay a week with us. Mrs Mary Davis & John Davis has taken supper with us.

[May 8, 1873-Thursday] 8 M Hall and Denem Bell is here to night.

[May 9, 1873-Friday] 9 Mart has been to take his Mother up to the railroad & did not git back till eleven o clock to night.

[May 11, 1873-Sunday] 11 Sabeth evening we had cousin Wille & Eliza Davis, cousin Ginny Brown & Mart with us last night. Mag is gone home with Mart.

[May 12, 1873-Monday] 12 aunt Emily & Jane is with us to day.

[May 13, 1873-Tuesday] 13 aunt Emily is gone to Mr Cains & Mr & Mrs Jonson is with us to day & Miss Nancy Peters.

[May 14, 1873-Wednesday] 14 aunt Emily & I have taken dinner with unckle Bille to day.

[May 15, 1873-Thursday] 15 Lawsons John Jackson was born May the fifteenth. Jackson & aunt Emily & I have taken dinner with them to day, they are dooing fine.

[May 17, 1873-Saturday] 17 I have been down to see Sally, taken supper with her & then we went to Ruffs, stayed all night, home this morning. All well.

[May 18, 1873-Sunday] 18 Mart & Mag & Jaily is gone to Bethany to a communion.

[May 19, 1873-Monday] 19 Mrs Bell & Sue is here to day & Joe & Sally came up this evening & Sue stayed all night.

[May 23, 1873-Friday] 23 Sally, Mag & Jaily is all gone to Bells last night. Fannie & I have been at york to day.

[May 24, 1873-Saturday] 24 Sally is not well.

[May 29, 1873-Thursday] 29 Ruff was up to day, all well.

[June 1, 1873-Sunday] June 1 Jaily & Wille is gone to Smerny to a communion to day.

[June 5, 1873-Thursday] Mag mooved June the 5 1873, Jaily went with her.

[June 8, 1873-Sunday] 8 Lawson & Mag was over last night with the little stranger & Wille is gone over to his aunt Janes. Fannie & I have been over to

Zion to preachen to day. Fanny was sick. Heard a great sermon from a Mr Marten of Collumbia. Bob Whisent & Sue Jackson was married June the 3 1873 by Mr Jonson.

[June 13, 1873-Friday] 13 Eliza came up yesterday morning & we went over to see Mart & Mag. She was pleased to see them so well fixed. Ruff came up last night & they are gone home.

[June 15, 1873-Sunday] 15 Bob Alexander & his wife was here to day. He had several fits that day.

[June 22, 1873- Sunday] 22 Sally is gone to stay this week with us.

[June 24, 1873-Tuesday] 24 Sally & Jaily went over to see Mag to day & Rit run off with them this evening. They did not git much hurt.

[June 25, 1873-Wednesday] 25 Joe could not let Sally stay a week but came after her last night. Aunt Caty & Jane has been helping her quilt to day got it out. Joe & Sally is gone home.

[June 29, 1873-Sunday] 29 Wille is gone fore the Dr fore unckle Bille. Wille Thomison was here last night. Jackson was sick this morning, could not go to preachen. Oure preacher is sick, we have no preachen to day.

[July 1, 1873-Tuesday] July 1 1873 I was over to see Mart & Mag yesterday. Mag has come home with me to stay this week. Mag & Jaily is gone up to see unckle Bille. He is verry porrly. Jaily & Mag is gone over to see Mrs Scoggins to night

[July 3, 1873-Thursday] 3 Mag is verry busy macking her a new dress & Jaily is helping her. Bille is no better the Dr is still waiting on him.

[July 6, 1873-Sunday] 6 M Hall come over last night & we all went to preachen to day. We are all gitting out with our preacher. The fault may be oures, if so I pray the Lord in mercy to open oure eyes to see oure faults beffore it will be too late. Mart and Mag is gone home.

[July 8, 1873-Tuesday] 8 I was down at York this morning, heard nothing new. I have been down to see Mrs Mary Davis. Had a plesent visit, can enjoye my self fine with her.

[July 13, 1873-Sunday] 13 Sally was up with us last night. Joe & Mag came up this morning, all gone home.

[July 14, 1873-Monday] 14 aunt Caty & I have been down to see ould Mr Coldwell. He is still living, an object of pyty & sorow to be hold what human nature can suffer, and by the grace of God, he beares it with out a murmiring word. Macy Bell & Mag Scoggins is with us to night.

[July 19, 1873-Saturday] 19 I have been down on a visit to see Eliza & Sally. They are all well but Joe & Ally. They are both unwell. Ally was verry sick on yesterday. I left Fanny to stay a week.

[July 20, 1873-Sunday] 20 Cate & Wille is gone to Center to the communion. Ould Mr Coldwell died this morning, July the 20 1873, on a sunday morning. Lawson & his Paw is gone down to Mr Coldwells. Mag & the children is here.

[July 21, 1873-Monday] 21 well we have laid ould unckle Breathy away in the cold and silent grave. Theire was a large buryen. Mr Ross gave an adress at the house. He spoke verry nice. R J is gone down to Ruffs little _____ has been verry bad sence I left.

[July 22, 1873-Tuesday] 22 have had company to day, sister Harriet & sister Jane, Mart & Mag, Lawson & Mag, Cal Parish, George Cabinest, John OPharal. The boyes is out macking up a pick nick dinner at Quins school house. Cate wont go.

[July 25, 1873-Friday] 25 Davis & Ann & Mag Scoggins was here last night. Bob Jackson, Jaily & Wille is all gone over with them to Scoggins to day to take dinner with them.

[July 27, 1873-Sunday] 27 we have all been at preachen to day. Mr Douglass tex was in John the sixth chapter thirty seventh verse these are the words, "All that the Farther giveth me shall come to me." He preached a verry good sermon but it dose seem that he preaches in self deffence. It dose seem so to me. Whether it be imagination ore whether it be soo I canot tell. We have commenced a new sabbeth school to day ore rather organized one. We have a large bibble class, one fore the little boyes, one fore the little girls, an other infant class. Cousin Wille Davis is suppertendent. He sung a hymn & made a prayer. He takes charge of the bibble class, Mr Lowry Smyth of the boyes, Mrs Cain of the girls, Mrs Burns of the infant class. So you see we have foure classes. I hope that ould Beershaba is not dead yet although it seems as if we have manny crosses to come through. I pray thee oh Lord God bee with oure church. Bee with oure sabbeth school, bee with oure people. Oh God let thy blessings rest on our young elder that this day has in oure church gave a prayer before the congration, what I have never heard one of oure ould elders doo. Lawson had his babby baptised to day. His name is John Jackson. Joe & Sally, Mart & Mag, Lawson & Mag, Hiram & Harrieet, Wille & I is all at preachen to day, all gone home. I was to see Mrs Davis yesterday.

[July 28, 1873-Monday] 28 unckle Bille is very porly yet. I was with him last night.

[July 29, 1873-Tuesday] 29 I was up to see Mrs Bell to day. She is sick. John Brown came home this evening found his Farther verry unwell. He has been gone near to years. Unckle Bille is worse. He is deranged, hardly can reconize John. He sayes they tell him John is home.

[August 1, 1873-Friday] August 1 Ruffe & Eliza was up last night to see unckle Bille. [He is] entirly deranged, has had his neck blistered. Sue Bell was here to day. Her & Jaily is gone up to see unckle Bille. Jackson is gone fore aunt Emily.

[August 2, 1873-Saturday] 2 Bille is verry bad. The Dr has no hopes of him. He has the brain dropesy. The Dr has foure blisters on him. Olde unckle Tommy Whitesides & Sally has come up to see him to day. He is badly deranged & the house is crowded with company.

[August 3, 1873-Sunday] 3 M Hall & Mag came over last night to see theire unckle. Wille Thomison & Sally, Jackson & I was with him last night. He is a little better, at him self this morning, but i don't think he will ever git well. Eliza & Sally, Mart & Mag & Wille Thomison is with us to day & to see unckle Bille.

[August 4, 1873-Monday] 4 Bille is still living. I can see no change fore the better.

[August 5, 1873-Tuesday] 5 I was up with unckle Bille, set up most all night with him. He is verry low. He is lasting so long i sometimes think he may git up again. They have plenty of company, aunt Emily, aunt Sally Coldwell is staying with them.

[August 6, 1873-Wednesday] 6 Ruff came by from york, took Jaily home with him to go to the Sabbeth school celabration at mount Vernon.

[August 7, 1873-Thursday] 7 Billey took a chill this morning about day light & has been verry bad all day. Sufferd dreadfull this morning has got more calm to night.

[August 9, 1873-Saturday] 9 Brother Bille died on Satterday morning at half past foure 1873. He took another chill last night but died a way verry easy. He said he was willing to die and tole us to pray fore ever and ever. He was taken in the church, Mr Douglass preached his funeral sermon his tex was in Psalms the nintieth chapter. He done verry well then we laid him in his grave.

[August 11, 1873-Monday] 11 Jackson is gone over to see Mag to day. Aunt Emily is here.

[August 12, 1873-Tuesday] 12 Jackson is gone to take aunt Emily home.

[August 14, 1873-Thursday] 14 Fannie is sick with the cold & swelled jaw & Ruff has come up fore Jaily to go down to stay with them a while.

[August 15, 1873-Friday] 15 Fannie & I have been over to see Mag. She has not been well, & git peaches.

[August 17, 1873-Sunday] 17 Wille & his Paw is gone to Smerny to preachen to day. Fannie & I am by oure selves to day.

[August 21, 1873-Thursday] 21 I have been down to see Mr & Mrs Cain. They have both been sick, is some better now.

[August 23, 1873-Saturday] 23 R G has brought Hatty up to stay a week.

[August 24, 1873-Sunday] 24 Sally has brought Cate home this morning. Joe is gone to the camp meeting. Mr Douglass tex was in Mathew the sev-

enth chapter, twelfth verse. He preached a verry good sermon. Not manny out. Wille is gone home with Sally.

[August 25, 1873-Monday] 25 Mag came over this morning fore Jaily to go & stay a week with her. She is gone with her.

[August 26 1873-Tuesday] Sally mooved August 26 1873.

[August 31, 1873-Sunday] 31 Fanny & Hatty and I have had a big trod to york yesterday, took dinner with aunt Emily, out & stayed all night with aunt Harriet, to union to preachen to day, heard Mr David Thomison preach. He preached a fine sermon. His tex was, "Fore God so loved the world that he gave his only begotten son that whoesoever beleveth on him should not die but have everlasting life." Jackson, he was down at Sharon, called to see cousin Margarets people, all well.

[September 1, 1873-Monday] September 1 Mag has brought Cate home & stayed all night, all well.

[September 4,1873-Thursday] 4 Jaily, Wille & Fanny is all gone down to mineral spring to day to a pick nik.

[September 5, 1873-Friday] September 5 Jackson is gone down to see Joe & Sally.

[September 8, 1873-Monday] 8 a cold damp day. We had a dreadfull rain last night, the creek was higher than it has been this summer, has injered the corn badly, all well to night.

1874

[July 5, 1874-Sunday] July the fifth young Mr Sprat preached to day. He dose only tolerable. His tex was in Ephesians, fifth chapter, second verse. He came home with us and stayed all night.

[July 11, 1874-Saturday] 11 we have had a fine rain this evening, greatly needed.

[July 12, 1874-Sunday] 12 Mr Miller preached this morning. He done fine, I think. He is an exceptional young preacher. He can make a good prayer. Young Mr Willson gave an address this evening. He lectured on the talents, he done fine. He is not through in simanary yet. Mr Miller was with us last night.

[July 14, 1874-Tuesday] 14 Joe & Sally came up this morning & I went to york with Joe. Sally stayed with Jaily.

[July 17, 1874-Friday] 17 Fanny Daubson, Vilet enloe, Cate, Fanny & myself have all been at aunt Emilies to day. Jackson is gone down to see Eliza & Sally.

[July 19, 1874-Sunday] 19 Jackson & I have been up to Center to day to a communion. Theire was a large congragation of people theire. Mr Douglass preached one of his ould sermons that I have heard him preach beffor.

[July 26, 1874-Sunday] 26 Ruff & Eliza & the children all came up last night, all well. It has been a verry wet morning, rained till about ten o clock, a bad day fore preachen. Young Mr Mcomic preached to day. This is the first day that young Mr R L Mcomick preached at Bershaba. He was raised in Chester. He is just from the Seminary, is licend to preach. He appears to be a verry gifted young man. His morning tex was in Romans sixth chapter, 23 verse. In the evening, Mathew 11 chapter, 28 verse. He done well. He is verry young & boy looking. Had a bad day, not manny out.

[July 27, 1874-Monday] 27 Lawson, Mag & Jaily has all gone over to Marts to day.

[July 29, 1874-Wednesday] 29 I have been down at Billy Coldwells to preachen this evening, Mr Ross preached. His tex was in Ephesians 2 chapter 8 verse. Mrs Coldwell & Gim is both unwell. Wille has gone down on a visit to see Eliza and Sally this evening and I have been down to Mr Billey Coldwells to preachen this evening. Mr Ross preached. His tex was in Ephesians 2 chapter 8 verse. Mrs Coldwell & Gim is both unwell.

[August 1, 1874-Saturday] August 1 Wille has come home & brought Sally home with him. Young Mr Perry preached to day. His tex was in Luke 10 chapt, 24 verse. He ant much of a preacher. He is verry large young man & bald headded. He is good looking. We have had foure young men to preach to us from the Siminary, Mr Sprat, Mr Willson, Mr Miller, Mr Perry & Mr Mcomick. Mr Mcomich is my choice of them all. All four of these young men was licend this spring. We are in hopes we will git Mr Miller to preach fore us till Christmas. Mr Douglass sayes we shant have no preachen but we will show him better than that.

[August 4, 1874-Tuesday] 4 Robbert Black & Mag Scoggins was married August the 4 1874.

[August 11, 1874-Tuesday] 11 I have been down at Ruffs, they are all sick with the cold. Cousin Jonny & Laura Russells infant babe was burried at Bershaba to day.

[August 12, 1874-Wednesday] 12 Mag Whitesides & Alas Castle has been up on a visit to day.

[August 14, 1874-Friday] 14 Jaily, Wille & I was at Sharon to day, stayed all night with cousin Psalm & Margaret. Ginny was theire with her babe, calls him Psalm.

[August 17, 1874-Monday] 17 I was over with Mag last night. Her babe has been sick, has got better.

[August 19, 1874-Wednesday] 19 Mrs Mary Davis has spent this day with me.

[August 20, 1874-Thursday] 20 this is the day that Mag Whitesides & Jaily went to York fore ould Bob Whitesides & John Alexander. Mary & aunt Emily & Mag Hall was all here. Mag Hall, Mary Alexander and aunt Emily has spent the night with us.

[August 21, 1874-Friday] 21 I have been down at Ruffs. Little Mary has cut her thumb off in the cutting knife. It is dooing pretty well. Sally came home with me. Sally & I have had a big visit over to see Mart & Mag, unckle Hirams, aunt Janes, & Buttlers & she is now gone home.

[August 22, 1874-Saturday] 22 I have been down to see Eliza & helped her to quilt, went over & stayed all night with Joe & Sally, all well.

[August 24, 1874-Monday] 24 I have been to see Mrs Cain to day.

[August 26, 1874-Wednesday] 26 cousin Emiline Floyd & Harriet Land has been here to day.

[August 27, 1874-Thursday] 27 Mr Mcomick preached to day. Had a fine congragation out, pay him about ten dollars a day. Willie went to york fore him last evening. He stayed all night.

[September 5, 1874-Saturday] 5 Mrs Cain was here to day

[September 6, 1874-Sunday] 6 Mr Mcomick preached to day, has been all night with us. I think fine of him.

[September 8, 1874-Tuesday] 8 Mr McComick was with us last night, the first time he has been to see us. I am well pleased with him. R J has gone to take him to york.

[September 11, 1874-Friday] 11 I have been down to see Eliza, they are all sick with the cold & cousin Jonny & Laura Russels infant babe was burried at Bershaba to day.

[September 12, 1874-Saturday] 12 Jaily has come from Ruffs, they hant much better.

[September 14, 1874-Monday] 14 Jaily, Wille & I was at Sharon at a communion, stayed all night with cousin Psalm & Margaret. Ginny & her babe was theire, they are well. Ould cousin John Brown was their, he is verry porly.

[September 17, 1874-Thursday] 17 I was over with Mag last night. Her babe has been sick. Aunt Emily, Mary Alexander, Jaily & Fanny is all gone down to Mr Cains on a visit.

[September 19, 1874-Saturday] 19 Mrs Mary Davis has spent the day with me.

[September 21, 1874-Monday] 21 I have been down to see Eliza. Little Mary has cut her thumb off in the cutting knife. It is dooing perty well. Sally came home with me & aunt Margaret Floyd was here.

[September 23, 1874-Wednesday] 23 Sally & I have had a big visit, been to see Butler, Hiram Davis, aunt Jane, Mart & Mag & she is now gone home.

[September 27, 1874-Sunday] 27 Mr Mcomick preached to day had a fine congragation out, pay him about ten dollars a day. Wille went down fore him to york, brought him out last night. He is gone to Mr Douglass to night. He stayed all night.

[October 3, 1874-Saturday] Oct. 3 theire was a congrational meeting at the church to day to see what they could make up fore Mr Mcomick. Theire was but few out. They made up one hunderd & fifty dollars.

[October 5, 1874-Monday] 5 Mag Whitesides & Sally came up to day to help us quilt. They have helpet to take it out & bound it & gone home.

[October 8, 1874-Thursday] Oct 8 this is the day that Bethel presbatary meets at Ebenezer Church. R J has gone as a delagate from Bershaba. We are all well but a great manny deaths with the children from that dreadfull disease, dipthera.

[October 10, 1874-Saturday] 10 I was down with Eliza last night, Hatty was verry bad yesterday, is better this morning.

[October 12, 1874-Monday] 12 R J has got home, had a fine time, got the pasteral relation disolved between Mr Douglass & Bershaba.

[October 13, 1874-Tuesday] 13 Wille took Cate over on yesterday to stay a while with Mag & I have been down to see Mrs M Davis to day, had a fine time. R J was down at Ruff they are not well.

[October 15, 1874-Thursday] 15 R J & Wille is gone to the station with cotton. Fanny & I am here to night by oure selves. The dipthera is still ragging, three & foure in a family & some times too in one day, in one house.

[October 20, 1874-Tuesday] 20 I was up with aunt Emily & cousin Mary last night, all well. Mag Hall was over to day & the babe, Mary. It is growing fine.

[October 25, 1874-Sunday] 25 Mr McComick was here last night & preached to day. His tex was in st John, the fifteenth chapter, fifth verse, "I am the vine ye are the branches." He is with us to night. I have been down to see Eliza & Sally. Sally & I went over to aunt Lisyes to see ould Mrs Berry. She was a dying. Died last night. They are all well.

[October 26, 1874-Monday] 26 Mr McComic, Mary Alexander, & I have spent the day at Mrs Bells & family. He came home with me to night.

[October 27, 1874-Tuesday] 27 Mr McComic spent this day with Mr Cain then to John Davises.

[October 29, 1874-Thursday] 29 R J was over to see Hiram last night. He is verry bad conjestive chill.

[October 30, 1874-Friday] 30 I came from Hirams this evening, they think he is a little better to day.

[November 1, 1874-Sunday] Nov 1 Jaily & Wille was with Hiram last night. He is a little better but verry porly yet.

[November 3, 1874-Tuesday] Nov 3 this is the great election day. The radicals has beet us badly. Sally has been up to day & Cate has gone home with her.

[November 6, 1874-Friday] friday evening the 6 This is the commencement of oure communion. Mr Dickson & Mr Willson was both theire, intended to preach too sermons. Theire was so few out that they preached but one. Too great embasaders fore Jesus. Mr Henry Dickson preached, his tex was in second Corinthians, fifth chapter & twenteth verse. These are the words, "Now then we are embasenders fore Jesus, as though God did beseech you by us we pray you in Christ stead be ye recenciled to God." He preached a great sermon.

[November 7, 1874-Saturday] Satterday evening Mr Dickson preached this morning, his tex was in second Corinthians 32 chapt 25 verse. Mr Lowry Willson preached this evening, his tex was in Revelations 20 chapt, 11. 12. 13 verse. Mr Willson, Mrs Jones, Sally Whitesides, Hatty Whitesides came home with us. We had preachen to night Mr Willson. His tex was in Isaiah 55 chapter, 1 verse, a great man in the pulpet & at the fire side. We doo all love him.

[November 8, 1874-Sunday] Sunday evening Mr Willson this morning. His tex was in Luke 22 chapt, 19 verse. Mr Dickson this evening. His tex in Genases 19 chapter, 17 vers. Wille Davis babby baptised by Mr Dickson, Anny Eliza.

[November 19, 1874-Thursday] 19 R G brought me & little Ally home & took Jaily home with him. Eliza & the babe is dooing well.

[November 22, 1874-Sunday] 22 I have been down at R G & to see Sally, all well. Was at preachen to day. Mr Mcomick preached a good sermon. His tex was in Mathew 21 chap 28 vers, "Son go work in my vinyard to day." Eliza babby was born Nov 16, a monday morning, half past nine. Dr Allison, Mrs Whitesides & myself was all that was there. Mary Castle gave birth to a son a Thursday morning Nov 17 1874 and then died.

[November 24, 1874-Tuesday] 24 Mag Whitesides & I have been to york to day to git her wedding trimmings.

[November 28, 1874-Saturday] 28 Mag Hall has come over to stay a week.

Wille Alexander died the 28 of Nov 1874.

[December 4, 1874-Friday] Dec 4 Mag Hall, Fanny & I was with Eliza last tusday night. They came home & I stayed to help Mag Whitesides to bake her cake. Oure gin house got afire last night and came verry near being burnt up.

[December 6, 1874-Sunday] 6 Mr McComick preached to day, his tex was in Mathew.

John Newman Mcgill & Mag Whitesides was married Dec the 10 1874 by Mr Ross. R J, Cate, Wille, Fanny & I was all theire, had a fine wedding. Eliza was theire with her babe. I stayed till Satterday morning.

[December 14, 1874-Monday] 14 I have been over to see Mart & Mag, all well.

[December 24, 1874-Thursday] 24 Lawson & Mag & Cate is all gone over to stay with Mart.

[December 25, 1874-Friday] 25 Christmas day R J & I took dinner at Cains to night.

1875

[*January 1, 1875-Friday*] Jan 1 1875 Newyears day friday all well & at home. How manny great events have come to pass during the last year, the Heavenly bodies have mooved on, the great wheels, of nature have rooled on, the seasons come & go. How manny of my friends have gone, how manny came. Great God what am I in this wourld, an insect, a nothing? Oh now, a traveler to eternity, a monument of mercy, yes living to prais my God. Oh Heavenly Farther may it not be in vain that thou has spared this unprofitable life of mine to se the light of an other new years day. Enable me to spend it fore thy Glory & Honor, & fore the good of my own never dying Soul.

[*January 3, 1875-Sunday*] 3 sunday evening Joe & Sally was up last night. All been to preachen to day.

[*January 15, 1875-Friday*] 15 I have been down at Ruff, took little Ally home & brought Hatty home with me to go to School to John Alexander.

[*January 17, 1875-Sunday*] 17 Mr McComick preached today.

[January 19, 1875-Tuesday] 19 R J & Jaily has gone down to Joes. He is fixen his house. Cate is going to stay a week.

[January 20, 1875-Wednesday] 20 aunt Marget & aunt Emily is here to night.

[January 25, 1875-Monday] 25 I have been down to cousin Wille Davis this evening. Mart & Mag & unckle Frank Furgison is here tonight. R J is gone to the station & Mr Mc is here to night.

[January 28, 1875-Thursday] 28 Jackson is gone to the station & Mr Mc-Comick is here to night.

[January 31, 1875-Sunday] 31 cousin Wille Brown from noth caroliny took dinner with us to day & Fanny & Hatty has been over to see Mart & Mag.

[February 2, 1875-Tuesday] Feb 2 Wills Brown is working at the pulpit going to make it over in the new & R J is gone down to help Joe. Eliza has come up to day & brought Hatty back to school.

[February 4, 1875-Thursday] 4 verry cold & a big snow & sleet. Cate has been bad with a bealed ear.

[February 6, 1875-Saturday] 6 this is that day the grange meeting at Bershaba. Mr Harrison, Mr McComick & Mrs Davis took dinner with me. The grange[24] failed.

[February 7, 1875-Sunday] 7 Mr Mc preached a great sermon to day. His tex was in Daniel fifth chapter & the thirtieth verse.

[February 15, 1875-Monday] 15 Wille & I have been to york to day.

[February 16, 1875-Tuesday] Joe & Sally mooved to theire own house Feb the 16 1875. R J & I went down to help them. They are verry well fixed up.

[February 18, 1875-Thursday] 18 I have been up to see aunt Emily to day.

[February 19, 1875-Friday] 19 the rev Mr Jonson and Mr Mc took dinner with us to day.

[February 20, 1875-Saturday] 20 Lawsons little Jonny has been verry bad to day with the croop today.

[February 21, 1875-Sunday] 21 Mr Jonson preached a mishenary sermon to day. He has been a mishanary to Turk.

[February 23, 1875-Tuesday] 23 I have had a quilting to day. It has been a verry wet day. Got my quilt out. Expected to have a singing at night. It was so wet theire was not manny come.

[February 24, 1875-Wednesday] 24 all gone. Cate & Wille went home with Mag.

[February 26, 1875-Friday] 26 R J is gone over to help Mart to build his barn, & Sally has been up. Joe has got his foot badly cut. I have been to see Gimmy Love. He is verry bad with the pnewmonia.

[February 28, 1875-Sunday] 28 I was down at Love last night. Gimmy is bad yet. Wille, Fanny & Hatty is gone over to Zion to preachen.

[March 3, 1875-Wednesday] March 3 Mag came home with Cate last night & the creek has got up so she could not git home to day. Her & Cate is gone up to aunt Emilies to night.

[March 5, 1875-Friday] 5 Wille was down to set up with Gimmy last night. He is a little better. R J is gone down to Joes.

[March 7, 1875-Sunday] 7 this has been a verry wet day, another big fressh in the creeks. Eliza & the children came last evening to go to preachen to day but it has rained so that the creeks is all past crossing. Mr Mc & cousin Wille Davis went to the church but theire was no one theire, came on here & took dinner. Cousin Wille is gone home. Mr Mc, Eliza & the children is here, stayed all night. It has cleared of, verry cold & windy.

[March 8, 1875-Monday] 8 All gone home. R G came fore Eliza this evening.

[March 11, 1875-Thursday] 11 Lawson & Mag & the children was here to day, all well.

[*March 12, 1875-Friday*] 12 I have been over to see Mart & Mag. All well. Mart is busy pailing in a new garden. It has been so wet that we have mad no gardens yet.

[*March 13, 1875-Saturday*] 13 R J & Lawson has been at york to day, took down a load of fodder.

[*March 16, 1875-Tuesday*] 16 Jaily was down at Joes last night, all well. John Brown had a log rollen to day. Aunt Emily, cousin Mary, Mrs Cain & I was all theire. Aunt Caty was sick this evening. Mary Alexander came home with me.

[*March 18, 1875-Thursday*] 18 I have been over to cousin Joe Stephesons to day to see cousin Caty. She has the cosumption, she is better now.

[*March 21, 1875-Sunday*] 21 this is sabbeth night. We had a blind baptest preacher with us last night. His name is Mocanson. He preached fore us to day. His tex was in John 3c 16v. He done verry well. They made him up about ten dollars

[*March 22, 1875-Monday*] Lawsons Clarance was born March 22 1875.

[*March 24, 1875-Wednesday*] 24 Jaily & Fanny is gone to a quilting at Mr Cains to day.

[*March 25, 1875-Thursday*] 25 aunt Sally Coldwell, Mrs Cain & aunt Caty & I have been over to see Mag & the babe & took supper with them.

[*March 28, 1875-Sunday*] 28 sabbeth evening, all well, no preachen to day, a calm holly sabbeth day. Oh what a great blessing Gods holly Sabbeth day. Oh that I may make a right improvement of it, blessed emblem of the eternal sabbeth day in Heaven.

[*April 2, 1875-Friday*] Aprile 2 Mag Hall came over to day. Mag & I was over to see Lawson & Mag, they are dooing fine.

[*April 4, 1875-Sunday*] 4 Mag Hall & I have been down to see Eliza & Sally. They came home with us to preachen. Mr Mc gave us a fine sermon, his tex was in 2 Corrinthians 5c 21v. Sally came home with us & took Fanny home with her to stay a week. Mart came for Mag & they are gone home. MDBrown

[April 8, 1875-Thursday] 8 John & Mary Alexander was with us last night. Mrs Cain & aunt Mary Freemon has spent the day with us & aunt Emily to night. Aunt Caty is sick.

[April 9, 1875-Friday] 9 all well. Fanny has not got home yet.

[April 11, 1875-Sunday] 11 Sabbeth evening all well & at home. I have had a fine dayes reading Burket on the beloved evangelist John. He who lay on Christs breast seemes to breath the verry heart of Jesus. Oh what great promises, what faithfull asurence of Christs love if we will love him & serve him.

[April 13, 1875-Tuesday] Gimmy Love & Lissy Land run of & got married Aprile the 13 1875, went to Mr Lathen. He married them.

[April 14, 1875-Wednesday] 14 Sally came up this morning & brought Fanny home. Sally & Cate is gone over to Lawsons.

[April 15, 1875-Thursday] 15 Sally & Cate is gone up to see aunt Emily. Joe & Sally is gone home.

[April 16, 1875-Friday] 16 I have been over to see aunt Margaret to day & it has been a dreadful dayes wind.

[April 18, 1875-Sunday] 18 it is verry cold to day, plenty of frost & ice. The fruit is all killed & the gardens. Mr McComicks tex to day was in John the third chapter, "Verrily, verily I say unto you, you must be born again."Yes we mus be born again ore sink in endless wo, Oh endless wo.

[April 19, 1875-Monday] 19 Lawson & Mag & the children is all over to night.

[April 22,1875-Thursday] 22 Wille & I was over with Mart & Mag last night.

[April 24, 1875-Saturday] 24 I was up with aunt Emily last night & all well.

[April 25, 1875-Sunday] 25 Jaily & Wille is gone over to the schoolhouse to hear Mr Jonson preach to day. We are all well.

[April 28, 1875-Wednesday] 28 Jaily & I have been to york to day, got Cate

a new hat at foure dollars, I a bonet at three & a half.

[April 29, 1875-Thursday] 29 we have all been over helping Mag Brown to sow to day. All well.

[May 1, 1875-Saturday] May 1 Jaily & Wille has been to Center to a big May party to day. We have had a dreadfull storm of rain, wind & hail. It was perty much a herican. They was caught out in it but stoped on the road. God in mercy protected them & brought them home safe, all thanks & prais be to his Glourious name.

[May 2, 1875-Sunday] 2 Mr Mc preached one of his great sermons to day. His tex was in John, "Ye will not come unto me that ye might be saved." It was a great sermon. It seems to me that he is the beginning of a great man if he improves his talents & God in his wisdom adds lenth of days & wisdom as he has commenced. I fear we will not git leaf to keep him. Oure people is so slow and too poor spirited ever to have a good preacher. I pray God that he will awaken them to theire duty to theire own souls, theire duty to theire preacher, theire duty to God. MDB

[May 4, 1875-Tuesday] 4 Jaily & I have been at Ruff at a big quilting to day, did not get the quilt out, had a fine day & dinner & supper.

[May 5, 1875-Wednesday] 5 Jaily & I have been to Bels to day & Fanny to stay with aunt Emily.

[May 9, 1875-Sunday] 9 R J & Wille & Fanny is gone to Bethany to preachen to day, a communion. The first time Fanny was ever theire, Cate & I at home by oure selves, a good chance to read & spend a holly sabbeth previous to oure communion sabbeth, which in the provedence of God, we expect to celebrate on next Sabbeth. Blesed Saviour oh will thou cloth me with that marriage robe which thou did shed thy precious blood to wash away oure crimson guilt. May I come in faith relying on thy precious promises.

[May 12, 1875-Wednesday] 12 I have been verry unwell this week, I feel some better this evening. Mrs Cain has been to see me this evening.

[May 14, 1875-Friday] 14 this is the first day of oure meeting & communion. Mr Cooper has failed to come. Mr Mc preached himself. Aunt Harriet & Em

came home with us. Harriet & I have been over to aunt Margarets. Cousin Emiline has another son, her third. His name is_____. It was born the 7 of May 1875.

[May 15, 1875-Saturday] 15 Mr Mc preached to day. His tex was in Acts this morning 4c 12v. In the evening Daniel 5c 30v. He preached too good sermons. Sally W, Mag H, Butler, Jonny & Em & Lissy came home with us. I have been verry unwell to day. Poore frail dying worm am I. My life is but a span. It may bee nearly run, Oh why should I wish to stay here. Wean my heart from this wourld of sin & sorrow. Oh may I remember my sainted Mothers dy words, "What I say unto you, I say unto all, watch."

[May 16, 1875-Sunday] 16 sabbeth evening & Mr Perry came to assist Mr Mc to day but he is not ordained either. Mr Jonson administered the Lords Supper. Mr Perry preached this evening. His tex was in Math 19c 20v. He done tolerable well. I have been verry unwell. I have not enjoyed it as wel as I ought. Oh this cold stuped heart of mine, how cold & luke warm am I. Come holly spirit Heavenly Dove warm this cold dull stuped heart of mine.

[May 20, 1875-Thursday] 20 Ruff & Eliza & the children was all here to day. Little Alis stayed with me.

[May 23, 1875-Sunday] 23 R J & Jaily went down to Joes last night to go to Salem to day. Sally & Cate have never been theire. Mag has brought Fanny home today. I have got some better. MDBrown

[May 25, 1875-Tuesday] 25 I have been to see cousin Wille Davis little Psalmy. He cant walk none yet, his nee is all drawed. The rest all well.

[May 26, 1875-Wednesday] 26 Cate & Ally has been down to see Mrs Cain.

[May 30, 1875-Sunday] 30 John Alexander & Mary was here last night & Wille went down to Ruffs to go to Sharon to day.

[June 6, 1875-Sunday] June the 6 sabbeth evening Mr Mc tex was in Johns episle 2c 1v. He preached a fine sermon. Mr Mc oganised a sabbeth school to day. May the Lord prosper it. Oh Lord God, will thou own & bless both teachers & scholars.

[June 12, 1875-Saturday] 12 I have been a trip down to see Eliza & Sally, stayed several dayes. Ruff has brought me home this evening & taken Mag home. Lawsons Jonnie has the hooping caughf.

[June 14, 1875-Monday] 14 I have been sick, had a bad spell, am a little better now. Lawsons Jonny has the hooping caugh, got a letter from Eb that little Maud was bad sick.

[June 16, 1875-Wednesday] 16 Sally has been up to day. All well, but Eliza, she had a chill last night. Jonnie is no better, Gimmy has it too.

[June 18, 1875-Friday] 18 Mag Hall was over last night. They are all well. Sent Fanny over to Lawsons. She went to Lawson to keep Mammy from gitting it. Jonny, Gimmy & the babe all has it. Gimmy Loves wife is bad with the fever.

[June 20, 1875-Sunday] 20 Jonnie is bad, the Dr was to see him last evening. I think the babe is taken it. Jimmy caughf bad. John Brown is sick. Fanny has the caughf. Wille is gone to Smerny to day. We have had a heap of rain to day & wind. Looks like it will rain now.

[June 23, 1875-Wednesday] 23 R J & I was down at Hew Loves last night. Gims wife, Lissy is verry bad.

[June 30, 1875-Wednesday] 30 Jaily was at Bells to day to get sue to help her to make her dress & was going to stay with aunt Emily to night.

[July 1, 1875-Thursday] July 1 Fanny Daubson, Margaret Smyth & Cate was all at aunt Emilies to day. Mary & Emily came home with Cate.

[July 4, 1875-Sunday] 4 Mr Mc preached to day.

[July 5, 1875-Monday] 5 I was over to see Mart & Mag last night, all well.

Jackson & I have been down to york to day to get some of Daubsons cheap goods.

[July 10, 1875-Saturday] July 10 Mrs William Enloe gave birth to a daughter to day & died verry suddenly.

[July 11, 1875-Sunday] 11 Mrs William Enloe gave birth to a daughter yesterday morning & died verry suddenly & was buried to day. She looked verry natural.

[July 18, 1875-Sunday] 18 we had preachen today. Cate has went home with Eliza to stay a week with her & Sally.

[July 20, 1875-Tuesday] 20 Mrs Cain & Mrs Freemon was here to day.

[July 23, 1875-Friday] 23 R J is gone down to Joes to night fore Jaily. Lawson, Mag & the children is here to night. They have all got better.

[July 29, 1875-Thursday] 29 I have had a big visit to see Mart & Mag, aunt Harriet, aunt Jane, by york & now home. All well.

[July 30, 1875-Friday] 30 Jaily, Fanny & theire Paw is all at aunt Emilies to day & I have been over with Mag. The children caughf hard yet.

[August 1, 1875-Sunday] August the frist I have come from Ruffs to day. Maggie has the dipthera, was taken bad yesterday morning. Oh I was so afraid of it. The Dr sayes she is not bad but I think she is. Joe has the fever, is some better. Mr McComick preached to day. Jaily & her Paw is gone down to Ruffs to night.

[August 2, 1875-Monday] 2 R J has come home this morning. Maggie is no better.

[August 6, 1875-Friday] August the 6 Friday night little Maggie is no more. She died Thursday morning at too oclock, August 5, after five dayes sickness. The good shepherd has folded her in his arms & taken her home. The blessed Saviour, who while on earth said, suffer the little children to come unto him on earth said, "Of such is the kingdom of Heaven," has taken her home. Sweet little Maggie, I shall see you no more with my natural eyes, but I shall see you, yes & I shall know & spend a long eternity with you. Mr Ross preached her funeral. His tex, "Bless the lord oh my soul."

[August 7, 1875-Saturday] 7 Mr Harrison preached to day, a satterday. His tex was, "Come unto me all ye that labor and are heavly laddend & I will give you rest." Theire was a congregational meeting to day to see what we could make up

for Mr Mcormach. I think we done fine fore what was theire. Mr Harrison, Mr Mc, cousin Psalm Brown, Hiram & Ida Thomison came home with us & took dinner.

[August 8, 1875-Sunday] 8 all well, no preachen. Cate has not come home.

[August 9, 1875-Monday] 9 Ruff has brought Cate home. Eliza & Eddy both has a tetch of the sore throat but has got better but the whole neighborhood is nearly all down with the billious fever. I have spent this evening with aunt Caty & aunt Sally Coldwell.

[August 12, 1875-Thursday] 12 Sally has the fever. Joe has come fore me this evening. Ida Jones died August the 12, gave birth to a son. Both died, burried in one coffin, a metalic case, cost one hundred and five dollars.

[August 15, 1875-Sunday] 15 I have come home from Joes. I have been with Sally since last thursday till this morning. She has been perty bad but I hope the fever is broke. Mr Harrison preached to day fore Mr McCormick. He was to take the vote of the congration whether we would put in a call fore Mr Mc. It was such a wet day and a bad turn out, it was laid over fore another time. Mr Harris tex was in Math 2 "They would not come."

[August 16, 1875-Monday] 16 R J has gone to take Jaily down to stay with Sally. She is not dooing so well. Aunt Sally Coldwell & aunt Caty has spent this evening with me.

[August 18, 1875-Wednesday] 18 Fanny went over to see Mag Hall to day, all well.

[August 19, 1875-Thursday] 19 Ruff & Eliza was up to day, went to york and left Eddy with me. Lawson & Mag & the children is all here. I am verry unwell to day. Sally is better.

[August 21, 1875-Thursday] 21 Jaily has come home to day & brought Sally home with her. She looks worsted, stood the trip perty well. MDBrown

[August 22, 1875-Sunday] 22 this is a verry wet Sabbeth day. Sally, Mag, Lawson & John Brown is all here to day. I have been trying to make them improve themselves, reading, asking questions and singing.

[August 23, 1875-Monday] 23 Sally is still better. Wille is gone to take her home. Mart came fore Mag yesterday evening.

[August 24, 1875-Tuesday] 24 aunt Emily is here to day. I have been bad with my head and teeth.

[August 25, 1875-Wednesday] 25 Mrs Land & cousin Emiline Floyd was here to day.

[August 26, 1875-Thursday] 26 Cate is gone to help Sue Bell to quilt to day.

[August 28, 1875-Saturday] 28 Eliza & the children came up last night & I was bad with my teeth. The first visit they have had since little Maggies death. Theire is a picknick at the mineral spring to day. Jaily, Wille, Fanny, Hatty & Mary is all gone.Aunt Emily, aunt Caty, Jane, Lawson & Mag & the children, Ruff & Eliza & theire children, John & Mary Alexander has all been here to day. Ruff came fore Eliza & the children. I have not been well, all gone now, quiet & calm.

[August 29, 1875-Sunday] 29 this is the fifth sabbeth oure little Preacher is gone to mount vernon to preach fore Mr Jonson today. We are all at home. I feel some better. John Enloe died August the 13 1875. Cousin Wille Davis little Psalmy died at his unckle Deals in Chester August 26 1875 & was buried at Bershaba the 28.

[August 31, 1875-Tuesday] 31 R J & Jaily & Fanny is gone to a big Grange meeting & picknick at Smerny.

[September 1, 1875-Wednesday] Sept 1 Gim Love & his wife, Mary & Bell love spent this evening with us.

[September 5, 1875-Sunday] Sabbeth eveng the 5 Mr Mc preached too great sermons to day. These are the words, "Is theire no balm in Gilead, is theire no physion theire?" In the evening it was, "As fore me and my house we will serve the Lord."

[September 8, 1875-Wednesday] 8 cousin Psalm & Margaret Brown came up yesterday morning. Them & I went over to Mr Jonsons & spent the day, came back & stayed all night with us.

[September 9, 1875-Thursday] 9 I have been helping Mary Alexander to quilt to day.

[September 11, 1875-Saturday] 11 I have been down at Mrs Davis last night. Edner is verry bad with dipthera. Willes little Eddy is theire with it too. Edner in one room and Eddy is in another. I don't think Edner can live long. Edner Brown died a Satterday night at nine Sept the 11 1875. It seems that cousin Sue will go crazy. She takes her death so hard.

[September 13, 1875-Monday] 13 Lawsons Jonny has the dipthera perty bad. Dr Jackson was out to see him this morning. Edner was buried to day. Mr Jon-son preached her funeral and Mr Mc gave a prayer.

[September 15, 1875-Wednesday] 15 Sally was up yesterday. I went down with her to Ruffs. Little Mary was taken with the sore throat this morning. She was sleeping with me. She awoke before day. She said, "Grand maw my throat is sore." She said that she felt like she was going to dye. Her Farther & Mother arose & sent fore the Dr Alison & Dr Hamrite. They done all they could but poore little sufferer, they could doo her no good. Fanny has taken the sore throat & her Paw came after me to come home. Her throat is perty sore.

[September 17, 1875-Friday] 17 Cate & Fanny both has the Dipthera. The Dr has been to see them. They are not verry bad. John Davis & Mrs Mary Davis was here to day. Mrs Davis washed theire throats and burnt them out. Robbert love has buried his fourth chile with dipthera to day, has but one more and it has it. Mary is no better. Jonny is bad too.

[September 18, 1875-Saturday] 18 Wille & I was down at Ruffs last night. Mary is no better, dose suffer dreadfull. obbert Mcelwees little Caty died of dipthera the 18 of September 1875.

[September 19, 1875-Sunday] Sunday morning 19 Cate & Fanny is better, Jonny is no worse. Joe came fore me this evening to go to Ruffs, little Mary died of diptheria a monday evening after six dayes exquisit pain, asleep in Jesus, blessed sleep from which she shall never wake to weep. Mr Mc preached to day.

[September 27, 1875-Monday] 27 Wille & I went to the buring. Fanny & her Paw came home. Cate staid with her sister to help her to mind little Ally. She has it bad. It seemes that the Drs cant doo nothing fore it. Mag Magilles,

Thomis Dickson was born Sept 25 a satterday morning 1875. Little Ally died Sept 26, a Sunday morning 1875 of diphtheria. All was done that fond parents, Drs & friends could doo, but Gods will must be done. Oh that we may submit without a muring word.

Ruff Knox & Sue Bell was married Sept 28 1875 by Mr Jonson.

[October 1, 1875-Friday] Oct 1 this is the commencement of oure comunion. Mr Mc preached to day. His tex was, "Reppent ye fore the kingdom of Heaven is at hand." Ruff & Eliza came up to preachen this morning. They look verry lonley & solitary. Theire three darling babes gone.

[October 2, 1875-Saturday] 2 oure ould Mr White preached to day. His tex was in Job, "I know that my reddemer liveth." Frank Furgison, Sue Glenn & too children, & Davis, Butler & Nanny, Ida & Lis Thomison, cousin Addy Brown is all here to night.

[October 3, 1875-Sunday] 3 Mr White preached to day. His tex in Psalms, "Oh let me not forget Jeruselum." He preached a great sermon. He told us never to forgit ould Bershaba. Fanny has joined the church. Her name wrote in the Lambs book of life. Send thy holy spirit to santify her & lead her in the path of the Just fore Christs sake. Oh my God I have one son, too son in laws without God, without Christ, with out hope. Heavenly Farther though who a heart of adament can melt hasten that happy peried when they shall turn to the Lord with all theire heart & take thee fore theire portion fore time and Eternity, is the prayer of thy humble servent.

[October 8, 1875-Friday] 8 I have been down to see Mrs Cain to day. Jackson is gone to Ruffs. Little Eddy was sick last night.

[October 9, 1875-Saturday] 9 Eddy is better. Cate, Wille & Fanny is all gone to the schoolhous to a singing to day.

[October 23, 1875-Saturday] 23 Elizas little Eddy is sick, got the dipthera. Robbert Love has lost his last child. Robbert Mcelwee has lost three children in a short time with dipthera, all he had. Eddy is still sick. So many little children taken home, housed a way safe in Heaven. Eddy has got better.

[December 12, 1875-Sunday] Dec 12 Mr Mack preached to day, came home with us to night.

[December 13, 1875-Monday] 13 R J & Mr Mack is gone a visiting to Joe Neels & Aida Jacksons.

[December 14, 1875-Tuesday] 14 met the grange to day.

[December 17, 1875-Friday] 17 I have been over to help Mag to make Marts coat. It is verry cold & the children is gone to Jenkens to a singing.

[December 19, 1875-Sunday] Sunday the 19 I was up with aunt Emily last night & they have took them negroes to jail.

[December 22, 1875-Wednesday] 22 I have been down to see Eliza and Sally to day & cousin Andrew Lathem was on a visit here to day from Missippia.

[December 23, 1875-Thursday] 23 William & Matty Coldwell has buried theire babe to day. Mart & Mag was over & took fanny home with them.

[December 24, 1875-Friday] 24 Cate & Wille is gone down to Joes to day.

[December 25, 1875-Saturday] 25 Christmas day I have been here by myself. Cate & Wille is gone to Ruffs. Fanny is with Mag Hall. R J is gone a hunting. Aunt Emily is here to night.

[December 26, 1875-Sunday] sunday 26 have no preachen to day. Wille has come home.

[December 27, 1875-Monday] monday night 27 Wille has gone to a singing at John Knoxes. R J is gone to Marts. Im at aunt Catyes.

[December 29, 1875-Wednesday] 29 Cate has come home to day & brought Hatty. Wille is gone to Marts fore Fanny. Unckle Frank Furgison was here last night.

[December 30, 1875-Thursday] 30 Wille & Fanny is come home & Em has come with them. All gone to a singing at Mrs Scoggins to night. It is near the close of another year, a year that will long be remembered by many a heart stricken parent. This year, yes long will they remember 75.

1876

[*January 1, 1876-Saturday*] A new years day 1876 a satterday evening my God has spared this life of mine through another year to combat with sin, the flesh & the Devil. What another year will bring forth is known to God only. Heavenly Farther into thy hands i, this day, commend myself, my Husband & children & theire little ones & all that I have to thy care & keeping fore an other year. Take us all under thy care and keeping. Direct us by thy holly spirit, guide us through life, prepare us for death, receve us into Glory when thou hast done & served thyself with us blow fore Christ sake Amen. Teach me to say, not my will oh Lord but thine be done. Unworthy Mary

[*January 1, 1876-Saturday*] 1 there is a singing at the church to day, the children is all gone. A singing at Lawsons to night. Wille & Ida came up to go. Matty, Jeffry, Mammy Black all gone.

[*January 2, 1876-Sunday*] 2 Cate, Wille, Fanny, Emma, Thomison & Hatty Whitesides is all gone to a preachen to smerny to day.

[January 5, 1876-Wednesday] 5 Sally has been up to day, took Fanny & Em home with her.

[January 8, 1876-Saturday] 8 gone to a singing at the church to day. Cousin Wille & Eliza Davis is here to day.

[January 9, 1876-Sunday] 9 Mr Mc preached to day. His tex was in Amos 4c 12v, "Prepare to meet thy God."

[January 14, 1876-Friday] 14 Ruff & Sue Knox is here to night. R J is gone down to Ruffs.

[January 15, 1876-Saturday] 15 Eb & Em & four children came back from Tenesee Jan the 15 1876, left little Netty remains theire.

[January 16, 1876-Sunday] 16 theire has been a good manny in to see Em to day.

[January 17, 1876-Monday] 17 Mag Hall has been over to day.

[January 19, 1876-Wednesday] 19 Eliza & Sally & Joe has come up to day to see Em. Eb & Em & the children is all gone home with them.

[January 23, 1876-Sunday] 23 aunt Harriet & Wille came up last night. Eb & Em came back, all gone to preachen to day.

Eb & Em has been visiting over to Marts & Hirams.

[January 27, 1876-Thursday] 27 Lissy Love sent fore me last night but no go. Eb & Em & the children is all gone to Marts & Cate.

[January 29, 1876-Saturday] 29 Sally Hall has brought Cate home this morning & Em has come. All gone to the singing at Bershaba. John Brown is teaching a singing.

[January 30, 1876-Sunday] 30 fifth sabbeth, no preachen.

[February 4, 1876-Friday] Feb 4 Grange met to day. A singing here to night. Mag Hall & Sally stayed all night. Em & the children is gone to Meek Whitesides to day.

[February 13, 1876-Sunday] 13 Mr Mack preached to day his tex was in first Timithy 1 chapter this is a faithful saying.

[February 16, 1876-Wednesday] 16 R G and Eliza was up to day.

[February 17, 1876-Thursday] 17 this is the day that Eb raised his house.

[February 19, 1876-Saturday] 19 this is the last day of theire singing. I have been to York with R G.

[February 20, 1876-Sunday] 20 Wille & I have been over to see cousin Cate Stencen to day. Lawsons Clarence was baptised by Mr Mc, Jan 9 1876. Gimmy & Lissy Loves infant son was born & died Feb 14 1876. Mary Alexanders babe was born Feb 16 1876. MDB

[February 26, 1876-Saturday] 26 I have been a trip to see Eliza & Sally, all well. Sally came home with me, Joe came up tonight.

[February 27, 1876-Sunday] Sabbeth 27 Mr Mc preached to day his tex was in Luke the 11c 9 10 verses. Theire was a fine congragation of people.

[February 28,1876-Monday] Monday 28 Mrs Mary Davis, Mrs Sally Davis, Miss Mary Davis & cousin Sue Brown was all on a visit to see us to day.

[February 29, 1876-Tuesday] 29 Eb & Em mooved to the log cabbin on the hill Feb 29 1876.

[March 2, 1876-Thursday] March 2 I have been down to see ould Mrs Davis to day.

[March 3, 1876-Friday] 3 Grange met to day, a day long to be rememberd. A day of dark deeds to some living on this Globe, nothing but the blood of Christ can wash a way. Some that reads this will understand, some will never. MDBrown.

[March 5, 1876-Sunday] 5 ould Mr Robbert Whitesides died March 5 1876. I have been over to see Harriet & Mag, all well.

[March 10, 1876-Friday] 10 this is the first day that Wille has worked on the road.

These nine notebooks were used by Mary Davis Brown to keep a record of her thoughts.
They are housed in the Manuscripts Division at the South Caroliniana Library,
University of South Carolina and are in fragile condition.
The diaries may be accessed through microfilmed copies.
(Photo Courtesy of Betty Talley Stevens)

Mary Davis Brown
(Photo Courtesy of Joanne Thomas Smoak)

Robert Jackson Brown
(Photo Courtesy of Joanne Thomas Smoak)

Cotton Belt Elementary School circa 1901

Front row: Janie Land, Mary Jones, Rob Jones, Paul Brown, Banks Stevenson, Lewis Good, Bratton Land, John Land, Cortis Brown, Charlie Smith, William Brown. Second row: Unidentified girl, Mary Brown, Reba Cain, Janie Hall, Sallie Whitesides, Rob Brown, Jim Land, five unidentified boys. Third row: Hattie McAfee, Ethel McAfee, Mary Land, Jessie Carroll, Mary Whitesides, Will Land, Vance Whitesides, Howard Smith, Martin Whitesides
(Photo courtesy of Minnie Price Brown Talley)

Lawson Brown and Family.
Standing in rear: Lowry McAllison Brown, John Jackson Brown, Frances Inez Brown.
From left: Thomas Clanton Brown, Mattie Anolia Brown, Robert Lawson Brown,
Mary Florence Brown, Margaret Jane (Maggie) Castles Brown, Roy Grady Brown on lap,
James Castles Brown, his wife, Ola Mary Cline Brown, Stella Edith Brown on lap.
(Photo courtesy of Julian Brown McAuley)

**Sallie Dorcas
Brown Whitesides**
*(Photo courtesy of
Maurice Alsing, Jr.)*

**James D. and
Frances Vance
(Fannie)
Brown Land**
*(Photo Courtesy of
Jane Land Ratliff)*

Emily Brown Castles *(Photo courtesy of Rebecca Thomas Chambers)*

Daguerreotype of RJ and Mary Davis Brown with son Lawson and unknown couple in wagon. Taken at the Brown farm on Beersheba Road, York County, SC. (Photo courtesy of Maurice Alsing, Jr.)

**Margaret Hannah (Mag)
Brown Hall**
*(Photo courtesy of
Laura Settle Gibson)*

Daniel Martin Hall
*(Photo courtesy of
Laura Settle Gibson)*

Family of William Given and Mary R. Minnie Price Brown taken in 1929.

First row: Neil Brown, Joe Wallace, Robert Brown, Dewey Gentry, Howard Thomas, Jean Thomas, Laura Brown, Elizabeth Brown, Ruth Wallace, William Wallace. Seated: John Brown, Myrtle Brown, Peggy Brown with Jaily Cate Brown Whitesides, William Given Brown, Mary R. Minnie Price Brown holding Muriel Brown, Kate Neil, Mary Brown Wallace holding John Wallace, Robert Jackson Brown. Standing: Moffatt Thomas holding twins Moffatt, Jr. and Miriam, Wilene Brown, Pauline Brown, William Brown holding Edward, Margaret Brown and her sister, Annie Neil, Minnie Brown, Joe Brown, Alma Brown Thomas, Eva Brown, Lawson Brown, Kate Brown Thomas, Esther Brown Gentry, Paul Brown, Alice Carroll Brown, Fred Thomas. (Photo courtesy of Minnie Price Brown Talley)

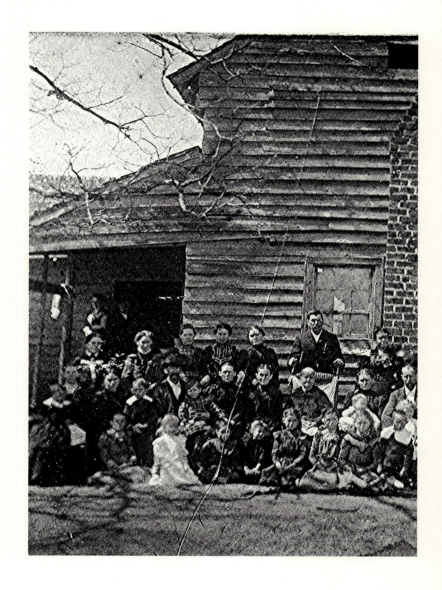

Mary Davis Brown and family pose in front of the Mary
and RJ Brown home. Mary moved to the house
(built around 1821) as a young bride.

**Photo of Mary Davis Brown at her 78th birthday on March 21, 1900.
Photographer, John R. Schorb.**

*On the roof: Vance Whitesides, Brown Whitesides, Will Land, James Land.
First row: Reba Cain, Sallie Whitesides, Esther Brown, Edith McGill, Mary Brown,
Kate Brown, Janie Land, Mary Davis Brown, Bratton Land, Minnie Given Brown,
Lawson Brown (on lap).
Children on knees: William Brown, John Land, Cortis Hay Brown, Paul Brown,
Rufus G. McGill, William E. McGill*

258

Children behind boys on knees: Haskell Land, Rob Brown, Martin Whitesides,
H. Bonner McGill
Second Row: Leslie Burns, Mary Whitesides, Mary Land, Ethel McGill, Jessie Land,
Mary Susan Hall, Sallie Brown Whitesides, Eliza Brown Whitesides, Frances Brown Land,
Jaily Catherine Brown Whitesides, William Given Brown, Mrs. S. H. Hay,
Margaret Castles Brown
Third Row: James D. Land holding Earl Land, Rachel Burns, Bell Whitesides, Jim McGill,
Maggie Brown Hall, Joe Whitesides, James C. Brown, Rev. Hay, Lawson Brown,
Rev. Oates, Hattie Whitesides McGill.
(Photo Courtesy of Joanne Thomas Smoak)

**Wedding Photo of William Given Brown and
Mary R. Minnie Price on February 2, 1887**
(Photo courtesy of Minnie Price Brown Talley)

Eliza Brown Whitesides and Rufus Grier Whitesides
(Photo courtesy of Roger Harold Whitesides, Jr.)

Sylvester S. Whitesides
*(Photo Courtesy
of Maurice Alsing, Jr.)*

**Jaily Catherine
(Katherine) Brown
Whitesides**
*(Photo Courtesy
of Maurice Alsing, Jr.)*

[March 12, 1876-Sunday] 12 Mr Mack preached to day, his tex was in 5 Zechariah 4c 13v.

[March 13, 1876-Monday] 13 I have been up to see aunt Emily to day.

[March 14, 1876-Tuesday] 14 I have been down to Mr Cains to day. Mr James Willson was here last night & spent the night. He is a fine young man studding for the ministery. He is under the care of bethel Presbatary.

[March 17, 1876-Friday] 17 I was down to see Ruff Whitesides. A mule threw him & hurt his shoulder & side, he is better. This has been a dreadful day of wind.

[March 18, 1876-Saturday] 18 Mart has brought Mag up to stay a few days & it is dreadfull cold.

[March 19, 1876-Sunday] 19 Press McAphee & John Brown & Mag is here to day, verry cold.

[March 20, 1876-Monday] 20 March 1876 there has been a big snow last night & still snowing and freezing, dreadfull cold.

[March 21, 1876-Tuesday] 21 Wille is gone to take Mag home. I have been over with Em in her new cabin.

[March 23, 1876-Thursday] 23 R J is gone down to see Eliza & Sally. Cate, Wille & Fanny is all gone up to see aunt Caty & I am by myself.

[March 24, 1876-Friday] 24 John & Mary Alexander & aunt Emily is here to night.

[March 26, 1876-Sunday] 26 sabbeth evening Mr Mc tex to day was in Psalms 126c 6v, a fine sermon.

[March 27, 1876-Monday] 27 I have been over to see Mag Hall & she is not verry well.

[March 30, 1876-Thursday] 30 I have been to York to day, took Cate down & left her with cousin Fanny to stay a week.

[April 1, 1876-Saturday] Aprile 1 Eliza & Sally came up yesterday morning & is now gone home.

[April 2, 1876-Sunday] 2 no preachen to day. Aunt Caty has been here to day we have been reading & asking questions.

[April 4, 1876-Tuesday] 4 Fanny is gone over to see Caty Jackson to day. They dont think she can live much longer. Em & Lenny is gone theire to night.

[April 5, 1876-Wednesday] 5 Caty Jackson died April 5 1876.

[April 6, 1876-Thursday] 6 John & Polly Brown from noth carolina has been here to day. Oure Grange met this evening. Mrs Margaret Johnson joined to day. Jaily has not got home. MDB

[April 16, 1876-Sunday] 16 Mr Mc preached to day, a fine sermon. His tex was in first Timothy second c fifth v "For their is one God and one mediator between God and men, the man is Christ Jesus." 16 sabbeth evening all well. I have been over with Mag for a few days. They are not well. Mart and Mag is both complaining.

[April 17, 1876-Monday] 17 R J and Wille is gone to the station to day. Eb and Em is here to night, all is well.

[April 18, 1876-Tuesday] 18 Mags Daniel was born April the 18, a Tuesday night. Dr Jackson, aunt Harriet & myself was all that was theire, she got along fine.

[April 21, 1876-Friday] 21 this is the commencement of our communion. I am still with Mag, her & the babe is dooing fine.

[April 22, 1876-Saturday] 22 this is satterday night Sally Hall came home with me this morning and went to preachen. Mr Cooper preached this morning, his tex was in Isiah 39c 4v, in the evening Ezekiel 36c 27v. He preached very good sermon. Wille, Ida & Em Thommison, Sally Whitesides, Hatty M is all that we have to night.

[April 23, 1876-Sunday] 23 the dog threw little Mary out of the porch & knocked her elbow out of place.

[April 24, 1876-Monday] 24 Hatty is with us this week & Cate is over with Mag.

[April 26, 1876-Wednesday] 26 I have been down to see Mrs Cain to day.

[April 27, 1876-Thursday] 27 Fanny & Hatty has been up to see aunt Cate to day and gone up to stay with aunt Emily to night. Ould Mr Sutton died April 27 1876. MD Brown

[April 30, 1876-Sunday] 30 Wille & Fanny went home with Hatty last evening & went to Smerny to day. Cate is gone to Smerny too. Fanny is going to stay a week with Hatty.

[May 2, 1876-Tuesday] May 2 Mrs Scoggins, Davis & Ann has spent the day with us.

[May 4, 1876-Thursday] 4 I have been over to see Mag & the babe to day. They are dooing fine & brought little Mary home with me.

[May 5, 1876-Friday] 5 Grange meeting to day.

[May 6, 1876-Saturday] 6 Mrs Cain was here to day.

[May 7, 1876-Sunday] 7 Sabbeth all well, no preachen to day.

[May 9, 1876-Tuesday] 9 Joe has brought Fanny home to day.

[May 12, 1876-Friday] 12 Mary and Lissy Love, Emily & the children is all here to day.

[May 13, 1876-Saturday] 13 Cate has been up to see aunt Emily.

[May 14, 1876-Sunday] 14 Sabbeth, Wille is gone over to Hirams to go to Shilo to the meeting.

[May 17, 1876-Wednesday] 17 aunt Emily, Em and Jane, Em and the children is helping me quilt to day.

[May 18, 1876-Thursday] 18 Press is here last night. We have all been at

preachen to day. Mr Mc tex was in Jeramiah 10v 25c, this evening Acts 13c 41v. "Behold ye despisers, and wonder, & perish."

[May 19, 1876-Friday] 19 this is the day that Fanny has started to school to Mrs Mary Davis. She boards at Ruff Whitesides

[May 21, 1876-Sunday] 21 this sabbeth I am at home to guard the house.

[May 23, 1876-Tuesday] 23 I have been over to see aunt Harriet & to see Mag to day, all well but Wille Thomison, he has a bad cold and pane in his head.

[May 25, 1876-Thursday] 25 I have been down to see Eliza, they are all well. Joe has the chills. Sally is not well.

[May 27, 1876-Saturday] 27 Cate was over with Mag last night. Mart is gone to cherryvill for corn.

[May 28, 1876-Sunday] 28 this is the day of the comunion at Bethany, it has been a wet morning. Cate did not go, Wille went.

[May 29, 1876-Monday] 29 Cate & Fanny is gone down to ould Mrs Davis to night, going to see cousin Wille & Eliza Davis tomorrow.

[June 1, 1876-Thursday] June 1 aunt Emily, John and Marg Alexander was here last night. Eliza & Sally has been up here to day helping us to quilt.

[June 2, 1876-Friday] 2 Mrs Cain, Mrs Freemon, aunt Caty & Em has been helping us to quilt. I have been to the grange.

[June 3, 1876-Saturday] 3 Mart brought Mag & the children up this morning. Mag and I went over & took dinner with Mrs Scoggins then supper with Em.

[June 4, 1876-Sunday] 4 Mr Mc preached to day, his tex was in Colotions. This is the words, "Grieve not the holly spirit." He preached a great sermon. Mart & Mag is gone home.

[June 6, 1876-Tuesday] 6 all well, cutting wheat to day. It is perty good. Eb & Ike Smith is cutting. Em and the children is over.

[June 7, 1876-Wednesday] 7 Lenny & I have been to York to fix Fanny to go to school.

[June 9, 1876-Friday] 9 Cate & Fanny is gone down to Mrs Cains. Wille is gone to Center.

[June 11, 1876-Sunday] 11 I was up with aunt Emily last night. John is gone to york. Cate, Wille & Fanny is gone to Zion to preachen.

[July 18, 1876-Tuesday] 18 R J is gone down to cousin Psalms Brown and to see Eliza and Sally, all well.

[July 19, 1876-Wednesday] 19 Sally has come home with her paw. Eb, Em & the children, aunt Emily & Sally is all here to day & Sally, Cate & Wille is all gone over to Ems. We are all well.

[July 22, 1876-Saturday] 22 Fanny & Hatty has come home to day to go to the picknick at the mineral spring to day.

[July 23, 1876-Sunday] 23 all well & preachen to day.

[July 24, 1876-Monday] 24 Cate is gone up to stay with aunt Emily to night.

[July 26, 1876-Wednesday] 26 aunt Caty & John took dinner with us to day.

[July 29, 1876-Saturday] 29 R J & I was over at Hirams last night. He has been sick, he has got better. R J & I have been to Center to preachen to day. They have been preachen their three dayes. The communion is to take place tomorow. They have four preachers, Mr Watson, Mr Lathan, Mr Luther Willson & Mr McComick. Mr Lathen preached this morning. His tex was in Isah 3c 11 verse. Mr Willson this evening, his tex was in Ruth the 16 17 verses. They both preached great sermons, trying to bring sinners to Jesus to love God.

[July 30, 1876-Sunday] 30 Cate & Wille is gone to Center to day. Margaret Ann Mcelwees William Coldwell landed back the 23 of this month safe & sound, brought Tompson & the babe with them, Martha Meek & her too youngest children, Nanny and Ruff. They look hearty and well.

[July 31, 1876-Monday] 31 Mrs Cain, Martha Meeks & her too children,

Nanny & Ruff, aunt Caty & John & Em & her children was all with us to day.

[August 5, 1876-Saturday] August the 5 Jackson & I have been a big trip up to noth Carolina this week. Went up to brother Johns a Tusday & stayed untile friday had a pleasent trip, found them generaly well.

[August 6, 1876-Sunday] 6 this is the sabbeth we was to have preachen to day but the minister failed to come, a young Mr Clifford from Union.

[August 7, 1876-Monday] 7 Ruff & Eliza, Hatty & Ed was all here to day.

[August 12, 1876-Saturday] 12 Fanny & I was over to see Mag last night all well. Ann Brown is worse.

[August 13, 1876-Sunday] 13 the sabbeth, no preachen. Ann is bad. Cate is gone over to see her. M D Brown

[August 15, 1876-Tuesday] 15 R J is gone down to the oule Dr Alisons to day. The Elders is to meet their to day.

[August 20, 1876-Sunday] 20 a sabbeth evening have been at preachen, have heard great preachen. Mr Macks tex this morning was in Revelations 21c 78 verse, in the evening, Psalms 10c 27v. He done a great dayes work. Ruff & Sue Knox had their first born baptised to day, Its name is Minna Jonson. Newmon & Mag Magill was here last night & Sally.

[August 21, 1876-Monday] 21 Sally & her paw has been over to see Davis & Ann. They are a little better & to see aunt Harriet & Mag, all well.

[August 22, 1876-Tuesday] 22 Lenny is gone to take Cate over to stay with Mag this week & olde aunt Mary & I have done a big dayes washing. John Caldwells Daughter, Emma was burried the 20 of August.

[August 27, 1876-Sunday] 27 Mag Hall came over last night & brought Cate home & is now gone home.

1877

New Years day 1877

[January 1, 1877-Monday] a monday evening It has been a dreadfrell day of wind & snow. The snow was about ten inches deep before. It has been the coldest winter I have felt fore years. Wille has come from Joes to day.

[January 6, 1877-Saturday] 6 Mart & Mag came over last night, had Mamy & Danne with them. Elizas, Jonny Wade was born Jan 5 1877.

[January 8, 1877-Monday] Mr McComick came here to bord Jan 8.

[January 9, 1877-Tuesday] 9 I have been staying with Eliza. Her & the babe is dooing fine.

[January 10, 1877-Wednesday] 10 Fanny is gone down to stay with Eliza & Mr Ruff Alison & Mr McComick is gone to Dr Camels.

[January 14, 1877-Sunday] 14 Mr Mack tex to day was in Romans, "Rejoice

with them that rejoice & weep with them that weep." We had Mr Thomis Scot with us last night. He is a from the Thornwell Orphenage. Fanny has come home to day. Eliza & little Wade is dooing fine.

[January 15, 1877-Monday] Mr Mack has commenced school to day up at the cross roads. Mary Bryan gave birth to too twin daughters, both dooing fine Jan 15 1877.

[January 16, 1877-Tuesday] 16 we had a singing last night. Wille, Ide, Em & Lizzy Thomison, Camel Jackson, & Richerd Mathes stayed all night. Em & Lis has started to school to Mr Mack to day. Cate has gone home with Will & Ida. Fanny went with Em to school to day. I dont feel well to day.

[January 20, 1877-Saturday] 20 Mrs Mary Davis has spent this day with me, the last that she may spend soon, as she is going to leave us. She is going to live with her Brother, John Black in Fairfield, I will miss her. Mr Mack has been down to see ould Mrs Davis to day.

[January 21, 1877-Sunday] 21 This has been a wet day & did not go to preachen.

[January 24, 1877-Wednesday] 24 I have been down to see Eliza. She is not well. I was to see Joe & Sally, all well.

[January 28, 1877-Sunday] 28 at preachen to day. Mr Macks tex was in Mathew 16 "Deny thyself." He preached a good sermon. Ruff Alison & Dudly Jones came home with us. Cousin Gus & Ginny Deal had theire children baptised to day, Psalm Miles, Agustes More.

[January 30, 1877-Tuesday] 30 I have had a housfull of company to day. All well.

[January 31, 1877-Wednesday] 31 I have been to see Mrs Mary F Davis to day. She is going to leave us. The Church will miss a devoted member & we will all miss a good neigbour.

[February 1, 1877-Thursday] Feb 1 I have been to york to day.

[February 2, 1877-Friday] 2 Mag Hall & the children has been over to day, all well.

[February 3, 1877-Saturday] 3 Mr Mack, Em, Ginny & R J & I have been down to Mr Cains today.

[February 4, 1877-Sunday] 4 This has been a wet sunday & I have not been at church.

[February 7, 1877-Wednesday] 7 R J & I have been to cousin Psalm browns to day to take a birth day with him.

[February 9, 1877-Friday] 9 Cate, Wille & Fanny is gone over to Marts to go to a singing at the Ginkens & John Brown, Em & Ginny is gone too. Mr Mack has taken Libby home.

[February 11, 1877-Sunday] 11 Mr Macks tex was in Ephesians, "Train up a chile in the way he should go." I tell you he gave us a hard sermon.

[February 15, 1877-Thursday] 15 I have been down to see cousin Sue Brown, went on & stayed all night with Eliza, took dinner with Sally & then home.

[February 16, 1877-Friday] 16 Mr Mack has gone home with Em & Ginny stayed.

[February 18, 1877-Sunday] 18 Mr Macks tex was in_____

[February 19, 1877-Monday] 19 Hatty has come up this evening to go to school.

[February 21, 1877-Wednesday] 21 Lawson & his Paw is gone up to the station to day & they have a singing at John Alexanders to night.

[August 2, 1877-Thursday] Aug 2 Cate & Fanny is gone over to the Chapple to a singing to day. Wille is gone to york.

[August 4, 1877-Saturday] 4 Cate & Wille is gone down on clarks fork to a picknick. R J is gone over to Mart Halls.

[August 5, 1877-Sunday] 5 sabbeth day R J is gone over to the chapple to preaching to day. Mr Mack is gone to Alison creek.

[August 7, 1877-Tuesday] 7 I & Em Furgison has been to york to day.

[August 12, 1877-Sunday] Sabbeth evening 12 Mr Lourry Willson has preached for us to day. He preached to the young Men this morning. His tex was in Psalms 1 19 verse 9. He preached to the young Ladies this evening. His tex was in first Timothy fifth c 2 verse. He is a good & great man.

[August 13, 1877-Monday] 13 this is the commencement of oure proctracted meeting. Mr Harison preached this morning. His tex was in Psalms the 15 chapt, "Lord, who shall abide in thy Tabernacle, who shall dwell in thy holy hill." Mr Luther Willson preached this evening. His tex was in Psalms 51 chapt, 12 13 verses. A great sermon. No company to night.

[August 17, 1877-Friday] friday evening 17 Mr Willson preached this Morning. His tex was in John 3 c 5 verse. Mr Henterson this evening, Hosey 10 c 12 verse.

1878

The new year of 1878

[January 1, 1878-Tuesday] A new year the ould is past & gone with all of its pleasures, all of its sorowers. Many of my friends & neighbors have gone to theire long home & I am here yet, the spared monument of thy grace. Thou still has something more fore me to do. O my Heavenly Farther prepare both soule & boddy, mind & will to make a better improvement of the dayes that thou hast granted unto me. They may bee few ore they may be many. Enable me from the heart to say, not my will, Oh Lord, thine be done.

Tusday, a new year day this is the day that John Alaxander mooved down to Beth shilo. R J is gone to hall him a load. Cousin Jaily Masabo is on a visit to see her friends. She has too nice little daughters, Lissy & Fanny. She is here to day & aunt Emily, Sally Whitesides, Hatty Whitesides & many another one. Theire is a singing at Mrs Blacks to night. Dudly Jones & Mr Elder is here.

[January 2, 1878-Wednesday] 2 Eliza came up to day to see Jaily Masabo & her sister, Cate went home with her.

[January 3, 1878-Thursday] 3 Milten Jackson & Alevia Land was married to day, also Ruffus Stepheson & Miss Lorena Dickson, by Mr Jonson.

[January 5, 1878-Saturday] 5 I have been down at Cains today. He has had a barn raised.

[January 6, 1878-Sunday] 6 Mr Mack preached to day. I was not theire. It was a verry cold day & I stayed at home & kept Mags children. Mart & her was here last night. Cousin Emiline Floyd & Emily & the children has been here to day.

[January 7, 1878-Monday] 7 Cate is down helping Mrs Cain to make her a new dress.

[January 8, 1878-Tuesday] 8 this is a verry cold day & is a snowing.

[January 11, 1878-Friday] 11 Mr Henterson took dinner with us to day, also Mag & the children. Davis Brown & Ann & theire three children is here to night. I have been over to see Ann to day. Ruff has brought Cate home this evening & she brought Eddy home with her to stay a week. Emily & Lenny is over to night.

[January 12, 1878-Saturday] 12 I have been to york to day. Sylvanas White-sides is here to night fore his last time.

[January 13, 1878-Sunday] 13 M Jackson has ould Mr McElwee a running of that land fore Lawson and Eb.

[January 15, 1878-Tuesday] 15 Bob Castle & Mary Whitesides is here to night. I have been on a visit to Mr Cains to day.

[January 16, 1878-Wednesday] 16 Mart has been over to day & bought Law-sons mare. Matty, Fanny is gone home with him. They have a party theire to night. Cate & Wille is gone.

[January 17, 1878-Thursday] 17 Sally came up to preachen to day but Mr Mack has changed his day till the 2 and 4. Wille & Fanny is gone over to the Chapple to hear Mr Jonson. Mrs Cain, Mrs Freemon, & aunt Sally Coldwell & aunt Caty has all been on a visit here to day.

[January 18, 1878-Friday] 18 we have had a singing here to night. Hatty Whitesides & Maggy Whisenhunt stayd all night.

[January 19, 1878-Saturday] 19 I have been over with Lawson & Mag to day.

[January 20, 1878-Sunday] 20 This is the sabbeth. I was not, did not go to church. Mr Macomick & Mart Hall came home with them. Cate & Wille has been down to see aunt Margaret Floyd. She is verry low. Ann & the children has been here to day.

[January 23, 1878-Wednesday] 23 R J & aunt Caty & John & myself have been over to unckle Hirams. He gave us a birth day dinner on yesterday. He was _____. Theire was a good manny their.

[January 24, 1878-Thursday] 24 I have been over to see Em this evening. I feel verry unwell.

[January 27, 1878-Sunday] 27 sabbeth evening Mr Mack has disapointed us to day. We all went to the church but he failed to come. Aunt Harriet & Em was here last night. I have been down to see the children. Joe is not verry well. Jonny Willson & Jonny Nickles was here last night, all well.

[January 30, 1878-Wednesday] 30 wensday evening a most dreadfull day. It has been verry cold. Davis and Ann Brown mooved to theire new cabben Jan 22. Aunt Margaret Floyd departed this life Jan 26, a tusday evening, 1878.

[February 3, 1878-Sunday] Feb 3 Mr Mack preached to day. His tex was in_____.

[February 19, 1878-Tuesday] Emit Walker & Miss Lissy Camel was married Feb the 19 1878.

[February 28, 1878-Thursday] 28 Mr Canidy was here last night. Wille has taken him down to John Davis.

[March 1, 1878-Friday] March the 1 all well, a beautifull day. I am working in the garden. Em Castle & the children was over this evening. Em Furgison & Fanny is gone over to John Mathews. MDB

[March 3, 1878-Sunday] 3 cousin Wille Davis brought Mr Canida up yesterday morning. He preached to day. He red the 37 chapt of Ezekle. His tex was in Colosians 2 c 10 verse. He preached a good sermon. I think he has improove a good deal.

[March 5, 1878-Tuesday] 5 I have been at york to day.

[March 6, 1878-Wednesday] 6 Jane is here putting in her web to day.

[March 9, 1878-Saturday] 9 Eliza & the children was up last night, all well. John & Mary Alexander & aunt Emily came up today.

[March 10, 1878-Sunday] 10 Mr Mack preached to day. His tex was in Philipians 2 c 12 verse, "Work out your own salvation with fear and trimbling." Aunt Emilies is all with us to night.

[March 12, 1878-Tuesday] 12 Mart has brought Mag & the children up to stay a while. Mag & Cate is gone over to stay with Emily to night.

[March 13, 1878-Wednesday] 13 I have been over with Em to day. Maud is sick.

[March 14, 1878-Thursday] 14 R J is gone to take Mag home.

[March 15, 1878-Friday] 15 Lawson had a house raising to day. I have been over theire to day.

[March 17, 1878-Sunday] 17 this is the sabbeth. We have no preachen to day. Aunt Emily is here. She is sick with the cold.

[March 19, 1878-Tuesday] 19 Ida Scoggins & a Miss Maggy Mathews is here to night.

[March 21, 1878-Thursday] 21 I have been up to see Hallbrook Good & his wife to day. I was verry well pleased with her.

[March 23, 1878-Saturday] 23 Ruff & Eliza is gone to york & left Wade with me.

[March 24, 1878-Sunday] 24 we have had preachen to day. Mr Mack has been gone a long time up to Morganton to see his girl. His tex was in first Timothy 2 c 5 vers. I dont think he done as well as I have heard him. The fault may be mine. I would be glad how soon he would marry fore I think he would doo better.

[March 25, 1878-Monday] 25 aunt Emily & I have been over to see Lawson & Mag to day.

[March 26, 1878-Tuesday] 26 this is the day that they have raised the tan yard house. Theire was a good manny here.

[March 27, 1878-Wednesday] 27 I have been down to see Eliza & Sally to day, found them all well.

[March 28, 1878-Thursday] 28 Fanny & I have been to cousin Gim Floyds to day.

[March 29, 1878-Friday] 29 aunt Emily & I have been over to see Emily to day, all well.

[March 31, 1878-Sunday] 31 Cate, Wille & Fanny is all gone to the Chapple to preachen to day & aunt Caty is sick. Aunt Emily is gone home. MD Brown

[April 5, 1878-Friday] Aprile 5 I was over at marts last night, all well. Called to see Ginny Curry. She has got a fall and bad hurt.

[April 7, 1878-Sunday] 7 Wille has been down to see Sally, all well.

[April 11, 1878-Thursday] 11 Cate went down to see Sally last night & she has come home with her.

[April 12, 1878-Friday] 12 I have been to york to day.

[April 15, 1878-Monday] monday 15 I have had a big trip down to bethshilo. Aunt Caty, John & Em and Jackson and I sence last satterday morning. Mr Lathen preached in the morning, Mr Mack in the evening. His tex was in Mathew 11 c 28 v, then we went home with Molly & Renes & took dinner with them, then went on to aunt Emilies. Was highly pleased to find them so well fixed. To preachen a sunday. Mr Mack preached. He did not doo much,

had the comunion, then home.

[April 16, 1878-Tuesday] 16 I have been over to see Polly Burns. She has got a fall and got hurt.

[April 17, 1878-Wednesday] 17 I have been helping Em to make Lennies close to day.

[April 21, 1878-Sunday] 21 Fannie and I have been over to Smerny to preachen to day. Mr Boyce preached this morning. He preached a fine sermon. His tex was in St. John 13 c 31 v.

[April 29, 1878-Monday] 29 oure meeting is over. Mr Cobbet of noth carolina preached a satterday morning, tex Mathew 19 c 42 v. Mr Henterson in the evening. Sally Whitesides & Lissy Thomison was all the company we had. Mr Cobbit preached a sunday morning. His tex was in Mark 8 c 34 v. He preached a good sermon. Then the communion services. Dr Cobbit done fine. Aunt Emily, John & his family came home with us. Eb was sick. Em did not git out.

[May 1, 1878-Wednesday] May 1 all well. Cate & Fanny was down at cousin Gim Floyds last night.

[May 4, 1878-Saturday] May 4 1878 Davis & Wille at the lime kill last night.

[May 5, 1878-Sunday] 5 Mr Dick Mathes & Mr John Waren was here to day.

[May 13, 1878-Monday] 13 I have been over to see Aunt Harriet & Mart & Mag, all well.

[May 18, 1878-Saturday] 18 I was down at cousin Wille Davises last night & we have had a hail, rain & win storme. Destroyed things bad. Had to plow some of the cotten up after it had been worked over.

[May 19, 1878-Sunday] 19 Cate, Wille & Fanny has gone over to the Chapple to preachen. Mrs Cain, Aunt Caty, Jane & Sally Whitesides has been helping Cate to quilt to day.

[May 22, 1878-Wednesday] 22 I have been to york to day, took supper with Sue Knox.

[May 25, 1878-Saturday] 25 Mr Henterson & Mrs Molly Fewel, Eliza Ann & Hatty was all here to day.

[May 26, 1878-Sunday] this is the Sabbeth evening & Cate has gone home with Sally & Joe to stay a week. Mr Mack was out to day with his new bride. He preached too good sermons. His tex was in Mathew 21, "Son, go work to day in my vineyard," this evening in Mark 2 c, "They that be holde have no need of a physician but they that are sick." Cousin Jonny Willson & Jonny Nickles last night. Mr Maccomick & Miss Minny pearson was married May 16 1878 by Mr Anterson at Morgaton. Mrs Ginkens died with a stroke of parralis May 18 1878.

[May 28, 1878-Tuesday] 28 Emily & myself have been over to se Ann Brown & Fancis Mathews.

[May 29, 1878-Wednesday] 29 I was down with ould Mrs Freeman last night. She is sick. Mrs Margaret Jonson & the children was here to day.

[June 2, 1878- Sunday] June 2 cousin Gim Floyd & his wife was here last night. Eb, Marg & Sally, Emily & Lenny & Wille is gone to Ruffs.

[June 10, 1878-Monday] 10 ould Mrs Freemon is here to day.

[June 15, 1878-Saturday] 15 Mr Henterson was here last night. He & R J is gone to Salem.

[June 16, 1878-Sunday] 16 Wille, Fanny & I have been over to the Chappel to preachen to day. Mr Jonson on the sin of Adom.

[June 17, 1878-Monday] 17 Em & I have been to see Mrs Cain to day.

[June 23, 1878-Sunday] 23 Gus Mathews & Jonny Warren was here last night & Joe brought Sally up. Mr Mack preached to day. John & Mary Alexander came up last night. Aunt Emily stayed.

[June 26, 1878-Wednesday] 26 I was at Ruffs last night, took Cate down. Ruff, Cate, Hatty & Lizzy Whitesides is all gone own to the Station to the commencement.

[June 29, 1878-Saturday] 29 I was over to see Mag last night. Aunt Caty & aunt Emily has been helping us to quilt to day.

[July 1, 1878-Monday] July 1 Mr and Mrs Mack & Miss Sally Pearcen has been here to day.

[July 2, 1878-Tuesday] 2 Em is sick last night.

[July 5, 1878-Friday] 5 theire was a big picknick at Cains spring on yesterday. Joe & Sally & Hatty was up. Ida & Em Thomison, Sally & Hatty stayed all night.

[July 6, 1878-Saturday] 6 Mary & Bill Love was here to day.

[July 7, 1878-Sunday] 7 this is the Sabbeth, no preachen. Wille is gone to see Mart & Mag.

[November 4, 1878-Monday] Nov. 4 Vilet Daubson was born_____

[November 6, 1878-Wednesday] Francis Mathews, Psamuel beafurd was born Nov 6 1878.

[November 9, 1878-Saturday] Mags son was born Nov 9 1878.

this is the time of oure fall Meeting. I have been staying with Mag & missed the meeting. They had fine preachen, Mr Leeper.

[November 13, 1878-Wednesday] 13 I have got home from Marts to day. Mag & the babe is dooing fine. Eliza, Emily, Sally & Cate was all to see her.

[November 15, 1878-Friday] 15 R J is gone to the sale at ould Mr Bryans.

[November 17, 1878-Sunday] 17 Fanny has come home from staying with mag, all well.

[November 20, 1878-Wednesday] 20 aunt Sally Coldwell, aunt Caty, aunt Mary Freemon all spent the day with us.

[November 21, 1878-Thursday] 21 Sue bell today.

[*November 30, 1878-Saturday*] 30 Cate & I have been down to york, stayed all night with Clem.

[*December 2, 1878-Monday*] Dec 2 I have been down to see Eliza & Sally. The first night that I have spent in theire new house. Mr Ross was theire too, all well. I spent this day with Miss Sally Davis.

[*December 4, 1878-Wednesday*] 4 Em & the children was here to day.

[*December 5, 1878-Thursday*] 5 Sue Knox was here to day.

[*December 6, 1878-Friday*] 6 Mr and Mrs Mack was here last night & to day. Miss Mag Mathews to night.

WHAT R J BROWN HAS BOUGHT IN 1878

coffy & soda in Jan 28	1.10
March 6 coffy	1.00
sugar & rice 1	1.50
salt 50 cents	.50
Aprile 12 shirting	1.65
buttens & thhread	.15
dye stuff	.40
Aprile 24	
24 sugar & coffy	2.00
25 fish	1.00
buttens	.25
Cate a pare shoos	1.50
June 12 sugar & coffy	2.00
July 25 sugar & coffy	2.10
September 13 sugar	1.11
meat & rice	2.75
soda ten soap ten	.20
chickens	1.00
sugar	1.00
coffy	1.00
meat	1.00
sugar soda	.50

On the bottom of this page she had the following addresses:

Jaily Massebea
Mrs Jaily E Massebea
Lydia P. O.
Darlington County S Carrolina
Mrs Mary L Davis
post office
ridgeway, Fairfield So Ca.

WHAT I HAVE BOUGHT 1878

one bunch yarn & pins	1.20
cards	.50
March 5 shoose	1.50
dress 80, needles 10	.90
soap 25 thimble 5 tea 10	.40
seeds 20, indig 10, paper 5	.35
paper & envelops	.25
pepper 10, one bunch yarn	1.20
fine comb 15 soda 10, musterd 10	.35
thread, needles, nutmeg	.25
lamp & hinges	.35
buttens, hooks, matches	.30
bucket, cake cutter	.40
lamp oil & Cologn	.25
yarn	1.00
white cloth & shoostrings	.75

WHAT I HAVE SOLD 1878

one pare pants	1.75
cloth Janes	4.20
butter	.45
bags March 5	7.80
eggs	.25
Aprile butter	.70
socks	.40
8 bags	5.20
May 22 butter	1.12
chickens & eggs	.65

Mr Mack too chickens May 30
too pounds butter   .50

it is the prayer of youre poor Mother that we will be among the sheep on the right hand of God to hear that welcom plaudit, "Come ye blessed of my farther where the kingdom prepared fore you from the foundation of the world." But if we should be found among the geats, oh that awfull sentence. You can read their doom in that chapter. Ruffus & Eliza, Joe & Sally, my dear children, acording to the flesh, Gods dear children by proffesion read his blessed word. See what great and presious promises he has made to his dear children. Also the awful threatnings to them that doo not love him. This is Gods blessed sabbeth day, blessed emblem of the eternal sabbeth in heaven. It has rained so we have not had eney preachen. Will went up to the church. Theire was a few theire but no preachen but I have had a fine sabbeth days reading Dr Plummers book, The Rock of Oure Salvation, also I have read the 25 chapt of Mathew & the explanation on it. I want you all to git it & read it. Read it & study it, also a tex. I want you to find & answer me, "Master which is the great commandment in the law & the second is like unto it." Also first John 4, the too last verses. I know not whether I shall ever behold one of your faces on earth again fore we know not what a day ore an hour may bring forth but I doo know that I shall meet you all the judgement bar of God.

1879

[*March 9, 1879-Sunday*] March the 9 this is the day that Mr Leeper has preached at Bershaba for Mr Mack. His tex was in Mathew the 11 chapt 28 verse. He made the greatest prayer this morning I think that ever I heard & as great a sermon as ever I would want to hear. May God grant that it may make a lasting impression on my mind.

[*March 10, 1879-Monday*] 10 I have been down at york to day.

[*March 15, 1879-Saturday*] 15 J Land is here to night.

[*March 16, 1879-Sunday*] 16 Wille & Fanny is gone to the chapple to day.

[*March 22, 1879-Saturday*] 22 I have been down to see Eliza & Sally. Joe & Sally have come home with me.

[*March 23, 1879-Sunday*] Mr Mack has preached one of his good sermons to day. He done fine. His tex was in Isah 40 chapt. 31 verse. He had his wife with him. He is a dear little man to me. It would been good fore manny an one if they had never been born the way they have persecuted him but I Beleve that God will bring him out victorious fore his own name sake. MD Brown

[March 30, 1879-Sunday] March 30 Eliza & Hatty came up last night. Hatty is away going to school now. A young soceder preacher by the name of Mr McClain preached fore us to day. His tex was in Romans 5 c and 8 v. He done tolerable well but he cant tetch oure little preacher. Ruff & Eliza, Joe & Sally, Mart & Mag all took dinner with us this evening. Cate went home with Mag to stay a week

[April 7, 1879-Monday] Aprile the 7 Jackson & I went up to Bethel on last friday morning to Presbatary. We had a fine time, had some great preachen, saw a heap of the preachers. Bethel is a great church, a fine conaragation of people. Ould Mr Watson preaches theire. He has preached theire fore forty one years, is now in eighty third year. Mr Lrethome preached a satterday morning. These are the words, "Another foundation can no man lay than that is laid which is Christ Jesus." Mr Leeper preached a sunday morning. His tex was in Mathew 27 c 42 v, "He saved others, himself he canot save." He preached a great sermon. We staid one night with Newton & Sue, one night with Gimmy & Mag. They are all gitting along fine. Sue has foure children, Henry, Ninny, Davis & Maggy, fine looking children. I had a bad cold & sore throat which made me not enjoy it as well as I would have done. Come home & found Cate bad with the sore throat.

[April 8, 1879-Tuesday] 8 Miss Minny May & Cousin Mag Jeffery is here to night.

[April 10, 1879-Thursday] 10 Cate & I have got better.

[April 12, 1879-Saturday] Cate & I have been to york to day the 12, a satterday.

[April 13, 1879-Sunday] Sabbeth evening 13 Mr Mack preached to day. His tex was in Mathew the 7 c 7 8 verses. He done well as ushal. Cousin Addy Brown is verry bad at this time. We had a stranger at preachen to day, Mr Tom Bell. Mag Hall is bad with the pains at this time. MD Brown

[April 17, 1879-Thursday] thursday 17 I have been over staying with Mag hall a few dayes. She is bad with the pains. Fanny is gone down to Joes to night.

[April 18, 1879-Friday] 18 Mag has got wors & sent for me this morning.

[April 24, 1879-Thursday] 24 I have stayed with Mag a week. She has had a bad spell but has got better. Aunt Harriet was up theire to day. Came home & found Cate bad with the pains.

[April 25, 1879-Friday] 25 this is the commencement of oure communion. Mr Mack preached to day. His tex was, "The foxes have holes, the birds of the air have nests, but the Son of man hath not whare to lay his head."

[April 26, 1879-Saturday] 26 Mr Canida from North Caroliny preached to day. His tex was in Genesis 28 c 12 v. His tex in the evening was about the Eagle. He is a good plaine preacher. The people was well pleased with him. Theire was 8 children baptised this morning, too joined the church, Mr Paul Rasulky & his wife.

[April 28, 1879-Monday] 28 I have been over to see Em today.

[April 29, 1879-Tuesday] 29 I have been down to help Mrs Cain to quilt to day.

[May 2, 1879-Friday] May 2 Fanny has been over to see Jane Furgason to day.

[May 7, 1879-Wednesday] 7 this is the day of the meeting at Smerny. Wille is gone.

1880

[January 1, 1880-Thursday] Jan the 1 1880 a thursday morning Here I am in health & strenth this beautifull new years morning, a monument of the love & mercy of my God that I am on the land of the living. Oh no, not the land of the living but the land of the dieing. In my Farthers house is the home of the living fore my saivioure has told me that he is gone to prepare a place fore me & that he will come fore me. When that day ore houre is to come is known only to my Farther in Heaven. He has told me to have oil in my lamp, have it well trimbed when the bride groom comes. Heavenly Farther I come before thee this day as I comence a new year. With thy grace strenthing with the aid of thy holy spirit to live a better life than I have done, the one that is past & gone. I often think that my dayes are to be but few. Not my will oh Lord but thine be done. I may have manny a hard struggle yet before the dross is consumed & the gold is refined.

Jan 1 thursday evening Lawson & his too sons, Gimmy & Jonny & Davis Brown has taken dinner with us to day. Ida & Ginny Thomison & a young Mr James Miller, Ginnys bow came up here this evening & we have had a singing to night.

[January 2, 1880-Friday] 2 Ida, Ginny, Miller & Cate is gone over to see Gimmy & Fanny.

[January 3, 1880-Saturday] Ann Browns ___ was born Jan the 3. John Alxander & family is up.

[January 4, 1880-Sunday] 4 sabbeth day the first sabbeth in a new year. We have no preachen but we have his holly word, his dying will & legacy to his children that we may eat & drink & never thirst again.

[January 6, 1880-Tuesday] 6 Fanny has been over to see us to day & I went with her as far as Mr Cains to see Mrs Cain. She is sick.

[January 7, 1880-Wednesday] 7 I have been over to see Em this evening. She is bad with her teeth acking.

[January 8, 1880-Thursday] 8 I have been over to see Ann & the babe. They are dooing fine.

[January 9, 1880-Friday] 9 I have been up to help Jane furgison to quilt to day.

[January 10, 1880-Saturday] 10 the deacens of oure church had a meeting at oure house to day. Mr & Mrs Mcomick, Hiram & Buttler Thomison, Mr Loury Smyth & Lawson, my son. Mr Mack went to John Davis, Buttler home with Lawson, Hiram with us.

[January 11, 1880-Sunday] Sabbeth evening 11 Mr Mack preached to day. His tex was in Romans the 12 c & 1 verse. He preached a good sermon on the commencement of a new year. Oh what unprofatable servents we are, oh how prone we are to let the flesh & the wourld draw us away from thee, oh my God, oh my God, leave us not, oh forsake us not. Draw oure hearts from the wourld. Thou hast said where youre treasure is theire will youre hearts be also.

[January 12, 1880-Monday] 12 Salvanas Whitesides was here last night. I have been down to see Mrs Cain. She has the fever. She is gitting week. Cate is gone over to see Fanny.

[January 13, 1880-Tuesday] 13 aunt Emily was here to day. Jane Furgison,

Emily Castle & children, Wille & Mr Houser, that is oure shoo maker, is gone to Marten Dixcens to a singing to night. MD Brown

[January 15, 1880-Thursday] 15 aunt Emily, aunt Caty & I have been over to see Emily to day.

[January 16, 1880-Friday] 16 Cate has been to see Mag Hall to day, all well.

[January 18, 1880-Sunday] 18 Wille & Howser is gone to the chapple to day.

[January 19, 1880-Monday] 19 R J has gone to take aunt Emily home.

[January 20, 1880-Tuesday] 20 Sally & I have been to see Gimmy & Fanny to day, all well.

[January 24, 1880-Saturday] 24 I have been over at Marts to stay with the children till they would go to the station to see Dr Ray. They have all the fever. They are mending slowly. Mrs Jane Ray died Jan 12 1880.

[January 25, 1880-Sunday] 25 sabbeth evening I have been sick with the cold but was abble to go to curch to day. Heard Mr Mack preach one of his good sermons. His tex was in Rev 2 c 10 verse, "Be thou faithfull untill death & I will give thee a crown unto life." Oh my Heavenly Farther, the spirit is willing but the flesh is weak, consume thou the dross that the gold may be refined, that I may be worthy of that crown of life.

[January 26, 1880-Monday] 26 Cate has been down to see Mrs Cain. She is no better.

[January 27, 1880-Tuesday] 27 Cate, Wille & Howser is gone over to John Matheus to a singing to night.

[January 29, 1880-Thursday] 29 Gimmy & Lenny was over last night, all well. Cate is gone down to see Sally. She is sick. Here I am all alone, oh no, I have the best of company, my God & my Bible. The pleasentest houre that I enjoy, sweet solitude, sweet solitude.

[January 30, 1880-Friday] 30 Ruff & Eliza was up last night. The little stranger is growing fine. They have gone back.

[January 31, 1880-Saturday] 31 cousin Robbert Brown, cousin Hollman, Emiline Floyd was here to day. Emily & the children is over here to day.

[February 1, 1880-Sunday] Feb 1 Sabbeth evening I have been over to see aunt Harriet to day. She is some better. She has had the shingles.

[February 2, 1880-Monday] 2 We have a big snow to day & verry cold.

[February 3, 1880-Tuesday] 3 Cate & Wille has gone over to see Fanny to night.

[February 5, 1880-Thursday] 5 Emi Thomison has come up this evening. Cate, Wille & Ema is gone up to John Coldwells this evening to a party.

[February 7, 1880-Saturday] 7 I was over with Ann last night. Her & the baby is both sick.

[February 8, 1880-Sunday] 8 sabbeth evening I have been to the house of the Lord to day to hear what God the Lord had to say to me. Mr Macks tex was in Philippians 3 14 "Press forward toward to the prise of the high calling of Christ Jesus." Oh what poor gravling worms we are when we have such great & glourious promises of reward if we would hold out faithfull till the end. Mart & Mag has come home with us.

[February 9, 1880-Monday] 9 Emily, Mag & Cate is all gone over to see Fanny to day.

[February 11, 1880-Wednesday] 11 Lawson & Wille is gone to york to day. Fanny has been over to day.

[February 14, 1880-Saturday] 14 I was at a quilting at cousin Gim Floyds on yesterday. Sally came up last night & is gone home.

[February 18, 1880-Wednesday] 18 Cate & I have been down at york to day.

[February 19, 1880-Thursday] 19 Cate is gone over to see Fanny to night.

[February 21, 1880-Saturday] 21 Gimmy Land & Wille is gone to kingsmountian to a big celebration, George Washington birth day. Fanny is here.

[February 22, 1880-Sunday] 22 Mr Macks tex was in first Thessalonians 5c 22 v "Abstain from all apperances of evil." He gave the dancers a hard rub.

[April 1, 1880-Thursday] Aprile 1 I have seen Bethel Presbatary organized once more. A fine turn out of Ministers & Elders. We have three Ministers, Mr Watson, Mr Say & Mr Pratt, elder Mr Bookman. Mr E Brantley preached. His tex was, "The fool hath said in his heart, theire is no God." Ministers 16, elders 25.

[April 2, 1880-Friday] 2 day friday ministers 18, elders 28. Too candidates for the ministary. We have with us to night, Mr Watson, Mr Say, Mr Pratt, Mr Lourry Willson, elders, Mr Bookman, Mr Davidson, & Sally Whitesides.

[April 3, 1880-Saturday] satterday evening Bethel Presbatary has closed. They have licend too young men to preach. They both preached theire trial sermons this morning. Mr Mathews, Mr McClure. His tex was in John 14 c 11 verse. They both done fine. I love Mr Mathews best. Our Preachers is all gon, that is, all that staid with us. Mr Bookman is here, Ruff & Eliza & the children & Sally is all we have to night.

[April 4, 1880-Sunday] Sabbeth evening I was sick last night. Went to preachen this morning, heard Mr Mills preach but felt so bad that I have not enjoyed it. His tex was in Acts 2 c 38 v. John & Mary Alexander is with us.

[April 6, 1880-Tuesday] 6 Em & the children was over to day & Fanny. We had a big hail storm on yesterday.

[April 8, 1880-Thursday] 8 of Aprile this has been a cold day, rain & snow. If the ground had been dry we would have had a big snow.

[April 10, 1880-Saturday] 10 R J & I went down to see Joe & Sally on yesterday, took dinner with them then went over & stayed with Ruff & Eliza. All well. I stoped & spent the day with ould Mrs Davis. She was sick.

[April 11, 1880-Sunday] Mr Mack preached to day 11. His tex was in Romans 11 c 36 v, evening tex Ephesians 2 c 1 verse. He preached too good sermons. MD Brown

[April 16, 1880-Friday] James Coldwell died Aprile 16 1880.

[April 21, 1880-Wednesday] 21 I have been over to see Fanny. Her & James came home with me.

[April 22, 1880-Thursday] 22 John Alexander has come after aunt Emily this evening.

[April 25, 1880-Sunday] 25 I have been over with James & Fanny. James has been bad with the colic, has got better. Mr Mack preached today.

[May 1, 1880-Saturday] May 1 Cate & Wille, James & Fanny & a company of them is gone to Kings mountin to day to view it.

[May 5, 1880-Wednesday] 5 Mrs Cain was here to day. She is gitting better.

[May 6, 1880-Thursday] 6 aunt Caty, Jane & I have been to see Fanny to day.

[May 9, 1880-Sunday] 9 James & Fanny has both been sick, have got better. Wille is gone to Sharon to day to the communion.

[May 14, 1880-Friday] 14 Ruff & Eliza & all the children, Amanda Whitesides & Sally was all here to night. Hatty & Amanda is going to school at york.

[May 16, 1880-Sunday] 16 Wille & I was at Marts last night, went to the Chapple to preachen to day. Mr Carliles preached in the morning. His tex was, "Theire remaineth a rest to the people of God." Mr Booser this evening. They done verry well.

[May 23, 1880-Sunday] 23 sabbeth evening. Mr Mack preached to day. It has been a wet morning for preachen.

[May 27, 1880-Thursday] 27 I have been to see Fanny to day.

[May 28, 1880-Friday] 28 I have been to see Em to day.

[May 29, 1880-Saturday] 29 Cate & Gimmy is gone to york this evening.

[May 31, 1880-Monday] 31 Davis & Ann has been sick. I have been theire sence yesterday morning. They have got better.

[June 4, 1880-Friday] June 4 Aunt Harriet & Ginny has been up on a visit. They have been to see all. We have been to see Fanny today, all well.

[June 6, 1880-Sunday] 6 Gimmy & Fanny was over last night.

[June 8, 1880-Tuesday] 8 Em & Cate has been over to see Fanny & help her sow.

[June 13, 1880-Sunday] 13 sabbeth evening. Mr Mack preached to day. His tex was in Ezekiel 33 c 7 verse, baptised thre children, one for Davis & Ann Brown. They called her Ela Davis, one for Buttler & Nanny Thomison, _____ Hunter, one for William & Mag Burns.Its name, Nancy Francis. Eixany organised oure sabbeth school.Sylvanis Whitesides has got back, was here last night.

[June 15, 1880-Tuesday] 15 Emily & I have been over to see Gimmy & Fanny to day, had a fine rain. Wille is gone dow to see Sally.

[June 20, 1880-Sunday] 20 Jackson is gone over to see Mart & Mag last night, going to Bethshilo to day, going to see aunt Emily to night.

[June 21, 1880-Monday] 21 Fanny has been over to day, Cate is gone down to Cains with her.

[June 26, 1880-Saturday] 26 Mr McComick has had a meeting at the church this evening asking questins, preached a short sermon. His tex was,"Search the scriptures fore in them ye think ye have eternal life." MD Brown

[June 27, 1880-Sunday] 27 Sabbeth evening Mr Mack preached to day. His morning tex was in the Acts of the apostles 20 c 28 verse. He preached a sermon to the elders then sunday school. I have a class of little boyes, Sue Brown little girls. His tex was "Love youre enimies."

[July 2, 1880-Friday] July 2 I have been up helping Aunt Caty to quilt to day. Aunt Sally Coldwell is helping her. Eb & Em & Fanny has been over this evening.

[July 4, 1880-Sunday] 4 Cate & Wille has been over to Smerny to preachen to day. Lawson & Mag was at Meek Whitesides last night.

[July 6, 1880-Tuesday] 6 I have been at york to day.

[July 7, 1880-Wednesday] 7 Fanny is over to day. James & Eddy Land, Wille is all gone to the river a fishing.

[July 8, 1880-Thursday] 8 I have been over to see Francis Mathes. She was taken verry bad this evening. We have had a fine rain. Lenny is gone home.

[July 10, 1880-Saturday] 10 John Brown & Cate is gone to Union to a pick-nick to day.

[August 16, 1880-Monday] Aug 16 I have been down at Bethshilo to a com-munion meeting. Heard Mr Talor preach. I think he is a good preacher and a good man. His tex was, "In forty days Ninava shall be destroyd." I was well pleased with him. He is a new man in our Presbatary. Wille & I went & stayed all night with aunt Emily to see Mary. She is verry bad with the consumption, cant live long, came on back & stayd a day & night with Fanny. Wille, Gimmy & Edy is all going to a writting school.

[August 17, 1880-Tuesday] 17 Fanny came home with me. Cate & Fanny is gone over to Davis to see Ida Waren & the baby.

[August 19, 1880-Thursday] 19 Sally has been up to day, gone home. Sylva-nis is here to night.

[August 22, 1880-Sunday] 22 sabbeth evening we have had no preachen to day, oure preacher has gone away on a mountian trip.

[August 24, 1880-Tuesday] 24 Cate & her Paw has been down to see cousin Mary. She is no better. MDBrown

[August 26, 1880-Thursday] 26 I have come through another hard and trying scene. We have seen oure little Wady sicken, suffer & dye. A solom warning it out to be to us all to see what sin has done. To see a sweet inicent chiled suf-fer, so his work is done, gone home as a jewel to deck the Crown of his Blessed Saiviour. He sufferd and died for Adams sin. He lives fore Christ has died. Dear little Wady died August the 25, a wensday evening, Heavenly Farther give us grace, give us a submissive heart to say, not my will be done but thine. Oh Lord enable the heart stricken Parents to beare it with submission feeling that they have greater treasure in Heaven, fore Christ has told us whare youre treasure is theire will youre heart be also. Eb & Em, Fannie & I have come on home. We did not go to the burring. Cate is gone to stay till sunday.

[August 29, 1880-Sunday] 29 Mr Talor preached for us to day. His tex in the morning in first Kings 6 c 7 verse in the evening it was in ___. Ruff has brought Cate home this morning. They are all well but the babe has a bad cold. Newton & Sue Genn & theire children was all here last night & Jonny Riddle.

[August 31, 1880-Tuesday] 31 we have a barn raisen to day. Fanny is over.

[September 3, 1880-Friday] Sept 3 I was over to se Mart & Mag last night. Jonny has been sick but better. Jane Furgison is sick.

[September 5, 1880-Sunday] 5 Cate & Sylvannas is gone to Bethany to day. This is the time of theire Presbatary.

[September 8, 1880-Wednesday] 8 Ruff & Eliza, Hatty & the little children all came up yesterday & went to york, came back & stayed all night & is now gone home. Cate is gone to see Fanny.

[September 9, 1880-Thursday] 9 Cate & Fanny has come home to day.

[September 12, 1880-Sunday] 12 this is the Sabbeth day. I have been over at Marts sence last thursday. Little Jonny is verry sick, no better. The Dr sayes it is dispepsy. Mr Mack has got back. He preached to day. His tex this morning was in Philippians 1 c 6 verse, in the evening in Genesus about Noah preachen to the people. Mr and Mrs Mack came home with us. Cate & her paw is gone over to Marts, cate is going to stay.

[September 13, 1880-Monday] 13 Mart has brought Mag & the children up to stay a while. Jonny is a little better but verry poorly yet.

[Sepember 14, 1880-Tuesday] 14 Mag, Fanny & myself have all been over to see Em to day.

[September 15, 1880-Wednesday] 15 Eliza & Sally has come up to day to see Mag & the babby. Mart has come fore them and they are gone home. Jonny has got some better. Mart is not well.

[September 17, 1880-Friday] 17 Miss Rachel Coldwell has been here on a visit, the first time she has been here in years.

[September 18, 1880-Saturday] 18 Fanny came over this evening & took Cate home with her. It goes verry hard with them to be parted. They are so much set on each other.

[September 19, 1880-Sunday] 19 sabbeth evening R J, Wille & I are by oure selves to day. A fine day fore reading, praye & meditation. Often doo I repeat that sweet hymn of Muhlenbery, "I would not live alwayes, I ask not to stay." Dear Children when you sing this hymn think of youre Mother. Christ has said, "In the world you shall have tribulation but be of good cheer."

1881

A new years day 1881

[January 1, 1881-Saturday] satterday morning we have a big snow & verry cold, all at home.

[January 2, 1881-Sunday] 2 I have been over at Ebs to see Neel. He is sick.

[January 4, 1881-Tuesday] 4 Wille has gone to take Cate & Mary Hall over to Fannies.

[January 7, 1881-Friday] 7 Sally, Hatty & Eddy came up this morning. Em & Eb & the children & Sally & Hatty is gone home & it is a snowing.

[January 9, 1881-Sunday] 9 it is the sabbeth but the ground is all coverd with ice. I did not go to church. Mr Mc was theire. Mart & Mag was over.

[January 10, 1881-Monday] 10 this is the day Eb & Em mooved to the gorden house. John & Em Quinn & Ida is here to night.

[January 11, 1881-Tuesday] 11 John & Em & Ida is gone home. Cate is gone home with them to stay a few dayes.

[January 14, 1881-Friday] 14 Cousin Will Davis has taken dinner with me to day.

[January 15, 1881-Saturday] 15 I have been over to see Fanny to day. She is not verry well.

[January 18, 1881-Tuesday] 18 Fannies babby was born a tusday morning at ten, lived till six the next morning. It was a son, burried at Bershaba that evening. I staid with her till friday evening. I came home sick. Left Cate with her, she is not gitting allong well.

[January 23, 1881-Sunday] 23 I have been sick sence I came home. Cate came home this morning to go to preachen but I was so bad that she did not go. Mr Mack preached a great sermon to day the rest said. Emily is sick, sent for me to go theire to night.

[January 25, 1881-Tuesday] Jan 25 I feel some better this morning. Cate is gone over to see Eddy & Fanny & Eliza & Sally has come up to see me.

[January 26, 1881-Wednesday] 26 Eliza, Sally & Cate is gone over to see Fanny to day.

[January 30, 1881-Sunday] 30 I have been staying with Fanny sence thursday. She has had chills & not gitting along well. I have left Cate with her, was at ould Mr Dave Stincens buring this evening.

[February 4, 1881-Friday] Feb 4 Jackson was over to see Ida last night. She is better. Cate has come home, Fanny is better.

[February 5, 1881-Saturday] 5 I have been down to spend the day with Mrs Cain to day. Wille is gone down to Ruffs to night.

[February 10, 1881-Thursday] 10 Mrs Cain & I have been to see Fanny to day. Lenny is here to night. I am bad off with a pain in my leg.

[February 12, 1881-Saturday] 12 Emily was over to day & Mart, Mary &

Dan all well. Fanny has come over to night for the first time in a long time.

[February 13, 1881-Sunday] 13 this is the Sabbeth. Mr Mack preached to day. Eliza & Fanny staid with me.

[February 15, 1881-Tuesday] 15 Fanny has been staying with me a few dayes. I feel some better. Gimmy Land & Wille is working at the porch. Gimmy & Fanny is gone home to night.

[February 18, 1881-Friday] 18 Emily & Lenny came over to see me last night, Gimmy & Fanny. Gimmy has finished the room, all gone home.

[February 22, 1881-Tuesday] 22 Jackson, Wille & Cate is all gone to york to day. Cate got her a new bureau.

[February 23, 1881-Wednesday] 23 I was bad with the pain in my leg last night, some better this morning.

[February 27, 1881-Sunday] 27 have been at preachen to day, heard Mr Mc preach a good sermon. His tex was, "I come not to call the richous but sinners to repentance." The first time that I have been theire in a long time.

[March 5, 1881-Saturday] March 5 I have been down to stay a few dayes with Eliza & Sall, all well. Lawson & Davis has been a trip of with the waggon.

[March 6, 1881-Sunday] 6 Cate, Wille & I have been over to Ebs schoolhous to preachen. Mr Lathen preached. His tex was in Hebrews 6 c 12 verses. I love to hear him preach.

[March 11, 1881-Friday] 11 I & Fanny was over to see Mag on yesterday & came back & stayed all night with Eb & Em in theire new home. All well but Mag is bad with the cold & cough.

[March 13, 1881-Sunday] 13 Ruffus & Bell Allison had theire first child baptised to day. Its name was Robbert Byers. Jonny & Ella Byers had theire first child baptised today. Its name was _____. Mr Mc was here last night. Cate has gone home with Mart to stay a week with Mag.

[March 14, 1881-Monday] 14 Fanny has been over to day.

[March 17, 1881-Thursday] 17 I have been over to see Fanny to day, all well.

[March 19, 1881-Saturday] 19 Lenny has brought Cate home this evening. Wille & Lenny is gone down to see Sally.

[March 20, 1881-Sunday] 20 cousin Fanny Daubson is verry bad. I dont think shee can live.

[March 22, 1881-Tuesday] 22 Cousin Fanny Daubson died March 22, a tusday morning, leaves thre little boyes, Hascal Brainard & a young babby too months ould. She buried the 23 at york. R J & I was down theire, the largest buring I ever seen. Fanny was over to day.

[March 26, 1881-Saturday] 26 Mr Mac & wife, Mr John Davis, Mr Frank Walker was here this evening to attend to Church matters. Mary & Sally has come over to night.

[March 27, 1881-Sunday] 27 Mr Mc tex was in Mark second chapter 17 verse.

[March 30, 1881-Wednesday] 30 R J & I was over at Marts last night, all as well as common. Had a big storm. Sue Walker was here with Cate & Wille.

[March 31, 1881-Thursday] 31 Cate is gone over to Fannies.

[April 1, 1881-Friday] Aprile 1 a dreadfull dayes wind & cold, plenty of ice.

[April 3, 1881-Sunday] 3 Sabbeth evening, all well & at home.

[April 5, 1881-Tuesday] 5 Fanny has been over to day.

[April 8, 1881-Friday] 8 aunt Sally Coldwell & aunt Caty has been here to day.

[April 10, 1881-Sunday] 10 sabbath evening. We have had a fine sermon to day. Mr Macks tex was in Luke about the prodigal son.

[April 12, 1881-Tuesday] 12 I have been over to see Mag. She is still on foot. I was over to see sister Harriet. She has been sick, is some better. Came by york and home.

[April 14, 1881-Thursday] 14 Fanny has been over to day. Cate is gone home with her. I am here allone, yet not allone. My dearest and best friend is near, yes, verry near. Yes his own word sayes he will dwell in this frail tabarnickal of mine if I will obey his command. I know I am weak and sinfull but Christ is all sufficent. MDBrown

[April 16, 1881-Saturday] 16 Fanny is bad with her head & teeth & sent fore Cate to go over theire this evening.

[April 23, 1881-Saturday] 23 oure communion commenced to day. Mr Mc-Commic preached too good sermons to day, one on prayer, the other on the holly spirit. Mr & Mrs Mack was here last night. I have got home from Mart Halls, have come through a great seen. Mags babby was dead born a sunday morning at nine, Aprile 17 1881. She was bad but God has spared her life to be with her Husband & little children. I pray God that it will make solom & lasting impression on both of theire minds as God has taken theire i[n]fant daughter to deck Emanuels crown. Oh that they may set theire hearts more on the one thing needful, renew theire vows & consecrate theire lives anew to the Lord & his service is the prayer of there Mother.

[April 24, 1881-Sunday] 24 sabbeth evening Mr Mack done all the preachen. He had no one to help him. He held out fine. Another communion over. My Saiviour has said to me, "Doo this in rememberence of him." I have said this day that I love the, that I am on the Lords side. Oh my Heavenly Farther, so deare a name, thou knowest this heart of mine. Thou knowest every thought, word & action. My enemies are many, theire name is legion. Saten, the great adversary, the world & the worlds trinity. The lust of the eye, the lust of the flesh & the pride of life. Heart traitors bosom sins But he that is for me is greater far than all that can be against me. He is stronger than the strong man, Christ the power of God, my great high priest who is now interceding in my behalf who has said, "Lo I am with you allways, even to the end of the world." MDBrown

[April 25, 1881-Monday] 25 unckle Franklin Furgison, John Alexander, Robbert Furgison was all with us last night. John & Emma Quinn, Mr Warlick, Ida & Ginny Thomison, Miss Wille Williams & Emma Furgison was all here a satterday night of our meeting. Sally & Lenny went over to see Mag. She is still mending.

[April 26, 1881-Tuesday] 26 Fanny was over this evening. Her and aunt Caty took supper with us.

[April 28, 1881-Thursday] 28 I & Wille was over at Marts last night. Mag is still mending but is verry week. Stoped & spent the day with Mrs Cain. She is verry porly. Emily & Fanny was both theire.

[May 1, 1881-Sunday] May the first, a sabbeth morning. Jackson & Cate is gone to Bethshilo to a communin to day, are going to stay with aunt Emily to night.

[May 2, 1881-Monday] 2 R J & Cate has come home, found them all well. Cate is gone over to see Fanny. I feel verry unwell. My back & leg hurts so bad. The dross must be consummed, the gold to refine. Fear not it is I, utter not a murmering word. MDB

[May 8, 1881-Sunday] 8 Mr Mack preached a great sermon this morning. His tex was in Luke 12 c 15 vers. These are the words, "Take heed & beware of covitinouss." Joe & Eliza Bell had a chile baptised, Ellwood Fisher.Martin & Mace Bryan had a chile baptised, Susan Bell. Cate went home with Eb & Em this evening to stay a few dayes.

[May 9, 1881-Monday] 9 I have been down to see Mrs Cain this morning. I dont see that she is eney better.

[May 10, 1881-Tuesday] 10 this is the day that Eb has had his examination. We was all over, had a nice time. Mr Lathen, Eb Castles, and General Law all spoke speeches & dialogues from the children. Joe & Sally was up.

[May 11, 1881-Wednesday] 11 I have been over to see the Scoggins children to day. They are dooing fine. It shows that a covinent keeping God has watched over them.

[May 12, 1881-Thursday] 12 Cate is gone over to Fannies.

[May 15, 1881-Sunday] 15 Cate & Wille is gone to Smerny to preachen.

[May 17, 1881-Tuesday] 17 Cate has been down to see Eliza & Sally. Eliza has been sick, is not well yet.

[May 19, 1881-Thursday] 19 Fanny has been over to day.

[May 25, 1881-Wednesday] a wensday 25 Fanny & I have been down to see Eliza & Sally. All well but Eliza. She is better.

[May 26, 1881-Thursday] 26 this is the day that Mrs Cain has gone up to Margaret Anns to see if it would doo her eney good. I fear she will never come back alive.

[May 29, 1881-Sunday] May 29 aunt Caty & ould aunt Mary Freeman has spent the day with us. She is badly hurt about Mrs Cain. Sabbeth evening Mart & Mag was over last night, all at preachen to day. Mr Mack had a fine sermon. His tex was, "Then all ye the sons of God." My children and grandchildren was all theire but one grand daughter, Hatty Whitesides. She is at York going to school. I had too sons, five sun-in-laws, eleven grand sons, six daughters, one daughter-in-law, six grand daughters. Ruffes & Eliza is members of Smerny, all the rest are members of my ould & bloved Bershaba, name ever dear to my heart, except one, Gimmy Davis Land. May God by his all mighty power melt & renew his heart. Mart & Mag has not had theire little Jonny baptised, all the res are baptised members of thy curch militant. Oh my Heavenly Farther, I humbly pray thee that they may all be members of thy Church tryumphant. Oh my God may theire not one be lacking when thou comest to make up thy jewels, yes thy own jewels to deck Emuals crown. I am this day fifty nine years, too months and seven dayes ould to day. I may never meet my children all at one time again on that hallowed spot, but we will all meet again. Yes when thou, my dear Saiviour shall come again in all thy Glory to awak the slumbering dead to come to Judgement. Oh my God that we may meet an unbroken family theire to spend an unding Eternity theire praising the, world without end, Amain. MDB

[June 3, 1881-Friday] June 3 Mrs Cain is no better.

[June 5, 1881-Sunday] 5 Sabbeth evening One sweet & Holy Sabbeth day without company to mar Gods Holly sabbeth day.

[June 8, 1881-Wednesday] 8 Aunt Caty & John is gone up to see Mrs Cain. She is no better.

[June 11, 1881-Saturday] June the 11 1881 I have seen the last of Mrs Cain, seen her die, seen her laid in the cold & silent grave.

[June 18, 1881-Saturday] 18 Aunt Harriet & Ida was up to day.

Gimmy Loves, Hew Walter died July 12 1881

Crow Warlick & Ida Thomison was married July 13 by Mr Mack.
He is from Waco. Cate & Wille is gone to the infare.

[July 23, 1881-Saturday] 23 I have been down staying with Eliza. Sally, Joe & Sally came home with me.

[July 25, 1881-Monday] 25 Crow & Ida was with us last night.

[August 6, 1881-Saturday] 6 Mart & Mag & Cate has a big visit over to Spartenburg to see Sue.

[August 16, 1881-Tuesday] Aug 16 cousin Mary Ramsey & her son, Wille Quin was with us last night. I went with her to Billy Coldwells & Bobs. Mrs Coldwell is verry porly. Mart & Mag was over to day.

[August 25, 1881-Thursday] 25 Aunt Caty & Fanny has been helping Cate to quilt to day. My leg is hurting me bad, bad. Emma Furgison died August 21, sunday morning, 1881. Wille & Cate is gone down. Theire was burrie at Bershaba. Aunt Emily & John came home with us.

[August 27, 1881-Saturday] 27 John Brown & Cate is gone to Bethany to a singing to day.

[August 28, 1881-Sunday] 28 I was abble to go to preachen to day. Lawsons babby is sick.

[August 30, 1881-Tuesday] 30 The babe is no better. John Lawson & Davis & Gimmy Land has been here converring oure house today. Got a fine ruff on it & Cate is gone home with Fanny.

[September 1, 1881-Thursday] September 1 I feel some better this morning. The babe is no better.

[September 3, 1881-Saturday] 3 James Mcninch of Chester & Mary Brown & sally W was here to day. Mart has brought Mag & the children over to stay

a while with me.

[September 5, 1881-Monday] 5 I feel some better this evening. It may be but a short reprieve, life at best is frail, short & uncertain, but Oh that glourious home that I hope soon to enter. Theire is no pain, sorow, sickness nor death. Oh happy day for all that is ready to go home.

[September 11, 1881-Sunday] sabbeth evening 11 I have been blessed to be abble to go to Gods house of worship once more. Heard Mr Mack preach to great sermons. His tex was in John 5 c 28 29 verses. He was preachen on the reserection of the boddy. What a glourious day that day will be to them that sleep in Jesus. His evening sermon was, "All things shall work together for good to them that love God."

[September 17, 1881-Saturday] 17 Cate & Wille is home. Had no company.

[September 18, 1881-Sunday] sabbeth evening been reading Edwerds on redemption. A great book from his droctron. It is to be feared that few proffessers an interist in Christ.

[September 20, 1881-Tuesday] Ginny Curry died September 20 1881.

[September 21, 1881-Wednesday] 21 aunt Harriet was over to day.

[September 29, 1881-Thursday] 29 aunt Sally Coldwell, aunt Caty & I have been over to see Fanny to day.

[October 7, 1881-Friday] Oct 7 Cate & I have been down to see Eliza & Sally. I left Cate to stay a week.

[October 9, 1881-Sunday] 9 Mr McElhanny, the blind preacher preached for us to day. He done verry well.

[October 22, 1881-Saturday] 22 this is the time of our communion, satterday night. Mr Macks tex this morning was in Hebrews 3 c 12 v. He has no help. Sally Whitesides, Will Thomison, Bob Furgison is here.

[October 23, 1881-Sunday] 23 Mr Macks tex this morning, "Ye are Christs," A good many theire.

[*October 24, 1881-Monday*] 24 Wille is gone with the ginners this week.

[*October 25, 1881-Tuesday*] 25 Fanny is gone home & Cate with her.

[*October 27, 1881-Thursday*] 27 Ruff took dinner with us to day. All well.

[*November 2, 1881-Wednesday*] Nov 2 I have been over to see Emily & aunt Harriet & Marts Mag has the pains, can hardly walk. Mart is gone with the gin. Fanny & Lenny came home with me.

[*December 14, 1881-Wednesday*] Dec 14 Irskin Whitesides & Ginny Thomison was maried Dec 14 1881 by Mr Mack. My Wille, Eddy Land & Brooks Neel all started for Arcancis Dec 12 1881.

[*December 20, 1881-Tuesday*] 20 Wille has landed home safe from his Arkancis trip this eveing. He has got enough of the west. Russel brought him from kings mountain this evening, all right.

1882

[July 2, 1882-Sunday] July 2 sabbeth evening all well. No preachen.

[July 3, 1882-Monday] 3 Mart Hall has thrashed our wheat to day with his steam engine & sepperater. Cate has gone home with Mart to stay a week.

[July 4, 1882-Tuesday] 4 Aunt Caty & I have been over to see Fanny to day.

[July 9, 1882-Sunday] 9 Mart has brought Cate home to.

[July 10, 1882-Monday] 10 Gim, Fanny & I was over at aunt Harriets last night. Ida Warlic is at her Mothers, had a son the 8. Not dooing well, neither of them.

[July 12, 1882-Wednesday] 12 Eb & Emily has been over to day, the first time with her new babe. Fanny was over too helping Cate to quilt.

[July 14, 1882-Friday] 14 Wille & Cate has been to york to day. Cate has treated her self to a new sewing mashene.

[July 19, 1882-Wednesday] 19 Fanny was over this evening. Cate is going home with her.

[July 21, 1882-Friday] 21 Cate & Wille was over at aunt Harriets last night to see Ida. Her & the babe is better, come by to see Mag. She is better.

[July 23, 1882-Sunday] 23 sabbeth evening Mr Macks tex this morning was in Romans 12 c 2 verse, evening tex, Luke 12 c 14 verse. He preached to great sermons. Eb & Em had theire babe baptised this morning, Jonny Ruffus. Aunt Emily, John & Jane was up last night. Mrs Gimmy Davis was at preachen to day & her too sons, Johny & Adams, Ema Thomison, G C Quinn & her little daughter was theire.

[July 26, 1882-Wednesday] 26 Sally & Eddy & I have been over to see aunt Harriet & Ida, stayd all night with Mart & Mag. Spent the day with Em & Fanny found them all well.

[July 28, 1882-Friday] 28 Sally & Eddy is gone home.

[July 29, 1882-Saturday] 29 Mag Halls Sally was born July 27 1882.

[July 31, 1882-Monday] 31 I have got home from Marts. Mag and the babe is dooing fine.

[August 4, 1882-Friday] August 4 Jackson & Lawson is gone over to see Mr Amos Burns. He is verry bad.

Mr Amos Burns died August 6 1882.

[August 11, 1882-Friday] August 11 this is the commencement of our summer communion. Mr Inglish from York preached to day, a great sermon. This is the tex, "The son of man goeth as it is written of him, but woe to that man by whome the son of man is betrayed, it had been good for that man if he had not been born." Theire was too joined the church to day, Miss Sally Baty, Mr Robbert Baty. Mr Inglish & Mr McComic both came home with us.

[August 12, 1882-Saturday] satterday evening 12 Inglish preached this morning about raisen Lazarus from the dead. Jesus said, "Take ye away the stone." A great sermon. Gimmy & Fanny had theire son baptised, called him Wille Edward. Lowry Smyth, one baptised, name Anny. Theire was too joined the church, Hallbrooks Good & Macy B Castles. Mr Inglish is gone home. Mr Mack has preachen to night. I did not feel abble to go. We hav a good deal of company.

[August 13, 1882-Sunday] 13 Mr Mack preached to day. He had no help. His tex was in Luke 14 c 24 v, had fine preachen & a good congragation. Gimmy Land has joined the church. A glourious thing to see the last one of my numerious family enlisting under the banner of oure great capten, oure Lord & saviour, Jesus Christ, and a grand daughter, Mary Brown Castles. Oh my Heavenly Farther as theire names is now regesterd in thy church militint, oh will thou enroll theire names in thy book of life, that when thou comest to make up thy jewels, yes thy own presious jewely, they may not be lacking. Mr Mack preached a verry solom sermon to night. "How shall you escape if you neglect so great salvation."

[August 14, 1882-Monday] 14 Mr Inglish preached to day, his tex was in Mathew 7 c 21 v, "Not every one that sayeth unto me, Lord, Lord, shall enter into the kingdom of Heaven, but he that dooeth the will of my Father which is in Heaven." Oure meeting closed with too more joining the church, Mrs Lizy Love, Miss Laura Clark. Mr Mack was gone down to see his Mother, came back here to night. Ann Brown is verry porly, was not abble to go to church.

[August 16, 1882-Wednesday] 16 Mrs Mary F Davis of Wallholla & Mrs Sally Davis & children was all to see us & Fanny & little Wille & aunt Caty, all gone. Ann is no better.

[August 19, 1882-Saturday] 19 John Brown & Cate & Wille is gone to Beth-shilo to preachen, the time of their communion. I have been over to see Ann. She has the consumption. I fear she will never be eney better. She seemes to be resined. She sayes she puts her trust in God & is resined to his will.

[August 20, 1882-Sunday] 20 Calm & peacfull sabbeth evening. Blessed emblem of the eternal sabbeth in Heaven. MDB

[August 24, 1882-Thursday] 24 Unckle Franklin Furgison has been here to day.

[August 26, 1882-Saturday] 26 Unckle Frank & I have been down to see ould Dr Alison. He is verry porly. Went on over to see Ruff & Eliza, took dinner with them, went & stayed all night with Joe & Sally & come home sick. Aunt Caty is sick too.

[August 29, 1882-Tuesday] 29 Ann is some better. They have brought the babby home sick.

[August 31, 1882-Thursday] 31 this is the first of theire singing. Mr Robbert Alison sung yesterday & to day. Fanny was at the singing to day, came on here. Wille is gone home with her.

[September 1, 1882-Friday] September 1 I was down at ould Mrs Davis to see Mrs Mary Davis. She leaves in a few dayes for Wallhollow. This is the night of Ebs Tablo [tableau]. Cate & Wille is gone. Lawson & the boyes, Mag & the children is here.

[September 2, 1882-Saturday] 2 Cate has come from Ems. She has the pains.

[September 3, 1882-Sunday] 3 I am going over to stay with Em a while. Em has been bad, cant moove herself. The friends has all been to see her. Sally & Hatty was up.

[September 10, 1882-Sunday] 10 Sabbeth we are all at Ebs, a dreadfull days wind & rain & Em is no better.

[September 12, 1882-Tuesday] 12 I think Em is a lettle better. I have come home & brought Jack & Neel home with me, left Cate with her.

[September 18, 1882-Monday] 18 Em is some better. She has walked to the door to day & I have come home & left her.

[September 22, 1882-Friday] 22 singing yesterday & to day. Alison was here last night. I have been over to see Ann & Mag. They are both porly.

[September 24, 1882-Sunday] 24 Mr Mack & Mr White was up to day. Mr White preached to day, had but one sermon. This is the time of Presbatary at Bulixcreek. They had to go back this evening.

[September 25, 1882-Monday] 25 Cate has been to see Mag Hall & Em. Mag children has the sore eyes. Emily mends but slow.

[September 29, 1882-Friday] 29 Wille & Cate was over with Em last night, poorly yet.

[September 30, 1882-Saturday] 30 Cate & I was up to see Ginny Whitesides this evening. Her & the babe is dooing fine. It was born the 24 of september, a daughter.

Daisy Whitesides was born Sept 1882.

[October 1, 1882-Sunday] Oct 1 sabbeth evening No preachen. I am not feeling well to day. My back hurts me bad.

[October 10, 1882-Tuesday] 10 R J and I have been over to see Mag to day, all well. Cate over with Fanny.

[October 17, 1882-Tuesday] 17 I have had a big trip down to see Eliza & Sally to see the ould Dr, he is suffering bad. I was at Smerny at preachen one day. Mr Boice preached. Ruff has brought me home this morning, all well.

[October 22, 1882-Sunday] 22 Eb & Em was over last night, all well. Gone home

Dr Alison died a sabbeth morning Oct 22 1882 and was burried at Bershaba a sabbeth evening. Mr Ross preached his funeral sermon at his house. Mr Mack was gone to Synod. Cate is gone home with Fanny, going to York tomorow.

[October 24, 1882-Tuesday] 24 R J & I have been to york to day.

[October 27, 1882-Friday] 27 Eliza & Sally have been up. We was all over to see Fanny to day. They are now gone home.

[November 1, 1882-Wednesday] Nov 1 Fanny has been over to day for Cate to help her with her new black dress.

[November 4, 1882-Saturday] 4 Mag Hall & the children has been over a few dayes. Mag has the sore eyes.

[*November 5, 1882-Sunday*] 5 Wille is gone to Beth shilo to a Communion to day.

[*November 10, 1882-Friday*] 10 Cate is sick to day. Miss Betsy Black was here.

[*November 11, 1882-Saturday*] 11 satterday evening of our communion. Sally, Hatty & Eddy is with us. Mr Mcomic wanted his salery raised from three hunderd to foure. They raised over foure hunderd dollars. He preache a good sermon. "Go work to day in my vinyard," a verry suitable sermon.

[*November 13, 1882-Monday*] 13 Fanny was over to day. Little Wille is sick. Cate is gone home with her.

[*November 17, 1882-Friday*] 17 I have been with Fanny fore a few dayes. Little Wille has been bad with colar fever. Not much better.

[*November 18, 1882-Saturday*] 18 Mr Robbert Alison sung at the church yesterday, had a singing here last night. This is his last day. I am going back to Gims to night.

[*November 19, 1882-Sunday*] 19 Gimmy has brought me home & took Cate home with him.

[*November 25, 1882-Saturday*] 25 R J & I was down at ould Mrs Davis to a prayer meeting.

[*November 26, 1882-Sunday*] 26 Mr Mack preached a good sermon to day, "If ye gather not with me, he scathereth." He came home with us, had dinner then on to the schoul hous to preach, then on to Ebs to stay all night. Miss Minny was with him.

[*November 28, 1882-Tuesday*] Nov 28 this is the day of the sale at the ould Dr Alisons. Gimmy has brought Fanny on here & left her. It is a cold & stormy morning.

[*November 29, 1882-Wednesday*] 29 Cate & her paw is gone down to Ruffs.

[*December 1, 1882-Friday*] Dec 1 This is the morning ould Tailor died.

[December 4, 1882-Monday] 4 sabbeth evening. All well, all at home.

[December 25, 1882-Monday] 25 Christmas day Cate & Wille is gone over to Ebs.

[December 26, 1882-Tuesday] 26 Lenny & Mary came home with us. Cate all gone down to see Eliza & Sally.

[December 27, 1882-Wednesday] 27 All come back & Hatty & Eddy came home with them, all gone up to John Coldwells to a party to night.

[December 29, 1882-Friday] 29 R J is gone over to see aunt Harriet, caught out in a big snow.

[December 31, 1882-Sunday] 31 Gim & Fanny was over last night. Cate is gone home with them.

Aunt Emily Alexander died Dec 20 1882
Robbert Alison & Eliza Scoggins was married Dec 20 1882
Hatty Whitesides started to Dew West Jan 2 1883
Mr Gim Cain & Sue Willey was married Oct 12 1882

1883

[January 1, 1883-Monday] A new years morning on monday 1883 new years evening I a poor ould wicked sinner spared to see a new year. My work is not done. God has something more fore me to doo. Oh that he will give me grace to mak a good improvement of the talent he has give me, if it is but one, may I improve it well. Within the last year so manny is gone home to glory. Some to that home of woe, woe, woe, into thy hands Heavenly Farther do I commend myself for life or death fore time & Eternity. MDB

Jim has brought Cate home this evening, all well & at home.

[January 7, 1883-Sunday] 7 I have been over to see Eb. He has been sick, is better, & to see Fanny. She has come home with me.

[January 8, 1883-Monday] 8 Eliza Scoggins Alison & Mary & Nanny was all here to day. Another big snow.

[January 13, 1883-Saturday] 13 R J is gone down to see Sally to day. Eddy

Land is here to night, he is going off to peddle. Mr Mack preached a good sermon, "They that serve the Lord shall renew theire strenth." Mrs Jane Jonson & her son, Wille, landed home from Arcancis Jan 13 1883.

[January 15, 1883-Monday] 15 Fanny was over to day. Cate is gone home with her.

[January 17, 1883-Wednesday] 17 Sally is up to day. Her & Cate is gone over to see Fanny. Gim is putting him up a new dinning room, Wille is helping him.

[January 20, 1883-Saturday] 20 I dont feel well to day.

[January 27, 1883-Saturday] 27 Eb & Em, Ruff & Eliza & the children is all there to day. Eb & Em is gone home, the rest stayed all night.

[January 28, 1883-Sunday] 28 This is the day that we have had thre new Elders and too new deacons ordained, elders, William Jackson, William Burns, Lawson Brown, deacons, Hallbrooks Good, William Coldwell.

[January 29, 1883-Monday] 29 Cate & Fanny is gone over to see Mag Hall.

[February 1, 1883-Thursday] Febuary the 1 all well & at home.

[February 4, 1883-Sunday] 4 Sabbeth evening no company, a great day to read Christs dying legacy. M Smoke & Duff Brown was married Feb 8 1883 by Mr Mack. R J was at the wedding.

[February 11, 1883-Sunday] Sabbeth evening 11 Aunt Harriet Thomison & Wille was here last night. Mag Hall & the children, John Alexander was all here last night, all went to preachen. Mr Mack preached a great sermon. It seems to me every sermon is the best, tex was John 6 c 61 v Mr Mack came home with us.

[February 12, 1883-Monday] 12 Mr Mack is gone home. Cate is gone over to Fannyes. Wille & Gim is gone over to Joe Neels to paile in the yard. I am setting here all alone.

[February 15, 1883-Thursday] 15 Cate has got home. Fanny came home with her. They was all at Emilyes yesterday at a quilting. Lawsons _____was

born February 18 1883. Dr Wister was theire.

[February 20, 1883-Tuesday] 20 Mag & the babe is dooing fine. Her Mother is with her.

[February 21, 1883-Wednesday] 21 Lissy Whitesides & Sue Walker was on a visit to day.

[February 23, 1883-Friday] 23 Cate & I was at York to day, a cold wet day.

[February 27, 1883-Tuesday] 27 I have been over with Fanny a few dayes. She has had the tooth ack & cold, is some better this morning. Wille has a log rollen this evening.

[March 1, 1883-Thursday] March 1 Cate, Mrs Cain & aunt Caty is all gone over to see Fanny today. She is not well yet.

[March 2, 1883-Friday] 2 Francis Mathews & Ann Brown, Gimmy Scoggins & aunt Caty & unckle Frank Furgison has all been her to day.

[March 4, 1883-Sunday] 4 Sabbeth evening Wille & Lenny has gone over towards Smerny last evening, not got home yet. Dr Alison has been verry bad sick, has got better.

[March 7, 1883-Wednesday] 7 Em & Lenny & Mary has been over to day. I am going down to Ruffs to night. Mary is going to stay with Cate.

[March 11, 1883-Sunday] 11 I have had a fine visit to see the children, all tolereble well but some cold. Sally and I went to John Whitesides on a visit one day. They all came home with me to preachen but Joe, he has the cold. Mr Macks tex was, "Ye are Christs."

[March 15, 1883-Thursday] 15 Cate was over with Fanny last night, all well.

[March 18, 1883-Sunday] Sabbeth evening 18 No preachen, all well. Wille is gone to the Chapple.

[March 21, 1883-Wednesday] March 21 1883 I am sixty one years ould to day. Whether I will live to see the year 1884, not my will oh Lord but thyne be

done. Heavenly Farther, give me grace to live fore thy glory. Elivrfan Ann & Sally has come up to day.

[March 22, 1883-Thursday] 22 Ruff has come up to day & they are gone home. A cold, stormy day.

[March 23, 1883-Friday] 23 Fanny has been over to day. Cate is gone home with her.

[March 24, 1883-Saturday] 24 Aunt Caty & Mrs Margaret Ann McElwee was to spend the day with us to day.

[March 25, 1883-Sunday] 25 I have been at preachen to day. It has been a cold, wet day. It has rained, hailed & snowed to day but few out. MDBrown

[March 28, 1883-Wednesday] March 28 R J & I have been to see Em & Mag, only tolerable well.

[March 31, 1883-Saturday] 31 I have been over with Em fore a few dayes. She has had some chills & not well but is some better.

[April 1, 1883-Sunday] Gim & Fanny came home with me this morning, all well, April 1.

[April 4, 1883-Wednesday] 4 Aunt Caty & I have been down to see ould Mrs Davis to day.

[April 8, 1883-Sunday] Sabbeth evening 8 Mr Mack was with us last night. Preached a great sermon to day. His tex was in Daniel fifth c 30 v "In that night was Belsazzer, the king of the Chealdeans slain." Mr Mack took dinner with us & is gone home. Lenny went home sick this morning.

[April 9, 1883-Monday] 9 Ann & I have been to york to day, got a good wetten.

[April 10, 1883-Tuesday] 10 Ann has been sick. I have been over to see her. Eb has come for me. Lenny is sick. I am going home with him.

[April 12, 1883-Thursday] 12 I have got home. Lenny is better. Sally is sick

& Em. They are most all sick. Come by took dinner with Fanny, then Gim brought me home. Found Cate sick with the could. I was over to see Lawsons babby. It has been sick, got better.

[April 15, 1883-Sunday] 15 R J went to Ebs last night & going to york to Presbetary to day. Bethel Presbatary met at york this spring.

[April 16, 1883-Monday] 16 R J has been down to see Eliza & Sally to day, all well.

[April 18, 1883-Wednesday] 18 Jackson is verry bad with the gravel last night & to day.

[April 20, 1883-Friday] 20 Jackson is still unwell. Fannys babby was bad with the croop last night. I have been over theire awhile to day. He is better.

[April 21, 1883-Saturday] 21 Jackson is still unwell. Dr Jackson was out to see him to day. This is satterday of our communion. Ould Mr Taylor preached. Wille stayed home with his Paw. We have no one with us but Sally. Cate & Sally has gone over to see Wille awhile.

[April 22, 1883-Sunday] 22 Eliza stayed with her Paw to day. Mr Taylor preached about the bitter watters of mara. A good congragation of people & a fine day. Mr Taylor & Mr Mack came home with us & stayed a while.

[April 23, 1883-Monday] 23 Aunt Sally & aunt Caty is here to day. Mag, Lawson & Mr Cold all to see Jackson. He is some better.

[April 25, 1883-Wednesday] 25 Mag Hall & children was up last night. Gone over to see Fanny to day, her & Cate. Will is better.

[April 26, 1883-Thursday] 26 Fanny is over. Wille is better. Ann & her children, Mrs Cain & aunt Sally Coldwell all here to day. R J is a little better.

[April 29, 1883-Sunday] 29 the fifth sunday in Aprile R Jackson was bad last night, better to day. Eb was over a while, no preachen to day.

[May 5, 1883-Saturday] May 5 R J is no better. Eliza was up last night & Fanny.

[May 6, 1883-Sunday] 6 Wille is gone to Ramma to preachen to day. I have been over to see Ann. She is verry bad with a pain in her head.

[May 8, 1883-Tuesday] 8 Ann is no better. Jackson is better. Aunt Harriet & Fanny is here to day.

[May 14, 1883-Monday] 14 John Alexander & Jane has been to see us. R J is better.

[May 20, 1883-Sunday] 20 Cate & Wille is gone to Smerny to preachen to day. Wille bought him a new buggy yesterday.

[May 22, 1883-Tuesday] 22 Fanny is over to day & it is verry cold.

[May 23, 1883-Wednesday] 23 a big frost this mornin. I can write my name in the frost. It has done a good deal of damage, cilled the cotton some.

[May 24, 1883-Thursday] 24 Jackson & I have been over to see Fanny to day. All well.

[May 25, 1883-Friday] 25 Lawson & Cate is gone to york.

[May 27, 1883-Sunday] 27 we have all been at preachen once more. Mr Mack preached to fine sermons. His tex was, "Straight is the gate, narow is the path that leads to life." Theire was foure children baptised, Jonny & Ela Byers second chile, Edward Gorden, Lawson & Mags sixth son, Robbert Claud, Robbert & Sue Love, Walter Wheeler, William & Mat Coldwell seventh chile, Sally Cain.

[May 28, 1883-Monday] 28 R J & I have been up to spend the day with aunt Caty.

[May 29, 1883-Tuesday] 29 I have had a house full to day, Aunt Caty & John, Mrs Sue Cain, Ann Brown Davis & the children, Lawson, Fanny & little Will, all gone.

[June 2, 1883-Saturday] June 2 Jackson & I have had a big visit down to see Eliza & Sally, found them all well, a gitting along fine.

[June 3, 1883-Sunday] 3 Cate & Wille went over to Mart Halls last night, drove Rolly. I am verry uneasy for them to come home. R J & I by oureselves. I am not feeling verry well to day. MDBrown

[June 8, 1883-Friday] 8 Cate has been staying a week with Mag Hall. Wille has went fore her to day & brought her back to Fannies & is home this evening.

[June 13, 1883-Wednesday] 13 Eliza & Sally was up to day & Cate is over at Fannies.

[June 16, 1883-Saturday] 16 R J & I was down at york this morning.

[June 18, 1883-Monday] 18 Jackson & I have taken dinner with the Scoggins children to day.

[June 24, 1883-Sunday] June 24 Mr Mack preached to day. His tex was in Mathew 1 21. Ould Mrs Davis is verry sick & William Davis little Bratten with the flux. Cate & Wille is gone down to see them. We have had a fine rain this evening. We was suffering bad.

Ould Mrs Eliza Davis died June 26, a tusday morning 1883, would have been eighty one in August. Oure ould preacher, Mr William Davis has been dead 28 years. Aunt Caty & I was down theire all night. Mr Mackomick preached her funeral sermon. He done well. He had good grounds. She was a Mother in Iseral. Her house was the home of the Ministers. She has gone home to hear the welcolm plawdit, "well done good & faithfull servent, enter though into the joyes of the Lord." Mr & Mrs Mack, Gim & Fanny came home with us & took dinner & gone home. Cate is gone with Fanny.

[June 27, 1883-Wednesday] 27 We had a dreadful rain last night. The creek was the highest it was ever knowned to be. It washed away near a hunderd dozen of wheat, the finest kind of wheat. They went down the creek & pulled some out of the mud & halled it up.

[June 30, 1883-Saturday] 30 Cate & Wille is gone down to Ruff Whitesides to night. This is the day that Hatty is to come home from school from Dew West.

[July 1, 1883-Sunday] July 1 All well. Gods holly sabbeth day. Cate & Wille

is gone to Smerny to hear the young Mr Mack Oats preach.

[July 4, 1883-Wednesday] 4 Cate has been sick for a few dayes. Theire is a pick nick over at Ebs school house to day. Wille is gone over this evening.

[July 8, 1883-Sunday] 8 Mr Mack has preached to day & has gone on over to Mr Joe Neels to baptise some of theire children.

[July 9, 1883-Monday] 9 this is the day Milt Jackson came to thrash our wheat & broke down. I was down to help Emiline to make jelly to day. Gim & Fanny is here to night. We have had a fine rain.

[July 13, 1883-Friday] 13 Hatty & Eddy came up this morning. Cate & Hatty is gone over to see Fanny.

[July 14, 1883-Saturday] 14 Theire is a singing up at the curch to day. Cate & Wille, Hatty & Eddy is all gone. Wille & John is gone home with Hatty.

[July 15, 1883-Sunday] 15 Jackson is gone over to the Chapple to preachen to day.

[July 16, 1883-Monday] 16 I have taken dinner with Davis & Ann to day. Ann is verry porly.

[July 17, 1883-Tuesday] 17 Cate & I have been at york to day, verry dry & warm.

[July 18, 1883-Wednesday] 18 Cate is gone over to see Fanny.

[July 20, 1883-Friday] 20 Gim & Fanny is here.

[July 21, 1883-Saturday] 21 I have been up to Aunt Catyes to day & spent the day with Ruffus & Martha Meek. Ruff & Martha, three daughters and one son landed here last week from Arcancis on a visit.

[July 25, 1883-Wednesday] 25 had a fine rain this evening, needed it bad.

[July 26, 1883-Thursday] 26 Lenny is bad with the cramp colic. Jackson & Cate is gone over to see him. Ed Land came home last everning on a visit. Cate

& Wille is gone over to Gims to see him.

[July 27, 1883-Friday] 27 Mrs Marth Meek, Sue Meek, Nanny Meek, aunt Caty & John, Mrs Sue Cain & Fanny all here to day. Lenny is verry bad. They have sent fore me. Fanny & I is gone theire to night.

[July 28, 1883-Saturday] 28 Had a big singing at Bershaba to day. Bob Castle, Waren Whisenhunt & Ed Land is all here to night.

[July 29, 1883-Sunday] 29 I have been over with Lenny to nights. He has been bad. I think he is a little better this morning. Cate & Wille is gone over to see him.

[July 30, 1883-Monday] 30 Cate & Wille has come home. Lenny is better.

[August 2, 1883-Thursday] Aug 2 John Brown & Cate went up to see Sue Walker to day. She was not at home. They went on & spent the day with Mart and Mag. Lenny & Mary Castle was over to day.

[August 5, 1883-Sunday] 5 Cate & Wille has been up to see John & Fanny Mathews & to a communion at Clover. Mr Mack from Columbia was theire preacher. Greatly beloved Cate has come home & left Wille with the Widow.

[August 10, 1883-Friday] 10 I was over with Fanny last night. Ann Brown has been taken bad up at John Caldwells satterday night.

[August 11, 1883-Saturday] 11 this is the commencement of oure summer communion. Mr Kirtpatrick from Clover preached this morning. His tex was in James 1c 15 verse. He preached a great sermon & gone on down to Bulix creek curch to hold a communion, will be back a monday. Cousin Margaret Brown, cousin Laura Russel & her little daughter, Adda, Hatty Fewel, Mary & Sally Castle, Mr McComick & his little nephew, Hal Shuffard are all with us.

1884

The Year 1884, Tuesday mornin a new years day My God thou hast brought to see a new years day, brought through seen after seen, a living monument of the Love of God. Oh my God fit & prepare me fore what is thy will, fore life or death, fore time ore Eternity is my prayer to thee this morning.

[January 5, 1884-Saturday] 5 Sylvanis Whitesides is here to night. Has been in Texas fore three years, a dreadfull cold day.

[January 6, 1884-Sunday] 6 No preachen. Dreadful cold.

[January 12, 1884-Saturday] 12 A big snow & still very cold. S S Whitesides is here to day.

[January 14, 1884-Monday] 14 Cate is gone down to see Sally & Eliza.

[January 16, 1884-Wednesday] 16 Cate, Wille & I have been at York to day, got her wedding trimmens. I am feeling better. Hatty has come up to help Cate

to sow & Fanny is here & Cate & Hatty is gone home with Gim & Fanny.

[January 23, 1884-Wednesday] 23 Fanny & Mary Castle is helping Cate to dress her cakes. Mag Hall & children is up.

[January 26, 1884-Saturday] 26 S S Whitesides was here last night. Eliza is up to day. John Alexander & his son, Hew came out here the 19 of the month.

[January 28, 1884-Monday] 28 Sally has come up this evening to stay till the wedding is over.

[January 30, 1884-Wednesday] Sylvanis S Whitesides & Jayly Catherine Brown was married January 30 on Wednesday evening by Mr Kirtpatric of Clover. We had all the children.

[January 31, 1884-Thursday] 31 My dear Cate is gone. John Brown, Wille & Lenny is all that went with them, the rest of the children is all gone home but Fanny. She hangs to me. Aunt Caty is here.

[February 3, 1884-Sunday] Feb the 3 Sylvanis & Cate has been to see Sally & Eliza & to Smerny to preachen today. Gim & Fanny is here. Wille got a pin in his throat eating a piece of pound cake. We was badly frightend awhile. Gim Land puled it out with the shears.

[February 5, 1884-Tuesday] 5 Cate has been over to see Fanny.

[February 6, 1884-Wednesday] 6 Mr Canady, the blind preacher, came here this evening to stay awhile.

[February 7, 1884-Thursday] 7 Wille & I have been to York today to get some things for Cate.

[February 10, 1884-Sunday] 10 Sylvanis came up last evening. They went over & stayed with Gim & Fanny & went to preachen to day to hear the blind Mr Canady preach. His tex, "We Have a friend that sticketh closer than a brother." He done fine. Oh how will such rise in judgement against manny that has eyes & makes a bad use of them. M D Brown

[February 12, 1884-Tuesday] Feb the 12 This is the day that my dear Cate has

left me & gone to a house of her own to battle with the wourld. They have not got much of this wourlds goods but I believe they have treasure in Heaven which is far better. Her Farther gave her nothing neither one way nor another. What is to come of me poor, ould trifling creature, but I know that I have a friend that sticketh closser than a brother. I have raised seven girls now left without one. I have no fear of ever suffering or lacking eney thing. Fanny is gone home & want be back soon.

[February 16, 1884-Saturday] 16 I have been over to see Fanny. Stayed too days & a night. She is doing perty well & little Will.

[February 17, 1884-Sunday] 17 Mr Canady preached to day but it is a verry wet day. I did not go.

[February 20, 1884-Wednesday] 20 I have been down to see Sally & Eliza. They are all well. Last night was the night of the great hericin in our own state, the like was never known in this country.

[February 24, 1884-Sunday] 24 Mr Canady preached to day. He is going to leave us now. His tex was, "Seek first the kingdom of God & his richeness & all necesery things will be added to you."

[February 25, 1884-Monday] 25 I was over at Ebs last night.

[February 28, 1884-Thursday] 28 Joe & Sally has mooved up in Lawsons house to day. I am so glad to have Sally so near. Took dinner with them. It is verry cold. John Alexander came home with me.

[March 1, 1884-Saturday] March 1 Cate & Sylvanis came up tonight the first time. All well.

[March 6, 1884-Thursday] 6 I was over with Fanny last night.

[March 8, 1884-Saturday] 8 Eb has a log rolling this evening.

[March 10, 1884-Monday] 10 Wille was down with Cate last night.

[March 11, 1884-Tuesday] 11 Ruff has brought Eliza & the children up to stay a few days. Joe & Sally, Cary & Lenny & Wille is all gone to York. Butler is here to night. Mart & Mag & the children is all up. Mag & Mart went home with Sally.

[March 12, 1884-Wednesday] 12 All gone home.

[March 14, 1884-Friday] 14 It is a verry wet day. Joe & Sally is here to day. Joe & Wille is working the road.

[March 15, 1884-Saturday] 15 Aunt Caty & John was here to day.

[March 23, 1884-Sunday] 23 I have just got home from staying with Fanny. She has a fine daughter. It was born Hetty Catharine March the 20, a thursday evening. Getting along fine. Wille went down & brought Caty up to stay a week with Fanny. I have left her with her & ould aunt Narcissa.

[March 25, 1884-Tuesday] 25 Cate & Wille was over to see Mart & Mag last night. All well. Sally & Cate is with me to day. Went up to see Aunt Caty this evening. She has been verry ill this winter. Cate went home with Sally.

[March 26, 1884-Wednesday] 26 Sally, Cate & I & theire paw has all been over at Ebs to day getting along fine.

[March 28, 1884-Friday] March 28 Cate & Mary Castle went over to stay with Fanny last night. Fanny & the babe is dooing fine. Sylvanis has come up fore Cate & they are gone home.

[March 30, 1884-Sunday] Sabbeth evening 30 Mr Kirkpatrick preached to day. His tex was in Psalms 34 chapter. These are the words, "Manny are the afflictions of the richous but the Lord will deliver him out of them all." He is a fine preacher. We was in hopes we would git him to preach four us but it has failed. I hope God will send us one in his own good time. MDB

[April 2, 1884-Wednesday] April 2 I have been over to see Fanny to day. Her & the babe is dooing fine. It has been a dreadfull day of wind & fire. It took hard work to save the church.

[April 4, 1884-Friday] 4 Mag has come to day to weave for me & Sally has made me too pots of good soap.

[April 6, 1884-Sunday] 6 Sabbeth all well, no preachen to day.

[April 12, 1884-Saturday] 12 I have been over to see Mag to day. The children has all been sick. Have got some better. Wille Jonsons youngest chile was burried to day.

[April 13, 1884-Sunday] 13 Jackson & Wille is gone to Clover to a communion to day. Ruff Stephensons youngest chile was burried to day. Ann Brown had a dead born babby on the 14. A fine big boy. She is dooing tollerable well.

[April 18, 1884-Friday] 18 Fanny came over last evening. The first time she has been over with her little Daughter. They are all dooing fine. A matter of great thankfullness to be abble to get back to Farthers house once more. We had went over to spend the day with Sally. Theire was bad luck befell them at home & they sent for her & I went home with her. All better now.

[April 20, 1884-Sunday] 20 This is the day of the communion at Smerny. Joe & Sally & Wille is gone over theire. R J & I have spent the sabbeth by our selves. A great to read & studdy & try to be prepared for that Sabbeth which has no end.

[April 22, 1884-Tuesday] 22 This is the night ould aunt Sally Coldwell fell out of the porch & got most killed & is bad off.

[April 26, 1884-Saturday] 26 Joe & Sally & Wille & I have been down to see Sylvanis & Cate. Found Ruff & Eliza Whitesides theire to. They are verry well fixed for a start if they can have theire health but is feared they will have the chills.

[April 27, 1884-Sunday] 27 Jackson is gone out to Clover to day to see something abbout getting Mr Kirkpatrick to preach for us. We expect to git him.

[April 29, 1884-Tuesday] 29 They have taken aunt Sally home to day.

[April 30, 1884-Wednesday] 30 Sally has been over to day to help me quilt. We have got it out.

[May 3, 1884-Saturday] May 3 Fanny & the babe has been over last night & to day. They are all dooing fine. Wille went home with her.

[May 4, 1884-Sunday] 4 I was over with Eb & the children last night. They have the cough. Jackson is bad off. Has got him down. The Dr was to see him this morning. Maud is bad off. Neel & Jonny is doing fine, the cough is all over the neighborhood. I am feeling tolerable well. MD Brown

[May 5, 1884-Monday] 5 I have been over to see Ann this evening. She is gitting along fine. The children has the cough.

[May 8, 1884-Thursday] 8 Jacky is bad off with the cough & fever. Sally & I have spent the day with Mrs Cain the second, had a plesant day. I think she is an excelent woman.

[May 11, 1884-Sunday] 11 This is the sabbeth day. Wille & Sally Castle, Joe & Sally & Lenny is all gown to Sharon. It is the time of the communion theire. I have been over to see Jackson. I think he is some better, able to set up some. MD Brown

[May 13, 1884-Tuesday] 13 Mrs Cain, Sally & I have been up to see Lawson & Mag, all well.

[May 14, 1884-Wednesday] 14 Ruffes has brought Hatty up this morning to stay a while with me. Sally is over this evening. Hatty is gone home with her.

[May 15, 1884-Thursday] 15 R J, Hatty & I have taken dinner with Sally. Hatty & Sally is gone over to Ebs to see Jackson & I have come home.

[May 16, 1884-Friday] 16 Hatty & I have been over to see Fanny to day. All well.

[May 18, 1884-Sunday] 18 Theire was preachen appointed for young Mr Hope but he has failed to come.

[May 19, 1884-Monday] 19 R J has gone to take Hatty home to day.

[May 20, 1884-Tuesday] 20 Sally is over this evening.

[May 21, 1884-Wednesday] 21 I have been over with Sally this evening. Joe & John is gone down to the ould place.

[May 23, 1884-Friday] 23 Sally & I have been down to see ould unckle Hugh Love to day. He is totering on the grave.

[May 25, 1884-Sunday] 25 Sylvanis & Cate came up last evening. We have all been to preachen to day. Young Mr Hope preached to day, a young man from the symanary. His tex was in Rommans the fifth chapter first verse. He done tolerable well. Sylvanis & Cate is gone home & I have had word that Eliza is verry sick. I am going down theire to night.

[May 31, 1884-Saturday] 31 Satterday I have got home from Ruffs. Been down theire since last Sunday. Eliza has been very low. We did not think she could live all this week. Had Dr Alison, Dr Bratton out. I think she is out of danger now. She has been verry low.

[June 3, 1884-Tuesday] June 3 Joe & Sally was down at Ruffs last night. Eliza is mending some. Jonny Davies was burried at Bershaba to day. He dyed at Clover. Fanny has left the children & come a houre this morning. She is affraid of the hooping cough as Wille has it, the second time for him. He is bad with it. Jacky has got better.

[June 7, 1884-Saturday] 7 Satterday evening of oure communion. Mr Kirkpatrick preached for us. His tex was in Hebbrews. "Go boldly to the throne of Grace & find grace to help in time of need." His evening tex was the parable of the ten virgins. He did preach to great sermons. Theire was three joined the church, Miss Allis Stephen, Miss Sally Castle, my disceaced darling Emilys second daughter, Mr Wille Adams Davis oure late, late pastor, the beloved James Davis youngest son, Mrs Gimmy Davies & her son Gimmy by syrtificate from Wallhollow. Cate came up this morning in the buggy by herself. Sally & Cate is gone over to stay with Fanny to night. Sabbeth evening another good meeting over, a pleasant meeting we have had. His tex this morning was in second Peter. "Whereby you are given unto us exceeding great & precious promises," his tex in the evening was in Isaiah 53c, "A man of sorrows & acquainted with grief." On Saturday theire was a subbriction to see how much we could rais for a young Mr Hope from the Symmanary during the vacation of foure months. The made about seventy five dollars & can rais more.

[June 9, 1884-Monday] 9 Cate is gone home this morning.

[June 10, 1884-Tuesday] 10 I have been over to see Fanny to day.

[June 11, 1884-Wednesday] 11 A beautiful morning, had a fine rain last night. Mary D Brown

[June 14, 1884-Saturday] 14 Sally & I have been over at Marts yesterday & last night.

[June 15, 1884-Sunday] 15 this is the Sabbeth. We have had a storm of rain & wind since last evening.

[June 17, 1884-Tuesday] 17 I have been down to see Eliza again. She has had another bad spell, a chill & cramps. I have stayed with her too nights. Left her better this morning. I am in hope shee will git allong now.

[June 19, 1884-Thursday] 19 Wille & I have been to york to day. All well.

[June 22, 1884-Sunday] 22 this is the first day that Mr Hope has preached for us.

[June 26, 1884-Thursday] 26 I have been over with Fanny for a few days. She has been sick. Got better.

[July 2, 1884-Wednesday] July 2 Sally Castle & I have been down at Ruffs. Eliza has mended fine since I was theire. Fanny has come over to day to go over & see Sally this evening.

[July 3, 1884-Thursday] 3 Gimmy has come for Fanny. Wille is not well.

[July 6, 1884-Sunday] 6 theire was to be preachen to day but was none. Aunt Harriet & Wille came to preachen & theire was none & they came on here & Mart & Mag too. This is the day that Mr Thomppsons little chile was burried.

[July 8, 1884-Tuesday] 8 Aunt Caty, Mrs Sue Cain & I have spent the day with Sally, & Bob Coldwell, is theire thrashing Lawsons wheat.

[July 9, 1884-Wednesday] 9 Cate is sick & sent for me to go & see her. Bob Coldwell is here thrashing our wheat.

[July 12, 1884-Saturday] 12 Satterday evening. I have got home from Cates. She has been bad with the billious fever her & Sylvanis both. Wille came down

for me & I left them both in bed but I think the wors is over. Mrs Martha Coldwell died July the 11 1884. Gimmy & Fanny came over this evening to stay all night.

[*July 13, 1884-Sunday*] 13 Mr Hope preached to day. His tex was in Proverbs the 18 v "But the path of the just is as the shining light that shinith more & more until the perfict day."

[*July 18, 1884-Friday*] 18 Ruff & Eliza has been up fore a few dayes. She has got tolerable well. They have all gone home this morning.

[*July 19, 1884-Saturday*] 19 Sylvanis & Cate has come up this morning. They have got better but lookes baddly worsted. Sylvanis is gone home & left Cate to stay a week.

[*July 21, 1884-Monday*] 21 Cate & I have been over to see Ann this evening.

[*July 22, 1884-Tuesday*] 22 Cate & her Paw & Sally & I have been over to see Fanny to day & I feel verry unwell this evening. Cate stayed with Fanny.

[*July 26, 1884-Saturday*] 26 Satterday evening. I have had a perty hard spell of billious fever but feel a little better this evening but Wille has had a chill. I fear he is taken it too. Sylvanis has come up for Cate to day. Bell has the fever. I was not fit for her to leave & she is not well herself.

[*July 28, 1884-Monday*] 28 Cate has had a chill & has been verry bad to day. Had Dr Bratten out to see her. I feel some better. Wille is feeling bad.

[*July 29, 1884-Tuesday*] 29 Dr Bratten was back this morning. He thinks Cate is dooing verry well.

[*July 30, 1884-Wednesday*] 30 Ruff & Hatty came up this morning. Hatty is going to stay. Ruff is gone on to york.

[*July 31, 1884-Thursday*] 31 Cate is better. Hatty is gone home. Wille has been bad to day.

[*August 1, 1884-Friday*] August 1 Dr Bratten was back to see Cate this morning. He thinks she is dooing fine. Wille is better & I am up but feel bad. Fanny babe has been bad, but is better.

[August 2, 1884-Saturday] 2 Fanny has come over this morning. She has been sick with the cold & ear ach. The babe is better but has a bad cold. Sylvanis has come up to day. He has got better & Bell to, through the loving kindess & tender mercies of oure God we have all got better once more. It may be but a short reprieve, prepare to meet thy God. Mag Hall came over this morning & her Paw went home with her.

[August 3, 1884-Sunday] 3 Sabbeth evening. The Bulix creek preacher preached for us to day. Cate, Fanny & I was not abble to go. Sylvanis is gone home & left Cate.

[August 4, 1884-Monday] 4 Cate is with Sally to day.

[August 5, 1884-Tuesday] 5 Sally, Cate & Wille is all gone up to Lawsons to day.

[August 6, 1884-Wednesday] 6 Lawson, Mag & the children is all here to day.

[August 7, 1884-Thursday] 7 Sylvanis has come fore Cate to day. He has mooved from the place he first mooved to. It was so sickly that they could not live theire. They have mooved this side of Sharon.

[August 9, 1884-Saturday] 9 Wille has been over to see aunt Harriet & Mart & Mag.

[August 10, 1884-Sunday] 10 Wille, John Brown is gone to Beth shilo to preach. They have a protracted meeting theire now.

[August 12, 1884-Tuesday] 12 R J is gone down to see Ruff & Eliza, John & Mag Whitesides, Joe & Sally, Mrs Mary Davis was all to see me this evening.

[August 14, 1884-Thursday] 14 Cousin Mary Ramsy & John Hallsman & Cate Coldwell was all here to day. Gim & Fanny & Wille has all been down to see Sylvanis & Cate, all well. R J & Lawson is gone to Clover to the candates speaking.

[August 16, 1884-Saturday] 16 Wille is gone to Smerny to a singing to day.

[August 17, 1884-Sunday] 17 Mr Hope preached to day, this morning in Hebbrews 4 c 15 & 16 verses, the last day that he will preach for us. He wants to go up in the mountians for his health.

[August 18, 1884-Monday] 18 Wille is gone to work the road & I have been over to see Mary Scoggins. She has been sick.

[August 23, 1884-Saturday] 23 I have been down with Cate sence last tusday morning till this morning, satterday morning. She has had a miscarrige. Is gitting allong fine. The men is all gone to York to hear the candates speak to day. Fanny has been over a while this evening.

[August 24, 1884-Sunday] 24 RJ is gone over to zion to preachen to day. Wille is down to Bethshilo today. I am not feeling well to day but it is a pleasent day to read & meditate on Gods word, prepare for that sabbeth which has no end. MDB

[August 25, 1884-Monday] 25 I have been over to see Fanny to day. The children has the sore eyes.

[August 29, 1884-Friday] 29 Wille had a cotten house raised to day. Eliza Allison was here, aunt Caty, Sally & Ann Brown, all well.

[August 31, 1884-Sunday] 31 Sabbeth. Wille is gone to Suttons Springs to hear the Eppiscople preach. MD Brown

[September 2, 1884-Tuesday] September 2 Fanny has come over this evening & is gone over to stay with Sally to night.

[September 6, 1884-Saturday] 6 Mag Hall & her too children, Mary & Sally, R J & I have had a big visit to see Eliza & stayed with her a day & night. She is not well. Looks bad. The rest is well, then went on to posim town to see Cate. She has been sick but has got better. We came back by Fannies & took dinner with her. Mag went on home, came home found all things right.

[September 11, 1884-Thursday] 11 this is the day of the prymary election & it has been a verry wet day & Mrs Manervy McAfee died Sept 9 1884. R J and I have been over to see aunt Harriet & Ida. Ida is very sick at this time & Nanny has another son. Was at Marts, took dinner, all well.

[September 20, 1884-Saturday] 20 Fanny has been over to day & dyed & sized her web.

[September 24, 1884-Wednesday] Mag & Bobs babby was born September 24 1884.

[September 25, 1884-Thursday] 25 Mrs Mary Davis & Adams & Matty Davis has been here on a visit to day.

[September 27, 1884-Saturday] 27 I have been over with Fanny. She has a verry sore throat, the dipthera.

[September 29, 1884-Monday] 29 I have been back with Fanny. Her throat is not much better. Sally is with her to day & Cate came up this morning to stay with her a few days.

[October 1, 1884-Wednesday] Oct 1 Cate has come home. Fanny has got better.

[October 2, 1884-Thursday] 2 Sally & Cate has spooled & warped theire web to day & is gone up to see aunt Caty & they have a little singing to night & Sylvanis has come up for Cate.

[October 3, 1884-Friday] 3 Sylvanis & Cate is gone home.

[October 4, 1884-Saturday] 4 Gimmy & Fanny is over to night.

[October 9, 1884-Thursday] 9 Sally has been over & we have put in oure web.

[October 10, 1884-Friday] 10 Bob & Wille is gone to york with cotten. Joe & Sally is gone down to John Magills. Sue is bad with dipthera.

[October 11, 1884-Saturday] 11 John, Alex & Wille is gone over to Gims.

[October 14, 1884-Tuesday] 14 Fanny is gone over to stay with Sally to night. She is here weaving.

[October 17, 1884-Friday] 17 Mag Hall, Mary & Sally is come to see me to

day. R J & Davis is gone to Blacks station to night.

[October 20, 1884-Monday] 20 I was over at Ebs last night. Mary & Sally is both sick.

[October 22, 1884-Wednesday] Eliza Ann & Hatty, Mary & Brown here to day & Fanny.

[October 24, 1884-Friday] 24 Wille & I have been to york to day.

[October 25, 1884-Saturday] 25 Fanny has come back to day & put her web out & stayed all night.

[October 28, 1884-Tuesday] 28 I have spent this day with aunt Caty B. I have been over with Fanny too nights.

[November 3, 1884-Monday] Nov 3 Wille has the dipthera but is not bad. Wille was down with Cate last night. She has the dipthera perty bad.

[November 5, 1884-Wednesday] 5 Sally & I was over with Fanny yesterday. Wille is better. Dr Bratten was waiting on him. Wille is gone to help Gim build a house for John Jackson.

[November 7, 1884-Friday] 7 Sally & I have put in oure second web of janes to day.

[November 10, 1884-Monday] Nov 10 I have been over with Fanny sence satterday. She has had another spell of dipthera. The clauset door cut open, the house door locked. Sally was here. She got in at a window, but Christ my dear redeemer has opened a door which no man can lock, nor cut open.

[November 13, 1884-Thursday] 13 Cate has come up to stay a few dayes & weave her cloth. Ann & Mag Brown is here to day & Cate has went home with Sally to night.

[November 15, 1884-Saturday] Nov the 15 a day long to be rememberd by me. Such a day I have never spent & I pray God I never may, Cate has come home from Fannies verry sick all day. Aunt Caty is with us. Wille is gone to the singing. Mr Shell was at Bersheba the 2 sabbeth in Nov, preached that day &

organised a Sabbeth school. I was not theire.

[November 16, 1884-Sunday] 16 Sylvanis has come up for Cate & she is going home. She has got better.

[November 20, 1884-Thursday] 20 I have been over to help Fanny to make Gims coat to day.

[November 23, 1884-Sunday] 23 Mr Shell, the mishanary Methedist preacher, preached at Bershaba to day. His tex was in Nehemia, "Oh Lord strenthen my hands." He has been here sence satterday morning, is gone up to preach at a school house this evening.

[November 27, 1884-Thursday] 27 Fanny & I was over with Joe & Sally last night. She is gone home.

[November 29, 1884-Saturday] 29 I have been over with Fanny to day to git her to help me on Wille coat. We got it done.

[November 30, 1884-Sunday] 30 I have been to Sabbeth school to day. Cousin Wille Davies red a chapter & made a prayer. Theire was a good manny out.

[December 4, 1884-Thursday] Dec 4 Sally & Fannie is both here to day. Have put out theire web & both gone home.

[December 5, 1884-Friday] 5 We have killed hogs to day.

[December 7, 1884-Sunday] 7 at Sabbeth school to studdy shorter catacism & questions, have got to the fifth commandment.

[December 9, 1884-Tuesday] 9 Aunt Caty has mooved down to Mr Gim Cains to day. Davis & Ann mooved in theire house. John is gone to York. Wille is helping Gim to build a house this week. Had a singing here to night. Mr Elder was here all night. He is out selling books.

[December 10, 1884-Wednesday] 10 Sally & Fanny was here to day.

[December 12, 1884-Friday] 12 John Alexander & Jane Furgison was here last night. Gone to york this morning. Gim & Fanny & Wille has set up my

new stove in the dinning room to day. It dos fine.

[*December 14, 1884-Sunday*] 14 Sabbeth evening a wet day. R J on the lounge sleeping, I in the corner by myself. Eddy Land & Wille is gone over to E P Castles. M D Brown

[*December 18, 1884-Thursday*] 18 this is the day that Lawson has mooved back to his own house from the Bell place, & Joe & Sally has mooved in Davis Browns house.

[*December 22, 1884-Monday*] 22 monday morning a dreadfull cold. Every thing is covered with ice. We have had a stranger with us sence satterday night. He is an agent for the Presbetarian papper. His name is Mr Fisher. I think he is a great man. He is a lay preacher.

[*December 24, 1884-Wednesday*] 24 Fanny has been over to day helping me to git reddy for Christmas.

[*December 25, 1884-Thursday*] 25 Christmas day I have been over & took dinner with Lawson & Mag & Hatty & Eddy Whitesides has come up this evening & Hatty & Wille is gone down to Bob Coldwells to a singing to night.

[*December 26, 1884-Friday*] 26 we have all been over to see Sally to day & Sylvanis & Cate has come up to night & we have had a nice singing to nght.

[*December 27, 1884-Saturday*] 27 Sylvanis & Cate, Hatty & Eddy is all gone over to Ebs to day.

[*December 28, 1884-Sunday*] 28 Wille is gone to Sharon to preachen to day. Going to Cates to night.

[*December 30, 1884-Tuesday*] 30 Wille & I was over with Fanny last night.

1885

[*May, 24, 1885-Sunday*] May 24 1885 God in his loving kindness & tender mercies has once more blessed us with a preacher. This is the first day that Mr McAlpine has preached for us. It was a wet morning, but theire was a good congration of people out. All seemes to be well pleased with oure new preacher. His tex this morning was in Revalation 3 c 20 verse, "Behold I stand at the door & knock," hymns, "Theire is a fountain filled with blood," "Nearer my God to thee." In the evening his tex was in Mark.

[*June 13, 1885-Saturday*] June 13 this is the commencement of oure communion. Mr English preached for us to day. His tex was in Matthew 12 c 30 verse. In the evening Luke 19 c 10 verse.

[*June 14, 1885-Sunday*] Sabbeth evening glory Hallugth when I git home to Glory I believe I will look back & see this days work. God of love & mercy has once more given us a Paster. His name is Mr John McAlpine, and has bee enstalled paster of oure church to day. This is the third paster I have seen enstalled in my dear ould church. My Farther in Heaven, I pray the to send thy holly Spyrit with power on the hearts of every member of oure Church doo oure duty, oure hole duty as thou will give us Grace & strenth to oureselves, our Paster & oure God thou may remove oure candle stick & leave us as sheep with out a shepherd to gravel our way in darkness, sin & sorow. Mr English had all the work to doo. Mr Mcomick, Mr Willson was appointed to come but failed. His tex this morning was in first Corinthians, first chap 17 18 verse. He gave the charge to the congragation & the Paster. I think he done well MDBrown.

[June 17, 1885-Wednesday] 17 Sally & I have had a fine visit. Been to see aunt Harriet, aunt Jane, Mart & Mag & Fanny. Got home safe. Foud all well.

[June 18, 1885-Thursday] 18 I have been down to see aunt Caty. She is porly. Mr Mcalpin call on us to day. He is out a visiting around now.

[June 28, 1885-Sunday] 28 Mr Mcalpin has preached for us to day. His tex this morning was in John 21 c 17 verse. The organised oure sabbeth school. I pray god that he will bless the effort that it will be a blessing to both ould & young & that it may train manny a soule for glory. MDBrown

[July 2, 1885-Thursday] July 2 1885 Eliza Brown & Eddy has been up to see us. All well. Cate & Bell was down this evening & took supper with me, all well.

[July 4, 1885-Saturday] 4 Fanny & the children has been over to day. Wille is gone to Chestnut Acadima to a picknick to day.

[July 9, 1885-Thursday] 9 we have had oure wheat thrashed to day, bad crops of wheat. We made seventeen bushels.

[July 10, 1885-Friday] 10 R J & I have been up to see Cate to day. They are all well & dooing fine.

[July 13, 1885-Monday] 12 a monday morning We have had a happy time sence last satterday. Oure bloved paster, Mr John McAlpine has been with us. He preached yesterday on the duty of the Elders. He tole them theire duty was a responcible one & one which God would hold them accountible. MDBrown

[July 14, 1885-Tuesday] 13 all well fitted for the dewtyes of another day. I pray God that he will keep us safe through another day & prepare us all for the

hour of death. Wille & I was a York yesterday, came by & took dinner with Fanny.

[July 15, 1885-Wednesday] 15 Fanny & I have been over to se Sally to day. R J is gone over to see aunt Harriet.

[July 18, 1885-Saturday] 18 we have had a fine picknick at the Mineral spring to day. A fine crowd & good behaiviour. Wille Thomison came home with us. Wille & Lenny is gone to take Maggy & Ella Jeffery home.

[July 20, 1885-Monday] 20 All well & home.

[July 26, 1885-Sunday] 26 Mr Mcalpine preached today on batism & then baptised seventeen children, Lawson & Mag one, William Wat, Davis & Ann one, Gim & Fanny one, Jessy Cate, Mart & Mag 3, John Quilla, Sarah Catharine, Hatty Mirtle, Ginny Whitesides too, Daisy & Blanch, Lizzy Love too.

[July 29, 1885-Wednesday] 29 Jackson & I have been down to see Eliza. They are all going to start off to the springs in the morning.

[August 3, 1885-Monday] August 3 I have been over to see Fanny. Jessy has been sick, is better this morning.

[August 7, 1885-Friday] 7 Jessy is better. Fanny has been over to day & Cate has been down. She is well.

[August 9, 1885-Sunday] 9 sabbeth evening Mr Mcalpine preached on the fourth commandment this morning. In the evening, "Rember Lots wife."

[August 12, 1885-Wednesday] 12 Sally, Mag & I have been over at Ebs to day backing his infare cake. Had good luck. A big meeting at the Capel. Wille is gone, went away last night. MDB

[August 19, 1885-Wednesday] my son in law Ebbernesar Castle & Miss Alas Whisenhunt was married Aug the 19 1885. I think it was a bad go. He has a large family, foure sons, three daughters. Lenny, Mary & Sally is all grown.

[August 21, 1885-Friday] Aug 21 this is the commencement of our meeting. Friday evening Mr Mcalpine & Mr Web of Bethel was both theire. Mr Webs tex was in John 11 c 56v, "What think ye, that he will not come to the feast?" Friday evening Mr Web Mathew 15c 23 v "But he answered her not a word."

[August 22, 1885-Saturday] satterday morning first Samuel 2 c 25 v. "If one man sin against another the Judge shall Judge him but if a man sin against the Lord, who shall entreat for him?" satterday evening, Ephesians 2 c 12 verse, "That at that time ye were without Christ, being aliens from the commonwealth of Isreal, & strangers from the covents of promis, having no hope, and without God in the world." Theire was foure children baptised this morning, Ruff & Bell Alison too, John & Pinkney, Jonny & Ella Byars one, Margaret Adams, Jonny & Laura Russel one, Psalm Brown. We have had great preachen. Ould unckle Eward & Theadore Byers has both joined the church.

[August 23, 1885-Sunday] Sabbeth evening Mr Web done all the preachen, too great sermons to day. Morning tex, Mathew 8 c 11 v, "And I say unto you, That many shall come from the east and west and shall sit down with Abraham and Isiac and Jacob, in the kingdom of Heaven." In the evening Hebrews 9 c 27 v, "And as it is appointed unto men once to die, but after this the judgment." We have had great preachen. Three joined by surtificate, John Alexander, Mrs Thompson, Mrs Jonson. My Farther in Heaven, make us all remember that we are not done with those great & momentious sermons. They will be a Saiviour of life unto life or of death unto death. I pray that this Solom time will make a lasting impression on me & mine. My children & Grand children was all theire but my darling Cate. She may never be theire again, not my will be done oh Lord but thine. MDBrown

[August 26, 1885-Wednesday] 26 Fanny & I have been up to see Cate to day. She has not been well. Fanny is gone home.

[August 30, 1885-Sunday] 30 this has been a wet Sabbeteh day.

[September 2, 1885-Wednesday] Sept 2 I have been down to see aunt Caty. She is no better.

[September 6, 1885-Sunday] 6 sabbeth evening all well. Gim & Fanny was over last night, all well. I was up to see Cate this morning. She is not well. Wille is gone down to see Eliza, has not got home.

[September 7, 1885-Monday] 7 this is the day that John Alexander has left us & gone to Bob Browns.

[September 11, 1885-Friday] 11 Eb has had a picknick at the school house to day.

[September 12, 1885-Saturday] 12 a singing at the church to day.

[September 14, 1885-Monday] 14 Fanny & I have been over with Sally to day. She is affraid of the measels. Peggy has had a chance of them.

[September 19, 1885-Saturday] 19 I have been up staying with Cate. She has a fine son. It is dooing fine. Cate is not so well. Sylvanis & Cates was born September the 15 1885. This is my 34 grand chile, nineteen grand sons, fifteen grand Daughters. My Heavenly Farther I humbly beseech the that when thou comest to make up thy jewels that they will all stars to deck Emanuels crown. This is the day that we have gave Mr McAlpin a poundin. He got a good deal. He had his new wife with him. I like her appearance verry well. He was married Sept 2 to Miss Lula Elliet.

[September 20, 1885-Sunday] sunday evening Mr McAlpin has preached to day, had his wife with him.

[September 22, 1885-Tuesday] 22 I have got home from Cates, have stayed near a week with her. Her & the babe is dooing tolerable well.

[September 24, 1885-Thursday] 24 Gim has had his barn covered to day. Wille & I have been over Joe & Sally & Elizas. Little Mary has been bad off to night, has got better. I feel not well & lonsem this evening.

[September 29, 1885-Tuesday] 29 Eliza & Eddy has been up to day & took Mary home with them. Fanny & the children is over to night.

[October 1, 1885-Thursday] Oct 1 Wille had a little shucking to night but it has rained & they had to stop.

[October 2, 1885-Friday] 2 Sally is over weaving to day.

[October 4, 1885-Sunday] 4 Sabbeth evening been to church to day. Mr McAlpins tex was in Hebrews 12 c 2 v. I was down with aunt Caty last night.

She is verry weak. Came by with Sally & stayed awhile.

[October 6, 1885-Tuesday] 6 Sally was over & put out oure web & I have put up a quilt. Had Mr & Mrs McAlpine last night. I think she is a verry nice lady.

[October 7, 1885-Wednesday] 7 Sally & I have been over & took dinner with Mag & Lawson. Went over to see Ebs in the evening.

[October 9, 1885-Friday] 9 I have been over a day & night with Fanny & Gim & Gim has brought me home this morning & Ebs new wife, Alas & Sally & little Jonny was all here to day. I have been down to see aunt Caty. She is worse.

[October 14, 1885-Wednesday] 14 I have been with aunt Caty for thre nights. She is bad.

[October 23, 1885-Friday] 23 Mrs Mary Davis, cousin Sue Brown, Cate & myself was all with Sally on yesterday, had a fine time.

[October 24, 1885-Saturday] 24 Cate has been down for a few dayes with her first born son. He is dooing fine, all but a burn on his chin is sore.

[October 26, 1885-Monday] 26 Fanny is with aunt Caty to night. She is no better.

[October 27, 1885-Tuesday] 27 Sally & I have been down to york to day.

[October 28, 1885-Wednesday] 28 Ruffes Whitesides has brought Hatty & Mary up to stay a few dayes.

[October 29, 1885-Thursday] 29 aunt Caty was verry bad last night & Wille is gone to take Hatty & Mary home.

[October 30, 1885-Friday] 30 I have been down to see aunt Caty. She is no better.

[November 1, 1885-Sunday] Nov 1 Mr McAlpin preached on the tithes to day.

[November 2, 1885-Monday] 2 Mag Hall & the little girls has been here, too las night, all well. Fanny came over this evening & we went over and took supper with Sally.

[November 4, 1885-Wednesday] 4 I was down with aunt Caty last. She was bad all night, better this morning.

[November 5, 1885-Thursday] 5 I have been to see ould unckle Hew Love today.

[November 6, 1885-Friday] 6 Sally & I went & stayed a while with aunt Caty & went on and took dinner with Fanny. Aunt Caty took worse & they sent for us beffore dinner. Sally & I stayed all night. Fanny went home.

[November 7, 1885-Saturday] 7 left Fanny Ann with her. She is verry low.

[November 9, 1885-Monday] aunt Caty Brown closed her eyes to this world Nov the 9, a monday morning at five oclock. I was with her from sunday morning till her death. Oh how happy to say & beleve that oure loved ones is gone home to heaven & to glory, no more to weep & suffer here. My Heavenly Farther prepare me for such an end.

[November 10, 1885-Tuesday] 10 Mr English was out, preached a funeral sermon. He read the 15 c 1 Corintheans. His discoures was abbout ould Simion, now Lord tellist thou thy servent, depart in peace, unveil thy bosom, faith tomb, take this new ___to thy trust.

[November 12, 1885-Thursday] 12 June Jane Furgison is with us now. She came up to see aunt Caty.

[November 14, 1885-Saturday] 14 Wille has gone to take Jane to york this everning.

[November 15, 1885-Sunday] 15 Mr McAlpine preached a good sermon to day, the best he has done in a good while.

[November 16, 1885-Monday] 16 Fanny & the children is over to day. I have not been well.

[November 17, 1885-Tuesday] unckle Hew Love died Nov 17 on a tusday in his ninety first year.

[November 21, 1885-Saturday] 21 I have not been well sence aunt Caties death. I hope I will soon be better. Jackson has sold Nel , a mule colt to Mart Hall to day fore seventy five dollars & gave Cate, Ginny & her calf, daisy.

[November 22, 1885-Sunday] 22 Sabbeth evening all at home. I am some better.

[November 30, 1885-Monday] 30 Fanny & Cate is with us to day & John & Bob is ginen cotten. Sally is gone down to help Hatty to bake her wedding cak.

[December 6, 1885-Sunday] Dec 6 this is a verry cold & windy day. Mr McAlpine has come from home this morning to preach for us.

[December 7, 1885-Monday] 7 Sally has gone over to see Fanny to day.

[December 10, 1885-Thursday] 10 Jackson & Sally & I have got home from Ruffs to the big wedding. Hatty Whitesides & James Magill was married by Mr Ross Dec the 9 1885.

[December 12, 1885-Saturday] 12 Fanny has been over to day & we went over to see Sally.

[December 17, 1885-Thursday] 17 Eliza & Eddy came up to night.

[December 18, 1885-Friday] 18 we killed oure hogs to day & Fanny has been over & helped me to put it all away & gone home. Gim Land & Wille is pitting up a house for Buttler Thomison.

[December 20, 1885-Sunday] 20 Mr McAlpin has preached to day. He preached on the talents. Cousin Wille Davis & John Brown is here to night. Joe & Sally mooved back to their ould house Dec the 15 1885. Cousin Emiline Floyd, Ruffes was born Dec 16 1885.

[December 23, 1885-Wednesday] 23 Mrs Mary Davis, Miss Mary Davis has spent this day with me. They are all going to Blacks station to live. Fanny was over to day. Her Paw has been bad with a pain in his shoulder.

[December 25, 1885-Friday] 25 Christmas day. Mag, Lawson & the children has been over to day. Not much company.

[December 27, 1885- Sunday] 27 Jackson & I have had a pleasent day, sabbeth, by oure selves, the last Sabbeth in the year 1885. The joyes & the sorrows, the pleasure & pain, the births & deaths of 1885 will last through the ceasless rounds of Eternity, oh that we may all live with oil in oure lamps & well trimed for in such an hour as ye think not the Lord comith.

[December 29, 1885-Tuesday] 29 Cate & Fanny been here to day & Mr James Magill & Hatty to night.

[December 30, 1885-Wednesday] 30 Jackson & I have been over to see Fanny to day. Buttler Thomison little Brown died with manegitus December 23 1885.

1886

[*January 1, 1886-Friday*] Friday, a new years morning 1886. the first figur I have made for 86. Whether I will ever mak 1887, my Farther in Heaven knows, not my will oh Lord but thine be done. Sally has come up to see us to day. We allwayes welcom her with a warm heart.

[*January 2, 1886-Saturday*] 2 Sally & her Paw has come up to see Cate. I am bad with a pain in my back & hench, can hardly walk. Sally & little Hew Alexander is gone home. She has taken Hew to live with her.

[*January 3, 1886-Sunday*] 3 the firs sabbeth in a new year, a verry wet day. Jackson & Wille is gone up to the church to preachen. I was not abble to go. I am suffering with a pain in my back & hench. I cant walk without help & feeling bad but why should a living woman complain, a punishment for my sins, but I have a great advocate with the Farther, even Jesus Christ, the richous, my proffet, Priest & King.

[*January 4, 1886-Monday*] 4 this is sale day. Wille is gone to York this evening.

[January 6, 1886-Wednesday] 6 Gimmy & Wille is gone back to work at Buttlers house & Fanny has been over to day. Mrs Gimmy Davis & Miss Mary Davis was to see me this evening. Theire last visit, soon if ever as they expect to go to Blacks Station tommoro for good.

[January 8, 1886-Friday] 8 we have had a big snow to day & strong wind & cold.

[January 9, 1886-Saturday] 9 Wille & Gimmy has got home. This is a dreadfull cold day.

[January 10, 1886-Sunday] 10 sabbeth evening, all well, most powerfull cold. Sylvanis & John Alexander is here.

[January 13, 1886-Wednesday] 13 it has been the coldest time & hardest freeze ould people sayes that has been in forty years, busted cans & jugs, jars & a lot of things too tedious to name. Young Jonny Alexander from North Caro & his farther was here last night. Wille & Jonny is gone down to stay all night with Sally & Hewe.

[January 15, 1886-Friday] 15 Wille has been out partridge hunting, caught over fifty.

[January 16, 1886-Saturday] 16 Wille has gone up to stay with Cate. Jonny Brown is with R J & I. The weather has moderated, quite pleasent.

[January 17, 1886-Sunday] Sabbeth evening we had no preachen to day, our preacher has gone off on a trip. I have had a pleasent day, no company, reading Gods holy word. I have read Debborah & Baracks songs. Scots notes.

[January 19, 1886-Tuesday] 19 a pleasent day. The snow most gone. Fanny, Wille & Jessy came over yesterday morning & stayed till this morning. All gone home, all well.

[January 26, 1886-Tuesday] Jan 26 I have been over with Fanny for a few dayes, caught over theire in a storm of snow & ice, all well.

[January 31, 1886-Sunday] 31 I have been up to see Cate. Little Vance is dooing fine & all well but colds.

[February 4, 1886-Thursday] Feb 4 Cate & I have been down to see Eliza & Sally, found them all well. Had a bad day to come home in snow & ice. Got home safe. Home is a great place although it be but a lowly one. It should make us strive hard to gain that home, that house of manny wheire Jesus is gone to prepare a place for all them that love & serve him. He has said he will come again & take us home, sweet home, that home of the blessed.

[February 7, 1886-Sunday] 7 sabbeth evening we was to have had preachen to day but got a letter from oure preacher that his wife was sick & could not come. A long recess from having preachen for seven weeks. Gimy & Fanny has been over.

[February 8, 1886-Monday] 8 Emiline Floyd has been up to spend the day with me to day & her new babe, Lawsons Mag too.

[February 10, 1886-Wednesday] 10 Lawson, Wille & I have been to york to day.

[February 11, 1886-Thursday] 11 Jackson is gone down to see Sally & Eliza on a visit.

[February 13, 1886-Saturday] 13 Wille & I was over with Fanny last night, all is well as common. Ann Brown & the children is here to day.

[February 15, 1886-Monday] 15 all well. I feel verry tired & lonesom but theire remaineth rest to them that love the Lord Jesus Christ. Oh glourous when shall I be at home, sweet home.

[February 16, 1886-Tuesday] 16 Jackson & I have been over to see Mart & Mag today, all well but Mag has a bad cold.

[February 17, 1886-Wednesday] 17 Mart & Mag has been over to day & Sally has been up to day, all gone home.

[February 27, 1886-Saturday] 27 Ann Brown is bad off with newralsy. I have been over with her a day & night.

[March 2, 1886-Tuesday] March 2 I have been over with Fanny for too nights. She is not well but better & Joe Whitesides is here to night.

[March 4, 1886-Thursday] 4 I have come home & Cate is gone to stay with Fanny till satterday. I will go back to see her.

[March 7, 1886-Sunday] 7 Sylvanis & Cate, Lawson & Mag, Gim & little ____, all helping Wille to pale in the garden to day. Mr McAlpin has preached today.

[March 8, 1886-Monday] 8 Fanny has a fine sone. It was born March 7, sunday night 1886. I have come home & left Fanny. I am feeling bad. Her & the babe is dooing fine. Fanny is dooing fine. Her Paw was over to see her to day.

[March 14, 1886-Sunday] 14 sunday evening. I have been over to see Fanny. She is dooing fine, the babe is perty cross. We went to the church but oure preacher failed to come.

[March 15, 1886-Monday] 15 Sylvanis & Cate came down this morning & got oure ould loom. Ruff & Eliza & all the children, Sally & Hewe was all up to day. Eliza and Sally & their paw went over to see Fanny a while, all gone home.

[March 16, 1886-Tuesday] R J & I have been sick with the cold but better. It is verry winday to day 16.

[March 21, 1886-Sunday] 21 this is oure preachen but oure preacher is sick & did not come. I have been over to see Fanny to day. She is sorty porly.

[March 28, 1886-Sunday] 28 Fanny & the babe has both been sick with the cold. I have been over theire for a few dayes.

[March 30, 1886-Tuesday] 30 Wille & I have been up with Cate last night. They are all well. Fanny has got better.

[April 1, 1886-Thursday] Aprile 1 Wille & his boy is down to help cousin Gim Floyd to rool logs to day. All well.

[April 7, 1886-Wednesday] 7 Fanny is over with the little stranger. He has the colic & is very cross. Haskel Daubson was out with us last night.

[April 8, 1886-Thursday] 8 Fanny is gone home.

[April 15, 1886-Thursday] 15 Cate & I have been to see Fanny to day. The babe is not dooing well.

[April 18, 1886-Sunday] 18 Mr Mcalpin has preached to day. His tex was in Acts, firs, "What must I doo to be saved? Believe on the Lord Jesus Christ & thou shall be saved."

[April 19, 1886-Monday] 19 Lawson & I went over to Gims last evening. Lawson went for Dr Jackson to come out to see the babe, think it will soon be all right. It cryes with the colic bad. MDBrown

[April 22, 1886-Thursday] 22 Jackson & I have been down to see Eliza & Sally. Eliza is not well, the rest is all dooing fine.

[April 25, 1886-Sunday] 25 Fanny & the children has all been over. The babe is some better. Wille is gone home with her & to go to york to preachen to day.

[April 29. 1886-Thursday] 29 we have had a fine rain. It was greatly needed. Heavenly Farther as thou hast sent us reffreshing showers of rain, oh send thy holy spirit down on these look warm hearts of oures, enliven them, cheer them.

[May 2, 1886-Sunday] Mr Mcalpine preached to day, May 2. He done verry well. His tex was in Kings, "Why halt ye if the Lord be God, serve him, if Balel, serve him."

[May 4, 1886-Tuesday] May the 4 a fine growing time, most too cool. MDB

[May 6, 1886-Thursday] 6 I have been over to see Fanny, all well. Fanny & Gim has been to york to day, got me a nice dress.

[May 9, 1886-Sunday] 9 Wille & I have been over to see Mart & Mag. Mag & Gimmy Ray went to Beth shilo to preachen to day. Mart & I stayed at home & minded the children.

[May 11, 1886-Tuesday] 11 Fanny was over to day. She will come to see me. Let what will happen, a tender loving Daughter. The lord will bless her. Mary D Brown

[May 15, 1886-Saturday] May 15 this is the commencement of oure communion. Mr McAlpin has no one to help him. His tex was in Luke 7 about the woman that washed oure Saviours feet with tears & wiped them with the hair of her head. Aunt Harriet & little Wille Warlick & Wille, Hatty & Eddy Fewell, Bessy Thomison, Sally Castle all came home with us from preachen.

[May 16, 1886-Sunday] Sabbeth evening May 16 Mr Mcalpins tex this morning in Luke 5 c 32 v. "I came not to call the richous, but sinners to repentance." I thought it was the best sermon that he had preached, then the Lords supper. I was well pleased with him. Too joined the church, Mrs Mige Smith, Miss Jane Jones. His tex in the evening was in Acts 12 c abbout Peter in prison. Now comes the trying time, a congragational meeting was held. No one but the Elders & Deacens knew what it was for and what was it for but to vote oure Paster away to leave the Church. All the elders & deacens went against him. 32 in number. Ten for him to stay. He was enstalled paster of Bershaba June 13 1885. Not a year sence he was enstalled paster here & then go & vote him out of the Church without eney warnen was a sin, shame & disgrace to God, oure preacher, oureselves & church. Oh my God all my help & trust is in thee, oh that thou will over rule all these things for thy glory & oure good. It has been a sore tryal. Not my will oh Lord but thyne be done. Mary D Brown

[May 21, 1886-Friday] May 21 we have had a big fresh. It has been raining sence tusday morning till friday. The creek is from hill to hill. Wille had his bottoms all worked over & in good fix. The ground is washed away & buryed up the corn. Gim & Fanny, Sylvanis & Cate has all been here to day. The boyes was gone a hunting.

[May 23, 1886-Sunday] 23 sabbeth evening, a beautifull sabbeth evening after such a storm of rain & wet. This world is not my home I know for sin & sorrow wound me. Then let my lot be what it may, come gladness or come sorrow. I am nearer my home today and may be theire to morrow. With heart resined I bid adieu to those I love & leav. I hope soon to meet you whare parting will be known no more. Mary D Brown

[May 26, 1886-Wednesday] 26 I was over with Fanny last night.

[May 31, 1886-Monday] 31 I have been over with Gim & Fanny. They have both been sick.

[June 2, 1886-Wednesday] June 2 Gim has been verry bad on yesterday, is some better to day. Cate has come down to stay a few dayes with them & I have come home.

[June 5, 1886-Saturday] Gim & Fanny is both better. Mrs Mary Davis & Mrs Sally Davis & children has been to see me this evening. R J is gone to Marts. Wille is gone to York with a bale of cotten.

[June 6, 1886-Sunday] 6 Another wet day. The creek is a full as ever.

[June 8, 1886-Tuesday] 8 Eliza & her children, Sally & Hew all came up this morning. Sally & Wille is gone to see Fanny.

[June 9, 1886-Wednesday] 9 Gim & Fanny came home with Wille & Sally. Had a big spreey, upset the buggy & the creek was verry full but no one got bad hurt & they are all gone home. Mags Baxter is bad sick.

[June 13, 1886-Sunday] 13 I have been up to see Cate, had a big visit to John Davis, then went to see Ginny Whitesides & her twin boyes. She has too little boyes, they are dooing fine & she is gitting along fine. Bell came home with me to stay till morning.

[June 16, 1886-Wednesday] 16 I was over with Fanny last night, all well but Wille is not verry well. I have been over at Lawsons this everning & by to see Bax. He is better. A fine rain last night, this is a beautifull day.

[June 20, 1886-Sunday] 20 Wille & I have been over to the Chappel to preachen to day. Mr Jonson preached a good sermon. His tex was in Romans first chap. Mags Dan has got his arm broke. We came by to see him a few mi-nets.

[June 21, 1886-Monday] 21 Lawsons little Wats is bad with the flux.

[June 22, 1886-Tuesday] 22 Wat is verry bad. I dont think he can live.

[June 23, 1886-Wednesday] Lawsons little Wat died June 23, a wensday eve-ning at foure oclock 1886. Mr Johnson preached his funeral. He spoke verry nice, came home with us & took dinner. We have been called to pass through deep waters.

[June 26, 1886-Saturday] 26 I have been down to see cousin Emiline Floyd to day. She is perty low down. Davis Brown has been bad with the flux & his little boy, Bunnion is verry bad to day.

[June 30, 1886-Wednesday] Davis & Ann Browns little James Bunion died June 30 1886, was Buried a friday. Ould aunt Sally Coldwell was buried the same day. Mr Jonson preached her funeral sermon. I have seen the ould & the young laid in the grave to day. Death is no respecter of persons. What I say unto you, I say unto all, watch. Death is a solom thing & it is busy in our neighborhood. The flux is verry bad, taken the ould & the young.

[July 3, 1886-Saturday] July 3 I was over with Fanny last night, came home & found Mag & Baxter both bad with flux.

[July 4, 1886-Sunday] 4 Mag is verry bad. I have been with her most all day. She is suffering bad.

[July 7, 1886-Wednesday] 7 Cate & Fanny has been down since yesterday morning, have been to see Mag & Bax. They are no better. They are both gone home. Sally & Hatty has been up to see us.

[July 11, 1886-Sunday] 11 Mag is no better. Joe Whitesides was up to day. Lowry Smyth buryed their babe yesterday.

[July 17, 1886-Saturday] 17 Fanny has come over to day & gone up to see Mag & Bax, is both bad.

[July 18, 1886-Sunday] 18 Mag Brown, Bobs wife died July 18 1886.

[July 21, 1886-Wednesday] 21 Bax is no better. Aunt Jane is staying with them.

[July 26, 1886-Monday] 26 I have been over with Fanny for a few dayes. She has had a bad spell, sore mouth, fever & weakness. Dr White waited on her. Cate has come down to stay a few dayes with her & I have come home. Bax is no better.

[July 28, 1886-Wednesday] 28 Baxter is no better.

[*August 1, 1886-Sunday*] Aug 1 I was over with Fanny. She is some better. Bax is living yet but cant live much longer.

[*August 2, 1886-Monday*] 2 Mag Hall & the children has come over to stay a week. Myrtle has been sick.

[*August 3, 1886-Tuesday*] 3 Mag & I have been over & took dinner with Lawson. His little Fanny is sick. Dr Bratten was theire to see her to day, flux & cold. Went over & took supper with Eb & Alis & the children, all well.

[*August 4, 1886-Wednesday*] 4 we had a stranger to day. Bessy Duff from Tenisee, Sister Eliza Duffs grand daughter, a verry nice girle & Wille Thomison brough her up. They are all gone over to Ebs to night & Wille has took Mag & the children over to Fannies to night.

[*August 6, 1886-Friday*] 6 Lenny & Sally Castle, Wille & Bessy is all gone over to Buttler Thomisons & to Union to preachen & Mag has come back. Mag, Cate & Fanny & the children is all here to day & Mart has sent for Mag. Little Baxter died August the 6, on friday evening. He lay thirty five dayes. It was a glourious change for poor little soule & boddy, gone home to his Saviour & to meet his sainted Mother, I hope, meet to part no more.

[*August 12, 1886-Thursday*] 12 John Alexander & I have been down to see Sally & Eliza. They are all well. Mr Cain & Gimmy is both down with the flux.

[*August 14, 1886-Saturday*] 14 I have been over to see Fanny, all tolerable well. Wille is gone to Bethany to a singing to day.

[*August 17, 1886-Tuesday*] 17 Fanny has been over to day. Gim & Wille is over at Joe Neels putting up a barn for him.

[*August 18, 1886-Wednesday*] 18 I have been down to see Cains. They are bad. Mr Cain is suffering bad with his bowles. John Brown has the flux.

[*August 19, 1886-Thursday*] 19 Mr Cain is no better. Gimmy is worse & Bob Gilfillen is down to day. John is no better. Wille has come home to night. He has the cold. I am feeling perty well. MDBrown

[*August 21, 1886-Saturday*] 21 Eliza & Ruff & children, Sally & Hew all came up yesterday morning. We all went up to see Cate & took supper with her & they are all gone home. Mr Cain is better. MDB

[August 22, 1886-Sunday] Sabbeth evening 22 Jackson & Wille is gone to Zion to preachen. I dont feel verry well. They think Mr Cain is better.

[August 24, 1886-Tuesday] 24 Mr Cain & Gimmy is no better. Bob Gilfillen is down to.

[August 26, 1886-Thursday] 26 Jackson & I have been over to see aunt Harriet & Mag, all well & dooing fine as to this worlds good.

[August 30, 1886-Monday] 30 Mr Cain & Gimmy is no better. It has turned to fever. I have been over with Fanny a day & night, all well.

[September 1, 1886-Wednesday] Wensday morning Sept 1 a day & night long to be remembered. The great earthquak of 1886, the like has never been felt in our country. The houses shook till the inmates in manny places left theire home, horry sticken, looking everry moment to see the earth open & all be swallowed up alive. The darkness was awfully frightening, all gone home but I have a guilty consience this night that the children came to Farthers house for comfert & advice in such a trying time & received no better advice & encouragement than they have got this day. My Farther in Heaven, I pray the thou would poor thy holy spirrit out on each one from this long to be remmerable day that by thy grace & by thy strenth we will live more to thy Glory & Honor & for the good of oure own dying soules.

[September 5, 1886-Sunday] 5 Mr Harrison preached for us to day. His tex was in Luke 18 c 4 verse last claus, "Thou I fear not God nor regard man." In the evening in Psalms 32, first few verrses. He done fine & mad out a report to send to Presberty.

[September 6, 1886-Monday] 6 I have been down to see the sick. They mend slow. Eliza & the Children came up this morning, gone over to Ebs to night. Gim & Fanny has come over to stay all night. The excitement of the earthquake is not got over yet. It is heard yet but not so bad. Charlston & Summervill is the worst. Theire is a hunderd thousand inhabitants in Charlston, their houses is nearly all shook down. They have fled to other places & living in tents.

[September 9, 1886-Thursday] 9 Jackson & I have been up to Clover to Presbetary for too dayes. Bethel Presbatary met theire September 7 1886. I did not find out much about it. They exammend a young Mr Blackburn. He stood a fine examination. He was to preach his tryal sermmon that night.

[September 10, 1886-Friday] 10 Wille has some hands helping to cover the wheat house to day & I have been verry sick all day. Fanny had to git them diner & stayed all night with me. Gone home this morning, is going to Beth- shilo to the communion.

[September 11, 1886-Saturday] 11 Cate & Bell & Sylvanis is gone down to Sharon. John Brown & Wille is gone to Clover.

[September 12, 1886-Sunday] 12 Jackson is gone down to Sharon to preachen to day. I am alone, no, not alone, my God is verry near & dear to me. Wille & John was to see cousin Sue Glenn while they was gone. All well.

[September 14, 1886-Tuesday] 14 Sylvanis & Lawson is helping Wille to cover the porch.

[September 16, 1886-Thursday] 16 Fannies babe has been sick with the cold & both of the others. Cate was down with her today.

[September 19, 1886-Sunday] 19 this is the day of the communion at Smerny. Wille is gone. I was not abble to go.

[September 20, 1886-Monday] 20 Cates little Vance was bad last night. Wille & I went up in the night. He is some better this morning.

[September 21, 1886-Tuesday] tusday 21 I was over with Fanny last night. The children is better. They have been making molses. Laws & Sue Neel mad theirs theire too.

[September 27, 1886-Monday] 27 this is the day of the election. I have been up at Cates. Vance is sick yet. I went up to Cates a sunday morning & stayed till monday morning. Left Fanny with her. I dont feel well & Lawson is bad with his head, a pain in it.

[September 29, 1886-Wednesday] 29 Lawson is better & Jackson is gone up

to Cates to see how they are now.

[*September 30, 1886-Thursday*] 30 I have had a little quilting to day. Mrs Coldwell, Ann & Mag & Fanny.

[*October 3, 1886-Sunday*] Oct 3 Gim & Fanny was over last night.

[*October 5, 1886-Tuesday*] 5 Cate & Bell was down to day to help me to quilt. Vance has got better.

[*October 7, 1886-Thursday*] 7 I have been over with Fanny to day. Wille & John was theire ginnen to day.

[*October 8, 1886-Friday*] 8 Mrs Cain was up this evening. We have taken out my quilt.

[*October 10, 1886-Sunday*] 10 Mr Harrison preached for us to day. He is going to preach till next Presbatary. Sally & Joe came home with us. Joe & Wille is gone over to Zion.

[*October 13, 1886-Wednesday*] 13 Jackson & I, Cate & Fanny have all been down to see Eliza & Sally. Had a fine visit. All Well. Fanny went home last night. Cate is gone home this morning. John & Wille is over at Mathews ginen.

[*October 15, 1886-Friday*] 15 Wille has got home to night. All well.

[*October 17, 1886-Sunday*] 17 Gim & Fanny was over last night, all well. Sabbeth evening all well, no preachen, no company, a pleasing Sabbeth day to read & study to prepare for the blessed Sabbeth which shall never end.

[*October 19, 1886-Tuesday*] 19 I have been over with Fanny to day & made a pare of pants for Wille & vest, all well.

[*October 22, 1886-Friday*] 22 John & Wille is down at John Coldwells a ginen.

[*October 24, 1886-Sunday*] 24 Mr Harrison preached to day. His tex was in Mathew 22 c 5 v, "But they made light of it." Some of our members is not coming to preachen. We are right smartely divided. My Heavenly Farther will thou by thy all mighty power over rull all things for thy glory & our good. We are wicked, we are sinfull but oh my God, leave us not nor forsake us not, but will thou unite this people & send us a pasteer that will feed thy sheep & feed thy lambs. Oh that my dear ould Church may bud & blossem like the rose.

[October 26, 1886-Tuesday] 26 Fanny & I have been over to see Lawson & Mag to day & Jackson has gone home with Fanny. John & Wille is ginnen down at the tan yard. MDB

[November 4, 1886-Thursday] Nov 4 I have been to see Fanny & Cate this week & Sally & Hew has come up this morning & Fanny is here too. John & Wille is ginning cotten for Gim. They are all gone home.

[November 7, 1886-Sunday] 7 aunt Harriet & little Wille Warlick was here last night, have all been to preachen to day.

[November 9, 1886-Tuesday] 9 Ruff & Eliza & the children was all up last night & Fanny & I have been to see Mrs Cain to day. Mr Parish fixed oure chimley yesterday & I have come home & been over at Lawson. He thinks little Cloud has the dipthery. Dr Hamright has been to see him.

[November 11, 1886-Thursday] 11 Cloud is no better & Fanny has it too.

[November 12, 1886-Friday] 12 aunt Harriet & Wille Thomison & little Wille has all been up to see Gim & Fanny to day & Jackson & I .

[November 13, 1886-Saturday] 13 I was over with Lawson last night. Cloud is bad. Fanny is not so bad yet. Her Mother is theire.

[November 14, 1886-Sunday] sunday 14 Sylvanis & Cate, Gim & Fanny here last night & Gim & Sylvanis was over at Lawsons last night. Cate & Fanny went over this morning. They are affraid to take the children over there. They are no better. All gone home.

[November 16, 1886-Tuesday] little Cloud died November the 16, a tusday night at ten oclock. A sore & hard death, just choacked to death. Oh my Farther in Heaven, thou has said wheire youre treasure is, theire will your heart be also. My heavenly Farther, I feel & hope I have great treasures in Heaven. My God, my Saviour & redeemer, too suns, too daughters, seven grand sons,

five grand daughters gone home to deck Emmanuel Crown. In this wourld of sin & sorow, I have five daughters & too sons, fourteen grand sons, ten grand daughters, Oh my Saiviour when thou comest to make up thy Jewels, thy own precious Jewels, may none of them be lacking. Oh my God, I humbly pray thee that thou would keep us from being tempted sin, support & deliver us when tempted. My Lord & my God through the strenth of thy holy spirit I commit my Husband, myself, my children & theire little ones to thy care & keeping for time & eternity & may we be all ready to say, "Come Lord Jesus, come quick."

[*November 17, 1886-Wednesday*] 17 Lawson has laid his little boy away. Foure little brothers lying side by side theire to rest till the great reserection morn.

[*November 20, 1886-Saurday*] 20 I have been over at Ebs to day to see Lenny. He has the shingles, right porly. Lawsons little Fanny is better.

[*November 21, 1886-Sunday*] 21 I have been at preachen to day. Mr Harison preached a good sermon.

[*November 22, 1886-Monday*] 22 I have been down at Ruffs to see my first great grand chile. Hatty Magill had a fine daughter November 20. They are dooing fine.

[*November 24, 1886-Wednesday*] 24 I am feeling bad, nervis rumatism in my back & leg.

[*November 25, 1886-Thursday*] 25 Gim & Fanny was over last night. Fanny will come to take care of me if i am not well, better than eney of the rest. She will not loss her reward.

[*November 26, 1886-Friday*] 26 I feel some better to day. Jackson is gone down to see Hatty & the stranger. Ruffes is gone to Columbia, a united states Jury man. Wille is gone down to cousin Gim Floyds to a singing. Gim & Fanny had theire third chile baptised last Sunday, Nov 21 by Mr Harrison, called him James.

[*December 4, 1886-Saturday*] Dec 4 this is the time appointed for oure communion. Wille went down & brought Mr Englis out on yesterday. He preached a great sermon. His tex was in Daniel 30 verses 16 17 18. He was preaching abbout, Shadrack, Mesack & Abendego, came home with us & took dinner & then Wille took him home. It was dreadfull cold when we got up this morning. Theire was a big snow & is snowing & sleeting on. Theire was no preachen to day.

[December 6, 1886-Monday] monday evening 6 we have a big snow, abbout 8 inches deep & is still some snow falling yet. We had no preachen but on friday. The weather has been so bad, Mr Harrison went home with Gim & Fanny & stayed till this morning.

[December 10, 1886-Friday] 10 Sylvanis & Cate came down this morning & Fanny has come this evening.

[December 11, 1886-Saturday] 11 Wille is gone to york. Lawson is gone to take Fanny home.

[December 15, 1886-Wednesday] 15 John & Wille is over at Marts ginning.

[December 19, 1886-Sunday] 19 we have been up to the Church to day but Mr Harrison did not come so we had no preachen.

[December 23, 1886-Thursday] 23 this is the day that Sylvanis & Cate mooved up to Johns Davis house. Lawson, Davis, Gim Land & Wille to help. Got along fine & well fixed up. A good house & every thing nice fixed. We left Wille with them. I was theire but came home tonight.

[December 24, 1886-Friday] 24 Hatty Fewel & Sally Bell Whitesides was here to day, gone back to Ebs.

[December 25, 1886-Saturday] Christmus day. Gim & Fanny & the children is over. All gone home.

[December 27, 1886-Monday] 27 monday Fanny had a big dinner to day. Jackson, I & Wille, Lawson & Mag, Sylvanes & Cate & Eb Land. Had a fine day of it

[December 28, 1886-Tuesday] 28 Sally, Hewe & Eddy Whitesides came up to day, had Lawson & Mag & the children, all over

[December 29, 1886-Wednesday] 29 Joe & Sally, Lawson & Mag, John

Brown & Wille all went up to see Cate to day. Joe & Sally stayed with Lawson to night.

[December 31, 1886-Friday] a friday night, the last night of 1886. Yes, nearly gone. It is a year long to be rememberd by manny a one. Sickness & death, flods of water, earth quakes.

WHAT FANNY HAS GIVE ME IN 1886
MDBROWN
March too dollars
May one dress & pan 1.25c

1887

[January 1, 1887-Saturday] The first day of 1887 has come. I have been spared to see it. My God has kept me here fore some purpus, what it is, God knows. Not my will but thyne be done. Oh my God give me grace, give me patiance, give strenth for to doo thy will. MDB

[January 3, 1887-Monday] 3 monday evening, Mr Harrison preached on yesterday. His tex was in Mathew, "Seek first the kingdom of God & all nessary things shall be added." Mr Harrison came home with us & stayed all night. Verry cold.

[January 4, 1887-Tuesday] 4 this day is dreadfull cold.

[January 5, 1887-Wednesday] 5 a wensday evening, another big snow & verry cold. Wille is gone home with Gim. I am not well.

[January 10, 1887-Monday] 10 I have been over to see Fanny. Little Wille has fell in the fire & got his head burnt, but not bad. Mr Arch Jackson died

Jan the 12 1887.

[January 14, 1887-Friday] 14 Mrs Cain has spent this day with us.

[January 16, 1887-Sunday] 16 Mr Harrison preached to day. Gim & Fanny was over last night.

[January 19, 1887-Wednesday] 19 Wille has been gone over to Parrits this week, him & Gim putting up a house. Ruff & Eliza was up this week, all well. R J is gone over to see Fanny & it is verry cold.

[January 22, 1887-Saturday] 22 Fanny came over yesterday to help to backe Willes weding cake & Jackson is gone up to see Cate & git her to make his pants & went on over to see Mag. All well as common. Wille has taken Fanny home & then going on to York to git his wedding trimmens & has swapt his mule for a gray horse seven years ould this spring.

[January 25, 1887-Tuesday] 25 Sally & Fanny is here to day trymming the cake, has got it all nice & well done.

[January 26, 1887-Wednesday] 26 Sally & Fanny has got through. Joe has come for Sally & Jackson has gone to take Fanny home.

[January 30, 1887-Sunday] 30 we have been up to the Church but no preachen. Mr Harrison failed to come. Eliza & Hatty was up but did not come by.

[February 2, 1887-Wednesday] Wille G Brown & Miss Minny Price was married Feb 2, a wensday morning by Mr Kirkpatrick at her Farthers & came on here for dinner. We had only part of the children. I have not been well & was not abble to make a big infare. Lawson & Sally, Joe & Sally, Gim & Fanny & Sylvanis was all of the children. Had a nice dinner & all got allong fine.

[February 3, 1887-Thursday] 3 all gone & left us.

[February 4, 1887-Friday] 4 Wille & Minny is gone down to Ruffs to day & to Joes to night.

[February 5, 1887-Saturday] 5 Wille & Minny has got back, gone over to stay with Fanny to night & it is verry cold.

[February 6, 1887-Sunday] 6 sabbeth evening all well & at home.

[February 7, 1887-Monday] 7 Wille & Minny went up home this morning & his Paw has taken sick this evening with a pain in his breast & Lawson & Davy is with us.

[February 8, 1887-Tuesday] 8 Jackson is porly. Wille has come home & gone over to Ed Lands & got nine gallons of molases.

[February 9, 1887-Wednesday] 9 Dr Bratten called to see Jackson & ingected some morphene in his breast. It has give him ease but it has affect him perty bad.

[February 10, 1887-Thursday] 10 Fanny has been over this morning for the first time. We was affraid it was scarlatena & it is catchen & they was all affraid of it but the Dr sayes it is not that. Ann is over this evening.

[February 11, 1887-Friday] 11 Cate came down this morning & her Paw is better & they are gone over to Fannies to night.

[February 12, 1887-Saturday] 12 Jackson had a bad spell last night at Fannies & Gim came over for me that night but he had got better beffore I got theire. Fanny came home with us & Cate is gone home

[February 13, 1887-Sunday] 13 I have been to preachen to day. Mr Harrison came home with us & stayed a while & went on to York. Fanny stayed with her Paw. He is still complaining some. John & John Brown is with us this night had some fine _____.

[February 15, 1887-Tuesday] 15 Fanny was over last night, gone home this morning. Jackson is up & abbout.

[February 17, 1887-Thursday] 17 Mrs Cain has been up this evening. I have sent Eliza & Sally word to come up to see theire Paw.

[February 19, 1887-Saturday] 19 Joe & Sally has come up this morning, Lawson Joe & Wille is all gone to York to the railroad election. Jackson had allowd to send for the Dr to come out to day but said he felt better this morning & would not send for him. Fanny came over this evening. Her & Sally is both here.

[*February 21, 1887-Monday*] Feb 20 1887 monday evening Oh my God! Oh my God! How can I write this awfull sene. My God thou hast said, "My grace is sufficient for thee." Oh for grace, oh for faith, oh for strenth to rely on thy precious promises, especily is such an hour as this. My dear ould Husband, Robbert Jackson Brown died a sabbeth evening at four oclock, setting up in his big arm chaire without a moan ore a struggle. The Dr had never been to see him till this evening. He said it was breast dropsy. He told him he could not cure him but he could give him something to releave him. He did not seem to be allarmed at all. When the Dr left he walked out in the porch & talked to him & came in & was talking as well a common. One sigh & the work was done. The Lord gave & the Lord taketh, blessed be the name of the Lord. I beleve he has gone home to God. Jesus has tole us in his Fathers hous theire are manny mansions if I go to prepare a place for you I will come again & receive you to my self that whare I am you may be also. My Lord & my God prepare me for that home, home, home. Mr Ingless came out & preached a funeral sermon. He read the ninthieth Psalm, the twelfth vers, "So teach us to number our dayes that we may apply our hearts unto wisdom." He gave us a solom address, sung 636 hymn "Oh for an overcoming faith, to cheer my dying hours." 630 "Why do we mourn departing friends or shake at deaths alarm."

[*February 22, 1887-Tuesday*] 22 a tusday evening, one more day & night with out a husbban & a Farther. My Heavenly Farther thou hast promised to be a Farther to the widow and farthaless verry thy promises to us all at this of oure deep sorow and affliction, these deep waters thou hast called us to pass through. Prepare the living for life, the dying for death. MDB

> 1 In vain the fancy strives to paint
> The moment after death
> The glories that surround a saint
> When yielding up his breath
>
> 2 One gentle sigh the fetter breaks
> We scarce can say Hes gone
> Beffore the willing spirit takes
> Its mansions near the throne
>
> 3 Faith strives but all its efforts fail
> To trace the spirits flight
> No eye can pierce within the veil

That hides the world of light

4 We know and tis enough to know
Saints are completly blesst
Have done with sin and care and woe
And with their Saiviour rest

5 On harps of gold they praise his name
And see him face to face
Oh let us catch the sacred flame
And run the heavenly race

unknown

Heavenly fellowship & society is an element of that blessedness into which the belever passes at death. It is called a family, the family of God whare all the family of Christ are gatherd together. A sweet & everlasting Home that the redeemed shall know each other in Heaven is in acordance with scripture. Death dose not dig an impassable gulf between us & our sainted ones. They are not lost, we shall meet them, and know them. If Lazarus knew Abraham resting in his bosom may not I know them too? If Paul could know in another the christians to whom he preached on earth, why shall I not know those with whome I have been intimatly associated with here. Our precious lost one found in glory with Jesus they glorified Redeemer wheire he has gone to prepare a place for all his loved ones. MD Brown

[February 22, 1887-Tuesday] Feb 22 Eliza & Fanny & the children stayed all night with us but no Farther to cheer the dreary night. Seens seraphic high and glorious now forbid his longer stay, see him rise ore death victorious, Angels becen him away.

[February 23, 1887-Wednesday] 23 A wensday evening Sylvanis & Cate came down & stayed with us last night, gone home.

[February 24, 1887-Thursday] 24 I have been over with Fanny a day & night.

[February 27, 1887-Sunday] 27 sabbeth evening I have been to preachen to day but no R J theire. I hope he is enjoying the eternal sabbeth day in that hous of manny mansions with Jesus & the glorified saints in Heaven abbove.

[February 28, 1887-Monday] Ebs wife & Sally has been here to day, Monday the 28.

[March 2, 1887-Wednesday] March 2 the children most all has been here to day, Eliza & Sally, Lawson & Mag, Mag Hall, Gim & Fanny.

[March 3, 1887-Thursday] 3 the children is all gone home & cousin Emaline Floyd is here to day.

[March 4, 1887-Friday] 4 we have been planting in the garden to day & Wille & Minny is gone up to see Cate this evening. John B & John A is with me. Oh what a miss, Oh what a loss, Oh when will I feel right again? When we meet in Heaven to part no more.

[March 6, 1887-Sunday] 6 Wille & Minny is gone to the Chapel to preachen. Fanny has been over a while. We went up to the graveyard seen the little hillock. How still and peaceful is the grave wheire lifes vain timults past the appointed hors by heavens decree, Recives us all at last.

[March 9, 1887-Wednesday] 9 I have been with Fanny sence monday till wensday evening. She has been to York & got some things for her & me & has made my new dress.

[March 10, 1887-Thursday] 10 Lawson, Wille & Joe has all been to york to day.

[March 13, 1887-Sunday] 13 sunday evening I have been up with Cate for too nights. They have had the cold & tooth ack. Sylvanis brought me down to preachen this morning. Mr Harrisen preached to day. His tex, "Lord be mercifull to me a sinner." Mr Harrison & aunt Harriet came home with us.

[March 14, 1887-Monday] 14 Wille & Minny is gone over to stay with Mart & Mag & Fanny has come over to stay with me.

[March 17, 1887-Thursday] 17 Wille has taken Minny up home to stay a few dayes.

[March 19, 1887-Saturday] 19 Wille is gone after Minny & they are working the road to day. Wille & Minny is gone over to stay with Fanny to night. John

B, John A is all with me to night.

[March 20, 1887-Sunday] 20 sabbeth evening I have had a fine day reading the saints everlasting rest. Oh what a glourious rest for them that love God. MD Brown

A sabbeth evening, one month this evening sence God took my dear ould Husband home. A long & dreary month it has been to me in this wourld of sin & woe but hush this wicked heart.

> When waves of sorrow round me swell, my soule is not dimayed
> I hear a voice I know full well, Tis I, be not affraid.
>
> I will meet you, I will love you, In the far off Eden land
> I will walk with you forever, I will hold you by the hand
> I will talk to you my darling, I will hear your sweet reply
> As we wonder by the river, That flows through paradice.
>
> I know theire is around you, A circle of the blest
> But I know when I behold you, I will know you from the rest
> I will know you by your singing, and the love light in your eyes
> Oh i'll know you & I'll love you, When we meet in Paradice.

[March 22, 1887-Tuesday] March 22 this is my birthday, sixty five long years, yes sixty five long years my God hast thou kept me in this world and I humbly thank thee for all the blessings & privaleges that thoust hast bless me with. Thou hast brought me through danger seen & unseen but abbove all I bless thee for that glouris hope that I have been born again, that this sin polluted soule of mine has been washed in the blood Christ. Oh my God prepare this soule of mine to ware the weeding garment arayed in that bright robe of Christs richeness which he has prepard for all them that love & serve him. My Heavenly Farther thoust has said that whare youre treasure is theire will your heart be. Also my God in Christ I hope & I believe that I have great treasures theire, Christ my great reedeme & advocate clothed in his glorified hummanity, high seated on his Farthers right hand, my sainted Farther & Mother, Husband & children & a host more gone home to deck Emaniels crown. My Heavenly Farther give me living grace, give me dying grace, that whenever it is thy will to take me home that I can say, come Lord Jesus, come quickly. MD Brown

[March 23, 1887-Wednesday] 23 Fanny has ben over to day. Dear chile, how glad I am to see her come.

[March 26, 1887-Saturday] 26 satterday night I have been over to see Mag to day, the close of another week. One sweetly solem thought comes to me ore & ore neeare my parting houre now than ere I was before. MDB

[March 27, 1887-Sunday] Sabbeth evening March 27 I have been to hear Mr Harrison to day, his last sermon. His tex was in Genisus the 7 chapter first verse. We are now left without a paster ore a preacher & but foure elders. Come oh Lord, come quickly with thy overrulling power for vain is the help of man.

[March 28, 1887-Monday] 28 Davis & Wille is gone to york.

[April 1, 1887-Friday] Aprile 1 I have gone up to stay a while with Cate.

[April 2, 1887-Saturday] 2 I went over to Marts this morning.

[April 3, 1887-Sunday] 3 I was at the Chappel at preachen to day. Mr Jonson preached. His tex was in Revelations first chapt, fifth verse.

[April 4, 1887-Monday] 4 Mag & I was over to see Ginny Whitesides to day. This is the time of Presbetary at Smerny. I failed to git to go. Cates & Sylvanis, Mary Bell was born Aprile the 8 1887.

[April 10, 1887-Sunday] 10 I have got home from Cates this morning. Her & the babe is doing verry well. I am feeling verry bad with the cold.

[April 13, 1887-Wednesday] 13 I have got home from Cates, her and the babe is doing fine. Wille, Minny & I have been over to see Fanny to day.

[April 19, 1887-Tuesday] 19 I have been down to see Eliza & Sally, all well, but ould aunt Betsy Black is sick at Ruffs. Ruff brought me home, found all well. I am feeling bad myself.

[April 20, 1887-Wednesday] 20 Fanny, Minny & I have been on a visit to Mr Cains to day.

[April 21, 1887-Thursday] 21 I have spent this day with Lawson & Mag.

[April 23, 1887-Saturday] 23 I have been bad with a pain in my side last night. It has got some better but I am verry porly yet. Wille went for Fanny this morning. She is with me, dear chile.

[April 24, 1887-Sunday] 24 Gods holly sabbeth evening. I feel theire is but a step between me & death. Theire is something the matter with my breast & heart. God may soon call me home from time to eternity to give an acount of the talent he has give me. Oh my God may I not be the slothfull servent who hid his Lords money. Give me grace to live that I may not be affraid to die whenever the sommons may come.

[April 26, 1887-Tuesday] 26 Eliza & Sally came up yesterday morning & stayed till this morning, gone home. I am feeling some better. Wille is gone to Cates & Mags & to york.

[April 27, 1887-Friday] 27 I am not feeling eney better. Dr Bratten has been out to see me to day. He seems to think it is heart disease that is hurting me. I am oppresed to git my breath. Fanny is here.

[April 28, 1887-Thursday] 28 Wille is gone to take Fanny home & hall cross ties fore Gim.

[April 30, 1887-Saturday] 30 Fanny has come back. Will & Gim gone to club meeting.

[May 1, 1887-Sunday] May 1 Wille & Minny has been to the Chapple to preachen to day. Fanny staid with me. I have been verry weak & bad to day from the medicen, feeling better this evening. Fanny is gone home.

[May 2, 1887-Monday] 2 Mary & Bell Love has been up to see me to day & Bell Whitesides.

[May 3, 1887-Tuesday] 3 Mag Hall & Mary, Sally & Mirtle was up last night. All gone over to see Fanny & John Alexander & Minny. I am feeling a heap better this evening, thank God.

[May 5, 1887-Thursday] 5 Cate has come down this morning & I have sent over for Fanny & she is here too, the first time Cate has been down with her little daughter. Both dooing fine.

[May 6, 1887-Friday] 6 Cate & Fanny is both gone home.

[May 12, 1887-Thursday] 12 I have been over with Fanny for a few dayes. She has been macking my black dress. I may soon need it to lay me in the cold & silent toomb. I am feeling some better this morning. Ould Dr Bratten has been out to see me this morning. He sayes I have heart disease & my nerves has give way.

[May 15, 1887-Sunday] Sabbeth evening 15 I have had a bad spell sence last thursday. I sent for Lawson & Fanny & Dr Bratten. He was here yesterday. I am feeling some better this evening. Eliza Ann & Sally & Joe was up to day.

[May 17, 1887-Tuesday] 17 Fanny was with me last night. She is a dear & true chile. I will never lack while she can doo eney thing for me. My God will reward her. Mag Hall was over yesterday evening. I am still feeling better, Gods will is mine. If it is his will to restore me to health & has eney more work for me to doo, with his strenth I will doo what I can. If he sees fit to remove me from time to Eternity, a jewel in Emmanuels crown to gem through eternity the fore-head that for me was once wreathed with thorns, shall I, can I murmer at any way my Savior sees meet to polish and prepare me for such an honor as this?

[May 19, 1887-Thursday] 19 Aunt Sister Harriet has been up to see me to day. She has not been well but still keeps going. Cate has been down & over to see Fanny. Gim & Fanny has been over this evening.

[May 22, 1887-Sunday] 22 Sabbeth evening am feeling better, have had a fine day to read Gods Holy word, Have had no company, a calm and peacefull sab-beth evening. Three long months, yes long they have been sence I laid my dear oull Husband in the cold & silent tomb & I am still here suffering pain, sickness & sorrow. Oh my wicked heart, murmer not at youre lot. God knows best.

[May 23, 1887-Monday] May 23 young Dr Bratten has been out to day, I am feeling better. I think it is time to dismiss him.

[May 25, 1887-Wednesday] 25 Joe & Sally has come up this morning. Sally & I went over to see Fanny. It has rained this evening & they have stayed all night.

[May 27, 1887-Friday] 27 Fanny & Mrs Cain is over this morning & I am feeling better.

[May 29, 1887-Sunday] 29 Wille & Minny went over to Gim Lands last night & to the chapple to day. It seems that we are a long time to have eney preachen at oure dear ould church. I dont feel well to day but have had a fine dayes readding.

> He is a God of soverign love, who promised heaven to me,
> and tought my thoughts to sore above, where happy spirits be.
> Prepare me Lord for thy right hand, then come the joyful day,
> come death & some celestral band, to bear my Soule away.

[May 31, 1887-Tuesday] 31 last day of May I am feeling a good deal better Fanny has been over this morning & we have had rain.

[June 3, 1887-Friday] June 3 I am feeling pretty well. All at home & all well. We have had a dreadfull rain this evening. Edward Black was found dead this evening down at the branch.

[June 4, 1887-Saturday] 4 I have witnessed a solem seen this day a brother & a sister brought in the church, laid side by side. Mr English preached the funeral sermon. His tex was in first Psamuel, "As the Lord liveth & as thy soule liveth theire is but a step between me & death," then took them to the grave & laid side by side. Margaret Black died sudden on the road from her unckles. We are dying, we will soon be all dead & the place which knows us shall soon know us no more forever. The time is short, the Master will soon come. Therefore it bee hooves us to bee all reddy for at an houre, when ye think not, the sone of man cometh.

[June 7, 1887-Tuesday] 7 I have been over with Fanny. She has been sick, is some better. Lawsons _____ was born June the 6 1887. Davis & Anns was born June 7 at too in the morning 1887.

[June 11, 1887-Saturday] 11 Eliza & the children was up last night, all well. Too of Minnes sisters too.

[June 17, 1887-Friday] 17 I was over to see Ann this evening & up to the graveyard to see the last resting place of my loved ones. MDB

[June 24, 1887-Friday] June 24 John & I have been down to see Joe & Sally, all well. Came on & took dinner with Ebs people & then home.

[June 28, 1887-Tuesday] 28 I have been over to see Fanny. She has not been well. She came home with me. We have been up to the church & sweept it out & cleaned up every thing nice with the hopes of having preaching next sabbeth. We have had a long fast from hearing the sweet sound of the word of God preached in oure dear ould church & in the grave yard to see last resting place of our loved ones.

[July 2, 1887-Saturday] July 2 Wille is gone to York for oure preacher that is to preach for us tommorow. John & Minny is gone over to see Ann, she is sick.

[July 3, 1887-Sunday] Sabbeth evening my God & Heavenly Farther has spared me to go to my dear ould church once more to hear the joyfull sound of Gods love to dying sinners. The preacher that preached for us to day is a Jerman, his name, the rev C R Birnback. I thought he done verry well. His morning tex was in Acts. In the evening 2 Timothy 1c 6v "That thou stir up the gift of God that is in you." He is preachen in Chester District, about 35 miles away. We had a fine congragation of people. It seemed that all was glad to git back to the ould church once more. Oh my God hasten the happy day when we shall have a paster to feed thy sheep, feed thy lambs. Help Lord for vain is the help of Man.

[July 4, 1887-Monday] 4 he stayed with us from satterday till this morning, a monday morning. Lawson is gone to take him to York. Wille & Minny is gone over to stay with Fanny to night. I have been over to see Ann. She is bad with her head.

[July 9, 1887-Saturday] 9 I have had a big visit down to see Eliza & Sally & down to see cousin Psalm Brown. He is at Chambers, he is in a bad fix he cant walk. He can set up in his big chair when he is set up in it. Cousin Margaret is verry porly too. Sally & I went over & stayed all night with Jonny & Laura Russel, back up to Joes. Ruff & Eliza & the children was all over their for dinner, then Joe brought me home. Found all well. Wille & Minny went home with her Farther.

[July 11 1887-Monday] July 11 Fanny has been over to day.

[July 15, 1887-Friday] 15 Fanny & I have been to see Mart & Mag, took dinner with them then to aunt Harriets stay all night. All went & took dinner with John & Emm Quinn then back home with Fanny. Stayed all night

with her then home. I have been over with Fanny a few dayes, her & little Gimmy has been sick.

[July 16, 1887-Thursday] 16 they have had a singing at Bershaba today & Jane Furgison has come to stay a week with us.

[July 18, 1887-Saturday] 18 I have spent this day with Mrs Cain.

[July 19, 1887-Sunday] 19 Jane & I have been up to see Cate to day, all well. I have been staying with Fanny. Little Gimmy is sick.

[July 30, 1887-Thursday] 30 I have come home. I have left Cate to stay with Fanny, the boy is some better.

[August 1, 1887-Monday] August 1 Little Gimmy is some better. They have all been over a day & night. We have had heavy rains, the creeks is full.

[August 6, 1887-Saturday] 6 this has been the Club picknick day. The brass band played. Theire was three spoke. A large crowd & plenty of diner. Sally has come home with us.

[August 7, 1887-Sunday] Sabbeth evening Aug 7 1887 young Mr Mackelwain of Lankester preached for us to day, the first time he has ever preached for us. He is going to preach too month during his vacation. His tex was in Mathew 5c, "Ye are the salt of the earth." I was well pleased with him.

[August 10, 1887- Wednesday] 10 oure preacher went to Mr Cains to stay all night then over to Gimy Lands all night. He took him down to his other church. Wille & John is gone to york to day.

[August 11, 1887-Thursday] Aug 11 Wille & Minny & Davis all started up to Waco this morning to see Brother John Brown & all the rest of the friends

[August 12, 1887-Friday] 12 Fanny was over with us last night.

[August 13, 1887-Saturday] 13 Wille & Minny has got home. Found them all living. Brother John is still living, waiting & ready for the summouns to take him home.

[August 15, 1887-Monday] 15 Cate & Bell was down to day. Joe White-sides & Sally met with a sad misfortune last satterday night, got his too mules drownded in Clarks fork creek, worth thre hunderd dollars. Lawson & Wille is gone down theire to night to see them.

[August 19, 1887-Friday] 19 I have been over with Fanny a few dayes.

[August 20, 1887-Saturday] 20 theire has been a picknick at the Capel to day. Ed Price & John Brown is here to night. Mary D Brown

[August 21, 1887-Sunday] Sabbeth evening August 21 I have been to preachen to my dear ould church once more. Mr Perry preached us a great ser-mon to day. His tex in Acts 9c, "Lord what will thou have me to doo?" I hope we all will rember it & go to work better than we have been dooing for myself. I feel that working time is most gone. Lord I pray thee give me grace, faith & strenth for what ever is thy will. Not mine but thin be done, living grace & dying grace to tryumph over the monster death.

[August 24, 1887-Wednesday] 24 Ruff & Eliza has come up to day. Ruff is gone to York. Mr Gim Magill & Hatty, Eliza & I have spent to day with Lawson & Mag.

[August 25, 1887-Thursday] 25 Ruff is gone home. Eliza & I am going to see Cate to day.

[August 26, 1887-Friday] 26 Ruff & Eliza is gone home & left Mary with me.

[August 27, 1887-Saturday] 27 this has been a dreadfull dayes rain. The creek is from hill to hill.

[August 30, 1887-Tuesday] 30 Fanny & I have been to York to day. I have had my picture taken & Fanny had Jetty & Gimmys taken & Fanny has come home with me.

[August 31, 1887-Wednesday] 31 Gim is helping Wille to start his cook room.

[September 1, 1887-Thursday] Sept 1 little Mary Whitesides & I have been over to spend the day with Mr Retty Coldwell.

[September 3, 1887-Saturday] 3 John Alexander is gone down to Joe White-sides, Wille to york.

[September 4, 1887-Sunday] 4 Mr William McElwaine preached for us to day. His tex this morning was in Ephesians 5c 14v, "Awake thou that sleepeth & arise from the dead & Christ shall give thee light." In the evening, 1 Samuel 15:22.

[September 8, 1887-Thursday] 8 Cousin Sue Glenn & her oldest son, Henry, came down last night. We have been macking calls all day. Wille is gone with her over to Fannies now. Bell Whitesides & Minny is gone to see Mary & Bell Love.

[September 10, 1887-Saturday] 10 satterday evening of oure communion. Mr Robbert Perry & Mr William McElwain was both theire. Mr Perry preached this morning. His tex was in Ephesians 3c commencion at the 14v. Sister Harriet & cousin Molly Fewel & her too sons, Wille & Jonny was with us last night & Mr Perry.

[September 19, 1887-Monday] Sept 19 I have been over & helped Fanny to put in her web. She is gitting along fine.

[September 25, 1887-Sunday] sunday evening 25 I have been down with Eliza & Sally. Mary Brown has the dipthera, is some better. Joe has been having some work done on his house. Mr Perry preached to day, "Beleve on the Lord Jesus Christ and thou shall be saved."

[September 26, 1887-Monday] 26 Fanny & the children is here to day.

[October 1, 1887-Saturday] Oct 1 Wille & Minny is gone over to aunt Harriets to night.

[October 2, 1887-Sunday] 2 Gim & Fanny is gone over to the Chapel to preachen to day & I have stayed & minded the children.

[October 4, 1887-Tuesday] 4 I have been over with Fanny helping her with her web & brought oure part home. The children has the sore eyes.

[October 7, 1887-Friday] 7 I have been down to see cousin Gim Floyd to day.

[October 9, 1887-Sunday] 9 Sabbeth evening I have been to preachen to day, Mr Perry, a good sermon on the tithes. What a great priv it was to give of oure substance to the Lord.

[October 12, 1887-Wednesday] 12 Mrs Cain has been up to spend to day with us & Wille & Minny is gone over to Gim Lands to a shucking to night.

[October 14, 1887-Friday] 14 Fanny & I have been over to see unckle Joe Stincens this evening. He is verry low. I dont think he can live long.

[October 18, 1887-Tuesday] Unckle Joe Stincen died Oct 18, a Tusday morning & was burried at Bethel, a wensday. I have been staying with Fanny for a week.

[October 19, 1887-Wednesday] Mr Jonson is at Fannies to night 19, was down at Mr Joe Smiths to marry Mr Thomis & Miss Sally Smith.

[October 21, 1887-Friday] 21 I have got home from Gims & Sally is here & Sallly & I Wille & Minny is all going up to see Cate.

[October 22, 1887-Saturday] 22 Sally & I have been to see Mart & Mag to day. The children all has the hooping cough. Sally & Murtle is bad. Joe has come up to night, Gim & Fanny. Oh what a miss, no Farther to greet them with a smile & welcom. God has promised to be a God to the Fartheless & the widows stay, and as Farther pitheth his children so the Lord pitheth them that fear him. We have all been to preachen to day but Fanny. She is sick, not able to go. Mr Perry tex was in Act 27c 22 31 verses. He was preachen on election. I thought he preached a great sermon & mad it verry plain. Joe & Sally is gone home. Gim & Fanny is no better.

[October 24, 1887-Monday] 24 Fanny is no better & Minny is gone over to stay with her.

[October 26, 1887-Wednesday] Oct 26 Wille & Minny has come home. Fanny is some better & I am going over.

[October 29, 1887-Saturday] 29 Fanny is better & I have come home. Gimmy is helping Wille to cover his cook room.

[October 30, 1887-Sunday] 30 Wille is gone to the Chapel to preachen. It has been a cold, wet day. Came by Marts to see the children. They are bad with the caugf. Bessy Duff was to see us this evening.

[October 31, 1887-Monday] 31 Wille & Minny is gone down to cousin Gim Floyds to night to git honey. MD Brown

[November 1, 1887-Tuesday] Nov 1 Gim is helping Wille on his cook room & Fanny is over too & Minny is gone home with her.

[November 4, 1887-Friday] 4 Fanny & I have been to spend the day with Mrs Cain.

[November 6, 1887-Sunday] 6 sabbeth evening Fannys little Gimmy cut too of his toes most off yesterday but he is dooing fine & I have come home.

[November 7, 1887-Monday] 7 Wille & Minny & John is all gone to york to day.

[November 8, 1887-Tuesday] 8 Silvanis & Wille is gone to Blacks station with the waggon.

[November 10, 1887-Thursday] 10 Eliza, Eddy, Mary & Brown has been up to see us. We were all over to see Gim & Fanny last night, all well & gone home this morning.

[November 13, 1887-Sunday] 13 Sabbeth evening we have had no preachen to day, oure Preachers wife is sick. Joe & Sally, Gim & Fanny came by a while.

[November 19, 1887-Saturday] 19 I have had a tripp up at Cates. Went home with her a Thursday morning, spent that evening with Mrs Lissy Walker a friday with Mr Frank Walker & family. Had a plesent visit. Sylvanis has brought me home this evening, all well.

[November 21, 1887-Monday] 21 it is verry cold & we have killed oure hogs to day, foure fine ones. I doo feel verry humble & thankfull we have made bread & meat, plenty to doo us to live on.

[November 24, 1887-Thursday] 24 Mag Hall & the little girls came up last

night & stayed till this evening. She wont be back soon, if ever as she has a great seen before her. Wille & Minny & John Alexander is all gone down to Mr Gim Cains to stay till bedtime. I & Rob is here allone & I am feeling bad with a pain in my breast & shoulder. Blessed Saviour I devolve my every care on Thee. Thou art noting now on the throne, the pangs & sorowes of every burdend heart. All other love is imperfect. May it be my joy to serve thee, my privelege to follow thee & if need be to suffer with thee. May everry cross lose its bitterness by having thee at my side. Livin ore dying may I be Thine. Mary D Brown, Nov 24 1887.

[November 26, 1887-Saturday] 26 Fanny & the children has been over a day & night, now gone home. John Alexander is gone down to see Jane.

[November 27, 1887-Sunday] 27 sabbeth evening Mr Perry preached to day. His tex was in first Peter 48. Oh thou blessed advocate with in the veil. Thou who art now interceding for thy tried ones. Do thou impart unto me a constant supply of thy promised grace.

[December 3, 1887-Saturday] Dec 3 I have been over with Fanny for a few dayes, all well. Wille & Minny is gone up to her Farthers to night & to Enen to preachen tommorow. Minny is gone to git her sertificate to join with Wille.

[December 4, 1887-Sunday] 4 Sabbeth evening John & I have had to day by oure selves, a happy day & my soul never suppose amid the faithlessness of earths trusted friends that thou art doomed to thread thy way in loneliness & solitude. There is more than one Emmas journey, the Abiding Friend is left. He is alwayes the same. He fainteth not, neither is weary. His faith full-ness is a tried faithfulness. His word is a tryed word. His friendship is a tryed friendship. He is alwayes better than His word. He payes with usury. I love to think of thy faithfulness. O thou tried stone laid in Zion & thou art faithfull still. MD Brown

[December 6, 1887-Tuesday] 6 Wille is gone down after Hewe. They are go-ing to Bob Furgirsons. Mr Cain is here this evening.

[December 8, 1887-Thursday] 8 Gim & Fannie is here to night.

[December 10, 1887-Saturday] 10 satterday night Wille & Minny is gone over to stay with Fanny to night. Oh my God forgive their sin of breaking thy

Holly Sabbeth day.

[December 11, 1887-Sunday] Sabbeth evening Dec 11 Mr Perry preached to day on Justifacation, then we had an election for a preacher, Mr Kirkpatrick ore Mr Perry. Mr Perry got 22 Mr Krikpatrick 21. I lost my vote. I hope God in his loving kindness & tender mercy will make it all rite for his glory & the good of oure church.

[December 13, 1887-Tuesday] 13 John Alexander has left us this morning, him & Hewe. Wille is gone with them to york. I feel sorry for John.

[December 15, 1887-Thursday] 15 Wille is gone to york to day with the last of his cotton. He has sole eight bales, he has mad a fine crop.

[December 18, 1887-Sunday] Sabbeth evening Dec 18 1887 Mr Kirkpatrick of Clover preached for us to day. His tex was in First Corinthians 3c 11 12 13 verses. A great sermon he did preach.

[December 28, 1887-Wednesday] wensday 28 I have been over with Mag Hall. She has come through a great seen. She had a dead born daughter Dec 22, a thursday 1887. Dr White was with her. I did not like him much. She was verry bad. I stayed with her till monday, came back to Fannies. She came home with me & stayed too nights. She left sorowfull, not knowin whether she would ever be back again. Let us trust our God. He will do all things right. If he is for us who can be against us to harm us.

[December 29, 1887-Thursday] 29 Wille is gone to take Fanny & the children home. She is some better this morning. John Berry & his wife is here to night.

[December 31, 1887-Saturday] Dec 31 Sylvanis & Cate, little Vance & Mary was here to day & Eddy & Denim Price is here to night. A satterday night near the cloosing hour of 1887. My Lord & my God, heare I set seeted at my little table, a monymount of thy Grace, Love & Mercy. Oh that I may love and praise thee as I ought, but when I see thee as thou art Ill prais thee as I ought. Oh my God thou has called me to pass through great seens. Sence this night twelve month ago, my dear ould Husband was with me. Here I am in this willnerness, travling on as fast as time can moove. My Heavenly Farther, I have many & great things to thank thee for, for the good & kind children

that thou hast given me & for the hope, the glourious hope, that they a thyne own dear children. Oh my God I have soons in law, I fear for them. They are thy proffessed disciples. Oh my God if they have never been born oh send thy Holy Spirits with power on theyer hard & stony hearts ear it be too late that we may meet an unbrocken family when thou comest to mak up thy own precious Jewels to deck Emanieuls Crown. Oh my God thou has promised to be a father to the Fartherless & the widows stay. Verryfy thy God to the promis to me & mine is the prayer of theire poor Mother for Christs sake. Amane

1888

[January 1, 1888-Sunday] A new years Sabbeth evening 1888 this has been a pleasent new years sabbeth day. No company to mar Gods holy sabbeth day. I have tryed to spend it reading my bibble & studing its solom truths. I am this day a monument of Gods love & mercy. My Heavenly Farther as thou hast spared this life of mine fore some wise purpos, give me love, grace & strenth fore what ever is thy will.

[January 2, 1888-Monday] 2 Wille is gone to York and Ann Brown is here. Mrs Molly Thomson died Jan 5 1888 down on Clarks fork, left a Husband & too little children.

[January 6, 1888-Friday] 6 Joe, Sally & Eddy has come up to day. Sally & I went over to see Fanny.

[January 7, 1888-Saturday] 7 all gone home this morning.

[January 10, 1888-Tuesday] 10 I have been over with Fanny fore a few dayes.

Wille & Minny is gone up to stay with Cate to night & Jackson Castle, Loury Brown & Lissy & Clary Brown is with me to night.

[January 12, 1888-Thursday] 12 This has been a cold, sleety day. Jon & Wille is helping at the school house to day. I am going over to stay with Fanny till she gits through.

[January 30, 1888-Monday] Fannies _____ was born January 30 1888, a monday morning. She got allong fine, sent for Dr Bratten, was all over before he got theire. Mr & Mrs Cain, Cate & Sylvanis, Wille & Minny was all over to day.

[February 4, 1888-Saturday] Feb 4 I have come home this morning to stay a day & night & then gone back to stay while longer.

[February 9, 1888-Thursday] 9 I have got home this evening, left Fanny & the babe dooing tolerable well. A fine large girl to git reddy for preachen.

[February 11, 1888-Saturday] 11 this has been a cold, icy morning. We was to have preachen to day but no one went to York for the preacher, Mr Neevel, so we had no preachen. Mart Hall came home with us & went to the club meeting.

[February 12, 1888-Sunday] Sabbeth evening Feb the 12 Mr Neevels got out to day. He preached a great sermon. His tex was in Amos 6 c 1 verse, first claus, "Woe to them that are at eas in Zion." The hyms he sung, 317 391 & 397. After Mr Neevells sermon the congragation put in a call for Mr M R Kirkpatrick of Clover for half of his time & to unite Clover & Bershaba. Oh my God I pray thee that thou will own & bless what has been done this day, that we may once more have a paster to feed thy sheep & feed thy lambs.

[February 15, 1888-Wednesday] 15 I have got home once more. I hope to stay awhile. I have been with Fanny for near five weeks. I have left them tolerable well. They have all been sick, but is better. MB

[February 26, 1888-Sunday] 26 I have had a big visit down to see my daughters, Eliza & Sally. They have not been verry well but has got better. Had a fine visit. Joe & Sally came home with me this morning to go to preachen. When I come home I found Wille sick with the cold. We all went to hear Mr Inglis

of York preach this evening. He preached a fine sermon. His tex was in Luke 8 35, "Setting at the feet of Jesus & clothed in his right mind." Then they made up the money for the call of Mr Kirkpatrick. They got along fine, made up too hundred & sixty dollars & think they can easy rais one hundred more. The call was for three hundred. Joe & Sally is gone home.

[March 1, 1888-Thursday] March 1 I have been over with Mag Hall for a few dayes. She has had a spell of the pains for some weeks, is a little better now, abble to walk over the house. Found Mrs Price & her daughter here. Unckle Franklin Furguson is on a visit to see his kin.

[March 3, 1888-Saturday] 3 Fanny is over to day with her new daughter, the first time, Gimmy & all the children. John Alexander came up to stay a week.

[March 11, 1888-Sunday] 11 Mr Kirkpatrick preached to day. It has been a verry wet morning but few out. I was not feeling well. John Alexander, unckle Frank & Wille went.

[March 12, 1888-Monday] 12 Wille has gone to moove John Alexanders things down to Bob Furgesons this evening. Cal Whisenhunt & Sally Castle was married March the 14 1888.

[March 15, 1888-Thursday] 15 Mary Hall was here to day. Gim Ray is gone to the infare. They are gone home. I am feeling bad with my back.

[March 22, 1888-Friday] 22 I have been over with Fanny for a week & am feeling verry unwell, the dross to consume, the gold to reffine. Theire is a home for sweet repose on that celestral shore, home, home.

[March 25, 1888-Sunday] March 25 Sabbeth evening my God has been good to me this day. I have been to his house to day to hear oure belloved Paster preach to day. His tex was in Judges 6, "Giden, I have sent you." It was a good sermon. He compared himself to Giden. He said he felt that God had called & sent him to preach to us. Great God thou hast all power & I humbly pray & beseech the for Jesus sake for the sake of my never dying soule fore the soules of my children & theire little ones fore every member of oure dear ould church that thou would bless us with the outporing of thy Holly Spirit on us, that every voice may awaken & cry alloud to thee for help, for thou hast promised to help, when we cry to thee for help.

[March 28, 1888-Wednesday] 28 This is a wet day, has been raining for dayes. I feel verry solom this morning on hearing of the death of my dear friend, Mrs Dr Alison. How mysterious are thy wayes Oh Lord God Allmigty, thou hast taken the young mother from her dear children, three little girls left to baffel with this cold world without the care & love of a mother. Oh God watch over them in the path of wisdom. One son Jonny, a nice & promising young man & a devoted Husband, Dr Wister Alison. Oh God thou art a God of love, a God of wonders. The Dr has never owned the for his God. Who knows but it had to take this hard strok to bring to the cross of Christ. Mrs Rachel Alison died March the 27 1888.

[March 30, 1888-Friday] 30 Cate & Fanny & the children has been to see me to day. I have not been feeling well but I am up. All gone home.

[April 1, 1888-Sunday] Aprile 1 sabbeth evening I have not been feeling well to day. I have been tryin to spend it as well as I could but theire seemes a heavy weight on me to day, but Christ has said, "Come unto me all ye that are heavely laiden & I will give you rest."

[April 7, 1888-Saturday] Satterday evening 7 Wille & Minny is gone up to Mr Prices to night. I am feeling tollerabble well this evening.

[April 8, 1888-Sunday] 8 Wille & I have been over at the Chapple to day. Lawson got home from Presbatary last evening, had a fine time, a good turnout.

[April 9, 1888-Monday] 9 Fannie & I have been visiting Mrs Cain to day, April 9 & went home with Fanny & stayed a week. They was not well when I left them. I have been sick too.

[April 15, 1888-Sunday] Aprile 15 Gim has brought me home this morning. I have been not well all week, my back & breast.

[April 17, 1888-Tuesday] 17 Minny is gone over to see Fanny to day. Ans babby, Nanny, is bad with the hooping coughf. I am feeling some better.

[April 22, 1888-Sunday] 22 Ruffus & Eliza & all the children was up last night & all went to oure dear ould Bershaba to day. Heard a fine sermon from oure dear Paster, Mr Kirkpatrick, abbout Jachob ladder. A great sermon. Mart & Mag & the children came home with us. Mag is going to stay a few dayes.

She has had rumetism, hardly abble to go.

[April 24, 1888-Tuesday] 24 Mag & I have been over to see Fanny & Mag is gone home.

[April 28, 1888-Saturday] 28 Gim & Fanny & the children, Sylvanis & Cate & children has all been down to see Eliza & Sally. Found them all well. They went in the waggon. I stayed & kept house for Fanny. They have all got home this evening. Cate is gone home.

[May 1, 1888-Tuesday] May 1 Gim has brought me home this evening. I helpt Fanny to put her web in to day.

[May 3, 1888-Thursday] May 3 John Brown & Miss Cary Latamore was married May 3. She lived in Shelby. They was married in the morning, came down to Mr Cains that night. He took no one with him but Press McAphee, & Brown Wily. A Friday morning he brought her up home. Theire was but few theire. Press McAphee & his wife & children, Mr & Mrs Cain & Gimmy & Brown Wily, Margaret Ann Mc Elwee & myself. She is not perty but I think she will do all right.

[May 9, 1888-Wednesday] 9 Minny & I have been up to see oure new kins woman, Mrs John Brown this evening. I hope she will be all right. Lawson has had the flux but is better. We have had a heap of rain & freshet in the creek. I have a fine gardin.

[May 11, 1888-Friday] 11 Fanny & the children has been over a day & night. All gone home. John & Carry has been down to see us to night.

[May 13, 1888-Sunday] 13 sabbeth evening I have been to preachen to day, heard a great sermon oure dear Mr Kirkpratrick. His tex was in Mathew 28 c. These are the words, "Lo I am with you allwayes, even unto the end of the wourld." A great sermon to the belever that Christ is ever with them. Oh my God for a heart to love & prais the as I ought & to feel that thou art ever present.

[May 15, 1888-Tuesday] May 15 I have been up to stay with Cate too days & a night. Little Mary is not well with her bowels, from tething or flux. I hope she will soon be better. Mr Edward Byers died May 19 1888. He was at Church last sunday. To day he has been laid in the cold & wet grave. We have warning enough of sudden deaths to make us try to be prepared for the solem houre of death.

[May 25, 1888-Friday] May 25 a Friday evening I have been spared to go to my dear ould Bershabba to the commencement of another communion seasen. Mr English of York preached for us to day, a great sermon. His tex, "Ye are the salt of the earth." Mr English & a young preacher from Bethesda by the name of Mr Reed came home with us & took dinner & went back to york. Mr Kirkpatrick is gone to Mr Byers. Had three preachers & few hearers.

[May 26, 1888-Saturday] 26 satterday night May 26 we have had great preachen to day. Mr Reed of Bethesday preached to day. His morning tex was in Psalms 95, " To day, if ye will hear his voice, harden not your heart." In the evening Mark 12 34. These are the words, "Though art not far from the kingdom of God." Oh such warnings he gave the wicked to repent & beleve. John & Sally, Wille & Ada Thomison & little Wille Warlick & Jetty is all we have to night. Wille is sick.

[May 27, 1888-Sunday] May 27 1888 a sabbeth evening a great & happy day has this been to me that my God has spared me to see this day, that God in his great love has once more given us a paster. The Reverent Mr M R Kirkpatrick has been enstalled paster to day. The congration all seemes well pleased. He has started a sunday school with sixty schollars & 8 teachers. Mr Reed preached this morning. His tex was in Mark 10.15. We have had great preachen, Mr Reed this morning, then Mr English gave the charge to the paster, then to the congration. When he got through, all the congragation was invited up to shake hands with him, a short intervill & then the Lords supper. Theire was a good manny joined the church, my daughter in law Minny, by sertificate, three grand children, Maud Castles, Gimmy & Johnny Brown, Lawsons sons. Oh my Heavenly Farther I adore & bless thee this evening for the blessings of this day that thou hast brought me & mine all to thy house of prayer to day. My children & grand children most all theire once more, but no dear ould Husband & Farther with us, but I hope he is enjoying far greater blessings than we have this day. There was strange circumstance connected with oure meeting. The first work Friday morning was to preach a funeral of a chile of Mr Brackets. The last thing, a sunday evening, the funeral of Mr Thommises chile. Thus ends another great day. MDB

[May 30, 1888-Wednesday] 30 I have been over to see Fanny to day, all well.

I am feeling some better. We have had great rains, winds & hail, hard time for the farmers.

[June 6, 1888-Wednesday] 6 I have had a big visit over to see Mag & aunt Harriet. She is not well, has the flux & her head is not right. I staid with her too days & nights & Sylvanis came for me. Little Mary has been right sick. Staid with them too nights & then home. Found all well. Had John Brown & his wife to day.

[June 7, 1888-Thursday] 7 Had Mrs Cain, Mr Cain, Fanny & the children & Miss Nancy Peters all to day.

[June 8, 1888-Friday] Cousin Psalm Brown died June 8 1888 at Blacks station & was buried up their. Sister Harriet & I am the last of the ould Browns. MDB

[June 10, 1888-Sunday] June 10, 1888, a sunday evening I have been to preachen one time more. Oure dear Paster preaches fine & have the start of a good sabbeth school. He was preachen about David & Golliah.

[June 13, 1888-Wednesday] 13 Minny nor I is not verry well. Ginny & Cate Price is here to night.

[June 17, 1888-Sunday] 17 sabbeth evening Sylvans & Cate, Gim & Fanny was here a while this evening.

[June 24, 1888-Sunday] Sabbeth evening June 24 I have been to preachen to my dear ould church. Had a good sermon & sunday school. His tex was in Colossians 2.10, "Ye are complete in him."

[June 26, 1888-Tuesday] 26 we are all tolerable well this evening. I am feeling better than I have done in a good while. Oh that I may feel as thankfull as I ought for all Gods love & care. It is verry warm & dry, suffering for rain.

[July 1, 1888-Sunday] July 1 Sabbeth morning Fanny was with us last night, gone home. Wille & Minnys first born, Robbert Jackson was born July 6, a friday morning at day break. Dr Andrell Bratten was here, got along verry well, both dooing fine. A great blessing that God has been so good & kind to us all. My Farther in Heaven, give these children Grace & strenth to rais this little

one for thee, if it is thy will to spare its life & theires.

[July 6, 1888-Friday] 6 Fanny has gone home & Sally Berry is with us.

[July 8, 1888-Sunday] 8 Cate came down last night to see the little stranger. We have been to preachen to day. Mr Kirkpatrick preached a fine sermon. His tex was in John. Farther I will that those thou hast given me, Be with me to behold my glory. Minny & the babe is dooing fine.

[July 13, 1888-Friday] 13 Bob Coldwell has thrashed oure wheat to day, had forty too bushels. It has been a bad wheat year but that will make oure bread.

[July16, 1888-Monday] 16 Fanny has been over to day.

[July 18, 1888-Wednesday] 18 I was over with Gim & Fanny last night, all well.

[July 22, 1888-Sunday] 22 I have been to preachen to day. Mr R Kirkpatrick tex was in Mathew 6c 33 verse. I am going home with Sally to stay a few dayes.

[July 27, 1888-Friday] 27 I have got home from my visit to see the Children. Had a fine time, felt well & enjoyed myself fine. Eliza & Sally & I went up to see Hatty Magill, found them all well & theire too little children. One day with Mag. John Alexander came down for me. John & Hew came up yesterday to stay a while & when I came home, found unckle Franklin Furgeson & Ninny Glenn, his grand daughter from Bethel, on a visit ammong theire relations.

[July 29, 1888-Sunday] 29 had unckle Frank, Henry & Ninny Glenn. Wille & I & them all went to the Chapel to preachen. I was not well pleased with him. They went to Marts & then home. John Alexander & Fanny was here to day & I went home with Fanny.

[August 1, 1888-Wednesday] Aug 1 Mag Hall & her three children, Ginny Whiteside & her too twin boyes, Brown & Baxter & Hatty Fewel was all here on a visit to day.

[August 4, 1888-Saturday] 4 Gim Land & Wille is sawing lumber to put up a bridge at McAffes.

[August 9, 1888-Thursday] 9 John Alexander has been up to see Cate.

[August 12, 1888-Sunday] 12 have been to preachen to day, heard a fine sermon, Mr Kirkpatrick, "Lay up foure selves treasures in Heaven where moth & rust doth not corrup."

[August 13, 1888-Monday] 13 John Alexander & Hew has left this evening fore home, have been up near three weeks.

[August 14, 1888-Tuesday] 14 Minny & the boy is gone over to spend the day with Ann Brown. Wille is at the bridge.

[August 18, 1888-Saturday] 18 I have been over with Fanny for a few dayes.

[August 20, 1888-Monday] 20 I have been to preachen to day. Mr Kirkpatrick tex was in Mathew, "Lay not up for your selves treasures on earth." He gave us a good sermon. Oh that we would make the right improvements of so many good sermons. Some of us may never hear many more of them. Oh that we all will make good improvement of them, that we may be ready to give a good account of them when the great reckening day dose come.

[August 21, 1888-Tuesday] 21 Wille & Minny is gone down to see Eliza & Sally. Fanny is with me to day. It has been a cold, stormy & windy day.

[August 22, 1888-Wednesday] 22 Fanny is gone home & Wille & Minny has got home, all safe. I have not been feeling well, the pain & the ackes of this poor ould boddy. I hope theire is a brighter day a coming when this mortal shall put on immortality, when death shall be swalled up of victory.

[August 24, 1888-Friday] 24 I am still feelin unwell, not my will Oh Lord but thyne be done. MDBrown

[August 25, 1888-Saturday] Aug 25 theire has been a few that has been up to the church to day & have scowerd it out, Cate Whitesides, Fanny Land, Ann Brown, Minny Brown & I & the men was redding off the church yard. Cate & Fanny came with me & stayed till night, all gone.

[August 26, 1888-Sunday] 26 Mr Harrisen preached for us to day.

[August 29, 1888-Wednesday] 29 I have been up with Cate a few dayes. She has had a miss carriate but I think she will be all right now.

[August 30, 1888-Thursday] 30 this is the day of the election. Theire is right smart excitement about it. Fanny, Wille & I have all been to York to day & I am bad with my back.

[September 2, 1888-Sunday] Sept 2 Wille & Minny went up last night to stay with Cate & to Bethany to preachen to day & Fanny was over a while this morning. Sabbeth evening I am feeling unwell. My back hurts me & pains & acks but no one with me, but I am not lonsen nor affraid. I desire to take refuge at the cross of a crucified saviour here. Lord give me that grace Thou has promised to the lowly selfrenouncing & sin renouncing. I would seek to be exalted only in Jesus crying out, "God be merciful to me a sinner." Full of my own unworthiness I turn to the infinitly worthy one. I seek to be washed in his blood, santified by his spirit, guided by His counsel, depend on him for every supply of grace & feeling that without him I must perish. Oh my God I thank thee that I can so happy set here at my little tabble while the rain is falling in torrents, this thy Holly Sabbeth evening without the least no mortal ear near, no one to speak but my dear saviour is dear & verry near. Mary D Brown Sept 2 1888.

[September 7, 1888-Friday] 7 this day is the commencement of oure communion but Mr Kirkpatrick did not git here.

[September 9, 1888-Sunday] Sabbeth evening Mr Kirkpatrick preached to day, his tex was, "I was glad when they said let us go up to the house of the Lord." It has been such a bad time of rain, thee creeks are up that oure meeting is laid over until the second of Oct. Aunt Harriet, Joe & Sally is all we had last night.

[September 10, 1888-Monday] 10 monday morning we have had a dreadfull nights rain & wind. Willy, Minny & I have all gone over to Gims to day and they are gone home & I am staying a week.

[September 18, 1888-Tuesday] 18 I came home yesterday & Fanny & the children came home with me & we all have been over to see Lawson to day.

[September 23, 1888-Sunday] 23 Wille is gone to smerny to day to a communion. I am feeling only tollerable well. Sabbeth evening we have no preachen to day, oure preacher is gone to Presbatary but have had fine reading in Johns Gospel where Christ tells us that he is the bread of life. If a man eat of this bread he shall live forever, such as feed upon Christ shall live forever that those & only those that by faith, feed on him shall obtain a life of grace & glory. Oh my God give me hope that I may eat his flesh, drink his blood that I may live forever.

[September 27, 1888-Thursday] Sept 27 I have been over with Fanny. Little _____ has had the sore throat but is got better & I have come home.

[September 29, 1888-Saturday] 29 Minny & I have been up to see Cate to day. Vance is sick with the cold, took my web up to Mrs Barber to weave.

[September 30, 1888-Sunday] 30 Mr Kirkpatrick preached for us to day. His tex was in Psalms 51, "Cast me not away from thy presence." Ben Coldwell infant was burried to day at Bershaba. Ruff & Eliza came home with us.

[October 7, 1888-Sunday] Oct 7 Sabbeth evening Wille & Minny is gone to Union baptist church to preachen & Fanny & the children was over last night, all gone home. Mary Furgison died Oct 3. Lord how little am I influenced & impressed by the solem words of death all around me. Friend after friend is departing. The proclamation is ever pounding in my ears. Be ye also ready blessed.

[October 23, 1888-Tuesday] Oct 23 this is the day that Lawson, Wille & Davis, Eddy Land & Fanny has put down the carpet. It looks verry nice, cost about thirty three dollars.

[October 26, 1888-Friday] Oct 26 a friday night this day is the commencement of our communion servis but seems as we will have another bad time as this has been a cold, wet day & verry few out. Mr Kirk came home with us & took dinner & then went down to Gimmy Loves to stay all night & it is a dark, rainny night. MDB

[October 27, 1888-Saturday] 27 satterday night a bad day for preachen. Mr Kanedy would have been here but could not cross the creeks.

[October 28, 1888-Sunday] Sabbeth evening another communion sabbeth over. We had too new Elders ordained to day. Mr Ruffes Alison & James Land.

Mr Kirk preached a great sermon to them what was their duty & what was the peoples duty to them. The last of oure Elders that was gathered home by death was my dear ould Husband & now a Son in law has taken his place. Oh my God will thou make them God feering & God serving men. Theire was six new members, five by sertificate, John & Emily Gwinn, Lasly Burns & his wife & daughter, Lizzy, Mary S Hall, another Grand Daughter. Oh my Heavenly Farther as her name is now on thy Church Book, Oh that thou will write her name in the book of life that when thou comest to make up thy Jewells she will be one to deck Emmanuels Crown. It has cleared off & had a fine time for our meeting. I am going home with Joe & Sally.

[November 2, 1888-Friday] Nov 2 a friday night Joe has brought me home this evening, found all well. Had a fine visit with Eliza & Sally, Dear, good Children. My Children has kept the fifth commandment better than the most does. My God fulfill thy promis to them & theire little ones.

[November 4, 1888-Sunday] Sabbeth morning Nov 4 I went yesterday morning down to see ould unckle Bille Coldwell. He had a storke of paralis last monday morning & has been bad ever sence. When I went a satterday morning he said he new me but could not talk much. I was sorry I did not git to see him sooner for he had been asking for me all week. I was down with the children & could not git theire no sooner. He was consious of death & was perfectly resind & reddy to go saying, "Lord Jesus receive my spyrit." He died with out a struggle, ore a moan at foure oclock in the evening. Wille & Minny is gone to Bethany to the burrying. Unckle Franklin Furgison is with me.

[November 11, 1888-Sunday] 11 Mr Kirk preached to day abbout the faith of ould Abbraham. A good sermon & a good congragation. Wille has got head stones for his Farther, Harriet & Ruffe & got them up. They are verry nice. He paid seventy seven dollars for them. I was glad to see them. Gim & Fanny & the children was with us last night, has gone home this morning.

[November 25, 1888-Sunday] 25 I have been over with Fanny for a week, got home this morning, found all well.

[November 30, 1888-Friday] 30 Fanny & the children & I have spent this day with Mrs Cain, had a fine visit.

[December 4, 1888-Tuesday] Dec 4 I have been over with Fanny, minded the

children till she went to York. Sally was their & came home with her & Eddy Whitesides too. They came home with me & is now gone home.

[December 5, 1888-Wednesday] 5 Eliza Ann & Mary & Brown came up to see us yesterday morning & stayed till this morning. Eliza has not much health, looks bad.

[December 6, 1888-Thursday] 6 Wille is gone to Hickry grove to day with cotton. Little Robby is sick with the cold. I am feeling better than I have done in a long time. I pray that God would give me grace & strenth to serve him & doo all the good that I can the rest of the dayes of my earthly pilgramage.

[December 7, 1888-Friday] 7 we have killed our hogs to day, had three fine ones.

[December 9, 1888-Sunday] 9 Mr Kirkpatrick preached to day. He preached a good sermon, gave us plain warning how to act at Christmas times.

[December 14, 1888-Friday] 14 Min & I have been up to see Cate to day, all well & it is verry cold.

[December 15, 1888-Saturday] 15 Wille is gone down to york to lay in for Christmas.

[December 21, 1888-Friday] 21 William Burns burried their youngest chile to day. Mr Kirkpatrick preached a funeral sermon. Wille & Min went, I stayed & kept the boy at the fire, it is cold. MDBrown

[December 22, 1888-Saturday] 22 I was over to see Fanny last night. She has not been well. Gim brought me home this evening. Wille & Min had Mr Kirkpatrick for dinner. I had not got home. Wille has taken the new church tabble up. It is a verry nice one. It cost seven dollars. The ladyes has paid for the carpet & tabble & had one dollar & thirty five cents over which they sent to the Thornwell orphanage.

[December 23, 1888-Sunday] 23 Mr Kirkpatrick preached a fine sermon to day. His tex was in Hebrews 13 17. He preached a fine sermon.

[December 25, 1888-Tuesday] 25 a christmas evening Wille & Min is gone over to see John & Em Quin & aunt Harriet. Lawson & Mag & the children, Fanny & her children, Ann Brown & her children was all with me to day, all gone home & I am going up to stay with John & wife & her Mother.

[December 27, 1888-Thursday] 27 Sylvanis & Cate & Bell, Wille, Min & I was all at Fannies yesterday. Cate & Bell came home with us & is now gone home. Wille & Min is gone up to Mr Prices.

[December 28, 1888-Friday] 28 Wille is gone to Mr Magills for a molasses mill to day & I am here by my self. I doo enjoye myself fine by my self.

[December 29, 1888-Saturday] 29 Wille is gone over to aunt Harriets to git some fodder from John Gwinn. He is going to McConelsvill.

[December 30, 1888-Sunday] 30 all at home & no company this holly sabbeth, the last sabbeth of 1888. Who is to see the last sabbeth of 1889 is known to God only but we who is so near three score dose know that it will soon be oure last. Oh that we may all live that we will not be affraid of death & the grave, that we may be abble to say, "Oh death whare is thy sting. Oh grave where is thy victory."

1889

[January 1, 1889-Tuesday] Jan 1 a thursday evening all well and at home. Litle did I think thirty years ago tha I would be here on this earth to day and in tollerable health. Oh my God, I hope it has not been in vain that thou hast spared this life of mine so long. Give me grace to use the talent that thou hast given me fore thy glory and the good of my never dying soule. O eternity, eternity, Mysterious, mighty existance, a sum not to be lessened by the largest dections, an extent not to be contracted by all possible dimunitions. None can truly say after the most prodigious waste of ages, so much of eternity is gone, for when millions of centuaries are elapsed it is but Just commencing & when millions more have run their ample round, it will be no nearer ending. Yea, when ages, numereous as the bloom of spring increased by the herbage of summer bouth augmented by the leaves of autum and all multiplied by the drops of rain which drown the winter, when these & ten thousand times ten thousand more, more than can be represented by any similitude or imagined by any conception, when all these are revolved and finished, eternity vast boundless amazing eternity will only be beginning. What a pleasing, yet awful thought is this. Full of delight and full of dread.

Oh may it alarm my fears, quicken my hopes and animate my endeavers cense I am so soon to lanche into this endless and inconceivable state, let me give all diligence to secure an entrance into bless all is steadfass and immovable beyound the grave. Oh eternity, eternity, Oh, that I may allwayes have it before me & be living in readiness fore eternity. Mary D Brown

[January 2, 1889-Wednesday] Jan 2 John Brown & his wife & her Mother, Mrs Latamore, Mrs Sue Cain and Gimmy & Sally Whitesides has spent this day with us.

[January 8, 1889-Tuesday] 8 I went home with Sally & staid a ful day. Edy & Brown brought me home this evening.

[January 13, 1889-Sunday] 13 Mr Kirkpatrick preached a fine sermon. His tex was in John 13, "Having loved his own which were in the world he loved them unto the end."

[January 19, 1889-Saturday] 19 Mrs Minny Mcomick was here today, my beoved little Macks widow. She is teaching school in Ebs School house, is well liked.

[January 27, 1889-Sunday] 27 I have been over with Fanny & one night with Mart & Mag. I have not been feeling well. The rest is all well. I was not abble to go to church to day. It has been a wet & bad. Few out. Gim & Wille was out.

[February 1, 1889-Friday] Feb 1 Wille & Minny is gone down to see Eliza & Sally.

[February 2, 1889-Saturday] 2 Gimmy came over & stayed with me last nigt, by myself to day & not feeling well. Gim & Fanny, Sylvanis & Cate & children is all with me to night. Wille and Min has got home, all well.

[February 3, 1889-Sunday] 3 a Sabbeth evening have been reading a new book, the King of Gloen, a fine book, tells manny things that we dont git out of the Bibble. He gits it from ould histry.

[February 4, 1889-Monday] 4 this is the day that Wille has mooved bill Price to work with him.

[February 5, 1889-Tuesday] 5 Cary Brown & I have been over to see Fanny to day, & the neighbors & friends have bought Davis Brown a fine young mule on yesterday.

[February 9, 1889-Saturday] Wille has hired Nora & her too children & mooved them home to day the 9.

[February 10, 1889-Sunday] Feb 10 Sally & Eddy came up last night & we have all been to preachen to day. Mr Kirkpatrick preached a good sermon to day,"I am the way," and then the congragation made up one hundred dollars more & is going to take Mr Kirk fore the half of his time, that is foure hunderd dollars for the half of his time. Sally is gone home. MDBROWN

[February 13, 1889-Wednesday] 13 I am feeling baddly to day.

[February 17, 1889-Sunday] 17 unckle Frankline Furgison was with us last night. He is gone over to see Lawson & Davis.

[February 20, 1889-Wednesday] 20 Fanny was over with me last night & I am feeling some better. Wille is gone to york for his guianna to day.

[February 22, 1889-Friday] 22 we have had a big snow last night, the first we have had for too winters.

[February 24, 1889-Sunday] Sabbeth evening 24 I have been to preachen to day. It was so cold but few out. We had a new preacher to day oure evangless. His name, Mr Cook. His tex was in 2 Samuial 24c 24 verse.

[February 26, 1889-Tuesday] 26 Wille is gone down to see Sally. I am feeling better now. Jonny Robbert Whitesides died Feb 23. He was out hunting with some other boyes. They cut down a tree & a limb loged & fell & struck him on the head & broke his scull. He lived a few dayes & dyed. He was little Bobby Whitesides ouldest son, abbout twenty too.

[March 5, 1889-Tuesday] March 5, 1889 I have been over with Fanny a few days. Wille & Min came over to Fannys last night & I came home. All tollerabble well.

[March 10, 1889-Sunday] 10 I have been at preachin to day. Came from

Marts, his tex was in Mathew 4c 8 9v.

[March 12, 1889-Tuesday] 12 I have been over with Mag for a week. She had a fine son a thursday morning. It seemed to be dooing all right till dark. That night it took bad & dyed the next morning & was burrye at Bershabba a friday. Mag had a hard time & I think that was what was the matter with the babb. I staid with her till this eveng & Mart brought me home. I think she will be all right now. She took the death of her babe verry hard. It was a beautifull little boy, bud on earth to bloom in Heaven.

[March 15, 1889-Friday] March 15 Wille is gone over to see Lesly Burns to night. He is sick with Pnewmonia. Fanny was over a while to day, all well.

[March 17, 1889-Sunday] 17 I have not been feeling so well for a few dayes. Oppressed for my breath & not feeling well. Wille is been over to see Lasley. He is better.

[March 21, 1889-Thursday] March 21 my birth day. I am sixty seven years ould to day.

[March 22, 1889-Friday] March 22 I am feeling some better to day. Fanny & Mrs Cain is here this evening.

[March 24, 1889-Sunday] 24 sabbeth evening I have been abble to go to Church to day. Mr Kirkpatrick tex was in John 6 37. Ruffes & Eliza came home with us. Ruffes is gone home. Eliza & the Children has stayed all night. Mary & Dan Hall was over last night. Mag is dooing fine.

[March 25, 1889-Monday] 25 Eliza & the Children is gone home & Min & I have been over to see Fanny to day & Cate & Sylvanis too. The boyes has been bird hunting to day.

[March 28, 1889-Thursday] 28 all well & at home. I am feeling some better.

[April 2, 1889-Tuesday] Aprile 2 I have been up to stay with Cate a few dayes. They are all well. Sylvanis brought me home this morning. I am feeling some better. Min is gone over to see little Gim. He swallowed a screw when Fanny was over here last friday. They are uneasy about him. Wille & Bob Brown & Bob Coldwell is gone down to Sallies to go a sayning for fish. I am feeling some better. MDB

[April 8, 1889-Monday] Aprile 8 Mrs Minny McCmick has been with Fanny & us sence last friday till this morning. She is gone on to her school. I love her so much. I beleve she is a good woman. Gim, Fanny & Mrs Mc went to the Chaple yesterday to preachen. I staid with the Children.

[April 11, 1889-Thursday] 11 Wille Davis & more is all gone down to Sallies a sayning & I am feeling some better. I expect to go over & stay with Fanny this evening till Gim come back from Presbatary next week.

[April 12, 1889-Friday] Aprile 12 I am over staying with Fanny. Gimy is gone to presbatary, mets at Brackstocks.

[April 13, 1889-Saturday] 13 Mag Hall & the children was with Fanny & I is gone home.

[April 15, 1889-Monday] Aprile 15 Minny has come over for Fanny to help her make her fine black dress & Gimmy has got home, his first trip to Presbatary. He was well pleased, had a fine turnout of Preachers & Elders & every thing seems to be in a prouspers condition.

[April 19, 1889-Friday] 19 Gim has brought me home this morning, found all well & dooing well.

[April 26, 1889-Friday] aprile 26 a friday evening the commencement of oure communion seasen. My Heavenly Farther come & be in oure midts, poure out thy Holy spirit upon the saint & sinner. May their be shacking of the dry bones of oure dear ould church. I thank thee theire has one, an ould and hard-end sinner. It has been said that he did not beleve theire was a God, has made a publick proffesion of his faith in Christ & was baptised & then had his three boyes babtised, Butler and Nanny Thomison one, Hatty Prue. Mr Mclain from Alisons creek church preached for us to day. His tex was in Luke 23, verses 39. 40. 41. 42. 43. He preached a good sermon & went back home. We had no company. Satterday evening Mr Mclain. To day his tex this morning was in Mathew 7c.13.14. "Because strait is the gate and narrow is tha way." In the evening 2 Corrinthians 5c 10 vers, "fore we must all appear before the Judge-ment seat of God." He preached too fine sermmons and theire was seven joined the Church, Mr Robbert Black, too of Willias Dicksons children, Gimmy &

Lissy, too of William Burns, Meek, too of Davis Browns, Lissy Clary, Jackson Bury, by sertifacate from Smerny. We have Mr Kirkpatrick, unckle Franklin Furgison, Joe & Sally.

[April 28, 1889-Sunday] Aprile 28 Sabbeth evening oure meeting is over. Mr Kirk preached to good sermmons to day, had no help. His morning tex in Rev, "These are they that washed theire robes and made them white in the blood of the Lamb." His evening tex, "Is theire no balm in gelead, is theire no physian theire?" Mrs Sue Jackson joined this morning. We had a right smart storm this morning, wind, rain & hail. The congaration had mostly got theire before it com on. Cleard off and had a tollerabble good time. Marten Bryan had his youngist burried theire this evening. My Lord and my God I thank and bless the that thow has sparred me and mine, children and Grand children and Great Grand children all to meet in my dear ould church one mere to hear a messag from the Lord and have heard some great ones to. Its more than probable that we will ever all meet theire again. My Heavenly Farther give us faith grace & strenth to love thee more and serve the better than we have ever done before.

[April 30, 1889-Tuesday] 30 Fanny & the children was all over to day.

[May 5, 1889-Sunday] May 5 1669 Wille is gone to Smerny to preachen to day. Min, Robby & I am all sick with the cold.

[May 6, 1889-Monday] 6 a beautifull May morning, has been fine seasens so far. Fine prospict of fruit. Gim Land has drove him home a fine young cow this morning and a beautifull calf.

[May 9, 1889-Thursday] 9 Gim & Fanny & I have all spent this day with Mrs & Mr Cain. Little Robby is sick yet.

[May 10, 1889-Friday] 10 I have been over with Lawson & Mag to day.

[May 12, 1889-Sunday] May 12 sabbeth evening Mr __has preached to day. He was not verry well. His tex was in Mark about blind Bartemeus. Ould aunt Eliza Burns was burried this evening. Joe & Sally came by a while, gone home.

[May 14, 1889-Tuesday] May 14 Min is gone over to Lawsons. Little Matty is sick, Robby is better.

[May 18, 1889-Saturday] 18 Wille & Min is gone up to Mr Prices to night. Cary is staying with me.

[May 19, 1889-Sunday] 19 Wille and Min is gone to Ramma to preachen.

[May 21, 1889-Tuesday] 21 I have been over with Mag last night & with Fanny to day.

[May 24, 1889-Friday] 24 Mag Hall and the girls has been over to day.

[June 4, 1889-Tuesday] June 4 well I have got home from my big visit with Eliza & Sally. Have not been feeling well sence I was down. They are all verry good & kind to me in every thing. My children has kept the fifth commandment better than the most dos. The Lord fullfill his promis to them.

[June 6, 1889-Thursday] 6 Fanny & Miss Nancy & the children has been over to day.

[June 9, 1889-Sunday] 9 sabbeth evening this has been the childrens day. They brought in theire might boxes for the mishanary caus. Got a good sum. Mr Kirkpatrick came home with us & got dinner, then went to Mr Stepensons school hous to preach this evening.

[June 12, 1889-Wednesday] 12 Wille, Min & I was all over with Fanny last night, been having fine rains and everry thing is looking fine.

[June 13, 1889-Thursday] 13 Will, Min & I was up to see Cate last night & all well their. Sylvanis has a fine prospect for a crop.

[June 16, 1889 -Sunday] 16 John & Sally Burry & children & Ginny price gone home. Fanny has been over a while. Wille has got done cutting wheat. It is verry good. His crop looks fine.

[June 20, 1889-Thursday] 20 all at home & well. Verry warm & all verry busy & I am feeling better than I have been fore a good while.

[June 21, 1889-Friday] 21 Min & I have been helping Ann to quilt to day, did not git it out.

[June 22, 1889-Saturday] 22 all well, a beautifull morning.

[June 27, 1889-Thursday] 27 I have been over with Fanny for a few dayes. I am not feeling well. I have thought of sending for the Dr Bratten.

[June 30, 1889-Sunday] 30 Sabbeth evening I did not go to preachen to day. I was feeling bad. Gim & Fanny came home with them from preachen & we have had a powerfull rain. The creek is over the bottems again. The corn is all washed down the hillsides, washed away. Wille thinks he has lost too hunderd bushels of corn. It is Gods work. We must not murmer nor complain, it is not so bad but it might be worse.

[July 1, 1889- Monday] July 1 Gim & Fanny is gone home.

[July 4, 1889-Thursday] 4 Joe & Sally has come up to day to see me. I am not feeling eney better, gone home.

[July 6, 1889-Saturday] 6 Eliza & little Brown came up yesterday morning & Fanny was over, all gone home.

[July 8, 1889-Monday] 8 monday evening I have been a bad with a pain in my breast & side sence sunday morning. Wille went down & brought ould Dr Bratten out this morning. He thinks he can help me, ore sayes he can. He sayes it is my nerves but I feel that I am like Jobe in affliction, not in paticence, but I put all my trust in the great physian who can heal both soule & boddy fore time and eternity.

[July 12, 1889-Friday] 12 I have had a perty hard week with a pain is my side and breast & feeling bad, but is feeling some better this evening. If it is the Lords will I hope he will remove these pains & acks. Not my will Oh Lord, but thyne be done.

[July 14, 1889-Sunday] 14 sabbeth evening God has spared me to go to his house once more, theire to hear a mesage from the Lord to me & to a good congragrtion of people. This was the mesage, "as for me and my house, we will serve the Lord." He preached a good sernon, he is going to commence a proc-trad meeting next month.

[July 20, 1889-Saturday] July 20 I have been over to see aunt Jane & aunt

Harriet. Sister Harriet is dooing verry well, all but her eyes is no better. Adda is got a bealed breast, come back & stayd a few dayes with Fanny.

[July 22, 1889-Monday] 22 I have been up to see Cate. She is dooing as well as could expect.

[July 24, 1889-Wednesday] 24 Mr Henterson has commenced a singing scool at the church to day. Fanny & Wille is gone.

[July 27, 1889-Saturday] 27 we had a powerfull rain last, all over the bottoms again. Wille & Min is gone up to Mr Prices to day.

[July 28, 1889-Sunday] 28 Mr Kirkpatrick has preached a good sermon to day. His tex, "Christ the rock." Mr John & Sally Davis & daughter was their to day, with Cate last night.

[July 30, 1889-Tuesday] 30 Wille is gone to York, took some chickens to git some things we need.

[July 31, 1889-Wednesday] 31 Fanny is gone on to the singing. I have the children, all gone home.

[August 1, 1889-Thursday] August 1 Wille, Min & Fanny is all gone to the singing, unckle Franklin Furgison is with us to night.

[August 2, 1889-Friday] 2 Frank & Wille is gone to York to the Alliance meeting & Ruff Whitesides spent the day with us.

[August 3, 1889-Saturday] 3 this is the day that they are redding off the Church yard, a verry wet time. We are abbout to loss all of oure fruit, been macking sider.

[August 5, 1889-Monday] 5 still raining, drying no fruit.

[August 9, 1889-Friday] August 9 this is the firs day of oure meeting, fine weather & great preachen, three preachers, Mr Kirk, Mr Cook & Mr McElwain & a good congration for a friday. Mr Cook preached to day. His tex was in st John, third chapter, abbout Nickademus. He preached a great sermon & it was so plain. We have no company to night. The preachers all gone blow.

[August 10, 1889-Saturday] Aug 10 Mr Cook to day, had fine preachen. Cousin William & Eliza Davis, Mrs Mary Davis of Blacks burg is with us, Aunt Harriet, Sally & Eddy Whitesides.

[August 11, 1889-Sunday] Sabbeth evening we have had a fine meeting. Mr Cook has done all the preachen. Theire was several joined.

[August 12, 1889-Monday] 12 the meeting is going on. Mr Kirkpatrick, wife and foure children came home with us. Mr Cook & Mr McElwane preached at night. William Thomisons wife, Ada joined the church & was baptised & her babe, Hiram Calhoun. I was at preachen to night. Mr. Cook preached. This was his tex, "Come and let us reasen together, though youre sins be as scarlet they shall be as white and as snow, though they be red like crimson, they shall be a wool." A great sermon he did preach. Great God give us streanth of mind & boddy to make a good improvement of these great & blessed sermons that I have been to lisen too.

[August 13, 1889-Tuesday] Aug the 13 Wille is gone to take Mrs Davis to york this morning & from theire she will go home.

[August 14, 1889-Wednesday] wensday Mr McElwane preached to day, a mishanary sermon. His tex, "Go ye into all the world & preach the gospel to every creauter." He is going to Japan this fall. He was smartly affect, he is a nobble young man. He has gave soul & boddy, life & property to the Lord & master who gav his all for us & what have I done for him who has done so much for me? I have tryed to do something if it as litle as the widows mite. If from the heart, it will be excepted.

[August 15, 1889-Thursday] thursday evening oure meeting has closed. one weeks preaching. When the last great comes it will be a glourious rembernce to some that they spent those happy dayes in Gods house and to some a sad remberance. Sally is gone home. Mrs Davis and Mrs Mcomick gone home with Mrs Cain.

[August 18, 1889-Sunday] 18 Wille went down to stay with Eliza last night & to the new church to day. Mr Kirkpatrick & Mr Cook went on down theire to organise it at Sharan station. The name of it is Woodlawn. Cates _____ was born Aug 22 a thursday morning, dooing fine.

[August 28, 1889-Wednesday] 28 Sylvanis has brought me home this morning. Cate & the boy is dooing fine.

[September 1, 1889-Sunday] Sept the 1 I have been over with Fanny a few dayes, all tollerabble well, stayd with the children while she went to the singing the too last dayes, had had Henry Glenn and Mr Clinton one night. Lawsons _____ was born on Aug 30, a friday morning 1889.

[September 3, 1889-Tuesday] 3 Min I have spent this day with Margaret Ann Mcelwee at John Browns.

[September 4, 1889-Wednesday] 4 Sally Berry & children was here to day.

[September 6, 1889-Friday] 6 Fanny & children here to day.

[September 8, 1889-Sunday] 8 Mr Kirk a fine sermon to us. His tex, "If ye abbide in me and my words abbide in you ye shall ask what ye will and it shall be don unto you."

[September 10, 1889-Tuesday] 10 I have been over with Lawson to day. He is bad with his back. He got it strain.

[September 11, 1889-Wednesday] 11 this is the day of the big speaking at _____. Wille is gone and I am sick to day.

[September 12, 1889-Thursday] 12 I am feeling no better. Fanny has come over to stay with me to night & Joe is here.

[September 13, 1889-Friday] 13 Sally has come up to see me to day. I feel a little better.

[September 15, 1889-Sunday] 15 sabbeth evening Mag Hall & the children came up last night, unckle Frank Furgison. All gone home and I feeling some better, through the love of God, I am feeling better.

[September 16, 1889-Monday] Monday morning 16 I am abble to be up this morning. My Farther in Heaven, give me grace & strenth to live for thy glory.

[September 27, 1889-Friday] Sept 27 Cate has been down with her new babe. It is dooing fine. Wille is gone to take Cate over to Fannies, and Eliza & little Mary has come up to stay all night.

[October 2, 1889-Wednesday] Oct 2 I have been over with Fanny for a few dayes. Gim is gone to the wool factory.

[October 4, 1889-Friday] 4 Fanny is sick with cold & sore throat.

[October 8, 1889-Tuesday] 8 Fanny is better, has been over to day.

[October 11, 1889-Friday] 11 all well. Wille has got done halling up his corn, had a fine crop.

[October 13, 1889-Sunday] Minny babby, Mary Lilian, was born Oct 13 1889, a sabbeth morning. Dr White was here.

[October 14, 1889-Monday] 14 Fanny has stayed with us till to day. Wille has taken her home. Min and the babe is dooing fine.

[October 16, 1889-Wednesday] 16 Sally has been up all night.

[October 18, 1889-Friday] 18 Cate & the children & Bell has been down to day. Min & the babe is dooing fine.

[October 20, 1889-Sunday] 20 Gim & Fanny has been over this evening.

[October 22, 1889-Tuesday] 22 Fanny has been over to day. I have not been feeling well.

[October 29, 1889-Tuesday] 29 Gim Smyth has been her ginning cotten, has gined 8 bales, is gone. Ould Miss Polly Smyth died Oct 29 1889. I was up at the burring & seen her laid in the silent dust their to rest till the great reserection morn. Mr Johson made a verry good talk to the people. My Lord & my God prepare me for that day & hour. It may soon come. Oh that I may have oil in my lamp, have it well trimbed and brightly burning when the summons comes. MDB

[October 30, 1889-Wednesday] 30 all dooin tollerabble well. I am feeling some better. Min & the babe is dooing fine. It has the cold some. I want to go over to stay with Fanny a few dayes.

[November 5, 1889-Tuesday] Nov 5 I have been over with Fanny for a few dayes & she has made a coat for Wille & is busy sowing.

[November 9, 1889-Saturday] 9 this is the day of oure communion has commenced. Mr Kirkpatrick had no help. Sally is all the company that we have.

[November 11, 1889-Monday] 11 monday night I have been up with Cate sence yesterday morning. Sylvanis has got all rong, has lost his mind. This has been one awfull day. Sylvanis got so bad this evening that they had to hold him by force. I have come home & left Gim & Fanny theire. They have had Dr Camel & Dr Bratten both with him. He dose not eat nor sleep. The Dr think he will have to be taken to the assilum.

[November 14, 1889-Thursday] Nov the 14 a thursday they have taken Sylvanis to the assilum to day. Lawson Brown & Gim Land & Joe Whiteside went with him. Fanny & Min & myself is with Cate & Bell. An awfull thing to see a man when his mind is gone. The Dr think he wont have to stay long but they dont know.

[November 15, 1889-Friday] 15 all gone home & left me with Cate.

[November 17, 1889-Sunday] 17 Mag & the children was over last night, Mr John Davis to day

[November 18, 1889-Monday] 18 Gim & Fanny & the children was with us last night.

[November 21, 1889-Thursday] thursday 21 a week sence Sylvanis left, got a letter from Mr Griffen the suppertendent of the assulm. He is dooing some better.

[November 22, 1889-Friday] 22 a friday morning I have come home & bulah is sick. Fanny is with Cate.

[November 24, 1889-Sunday] 24 sabbeth Mr Kirkpatrick preached to day, a great sermon. His tex, "Wine is a mocker, strong drink is ragging." A great sermon, but Ephram is joined to his idles, let him alone.

[*November 25, 1889-Monday*] 25 Eliza & I went up to stay with Cate last night. They are dooing fine. Wille went & brought John Alexander up to day to stay with Cate, bulah is no better, wont eat eney thing but a little wheat bran. Eliza is gone home.

[*November 28, 1889-Thursday*] 28 Fanny & the children has been over to day & we have killed too of oure hogs to day. They was fine.

[*December 1, 1889-Sunday*] Dec 1 sabbeth evening Wille, Minny & I have been over with Fanny last night, all well, bulas is no better.

[*December 2, 1889-Monday*] 2 Wille & Min has been to York to day.

[*December 4, 1889-Wednesday*] 4 Fanny was over to day.

[*December 5, 1889-Thursday*] 5 Min has gone over to Fannies to git her help her to sow some.

[*December 7, 1889-Saturday*] 7 Sally & Eddy Whitesides came up this evening & is gone up to see Cate to night, bulas is dead. The Lord gave & the Lord taketh. Blessed be the name of the Lord. Oh my God thou has laid thyne chasting hand sorly on me & mine. Oh will thou give us Grace and strnnth both of boddy & mind not to murmer nor repine but say not my will Oh Lord but thine be done. They have got an other letter from Mr Griffen. Sylvanis is mending slowly. The said he wants to go home to see his wife & children. He is not nigh well & Cate must have paitiance.

[*December 8, 1889-Sunday*] 8 sabbeth evening Mr Kirkpatrick tex was in John 10c, "I know my sheep and they hear my voice."

[*December 9, 1889-Monday*] 9 John Alexander & Cate & Bell was all down to day. All gone home with Fanny.

[*December 10, 1889-Tuesday*] 10 Cate has got a letter from Sylvanis. He is better.

[*December 11, 1889-Wednesday*] 11 Eddy Price & Miss Bell Berry was married Dec 1 1889. Wille & Min is gone to the wedding. Mr Kirkpatrick married them & his horse died that night.

[December 12, 1889-Thursday] 12 Wille & Min is gone up to Mr Prices to day to take dinner with them & I am going to Fannies to night.

[December 17, 1889-Tuesday] 17 I have had a big visit to see Fanny, Mag & Cate. They are all well. Cate has got another letter from Sylvanis. He is better. Mart Hall is going down for to see if he can git him home.

[December 18, 1889-Wednesday] 18 Wille is gone to help Ben Coldwell to rais a barn. Wille has bought a young mule from Brooks Neel for one hunderd & twenty five dollars. Sally, Fanny & Min is all gone over to Davis Browns to help to pack a box to send to the Thornwell Orphanage for a Christmas present. They sent gifts, pillow slips, shirting, callico, orianges, apples, candy and too manny things to name. Gimy Land & Wille is gone to Mr MaGills to a sail and I am going home with Sally.

[December 29, 1889-Sunday] a Sabbeth evening 29 Joe & Sally has come home with me this morning & all been to preachen to day. Mr Kirkpatrick tex, "Enick was not for God took him." I have had a big visit down with Eliza & Sally. I left Eliza not well with the cold, pnewmon & Mag Magill & children & Sally & I spent Christmas day with Ruff & Eliza. The next day all of us with Sally. It has been a quiet Christmas. Joe has been taken too much dram, but not so bad.

[December 31, 1889-Tuesday] 31 Wille has killed too fine hogs to day. One weighed too hunderd & eighty six & one two & twenty five. He sold one, twenty one dollars. and now farewell to 1889 with all youre pleasures, losses and crosses. You are gone. Oure blessings have been great. We have a good preacher & good sabbeth school. We have had a fine fall, had but one cold spell & have plenty to live on. My health is not good but am abble to go & I try to be thankfull for all of these blessings. I have had some hard seenes, seen Sylvanis loss his mind till he was like a ravin maniac, but I thank God that he has got all right and will soon be home. A great blessing to his wife & children. They have all got allong & done fine sence he left.

1890

[January 1, 1890-Wednesday] A new years day on wensday all well & at home, warm & clowdy. I know something of the past but what the 1890 will bring is known only to the my farther which is in Heaven. I Pray thee that thou will give me grace & strenth to be resined to thy Heavenly will in all things. What I ask for myself do I ask the for my Children & their little ones, for time & eternity for Christs sake. amen MDB

[January 4, 1890-Saturday] 4 all well. Wille is gone to the Alliance meeting today. Clowday but no rain.

[January 11, 1890-Saturday] Jan 11 satterday evening I have been over with Fanny & then up at Cates. Sylvanis got home last nigt & seemes all right. He brought me home this, all right.

[January 12, 1890-Sunday] sabbeth evening Mr Kirkpatrick tex was in Heb 9 28v. Sylvanis was at preachen, all right.

[January 22, 1890-Wednesday] 12 Edward Land & Miss Emma Keller was married Jan 22 1890, a wensday evening by Mr Inglish. Jim & Fanny, Milt & Elevia Jackson & my Wille & Bob went and seen them married & then all came back to Gims. Had a fine supper. I have been over with Fanny for a week to help some. I have not been well, dont feel no better yet.

[January 23, 1890-Thursday] 23 Wille has brought me home this evening, rainen & freezen.

[January 26, 1890-Sunday] 26 Mr Kirkpatrick preached a good sermon to day. His tex, "Behold I stand at the door & knock." Wille & Min had theire first daughter baptised to day, its name Mary Lilian.

[January 29, 1890-Wednesday] 29 Fanny & the children was over yesterday. Had a big singing last night, a crowd of young boyes & girls. Had a fine singing. Wille is gone to Hickry grove to day with cotten & is cold & rainen.

[February 5, 1890-Wednesday] Feb 5 1890 all well. Wille is gone to Hickry Grove with cotten.

[February 11, 1890-Tuesday] 11 I have been over with Mag Hall fore a few dayes. Her little Sally has had a bad spell of Pnewmonia but has got the turn now & I have come home. Stayed with Fanny a few dayes. Gim has brought me home this evening. All well, but myself, feeling bad.

[February 16, 1890-Sunday] 16 sabbeth night I did not go to preachen to day as I have been feeling unwell. Mr Kirkpatrick is here to night.

[February 18, 1890-Tuesday] 18 Min, Fanny & I have been up to spend the day with John Brown & his wife & the ould Mother Latamore. Gim & Wille is helping Lawson to cover his new house, all gone home.

[February 19, 1890-Wednesday] Rewfus & Eliza was up to day. Eliza is dooing better 19.

[February 21, 1890-Friday] 21 Mag Hall, Sally & Myrtal came up yesterday evening & stayed till this evening Mag is not dooing well. I feel verry uneasy about her.

[February 23, 1890-Sunday] 23 Sabbeth evening I have been to church to day. Oure preacher was sick with the cold, lectured on Christs temptations. Wille was not well and did not go to church.

[February 24, 1890-Monday] 24 Wille is better, palen in the yard. The rest all well.

[March 4, 1890-Tuesday] March 4 I have had a big visit to see Mag & Cate. Helped Cate to make Sylvanis coat.

[March 8, 1890-Saturday] 8 I have been over at Fannies. Helped her put in her blanket web. Ann & the children was over to day.

[March 9, 1890-Sunday] 9 Sally came up last night & all have been to preachen to day.

[March 10, 1890-Monday] 10 Macy & Maud Castles was here to day.

[March 16, 1890-Sunday] 16 Sabbeth day & very cold.

[March 20, 1890-Thursday] 20 I have been over to see Mag Hall. She has a fine daughter. It was born March 20, a tusday morning. Dr White was with her

[March 21, 1890-Friday] 21 this is my birth day, sixty eight years ould. I am near my three score years & ten. Gods will is mine, be it long ore short. I dont feel like that it will be long, but I have thought that for the last years.

[March 23, 1890-Sunday] March 23 sabbeth evening Mr Kirkpatrick preached a great sermon to day. His tex was, "Know you not that ye are the temple of the Holly Ghost." A fine serrmon for us all to see if Gods holly spirit dwelleth in us. Oh that we would live better lives, that we may have oil in our lamps, trimed & brightly burning when the bridegroom comes to make up his jewels, his own precious Jewells. M D BROWN

[March 26, 1890-Wednesday] 26 I was over with Fanny last night, all well.

[March 29, 1890-Saturday] Eliza Stephenson dide March 29 1890. Wille is gone to the Aliance meetin. They are having some trouble abbout it now.

[April 5, 1890-Saturday] Aprile 5 I have been down staying a week with Eliza & Sally. Joe was on the Jury. They have most all been sick with the Grip. Eliza is porly yet. The rest, some better. Eddy brought me home. I have good Grand children. My own children is so good & kind to me the Lord will bless them for it for he has promised it. MDB

[April 9, 1890-Wednesday] 9 Wille has taken Min up to her Farthers. He is sick. Then going on to York, a witness for Psalm Wallace in the alliance suit.

[April 10, 1890-Thursday] 10 I was over with Ann last night. She had a bad night of it. Dr White came out to see her. She is dooing better this morning. Wille is gone down to Sallys to night.

[April 11, 1890-Friday] 11 Wille has come home from York & unckle Frank with him.

[April 12, 1890-Saturday] 12 this is the time of oure communion. Mr Kirkpatrick has no one to help him. His tex this morning was in Hebrews 4 16, "Let us therefore come boldly unto a throne of grace, that we may obtain mercy & find grace to help in time of need." Theire was foure children baptised, William Coldwell & Sue his second wife. Its name, Margaret Mcelwee, Lissy Love, Walter Brown, Martin Bryans Matty, Sylvanis & Cates Marten Silome, sister Harriets little Wile Warlick, Hatty Fewel, unckle Frank & Sally Whitesides.

[April 13, 1890-Sunday] 13 Sabbeth evening oure meeting is over.

[April 14, 1890-Monday] 14 monday the men is all gone to York to day on the alliance sueit.

[April 15, 1890-Tuesday] 15 the suit was not settled. The jewery made a miss trial.

[April 21, 1890-Monday] 21 I have been over with Fanny for a few dayes. Gim Brought me home this morning, all well. Went up & stayed with John & Carry. John has had the grip & not well. Sylvanis and Cate has been sick but we had not heard it.

[April 23, 1890-Wednesday] 23 Mag, Lawson & the Children was over this evening.

[April 24, 1890-Thursday] 24 Fanny & the children, Min & hers & I have all spent this day with Mrs Cain. Had a plesent day.

[April 27, 1890-Sunday] 27 have been to church to day, heard a good sermon. His tex was in John 13, "A new commandment I give unto you, that you love one another as I have loved you that ye also love one another. By this shall all men know that ye are my disciples. If ye have love one to another." He did preach a good sermon to his congration as theire is a good deal of disterbance in oure neighborhood about Vandora alliance & schools. If we would practes what he tole us I think it will do good.

[May 2, 1890-Friday] May 2 Cate was down with us last night, Sally Bury & children & Georgy Price to day.

[May 3, 1890-Saturday] 3 Gim & Wille is gone up on Kings creek a sayning. Fanny & the children is with us.

[May 8, 1890-Thursday] 8 I have been over to Lawsons to day & Ann Brown has been over this evening.

[May 11, 1890-Sunday] 11 Jim Land & Wille is gone to Bethany to preachen to day & Fanny is over with us.

[May 13, 1890-Tuesday] 13 I have been over with Fanny. Her & I went up & spent one evening with Ed & his wife. Sylvanis is rong again. Gim & Wille is gone up theire to night

[May 15, 1890-Thursday] 15 Sylvanis has got all rong & they have taken him to the asilum to day. Marten Hall, Irskin Whitesides, Davis Brown went with him.

[May 17, 1890-Saturday] May 17 This is the day that they haven taken Sylvanis to the asylum.

[May 22, 1890-Thursday] 22 I have come home from Cates. A sad thing to take Sylvanis away again & leave Cate & the little children & Bell by themselves. Gim Ray has gone to stay with her & work out the crop.

[May 25, 1890-Sunday] 25 We have been to preachen to day.

[May 27, 1890-Tuesday] 27 I have been over to see Fanny & Gim & Wille has been up to see Cate. Had heard from Sylvanis, dooin as well as could expect.

[May 29, 1890-Thursday] 29 Mag Hall & the children has come to Fannies & was affraid to come over here on the account of the hooping cough as Willes children had a chance of catching it. Gim came over fore me to go over to see her.

[June 1, 1890-Sunday] Sabbeth evening the firs day of June all well & no company. A holy happy sabbeth day to try to spend it in a right way.

[June 3, 1890-Tuesday] 3 Fanny & the children is over & Willes, Ely Price left him.

[June 4, 1890-Wednesday] 4 All well & at home, verry busy. A fine growing time. We have a fine garden, beans, potatoes, onions, cucumbers & beets, plenty of them.

[June 5, 1890-Thursday] 5 Mrs Sue Cain & Gimmy, John & Cary Brown & Mrs Latamore has spent this day with us. Had a plesent day.

[June 8, 1890-Sunday] 8 sabbeth evening this was the children day to bring in theire boxes. They gave thirteen dollars. Had no sermon, read the little leefllets & talked to the children. Gim & Fanny & the children & Mr Kirkpatrick for dinner, all gone.

[June 9, 1890-Monday] 9 all well. Wille is cutting wheat. It is not verry good, a beautiful day for harvest.

[June 13, 1890-Friday] 13 Wille, Min & I have been spending this day with Davis & Ann. Robby & Mary is bad with the caughf.

[June 22, 1890-Sunday] 22 this was oure preachen day but Mr Kirkpatrick did not preach. Mr Elder lectured in behalf of the American bibble socity.

[June 26, 1890-Thursday] 26 I have been with Fanny for several dayes. She is feeling bad, has got her a good cook. I hope she will feel better now. The children is caughufind bad.

[June 28, 1890-Saturday] 28 I have been over to see Lawsons children. They are bad with the caughf. They had a singing at the church to make up a school for Mr Henterson.

[July 3, 1890-Thursday] July the 3 I have been up with Cate for a few dayes. She has brought me home this morning. They have not heard from Sylvanis for a week. He is not mending much. Cate has had a hard time but they seem to be gitting allong fine, has a fine prospect for a crop & all well. Wille is gone to york to the big speaking, Tillmon Earl & Bratton for Govener. Had a big day & lots of candates.

[July 4, 1890-Friday] July 4 Wille is gone back to York. He is a diligate to the Alliance meeting to day. Cousin Newton Glenn was here.

[July 6, 1890-Sunday] 6 Cate has brought unckle Franklin Furgison down this morning. They are all well.

[July 7, 1890-Monday] July the 7 monday morning Willie has brought me over to stay with Fanny till she will be confined. She is complaining a good but our Heavenly Farther has promised to be with us in child bearing if we will put our trust in him. Heavenly Farther, I pray thee, if it bee thy holly will, that though would give her a safe delivery, a living Mother & a living chile, fore Jesus sake.

[July 10, 1890-Thursday] 10 all dooing as well as common. Gim is gone over to Willes. Mag Hall & the children was over this evening.

[July 13, 1890-Sunday] 13 I have been at preachen to day. Went by home to see the children. They are gitting better of the caughf. Mr Kirk preached a fine sermon to day. His tex was, "Theire is joy in the preasence of the Angels of God over one sinner that repentheth more than ninty & nine that need no repentence." Joe & Sally came up yesterday, took dinner with Fanny & me, then went up & stayed with Cate to preachen to day, now gone home.

[July 20, 1890-Sunday] 20 Cate has been down this morning, has got a card from the Dr. Sylvanis is no better. Fannys Children has the hooping perty bad & Fanny is verry porly. The Dr White has been out to see them to day, some better to day. I am with Fanny.

[July 22, 1890-Tuesday] 22 Wille & Min has been over to day. The Children still coughfs.

[July 26, 1890-Saturday] 26 we have had a few dayes of rain, a bad time fore the caughf.

[July 27, 1890-Sunday] 27 sabbeth evening I am feeling tolerabble. Fanny is dooing as well as could expect. The children caugh hard. This is oure preachen day but have none to day.

[August 3, 1890-Sunday] Aug 3 sabbeth evening I have been home to day to see little Mary. She is sick.

[August 7, 1890-Thursday] 7 Mag Hall has been over this evening, all well. Fannies _____ was born August 9, a satterday morning, Robbert Haskel, a fine big boy. Both dooing fine.

[August 10, 1890-Sunday] 10 Gim & Wille is gone over to the school house to preachen to day.

[August 12, 1890-Tuesday] 12 Joe & Sally has come up to see Fanny & the babe to day.

[August 16, 1890-Saturday] 16 I have left Fanny this morning, gone home to stay a few dayes.

[August 17, 1890-Sunday] 17 Wille & Min is gone to Union to preachen to day.

[August 20, 1890-Wednesday] 20 I have gone back to Fanny. She is not well.

[August 23, 1890-Saturday] 23 I have come back home this morning. Fanny & the babe is dooing better. Mammy & Dan Hall was here last night, all gone to the singing to day, Wille & Min. This is the last day of the singing. They have had a big day.

[August 24, 1890-Sunday] 24 Mr Glassgo has preached for us to day. He preached a fine sermon.

[August 29, 1890-Friday] 29 Cate & bell & the Children has been down. Was all at Lawsons yesterday. She was over to see Fanny this morning, all well.

[September 5, 1890-Friday] Sept 5 Joe has brought me home this morning, have had a visit down to see Eliza & Sally & to Hickry Grove to preachen. Mr White & Mr Chalmores preach fine sermons, their firs Comunion in their new church. Ruff & Eliza has mooved theire membership from Smerny, Joe & Sally from Bershaba. May God Bless them & their Church. Eddy, Ruffs son, joined the church. Wille is gone to York with his firs bale of cotten to day Sept 6.

[September 8, 1890-Monday] 8 I have been over to Fannies to see Libby Jackson. Gim & Fanny is to come over to night & Cate has sent for me. Vance has the dipthera. I am going up their.

[September 10, 1890-Wednesday] 10 I have come home this evening. Vance is better, dooing verry well.

[September 11, 1890-Thursday] This thursday Sept. 11 this is the firs day of oure protracted meeting. I have not been feeling well, did not go to preach. Wille & Minny went. Mr Kirkpatrick & Mr H B Garis, he is oure evanglist, came home with them.

[September 12, 1890-Friday] Friday evenig the 12 we have all been to preachen to day. Mr Garris preached. His tex, "Behold I stand at the door & knock." We have preachen every night.

[September 13, 1890-Saturday] 13 we have all been at preachen to day. Mr Garris preached again. His tex was abbout the blood on the lintles & door posts. A fine sermon. Gim & Fanny had theire son baptised, Robbert Haskel. Mr & Mrs Kirkpatrick & children, Minnes & Ethel, aunt Harriet, Joe & Sallie. Sallie is gone up to stay with Cate. Little Mary has the araciplas in her leg. They are gone to preachen to night. Mr Kirk has not went no night. He is not nigh well yet.

[September 14, 1890-Sunday] Sabbeth evening oure great preachen is over & preachers all gone. Mr Garris preached to day. His tex was in Mathew 27c 22, "What shall I doo with Jesus which is called Christ." A great sermon. Theire was ten joined the church, too men baptised, Newten Neel, Camel Robberts.

Oh my Farther which is in Heaven I pray thee to give me Grace & strenth to make a good imprvement of these great & momentious truths that I have heard. That I may put on the whole armour of God, that I may be abble to stand against the wiles of the flesh, the world & the devil, having my loins girt about with truth & having on the brest plate of righteousness & having oil in my lamp that I may be reddy to go forth to meet the bridegroon, for my three score years & ten is nearly run.

Awake my soule strech every nerve
And press with vigor on
A heavenly race demands thy zeal
And an emmortal crown

unknown

[September 20, 1890-Saturday] 20 I have come home from Cates this evening. The children has got better. Cate has got a letter from Sylvanis. He is improving, but slow. Cate is axinious to go see him.

[September 25, 1890-Thursday] 25 wet & a bad time for cotten picking.

[September 26, 1890-Friday] 26 I have spent this day with John & Cary Brown & Dr Coldwell & his wife was visinting their that day.

[September 27, 1890-Saturday] 27 Gim & Fannie was over last night. All gone home.

[September 28, 1890-Sunday] 28 sabbeth evening Mag Hall & the children was over last night, have all been at preachen to day. Mr Kirk was abble to git back. His sermon was abbout Lots last night in soddom. He preached a fine sermon. Not manny out. It has been a cold, drizely day. Joe & Sally went home.

[September 29, 1890-Monday] 29 this is a cold & drizely day. Wille is holling his cotten to the gin to day.

[October 6, 1890-Monday] Oct 6 I have been over with Fanny for a few dayes. Was at York last satterday, took dinner Ruff Parish, with Ned & Clem Jeffry, had a fine day.

[October 9, 1890-Thursday] 9 Wille & Min has been down to york this evening.

[October 12, 1890-Sunday] 12 Mr Inglish has preached for Mr Kirk to day.

[October 15, 1890-Wednesday] 15 I have been up with Cate. Her children has been sick. She had a corn shucking last. Had a fine chance of good corn. Wille has come home sick.

[October 16, 1890-Thursday] 16 this is the day of the sentcantalion at Bulix creek. Jim & Wille intended going but Wille is sick & it has rained so that it was bad to git out.

[October 24, 1890-Friday] 24 I have been with Fanny for a week. She has had a beeled jaw. The Dr lanced it. It run a heap. The children has all been sick with the cold, is a little better.

[October 26, 1890-Sunday] 26 we have all been to preachen to day. Mr Kirks tex was in Psalms fortyeth 3 verse. Joe & Sally was up. Fanny was not abble to come. Mrs Kirk was down to day. Cal Clak had to children baptised to day. Wille & Min is gone over to Davis to a singing. MDB

[November 2, 1890-Sunday] Nov 2 Wille is gone to enen to preachen to day. The children is sick with the cold. Unckle Franklin is here.

[November 4, 1890-Tuesday] 4 this is the day for electing Govener & other state officers. Robby is sick & Gimmy Land is gone for the Dr White.

[November 5, 1890-Wednesday] 5 Fanny & the children is over to day & Robby is better.

[November 9, 1890-Sunday] 9 Sabbeth evening I went home with Cate yesterday, come back. Bell & I have stayed with the children & let Minny go to preachen. Joe & Sally & Eddy Whitesides came by, gon home. I am going back to Cates. Robby has got better.

[November 11, 1890-Tuesday] 11 tusday evening Cate & her little Mart, my Wille, Gimmy Land, Mart Hall & his too boyes, Dan & Jonny Quilla, all started for Collumbia this morning. Cate to see Sylvanis Whitesides, & some of them to the Collumbia fare, Bell & the children, Vance & Mary. Unckle Fanklin Furgison is staying with Fanny.

[November 12, 1890-Wednesday] wensday Bell & Minny has been over to see Fanny this morning. She is not verry well. The rest is all dooing fine.

[November 13, 1890-Thursday] 13 thursday evening Min is sick & Lawson is gone down to York for Wille & Cate.

[November 14, 1890-Friday] 14 they all got back safe & sound, but perty tired. Cate came on here & stayed all night. Had a fine time. Found Sylvanis perty well, wanted to come home badly but the Dr did not want him to come yet but thinks it wont be long till he can come. The ould man came down fore Cate this morning, all gone home.

[November 15, 1890-Saturday] 15 Eliza & Eddy came up last night & stayed all night, gone back soon this morning. Wille is gone to the Alliance meeting this morning. The Alliance has gained the suit with Psalm Wallace. I am going over to Fannies this evening.

[November 21, 1890-Friday] friday the 21 I have got home again. Brought Fanny & the children home with me to stay till morning. Fanny is not well, has tak three doses of calamole this week.

[November 22, 1890-Saturday] Nov 22 Fanny is gone home this morning, not feelin eney better. Gim was going for Dr Bratten a soon as he went home. Mr Latamore went home with her.

[November 23, 1890-Sunday] 23 I have been to preachen to day. Mr Kirkpatrick preached us a great serrmon. His tex was in Psalms, "Whether shall I go from thy Spirit ore whither shall I flee from thy presence, If I ascend up into Heaven thou art therre, if I make my bed in hell, behold thou art there, If I take the wings of the morning and dwell in the uttermost parts of the sea, Even there shall thy hand lead me and thy right hand shall hold me." A great sermon.

[December 6, 1890-Saturday] Dec 6 Wille & Min & I have been down to see Eliza & Sallie, all well.

[December 14, 1890-Sunday] sunday 14 I have been to preachen to day, have elected too new Deackons to day, Davis Brown & Marten Bryan to be ore-dained next preachen day.

[December 16, 1890-Tuesday] 16 Wille has gone ore started to Gastonia with a load of cotten this morning. Davis & Ann Brown mooved to their new home to day.

[December 17, 1890-Wednesday] 17 Wille got back as far a Cates last night. It is verry cold , had a big snow last night.

[December 18, 1890-Thursday] 18 Fannie & children & Mrs Anna Jones was over to day.

[December 22, 1890-Monday] 22 Wille & I have been down to York this morning. Got a pare of new shoose & a fine shall.

[December 24, 1890-Wednesday] 24 christmas eve we have had some fine weather.

[December 25, 1890-Thursday] 25 Christmas morning Gim & Fanny & the Children has come over this morning. Wille & Min & all of Gims is gone over to take dinner with Lawson & Mag. Little Mary Land & little little Mary Brown stayed with me.

[December 27,1890-Saturday] 27 satterday I went home with Fanny yester-day in the frees & rain & stayed with her till this evening.

[December 28, 1890-Sunday] 28 sabbeth evening all been to preachen to day.

[December 30, 1890-Tuesday] tusday 30 Lee Willson from Georgy & Henry Glenn took dinner with us to day & Mr Price & his wife.

[December 31, 1890-Wednesday] 31 John Brown & his wife, Mrs Latamore, Mag Brown & her children, Clary Brown & Mrs Cain was here to day.

1891

[January 3, 1891-Saturday] Jan the 3 a satterday night Cate Whitesides has got mooved last thursday, a newyears day, to her own house. I hope she wont have to moove soon again. All got allong fine. Most every thing mooved. I staid with her till this evening & then left them.

[January 6, 1891-Tuesday] tusday evening 6 Eliza, Mary & Brown & Sally Whitesides came up yesterday morning & went to see Fanny. Cate came back & took dinner with us & then went back home, Fanny & her folks too, all gone home.

[January 11, 1891-Sunday] 11 sabbeth evening this has been a wet day. I did not go to preachen to day. Stayed with the children. Sylvanis got home last night from the asslum. His head dose hurt him yet, is looking well.

[January 12, 1891-Monday] 12 Min & the children is gone over to see Cate & Sylvanis.

[January 18, 1891-Sunday] 18 I have had a big trip over to see sister Harriet, Emma Quinn, Buttlers aunt Janes & Marts. Home this evening. Robby is sick & Mary is not well.

[January 20, 1891-Tuesday] 20 Ruff Whitesides was here to day, all well.

[January 21, 1891-Wednesday] 21 Dr Bratten has been out to see Sylvanis to day. Bell & Vance & Mary has been over this evening. Robby has got better. Mary is not well, got the cold.

[January 23, 1891-Friday] 23 Mag Hall & the little children came over last night. Mag, I & Joe Whitesides all took dinner with Lawson & Mag to day. Sylvanis, Cate & the children has all been over to day. Willes gone to take Mag over to Fannies. Cate is gone home to little Mary, is no better.

[January 24, 1891-Saturday] 24 this is a cold wet day.

[January 25, 1891-Sunday] 25 I have been to preachen to day. Mr Kirkpatrick tex was in Hebbrews 17 chapter. Eb Castel had too children baptised to day. Had too new Deacons installed today, Marten Bryen & Davis Brown. Had a good congragation out.

[January 31, 1891-Saturday] 31 I have spent this day with Mrs Latamore, John and Cary Brown.

[February 6, 1891-Friday] Feb 6 1891 I have been over with Fanny & Cate this week. The children has not been well. Have got back home this morning. Little Mary Lilion has got better.

[February 7, 1891-Saturday] 7 this has been a very wet day.

[February 8, 1891-Sunday] 8 I have been at preachen to day. Mr Kirkpatrick is talking of leaven us. His health has failed him so that he cant ride. It will be a sore chastisment on us. We thought so much of him & every thing seemed gitting allong so well. We may have a heap of trouble & dissatifaction before we will be as well suited again. Oh my God though has promised that all thing shall work for good to them that love God. We as short sited we cant see how it is best. If we cant see it, we can beleve, for it is thy own precious promis.

[February 10, 1891-Tuesday] 10 this is a beautifull evening. We have a long wet spell, the roads is nearly impasabble.

[February 13, 1891-Friday] 13 Cate & Fany has been over this evening.

[February 14, 1891-Saturday] 14 I was looking fore Joe & Sally up this evening if we had not had such a rain this evening.

[February 22, 1891-Sunday] 22 this is the day that Mr Kirkpatrick has preached his farewell sermon for us. It was a sad day for us to part with oure beloved Paster. His health had failed him so that he was not abble to ride. His tex was in Psalms 23c 1 verse his last him, "Jesus lover of my soule." I trust that God in his good providence will soon send us another to feed his sheep & feed his lambs.

[February 28, 1891-Saturday] Satterday morning I have spent this week with my dear children on clarks fork. Had a pleasent visit, such good & kind children. It is one great pleashure of life when one is ould to have such good children to doo for them as I have. One & all. Eddy brought me home this morning & is gone on over to Sylvanis. He has a house covering to day.

[March 8, 1891-Sunday] March 8 Sabbeth evening all well. Mr English was to preach for us to day but it has rained so that we have had no preachen. Ann Brown was with us last night.

[March 17, 1891-Tuesday] 17 I have been over with Fanny & Cate came home this evening.

[March 18, 1891-Wednesday] 18 all well. They have mooved the steem sawmile over to the tan yard this evening to saw some for Wille.

[March 19, 1891-Thursday] 19 another wet morning. It has rained all most every day & night this year. We have got nothing done in oure garden yet & verry little plowing.

[March 26, 1891-Thursday] 26 Gim & Fanny was over last night went up & took supper with John Brown & Cary, Wille & Min too. Have planted some in the garden.

[March 29, 1891-Sunday] 29 I have been to preachen to my ould church bershaba. The rev I McL Seabrook from James Iland preached for us to day. His tex was, "Ye are the salt of the earth, ye are the light of the world." He preached a fine sermon, a large congragation the church would not hold them, gone to Clover to preach this evening.

[April 6, 1891-Monday] April 6 we have a verry cold spell now, big frosts & ice. I am affraid the fruit is all killed. Min & little Robby is gone over to Cates.

[April 7, 1891-Tuesday] 7 Bell Whitesides & Min is gone up to Sue Neeis tablo at the school house. Mrs Latamore staid with me & helped mind the children.

[April 10, 1891-Friday] 10 Bethel Presbatary meets at Blacks to night. Lawson is gone as a delagate from Bershaba.

[April 11, 1891-Saturday] 11 another wet morning, to wet to plow. Wille is going to york with the wagon.

[April 12, 1891-Sunday] Aprile 12 Mr Hay has preached for us to day his tex. was in Hebrews 10c 30 31 verse part. It is a fearfuff things to fall into the hands of the living God. The people was well pleased.

[April 17, 1891-Friday] 17 I have been over with Fanny & Cate this week. Gim has been sick & Cate, both perty bad off. Dr Bratten was out to see them, both better.

[April 19, 1891-Sunday] Aprile 19 Mr Inglash preached fore us to day. His tex was in Acts 9c 11 verse & then had a election of a paster & the voted for Mr Hay. Will put in a call for him for four hunderd dollars. Joe & Sally was up, gone home.

[April 28, 1891-Tuesday] 28 Gim & Wille has bought a barl of suggar between them. The barl weyes three hunderd & thirty too. Wille is gone over to Gims & I am going with him.

[May 3, 1891-Sunday] May 3 I have been over with Fanny for a few dayes. Have been over to see Ebbs babby, is sick.

[May 6, 1891-Wednesday] 6 Wille & Min is gone to york to day. Mrs Lata-more & Min is gone over to Fannies to day.

[May 15, 1891-Friday] I have had a big visit down to see Eliza & Sally, all well. Went to Hickry Grove to preachen too dayes. Heard Mr Stewerd preach. Mag Hall, Dan & the babe came over this evening.

[May 17, 1891-Sunday] 17 sabbeth morning Gim & Fannie was over last night, all gone home.

[May 21, 1891-Thursday] 21 Cary had a quilting to day.

[May 24, 1891-Sunday] 24 Mr Hay has preached for us today. His tex was, "Behold I stand at the door & knock." He preached a fine sermon. His wife was with him.

[May 26, 1891-Tuesday] 26 Cary has had a miss to day, giting allon well.

[May 29, 1891-Friday] 29 Ginny & Cate Price was down last night. Fannie & Min is gone over to see Lawsons babe. It is sick. Theire is some sickness ab-bout now.

[June 2, 1891-Tuesday] June 2, 1891 I have been over with Cate & Fannie. They are both not well. Fanny has been bad with a pain in her head & shoul-der, is some better. Ruffes & Eliza has been up to day.

[June 6, 1891-Saturday] 6 I have been back to see Fannie. She is some better. Wille & Min is gone up to Ed Prices to night & to Clover tommorow.

[June 7, 1891-Sunday] Sabbeth evening I have had a fine sabbeth day by my-self. I call it a great privalige to spend a holly sabbeth day allone with my God, trying to spend it in reading Gods holy word & trying to make a sabbeth dayes journey towards my Heavenly home. My heavenly home is bright & fair, nor pain nor death can enter theire, in that blessed home that my blessed saiviour is gone to prepare a place for me, even me, a poor ould wicked sinner. Yes, dear, dear Saiviour, thou dids bleed & die for me, I humbly trust & hope.

[June 8, 1891-Monday] 8 we have had rain. A dreadfull stormy night, thun-der & litening & rain. All over the bottems, the creek was from hill to hill.

Lawsons babe is porly yet, something like gravel.

[June 13, 1891-Saturday] June 13 1891 this is the day that Mr Hay was in-stalled paster of Bershabba Church. Mr Inglas preached a great sermon this morning. His tex was in firs Corrinthians 12 chapter 27 verse. Had an interval, then Mr Fraisure gave the charge to the Paster & then to the people. My Heav-enly Farther will thou be pleased to overule this dayes work for thy Glory & for the good of oure Church & people. Mr Hay, sister Harriet, Wille Warlick, Joe & Sallie is all the company we have.

[June 14, 1891-Sunday] 14 Mr Hay preached this morning. Had but one servis & the Lords supper. Oure Preachers dont want to preach but one sermon now.

[June 16, 1891-Tuesday] 16 I have had a spell of colic this evening. Sylvanis is not dooing well.

[June 20, 1891-Saturday] 20 Cate & Sylvanis was here last night. He is no better. Him & Bell is gone home. Cate & the children staid with us.

[June 21, 1891-Sunday] 21 Sylvanis & Cate is gone home & Lawson with them. Wille Min & myself is going over to Gims.

[June 22, 1891-Monday] 22 Gim Land & Robbert Coldwell is gone to take Sylvanis to the Assylum this evening. A hard seen to see him sent away again.

[June 27, 1891-Saturday] 27 I have come home from Cates this morning. Staid this week with Fannie & Cate. Cate is left in a sad fix, a hard seen. Her & Bell & three little children.

[June 28, 1891-Sunday] 28 Mr Hay preached a fine sermon to day his tex, Mathew 25 c from the 31 verse out.

[July 4, 1891-Saturday] July 4 Wille & Gim is helping Cate to day & Min & Fanny is theire too. Sally Berry & her children is here to night.

[July 9, 1891-Thursday] 9 Fanny is over to day. Gim & Wille is helping Cate to day, they have got her crop perty well cleaned.

[July 11, 1891-Saturday] 11 satterday evening Min & I have been quilting on Willes fine quilt. Got it most out.

[July 12, 1891-Sunday] 12 Mr Hays tex to day was in Acts 4 chapt 17 verse. A good sermon, a good sunday school & a good congragation of people. Mr Hay & I went home with Gim & Fanny then Mr Hay & Gim went over to see Cate.

[July 18, 1891-Saturday] 18 a satterday evening I have spent this week with Fanny & Cate, all well.

[July 19, 1891-Sunday] Sabbeth evening all well & all at home, no company to mar Gods Holy sabbeth day, sweet day of rest. MDB
> Down lifes dark vale we wonder, till Jesus comes
> We watch & wait & wonder till Jesus comes
> Oh let my lamp be burning when Jesus comes
> for him my soule be yearning when Jesus comes

[July 26, 1891-Sunday] July 26 Mr Hayes tex to day was in John 2 10 verse.

[July 28, 1891-Tuesday] 28 they have got their new school house & Mr James Canida is teach for them & has 25 schollars.

[July 29, 1891-Wednesday] 29 Wille & I have been down to see Eliza & Sally, all well.

[July 30, 1891-Thursday] thursday the 30 Gim & Fannie is gone to york to the great reunion meeting of the soilders. I am stayen with the children.

[August 9, 1891-Sunday] Aug the 9 I have been to preachen to day. Mr Hayes tex, "Let me die the death of the richous & let my last end be lik theires." He preached a fine sermon. Eddy Whitesides was up with us last night.

[August 10, 1891-Monday] 10 It is verry warm. Wille is working on the road.

[August 13, 1891-Thursday] 13 I was at a pick nick down at the mineral spring to day, a big crowd. Joe & Sallie was up, gone home.

[August 14, 1891-Friday] 14 Wille, Min & I have all been at Cates gitting peaches & canen.

[August 18, 1891-Tuesday] 18 I have been over with Cate. She has had a bealed jaw, is better.

[August 20, 1891-Thursday] 20 Lawson, Wille, Gim & John Brown is all over at Cates to day covering her cook room.

[August 23, 1891-Sunday] 23 sabbeth evening Mr Hays tex, "Lest these slip from you." Gim & Fanny was over last night, gone home. Had a big rain this evening.

[August 25, 1891-Tuesday] 25 Wille, little Rob & I have all been up to see Davis & Ann Brown. Camel Caveny & Lissy Brown run of & got married Aug 15 a satterday night.

[August 28, 1891-Friday] Aug 28 Ruffes & Eliza Joe & Sally, Cate & her Children was all her to day. Ruff & Eliza is gone home. Joe & Sally, Mary Whitesides is all gone ove to Fannies to night.

[August 29, 1891-Saturday] 29 satterday morning Joe & Sally, Mary and I have come home, cold & wet. Joe & Sally & Mary is gone home.

[August 30, 1891-Sunday] 30 sabbeth no preachen to day. In my Farthers house theire is many a room And my Lord is gone to prepare a place for me. Oh can it be that I shall be with him theire. MDB

[September 11, 1891-Friday] Sept 11 Mr Paris has fixed oure chimney to day.

[September 13, 1891-Sunday] Mins _____ was born September 13, a sunday morning at one oclock 1891. Dr Andrew Bratten was with her, Mrs Latamore, Sally Berry & Fanny.

[September 16, 1891-Wednesday] 16 Min is not getting allong so well.

[September 19, 1891-Saturday] 19 Min is right porly. The Dr has been back to see her. Sally Berry & Fanny is both here to night.

[September 20, 1891-Sunday] 20 sabbeth evening Min seems to be some better. The Dr was out to day. He said he thought she would be all right now. The babe is dooing fine.

[September 22, 1891-Tuesday] 22 Joe & Sally was up last night, gone home this morning. Min is dooing better.

[September 25, 1891-Friday] 25 Wille is gone down to Ruffes for a young heiffer with her first calf, gave twenty five dollars for her.

[September 27, 1891-Sunday] 27 Ed Price & his wife was down to day. I have been to preachen to day. Mr Hays tex was in first Corinthians 16 c 2 verse. Ginny Price is gone home. Min is dooing fine.

[October 1, 1891-Thursday] Oct 1 1891 I have been over to see Fanny. She is not well & to see Cate. Mr Melon has left her to day.

[October 4, 1891-Sunday] 4 Wille & I have been over to the Chapel to preachen to day. Mr Christburg preached a good sermon. His tex was abbout the angels, are they not all ministering spirits sent forth to minester unto them that shall be heirs of salvation.

[October 9, 1891-Friday] Oct 9 a friday evening this is the commen commencement of oure communion, a small congration. Mr M J Mclain preached to day, a fine sermon. His tex was in James 5 16v "The effectuas fervent prare of a riceous man evaileth much." We have no company. Mr & Mrs Hay is gone to Robbert Loves & Mr I M Mclain is gone with them.

[October 10, 1891-Saturday] a satterday evening Mr I M Mclain came home with us & Emma Guinn, Mr & Mrs Hay will be here to night. Mr M I Mclain preached today his tex was in Acts 10, "Now theirefore are we all here present beffore God to hear all things commanded thee of God."

[October 11, 1891-Sunday] Sabbeth evening oure communion over. Mr Mclain preached. His tex, "Prove youre own selves, try youre own selves." Sue Coldwell, William Coldwells wife, joined by surtificate & had theire second chile baptized, William Franklin, one more chile baptised, Mr & Mrs Hay & theire too sones, Hary & Psalm & Mammy Hall was all the company we had last night.

[October 12, 1891-Monday] Bob Coldwell babby died Oct 12 a little after twelve to day it was near a year ould.

[October 13, 1891-Tuesday] 13 I have up to the buring to day. Mr Stephenson preached a verry nice little sermon abbout David & his dead chile.

[October 15, 1891-Thursday] 15 I have been over to see Fanny & Cate she has got better. Wille is hawling wood to York. Took Min & the children over to Cates the firs visit for the little new babe. I am here by myself a verry pleasent day.

[October 17, 1891-Saturday] 17 Wille & Min is all at Mr Prices.

[October 23, 1891-Friday] 23 I have been down to see Mrs Cain to day.

[October 25, 1891-Sunday] 25 Sabbeth evening I have not been abble to go to church to day. I have been bad of with this rupter for several dayes. Gim & Fanny, Joe & Sally came by to see me this evening.

[October 26, 1891-Monday] 26 I am feeling bad yet.

[October 27, 1891-Tuesday] 27 Mag Hall was over to day. Lawson & Mags babby was dead born Oct 21 1891, a daughter.

[November 22, 1891-Sunday] 22 I am a little better, am going over to stay a while with Fanny & Cate.

[November 28, 1891-Saturday] Cates _____ was born Nov 28, a saterday. She got allong fine, sent for Dr Bratten but did not git their.

[December 5, 1891-Saturday] Dec the fifth I have been staying with Cate for near five weeks. I have left her & the babe dooing fine.

[December 6, 1891-Sunday] Robbert Brown died Dec the 5 1891 with the typhoid fever. He lay too weeks & was burried at Bershabba the 6. Mr Hay his funeral sermon, sabbeth Evening & I went home with Fanny.

[December 11, 1891-Friday] 11 Fanny has come home with me this morning.

[December 13, 1891-Sunday] Sunday evening Fanny is gone home. Eddy Whitesides came by this evening.

[December 18, 1891-Friday] 18 Lawson & Wille was going to York in the waggon & I went over to Cates & to Fannyes that night. It is verry cold.

[December 25, 1891-Friday] 25 Christmas day Cate & Bell & their children, Lawson & Mag & their children & I have all spent this day with Fanny. Gim has brought me home this evening.

[December 26, 1891-Saturday] 26 Gim & Fanny & Children has come over this morning. Mrs Mary Francis Baty died Dec 12 & was burried at Bershabba on sunday 13. Mr Hay preached her funeral sermon. Ruffis & Eliza moved to theire new home Dec the 15 1891, the Billy Whitesides place. Gim Ray & Sally Jackson was married Dec 24 1891.

[December 28, 1891-Monday] 28 Ruff & Eliza & children came over this morning. Ruff took dinner with us & then went home. Eliza & I went to see Cate awhile, went on & stayed with Fanny all night & they are all gone home.

1892

[January 1, 1892-Friday] fryday morning new years day & new years day has come in perty sobber. I am not feeling well this morning, my head & ears is in bad fix.

[January 3, 1892-Sunday] 3 sunday evening Min has the grip, is feeling bad, & the babe.

[January 4, 1892-Monday] 4 Min is no better is suffering bad.

[January 5, 1892-Tuesday] 5 Sally Whitesides came up this morning, took dinner with us & gone to stay with Fanny to night & Cate tommorow.

[January 6, 1892-Wednesday] 6 Sally is gone home & Wille is bad with the grip. Little Mary & Gim & Fanny is over to night. Wille & little Mary is bad yet.

[January 9, 1892-Saturday] 9 Ould Mrs Arch Jackson was burried to day. Mr Hay preach her funeral sermon. Sister Harriet is with us to night & I am feeling perty bad.

[January 11, 1892-Monday] 11 I am feeling better. This is a cold morning, raining & freezang & blowing. We have all got better. Gim & Fanny is gone home & ould Mr Love is burried to day. Mr Francis Walker died Jan 9 1892. Bershaba church will miss him, he was one of oure elders.

[January 12, 1892-Tuesday] 12 Fannie has gone home & tacken the grip. I am going over theire to night.

[January 22, 1892-Friday] 22 I have been with Fanny near too weeks. She has had a bad time & all the rest has had it. All got better but her, she is not well yet. Mrs Jane Walker is burried to day, not too weeks sence her Husband died. I have just come from Fannies, was not well, did not go to the burring, Min & Wille went. Mr Hay & Mr Inglish was both theire. Mr Ivens is dead. We have had a great manny death with the ould.

[January 24, 1892-Sunday] 24 we have all been to preachen, had a great sermon. Sabbeth evening we have all been to preachen to day. Mr Hay preached a great sermon his tex was, "Master carrest thou not that we perish."

[January 26, 1892-Tuesday] 26 John Brown & Gim Land & Wille is all gone to Gastonia with cotten.

[January 30, 1892-Saturday] 30 All tolerabble well & at home. Wille is plowing.

[January 31, 1892-Sunday] 31 Gim & Fanny was over last night. She is some better, all gone home.

[February 10, 1892-Wednesday] Feb 10 I have had a big visit down to see Sallie & to see Eliza & Ruff in theire new home. I was well pleased with it. All well. Ruff brought me home this morning, all well.

[February 14, 1892-Sunday] Feb. 14 I have been to preachen to day.

[February 19, 1892-Friday] 19 I have had a visit over to see Mag Hall, sister Harriet. Found Mag perty bad of with the grip & the pains. Stayed too nights with Mag, one night with sister Harriet, took dinner with Adda, supper with Duff & Smoke, left & Marts folks most all sick. Gim Ray brought me over to Fannies, stayed all night with her, then home. Found them all well.

[February 21, 1892-Sunday] 21 Sabbeth evening all well. Preachen to day, had a big rain last night.

[February 23, 1892-Tuesday] 23 Min & the children is gone over to see Fanny to day.

[February 29, 1892-Monday] 29 I was not at preachen yesterday. Mr Hay came home with Wille & Min, stayed all night. Gone to see Fanny this morning.

[March 7, 1892-Monday] Monday evening 7 Fanny has been over to day, the first time in a long time. She has been sick. Mrs Latamore, both gone home.

[March 11, 1892-Friday] 11 I have been a few dayes with Cate & Fannie all well.

[March 19, 1892-Saturday] 19 Satterday night Wille & Min is gone up to Mr Prices. Jonny is staying with me. Cate has been over this evening.

[March 28, 1892-Monday] 28 Mag Hall came up a Satterday & stayed for preachen. Mr Hay tex was in 2 Pete 3. 9 verse, a good sermon. Wille is working the road to day, all well.

[April 5, 1892-Tuesday] April 5 1892 I have been with Fanny for a week helping her to weave her web. I am not feeling well.

[April 20, 1892-Wednesday] 20 Fanny has got part of her web out & I have got home, not feeling well.

[April 22, 1892-Friday] Aprile 22 this is the commencement of oure communion. I have not been feeling well, did not go to day. Wille & Min went. Had no company satterday night. Mr Hamiter of Bracks is helping Mr Hay. No company but Joe & Sallie.

[April 24, 1892-Sunday] Sabbeth evening Mr Hamilter preached a fine sermon. His tex, "This day shall thou be with me in paredice." Theire was seven children baptised yesterday, Mart & Mag one, Jannie, Wille & Min one, William Price, Cate one, Sally Dorcas & theire was foure joined the church, Mrs Anna Joens, Miss Ammieala Sthevenson, Dr Coldwell & wife by sertifficate.

It seemes that they have got to cut things verry short, one sermon & that verry short. It dont seeme to me like the preachen we usto have.

Have our hearts grown cold sence the dayes of ould
Have we left oure soules first love, neither cold nor hot
Has the God abouve oure supreme love doo, we own his name
Are we allwayes in the things we doo are we quite content
Dare a mortal say for a singal day, I have kept thy law oh God undefiled by sin
& say I am pure within.

[April 25, 1892-Monday] Aprile 25 Wille, Min & I have gone over to Gims to night & I am going to stay.

[April 30, 1892- Saturday] 30 I have got home.

[May 1, 1892-Sunday] May 1 I have not been feeling well. Gim & Fannie is over this evening.

[May 6, 1892-Friday] 6 I have been up to see aunt Latamore & Cary to day. The ould Laddy has been sick.

[May 8, 1892-Sunday] Sunday evening at church once more. Mr Hayes tex was in Psalms 84c 1 2 3 verses, a good sermon.

[May 11, 1892-Wednesday] 11 Gim & Fanny & the children has been over. Gim & Wille is dooing some work at the tan yard. Fanny & Min has been to see Aunt Latamore & over to Lawsons. All now gone home.

[May 12, 1892-Thursday] 12 all well & dooing the best we can. Not quite done planting yet.

[May 21, 1892-Saturday] 21 I have been over with Fanny & Cate for a few dayes.

[May 22, 1892-Sunday] 22 I have been to church to day. Mr Haye was preaching abbout Daniel.

[May 24, 1892-Tuesday] 24 Wille & Min went to york this morning.

[May 25, 1892-Wednesday] 25 Fannies to day.

[June 4, 1892-Saturday] June 4 1892 I have had a big visit to see Sallie & Eliza & attended the big evangilist Orr preach at Hickry Grove. He done some fine preachen. Some things I did not like but I hope he has done great good. Theire was seventy six joined the church. Wille, Min & I all went down last. They went a satterday night & Sunday then came home & I stayed, went home with Ruff & Eliza & stayed till to day. Eddy brought me home this morning. Had a powerfull rain this evening. The creek was fuller than it was ever known to be, washed the land badly, runind the bottems.

[June 8, 1892-Wednesday] 8 Gim & Mr Cain is gone seining. Fanny is here.

[June 12, 1892-Sunday] 12 Mr Hay was preaching abbout Daniel again.

[June 14, 1892-Tuesday] 14 Min is gone to York to have her tooth pulled this evening.

[June 16, 1892-Thursday] 16 Cate was over last night, all well.

[June 16, 1892-Thursday] June 16 1892 Wille & Min & the children is all gone over to stay with Gim & Fanny & I am going up to stay with Johns folks.

[June 17, 1892-Friday] 17 Wille is cutting wheat some is verry good some not so good.

[June 26, 1892-Sunday] 26 Sabbeth evening been to preachen to day. Mr Hays tex was in the songs of Solomen. He came home with us this evening took dinner then went down to see Mrs Ruff Allison. She is verry sick with the flux.

[June 27, 1892-Monday] monday evening 27 Mr Hay has come back. Mrs Allison is no better. Mr Hay is going to take me over to Fannies this evening.

[July 5, 1892-Tuesday] July the fifth I was over with Fanny last week help-ing her to weave her bags. Fanny 3 & Min 3. Went over & stayed with Cate one day & night. She is gitting allong fine. Has plenty of ould corn. Made 32 bushels of wheat. Came home this evening, found them all well. Wille has his wheat thrashed, had ninty bushels & a half. A great blessing, some has theire wheat in the field yet & it is raining every day. I fear they will loos it.

[July 6, 1892-Wednesday] 6 All well, Mrs Allison no better. Another wet day. MD Brown

[July 7, 1892-Thursday] 7 Wille & Min & Fanny is gone to York.

[July 11, 1892-Monday] 11 monday morning we have had a nother wet time. It rained so that we had no preachen yesterday. Mag Hall came over satterday & stayed till this morning. I am not feeling verry well this morning.

[July 18, 1892-Monday] July 18 all well & at home. I expect to go to Fannies in the morning for her to make my new dress, black satteen.

[July 25, 1892-Monday] 25 I have been over with Fanny & Cate for a week, all well.

[July 31, 1892-Sunday] Sabbeth evening have been to the church but no preachen, a good congration. Dr Camel died yesterday one of main Clover Elders. We thought that was the reasen, a good & a great man gone home to Heaven.

[August 6, 1892-Saturday] August 6 1892 satterday evening we have all been at a big picknick at Cains Spring to day. I have been over with Fanny, she has not been well this week. Joe & Sallie came up to Gims last night & Eddy Wh-itesides too. Eliza, Mary & Brown home with Wille & Min, have all been down to the picknick at Cains spring, all gone home.

[August 7, 1892-Sunday] 7 Sabbeth evening Wille & Min, Robby & Wille Price is all gone to Union to preachen. Little Mary & I are by oure selves. I doo enjoy a holly sabbeth allone without company, to read Gods Holly word. I have read Burkett, 1 Corrinthians, 15 chapter, on the reserection of the body when these vile boddies will be changed like unto his glouris boddy.

> We shall sleep but not forever,
> Theire will be a glouris dawn
> We shall meet to part no never
> On the resurection morn

We shall sleep but not forever
In the lone & silent grave
In his own good time Hell call us
From oure rest to Home sweet home

———————

Take my life & let it be
Consecrated Lord to thee
Take my hands and let them move
At the impulse of thy love

Take my will and make it Thine
It shall be no longer mine
Take mine heart it is Thine own
It shall be Thy royal throne

unknown

[August 8, 1892-Monday] 8 I have spent this day at John Browns with Mrs Margaret Ann McElwee & Mrs Cate Coldwell. They was both poorly.

[August 10, 1892-Wednesday] 10 Lawson & I have been over to see aunt Harriet & Mag to day, all well.

[August 14, 1892-Sunday] Sabbeth evening 14 I have been to preachen to day he was preachen abbout Annanias & Sopheia. Wille is sick, not abble to go to church.

[August 15, 1892-Monday] monday morning Wille is better. I am going back to Fannies to finishing putting up fruit. We have none at home.

[August 19, 1892-Friday] 19 I have got back home & Cate is over to day.

[August 21, 1892-Sunday] 21 sabbeth evening a poor spent sabbeth day, had John & Sallie Berry & children last night & to day.

[August 24, 1892-Wednesday] 24 Min & the children is gone to Fannies to git peaches & Wille has brought Jane Furgison over this morning.

[August 25, 1892-Thursday] 25 Jane Furgison & I have spent the day with

John Browns folks to day.

[August 29, 1892-Monday] 29 had Mr Hay for dinner to day, gone home.

[August 31, 1892-Wednesday] 31 have been over at Fannies. Lawson & I helping them to make Mollases, have mad fifty gallons & not near done.

[September 1, 1892-Thursday] Sept 1 this morning has come in like fall. We are dreadfully burnt up. Have suffered dreadfull from the drouth, cotten has made nothing in a month & a good deal of fever. Wille is going to commence making his molasses this evening. MDBrown

[September 2, 1892-Friday] 2 we have had Mrs McComick & Mrs Smith to day, Lasley & Rachell Burns. Lawson is gone to Rock hill to see abbout mooving theire.

[September 3, 1892-Saturday] 3 Wille has made his mollases, they are fine, made 45 gallons. Gim one hunderd & twenty five, Cate 45 & not done. A fine thing to have so manny nice ones for winter. It is so dry that we have got no turnips sowed yet.

[September 6, 1892-Tuesday] 6 Wille has been to Gastonia with wheat. Got nice flower, foure hunderd & fifty pounds. Took Min & the children up to her brother Eds to stay till he come back, all got home safe. Gim & Fannie staid with me.

[September 8, 1892-Thursday] 8 Mrs Latamore has been with us too dayes & nights. She is verry porly. John & Cary was down yesterday.

[September 11, 1892-Sunday] 11 sabbeth evening have been to preachen to day. Mr Hay preached a good sermon to day. His tex was about Philip & the Ethopian, a good congragation. I am not feeling well this evening. Oh that I may live in readiness for death, we know not what a day ore an hour may bring forth.

[September 13, 1892-Tuesday] 13 Wille is gone to york to the election. I expect Wille will take me up to stay a while with Eliza this evening. They have met with a bad misfourtin. Last sabbeth morning got his cribs, a fine faten & buggy burnt up, five loads of hay & some corn.

[September 24, 1892-Saturday] Sept 24 satterday evening have got home from a big visit with Eliza & Sallie. Sallie has come home with me. Fanny & the children has come over. I am not feeling well have not been well ever sence I have been gone. Had a long visit, near too weeks. Ruff & Eliza is dooing verry over their loss.

[September 25, 1892-Sunday] Sabbeth evening 25 we have all been to preachen to day. Had a large congragtion & a good sermon. My dear children was all their but Eliza. Eddy was their. He came home with us & took dinner. All gone home. MDBrown

[September 26, 1892-Monday] Sept 26 1892 I am feeling some better to day, took a dose of calimol last. Wille & Min, Psalm & fron is all picking cotton.

[October 2, 1892-Sunday] Oct 2 1892 sabbeth evening I am feeling better. If its Gods will I hope he will restore me to my usual health that I may use the talent that God has given me for his glory & my own good.

[October 9, 1892-Sunday] sabbeth evening 9 Mr & Mrs Hay came home with us & took dinner, gone home, preached a good sermon.

[October 10, 1892-Monday] 10 all well & busy picken cotton.

[October 25, 1892-Tuesday] 25 Cate has a cornshucking to night & we have killed oure pig, it is fine.

[October 27, 1892-Thursday] 27 I am going over to Fannies to stay a few dayes.

[November 6, 1892-Sunday] Nov 6 I have been over at Marts for a week. He has been verry bad, had hemerage of the stomic, has had three spells, has been in a dangerous situation but the Dr thinks he is out of danger now, Dr White.

[November 11, 1892-Friday] 11 friday night of our communion. Mr McAlster from Bethel preached to day. I think he is a fine preacher & a nice man. Mr McAlster & Mr Hay is both with us to night, also Ginny & Cate Price.

[November 12, 1892-Saturday] Satterday evening Mr McAlister preached too sermons to day, gone home this evening. Eddy Whitesides has got his hand

tore in the cotten Gin. Wille is gone over to see him. Oure communion is over.

[November 13, 1892-Sunday] Nov 13 Mr Hay done the preachen, no help.

[November 27, 1892-Sunday] Sabbeth evening I have not been feeling well, did not go to preachen to day.

[December 1, 1892-Thursday] Dec 1 1892 Mag Hall & the children has come over to night. Mart has got perty well.

[December 8, 1892-Thursday] 8 I have been over with Cate & Fanny for a week. Gim & Fanny & the children has come home with me this morning & Cate came over this evening & I am feeling bad.

[December 11, 1892-Sunday] 11 I have been to preachen to day, am feeling better. Mr Hay preached a great sermon abbout the rich man & Lazaris. A solom sermon it was, came home with us & took dinner.

James Castel Brown, Lawsons oldest son started to Texes Oct 31, a monday morning. John Jackson Brown, Lawson second son started for Floriday monday Nov 14, monday. John Jackson Brown has come back Dec the 23 1892.

[December 17, 1892-Saturday] 17 Wille & Min, Gim & Fanny was all down with Joe & Sallie last night. Jane stayed with me. Joe & Sallie was up this week.

[December 20, 1892-Tuesday] 20 Gim & Fannie, Wille & Min is gone to York with the children to see Santy.

[December 25, 1892-Sunday] 25 Christmas day, a Sunday evening we have all been at preachen to day. Mr L Loury of Georgia preached a mishanary sermon to day in behalf of Japan. A great sermon, came home with us & stayed all night.

[December 27, 1892-Tuesday] 27 Gim & Fanny & children came over last night & it is verry cold & snowing & they have gone home in the snow.

[December 30, 1892-Friday] friday evening 30 Wille & Min is gone over to Marts, coming back to Fannies to day. Jane Furgason is staying with me. She is gone up to John Browns to day. I am not feeling verry well, a pain in my back

& hench. Mary D Brown

[December 31, 1892-Saturday] Dec 31 the last day of the year. Ruffes & Eliza is here to day, Jane Furgison, Bob & his wife & children.

1893

[January 1, 1893-Sunday] A new years day 1893, a sunday. I have not been feeling verry well to day but that is nothing new. I have been complaining for manny a long day, yet I am here yet.

[January 9, 1893-Monday] Lawsons Gimmy came home from Texes Jan. the 9 1893.

[January 10, 1893-Tuesday] Eddy Whitesides and Hew Alexander was here for dinner to day.

[January 14, 1893-Saturday] 14 Cate was over this evening, all well.

[January 15, 1893-Sunday] 15 Mr Hay us a fine serrmon for the commencement of a new year. A verry cold day but a good congragation of people. We have had powerfull cold weather.

[January 18, 1893-Wednesday] 18 We have had a big snow.

[January 29, 1893-Sunday] 29 fifth sabbeth. Mr Hay was to give us this day but it has rained so he did not come. We had Joe & Sallie yesterday. Sister Harriet & little Wille Warlick, Mammy Hall & Mertie all went to church but had none.

[January 30, 1893-Monday] monday 30 I am going over to stay a week with Fanny & Cate.

[February 8, 1893-Wednesday] Feb 8 I have been over with Cate & Fanny for a week. All well. I am not feeling well, have a pain in my back & hench.

[February 11, 1893-Saturday] satterday 11 another wet spell. I have got the cold & feeling bad.

[February 14, 1893-Tuesday] 14 Min is gone over to help Fanny to quilt today.

[March 2, 1893-Thursday] March 2 Fanny had a quilten to day. Mag Hall & Mammy, Cate & Min got it out.

[March 4, 1893-Saturday] 4 I am over at Fannyes, verry cold & windy.

[March 7, 1893-Tuesday] 7 I have been a day & night with Cate. Wille came for me this evening. I am not feeling well.

[March 12, 1893-Sunday] 12 I have been to preachen to day. Mr Hay was preachen abbout the man that was going to pull down his barns & build greater. He came home with us & took dinner, him & Lawson & then he went down to Ruffus Allison to stay all night.

[March 14, 1893-Tuesday] March 14 Jane & Mary has been helping Min to quilt to day.

[March 18, 1893-Saturday] 18 cold & stormy, a big snow this evening.

[March 19, 1893-Sunday] 19 sabbeth evening. I have had a fine dayes reading abbout Joshua taken the children of Israel over Jorden into the promis land after their wandrings in the wilderness, everdently typifred the beleivers passage through death to Heaven when he has finished his course in this sinfull wourld.

[March 21, 1893-Tuesday] March 21 1893 this day seventy one years ago I was born. Cate & Fanny has come over to spend the day with me to day & brough me some birthday presents & help Min to quilt. My Heavenly Farther, I humbly thank for the manefestation of thy loving kindness and tender mercies, both spiritual & temperal & pray thy continuation of thy mercies the remmainder of my life for thou has promised my grace shall be sufficent for me. Wille & John Brown is gone to kings mountian with cotten. I am not feeling well. Wille has got back all right, got nine thirty five.

[March 22, 1893-Wednesday] 22 I am feeling some better. Min has got her quilt out.

[April 7, 1893-Friday] Aprile 7 1893 Mrs Sue Cain has been here to day. Ruff & Eliza came by from York to day, all well.

[April 9, 1893-Sunday] 9 Sabbeth evening Sermon abbout Paul being carried up to the third Heaven. A fine sermon.

[April 15, 1893-Saturday] 15 I have spent this week with Cate & Fanny. All well.

[April 17, 1893-Monday] 17 I am not feeling well to day, had a bad night of it but am abble to be up to day.

[April 22, 1893-Saturday] Aprile 22 Wille & Min is gone to york. Cate & Fanny is helping Min to sow to day. Cate is over too.

[April 28, 1893-Friday] 28 Ed Price & his wife was down to day.

[April 30, 1893-Sunday] 30 John Berry, wife & children came down to day. Mr Hay has preached to day.

[May 11, 1893-Thursday] May 11 I have been over with Mag Hall for a week. She had a fine sone May 3 1893. They are both dooing fine. Was over to see aunt Harriet & Ginny Whitesides & have got back home. Feeling tollerabble well.

[May 14, 1893-Sunday] 14 I have been at preachen to day. Mr Hayes tex, Heb 12, the last claus of the first verse. Mr Hay, Joe & Sallie came by with us

& took dinner. I am feeling bad.

[May 25, 1893-Thursday] May 25 oure communion services commenced to day. Mr Mclin from Chester has preached to day. His tex was in Mathew 6 c 6 v. He is a good preacher. Mr Mclin & Mr Hay both came home with us. Preachen to night.

[May 26, 1893-Friday] 26 satterday evening Mr Mclins tex was in John 21 c. "Simon Peter, son of Jonis, lovest thou me?" Theire was foure joined the church, Lourry Brown & Fanny Brown, Lawsons children, Cary Good, Jonny Thomison, too by sertificate, Mr & Mrs Good. Sabbeth evening Mr Mclins tex to day was, "The love of Christ." He preached a great sermon, all gone home. No company.

[June 3, 1893-Saturday] June the 3 Mary & I have been over to see Cate & Fanny. Mary is gone home. I am feeling bad.

[June 8, 1893-Thursday] 8 I have been down to see Sallie fore a few dayes. Joe brought me home this morning, am not feeling verry well.

[June 30, 1893-Friday] June 30 Mary Furgisons babby was born May 30 1893. Eliza Ann, Mary & Brown all came over to day. I was at Bobs. She went on & spent the day with Cate & here to night.

[July 1, 1893-Saturday] 1 gone home this morning, left Mary to stay a week.

[July 14, 1893-Friday] July Mag Browns Mary Floraree was born July 14 1893, a friday night. Dr White was with her.

[July 21, 1893-Friday] July 21 Joe & Sallie has come up to day, took dinner with us & went on to stay with Fanny to night.

[July 22, 1893-Saturday] 22 theire has been a big picknick at Cains Spring to day. Joe & Sallie & Ruff was theire, Wille & I this evening.

[July 26, 1893-Wednesday] 26 Cate & I have been over at Lawsons to day.

[July 30, 1893-Sunday] the 5 sabbeth have been at preachen. Sally up.

[August 13, 1893-Sunday] Aug 13 Fanny has come over & stayed with Min till we went to preachen.

[August 17, 1893-Thursday] Mins _____ was born August the 17 1893, a thursday morning. Dr Andrel Bratten was with her, all dooing fine.

[August 25, 1893-Friday] 25 Ruffes & Eliza has been here to day.

[August 27, 1893-Sunday] I have been to preachen to day. Mr Hayes tex was in Kings, "Sammary besiegd."

[August 28, 1893-Monday] 28 this has been a dreadfull nights & days wind & rain. It hase done great damage to the crops.

[August 31, 1893-Thursday] thursday evening 31 Wille & Bob has been to Kings mountian to mill, got back all right, got abbout six hunderd pounds of flower, verry nice.

[September 1, 1893-Friday] Sept the first this is a verry wet day, has been raining all day.

[September 5, 1893-Tuesday] 5 I have been over to see Cate & Fanny, all well. The great sorm of rain & win was Sept 3 1893. The eylands was washed over & thousand of people was drownd.

[September 9, 1893-Saturday] 9 this is a wet day & Wille & Bob is macking molases.

[September 18, 1893-Monday] Sept 18 I have had a fine visit to see Ruff & Eliza for a week. Eliza has been sick with the chills but has got some better, abble to go to church too dayes to Smerny. Mr Sthephen preached a satterday, his tex in the morning, "The precious blood of Christ." A mishanary sermon. Mr Knox a sunday. He preached too good sermons, had open communion. The first time that I ever communiond with the Soceders. Went to see Ebs Neel. He is bad with the fever. They think he is a little better, has been verry low. One day to see Hattie, had a nice visit, had a big turkey dinner. Ruff & Eliza, Mary & Brown Brown has been sick but has got better. Eddy has brought me home this, left them all tollerabble well. Found them all well at home.

[September 22, 1893-Friday] 22 all well. Wille is fast busy picken cotten, him and Psalm. It is opening.

[September 23, 1893-Saturday] 23 all well & at home. Wille is busy picken cotten.

[September 24, 1893-Sunday] 24 I have been over with Fanny last night. She is poorly, was at preachen yesterday. Mr Hay preached from the twelve last chapters of Acts, what oure sundy school has been on.

[October 1, 1893-Sunday] Oct 1 Sabbeth evening no preachen to day & no company. A great time to read & study.

[October 10, 1893-Tuesday] tusday 10 this is the day that I have come over to stay a while with Fanny till she is confined.

[October 11, 1893-Wednesday] 11 Min & the children is all over to day. Lawson & WIlle is gone to york.

[October 12, 1893-Thursday] 12 Mrs Cain is over this evening.

[October 13, 1893-Friday] 13 Mrs Jones here this evening.

[October 15, 1893-Sunday] sunday evening 15 Gim & I have been to preachen to day. Mr Hayes tex was in Mathew.

[October 18, 1893-Wednesday] 18 Wille & Min is gone to york & left the children with Fannie & I, the babe too.

[October 21, 1893-Saturday] 21 Fanny is still up yet. Mag Hall & the children has been over to day & Cate this evening.

[October 22, 1893-Sunday] 22 this has been a wet day. It is the time of bethel presbatary & Synod at Sharan, to bad to git out.

[October 28, 1893-Saturday] Fannies Jonney Ruffus was born Oct 28, a satterday eveing at too. Dr White was with her, got along verry well.

[November 2, 1893-Thursday] Nov 2 Gim is gone over to fix the ruff of her

house & Lawson & Wille too.

[November 3, 1893-Friday] 3 Gim & Cate is gone to york this evening to see abbout her land.

[November 4, 1893-Saturday] 4 Cate is over this evening helping aunt Norcis to doo the backen for sunday.

[November 7, 1893-Tuesday] 7 I have left Fanny & come home this morning, her & the babe is dooing verry well.

[November 10, 1893-Friday] Nov 10 1893 this is the day our fall meeting has commenced. The Rev Mr J R Millard of Richburg is issisting Mr Hay. He preached a good sermon.

[November 25, 1893-Saturday] Nov 25 this is the day Mrs Latamore fell & is verry bad. Ould Dr Bratten is waiting on her & Wille has swapped Jane for a bay mare, daisy.

[November 26, 1893-Sunday] 26 sabbeth evening it has been so cold that I did not go to church to day. Min had to go to stay with Mrs Latamore & I kept the children. She is no better & Fannie & Gim has come over to night.

[December 1, 1893-Friday] Dec 1 Eliza & Brown has come over this morning & we are going over to Fannies to night.

[December 3, 1893-Sunday] 3 I have been with Cate a few dayes, all well.

[December 9, 1893-Saturday] 9 I have been over with Fanny for a few dayes.

[December 14, 1893-Thursday] 14 Wille has killed three fine hoghs to day, over six hunderd pounds. It is verry cold.

[December 19, 1893-Tuesday] 19 Wille & Lawson is gone to Kings Mountian with wheat & cotten.

[December 24, 1893-Sunday] 24 Mr Hay preached a fine sermon abbout the prodigais son.

[December 25, 1893-Monday] Christmas day Fanny & her children, Cate & hers & Bell, Joe & Sallie, here, had a fine daye of it. All gone home.

[December 26, 1893-Tuesday] 26 Wille & Min is going to see Ed Price to day & I am going to stay with Fanny.

[December 28, 1893-Thursday] aunt Jane Brown, that is brother Lawsons wife, died Dec 27 in 1893 & I never got over to see her till she was dead. Buried at Bersheba a thursday evening. Mr Hay preached a funeral sermon about the ould tabbernical must fall but we have a building, a hous, not mad with hands eternal in the Heavens. Theire was a large buring, the boyes took it verry hard. I feel that I must be gitting ould when I can look back & think of them that is gone beffore, them that I wonce knew whare are they now, in Heaven ore hell, theire disembod soules dwell.

1894

[January 1, 1894-Monday] monday A newyears day 1894 Well I have arrisen to see the light of another new years morning. All at home & as well as commin. This ould tabbernical is standing but nature tells me it wont stand much longer & oh may it be my great business to be preparing for that house, not made with hands eternal in the Heavens.

[January 2, 1894-Tuesday] 2 Min & the children is gone to Caites. Wille is mooving Tailor over to the other place.

[January 3, 1894-Wednesday] 3 Wille is gone to Kings mountian to git his money fore cotten he sold some time ago.

[January 4, 1894-Thursday] 4 Wille is gone down to Sallies. Fanie & Min is gone up to see Mrs Latamore. She is mending.

[January 7, 1894-Sunday] 7 sunday it has been a verry wet day, Clover day.

[January 10, 1894-Wednesday] 10 a perty morning. We have had a wet time. Wille is gone to york with a load for sale.

[February 1, 1894-Thursday] Feb 1 1894 Eliza has come over to see me to day. She is lookin thin & bad.

[February 2, 1894-Friday] 2 I am feeling some better to day. Cate & Fanny is both here this evening.

[February 4, 1894-Sunday] 4 Mag Hall & the children was over last night. She is not well, hase the cold.

[February 5, 1894-Monday] 5 Min has gone over to see Fanny to day.

[February 6, 1894-Tuesday] 6 I have been up & spent the day with aunt Latamore & Cary. She mends slow.

[February 7, 1894-Wednesday] 7 Fanny & I have spent this day with Mrs Cain. She is verry unwell with the cold.

[February 8, 1894-Thursday] 8 William is gone over to Cates to help with a house for her tenant. I am still feeling better. A perty day.

[February 11, 1894-Sunday] Sabbeth 11 1894 I have been to preachen to day. Mr Hay tex was in Mathew. Sister Harriet & little Wille Warlick was with us last night. Went to preachen to day & gone home. Theire is a good deal of sickness. Mart Hall is sick, Fanny & her children.

[February 17, 1894-Saturday] 17 I have been over with Fanny & Cate. They have most all been sick, is some better. Wille, Min is gone up to see her Farther.

[February 18, 1894-Sunday] 18 Min is bad off with the cold & weed.

[February 21, 1894-Wednesday] 21 Gim & Wille is gone to Gastonia with some cotten & wheat, look for them home to night.

[February 22, 1894-Thursday] 22 Wille is gone to York, all got some better.

[February 23, 1894-Friday] 23 friday morning Wille Mare that he bought from Tenesee & mule is gone. I dont know whare they will go too.

[February 24, 1894-Saturday] 24 Wille, Lawson, John Brown & Lenny Castel is gone to hunt Wille mare. A cold and stormmy day. Wille has got back this evening, found the mare & mule, a great thing to git back home such a day as this.

[February 25, 1894-Sunday] 25 sunday this is a dreadfull day, snowing & sleetting & cold.

[February 26, 1894-Monday] 26 monday morning the sun has risen bright & clear, a dreadfull storm of snow.

[March 2, 1894-Friday] March 2 Fannie has been over to day & Bell this evening. Wille & Min is gone up to see her Farther, he is sick. Lawson is with me to night.

[March 8, 1894-Thursday] 8 we have had a fine spell of weather, made some garden & plowing.

[March 11, 1894-Sunday] Sabeth evening 11 I have been to preachen to day. Mr Hay, a fine sermon abbout Abbraham faith. Had a good congration. Gim & Fannie had theire little son baptised, Joney Psamual.

[March 12, 1894-Monday] 12 Joe & Sallie came over this morning. Joe is gone to York. Sallie & Min is gone over to see Cate.

[March 13, 1894-Tuesday] 13 Joe & Sallie is gone home. This is a perty morning.

[March 14, 1894-Wednesday] 14 I am not feeling well. My back hurts & not feeling good.

[March 24, 1894-Saturday] 24 I have been a week over with Cate & Fanny, all well. We have had the pertiest March that I have ever seen. The fruit trees in blewm & the gardens looks like the last of Aprile.

[March 25, 1894-Sunday] 25 Mr Hay preached to day. His tex was Abraham interceding for Soddom. Molly Enloe died March 24 1894, gave birth to a

daughter & both died.

[March 26, 1894-Monday] 26 Fannie has been over to day. We have been up to see aunt Latamore to day. She is right porly, up & down.

[March 27, 1894-Tuesday] March 27 a sobber looking day this is. Everry thing killed. It is freesing cold. It sets hard on us after such a warm spell. Some thinks the wheat is hurt.

[March 29, 1894-Thursday] 29 This is a cold & blustery day. It has rained & snowed & blowed & I am feeling better than I have done for some time.

[April 6, 1894-Friday] friday evening Aprile 6 this is the commencement of oure communion.

[April 7, 1894-Saturday] satterday evening Mr Hay has all the preachen to do. Mr _____ wife was sick & he could not come. Mr Hayes tex was in Reverlations. He was preachen about the golden candelsticks. He preached a fine sermon. Joe & Sallie came home with us, took dinner & then went over to Gims. Mr Hay is with us. Sabbeth evening oure meeting is over. Mr Hayes tex, "Christ manifested in the flesh." He preached a good sermon. Theire was no one joined the church, thre children baptised, Anna Jones, Mary Carliles, William & Ada Thomison Eliza, Lawson & Sue Neel, Margaret Ann. I have been spared to commerate my Saiviours dying love while so manny has gone home to meet their Saiviour.

[April 13, 1894-Friday] Aprile 13 I was up with Mrs Latamore last night. She is verry weak & porly. I expect Joe Whisonant to come for me to day.

[April 20, 1894-Friday] 20 Wille has brought me & little Mary home this morning, have had a pleasent visit down with Joe & Sally, all well & dooing well as to the things of this wourld. Sallie is living a christian life & trying to serve her God. Joe has quit drinking & is dooing fine.

[April 21, 1894-Saturday] 21 Gim & Fanny was over last night & went up to see aunt Latamore, gone home this morning.

[April 22, 1894-Sunday] 22 the sabbeth school has opend again to day. Mr Hay will miss too sundayes & they have opened the school now for everry sabbeth. Gim Land is supperetend. I pray God to give him faith, grace & strenth to fill the place he has been appointed to.

[April 25, 1894-Wednesday] 25 I have been up to see aunt Latamore this mornings. She is no better. Have been down to see Mrs Cain this evening. She is not well.

[April 27, 1894-Friday] 27 we had Ed Price, his wife & children & aunt Jane down on a visit to day, Cate & her children this evening, all gone.

[April 28, 1894-Saturday] 28 Min is gone up to see aunt Latamore. She is verry low. Wille has taken his mare up to the stand to day.

[April 29, 1894-Sunday] 29 I have been to sabbeth school to day. I think Gim done verry well. Had a good school.

[April 30, 1894-Monday] 30 Fanny has come over this evening to go up to stay with aunt Latamore, staid awhile & came back. Gimmy Brown is here to night. Aunt Latamore is no better.

[May 1, 1894-Tuesday] May the 1 I have been up with aunt Latamor. She is no better.

[May 6, 1894-Sunday] Aunt Mary Latamore died May 5 1894 at John Browns, his wifes Mother, burried at Bershabba a sunday evening. Mr Hay preached her funeral.

[May 7, 1894-Monday] May the 7 I am going over this evening to stay a week with Fanny. Wille & Min is allowing to go to york to hear the eveangilest, Mr Piercen, has been preachen their sence last week.

[May 8, 1894-Tuesday] 8 over at Fannies. I am sick to day, bowel disease & grip. Wille, Min & Gim is all gone to preachen. It rained so last evening Min did not git to go. I am not feeling no better.

[May 11, 1894-Friday] 11 I dont feel eney better. Eliza & her Mary was here last night. Friday evening I am not feeling eney better. Dr Andrewl Bratten has been out to see me to day.

[May 13, 1894-Sunday] 13 Sabbeth Min & Wille is both here. I am feeling bad. Wille is gone for the Dr. It has been a worrisom day, so much company & feeling so bad.

[May 22, 1894-Tuesday] 22 I have got home this morning & Fanny has come home with me. I have had a right bad spell, have been over at Fannies for too weeks. She has so good to wait on me & all the children is so good to wait on me. How good & kind oure Heavenly Farther is to us that has raised me up of a bed of sickness & pain & brought me back home again. The Lord is my Shepherd, I shall not want.

[May 25, 1894-Friday] 25 I have been over to stay a week with sister Harriet. She has the pains of the mussels & nerves, is right bad off, think she is some better.

[July 17, 1894-Tuesday] July the 17 I have been over to see sister Harriet & Mag. Aunt Harriet is some better. Marts all well. Wille came to Marts for me, came on back to Fannies. Min & the children was theire. Fanny had a big dinner, then we all came home. We are needing rain bad. It raining some this morning, crops is dooing perty well.

[July 18, 1894-Wednesday] July 18 1894 Joe & Sallie has been up to day, all well. Cate came over this evening, had a pleasent visit. Oh that I may feel thankfull to my Farther in Heaven for all the manifestations of his love & mercy while traviling throw this vale of tears.

[July 20, 1894-Friday] 20 Wille has been to york to day.

[July 23, 1894-Monday] monday evening 23 we have had plenty of rain, crops looks well. We have had Mr Lowry with us sence last satterday. He preached for us yesterday & last night. He is a good preacher & a good man, as far as I can judge. His tex was in second peter 26. I have spent this day with John & Carrie.

[July 27, 1894-Friday] 27 Wille is gone to Kings Mountian station with wheat.

[July 28, 1894-Saturday] 28 Wille & Min is gone to York to day to get theire pictures taken.

[July 29, 1894-Sunday] 29 Wille & Min is gone to Rama to preachen to day.

[July 31, 1894-Tuesday] 31 Wille has oure milk cow, has gone to york with her. I expect to go to Lawsons to day to see Mrs Castel.

[August 1, 1894-Wednesday] August 1 Mary Furgison & her sister, Hatty & their Mother, ould Mrs Thomison who has not walked in thirty years _____.

[August 4, 1894-Saturday] 4 We have all been at the church to day cleening of the yard & the church.

[August 9, 1894-Thursday] Sylvanis Whitesides died in the lunitic assylym at Collumbia August 8 and brought up & was burried at bershabba thursday 9. Mr Hay was theire & made a nice adress. His tex was in Psalms 66 c 5 vers, "Come & see the works of God. He is terrible in his dooings towards the children of men." Hymn- "God mooves in a misterious way."

[August 12, 1894-Sunday] Aug 12 Mr Harrison preached to day. His tex was the 27 Psalm. This is the beggining of oure summer meeting.

[August 13, 1894-Monday] 13 Mr Harrison again to day. His tex was in Salms. Theire was but few out waiting for the evangalist Mr Boggs.

[August 14, 1894-Tuesday] 14 well Mr Boggs has come. A good manny out. His tex, "As for me & my house we will serve the Lord." Mr Hay was with us last night.

[August 15, 1894-Wednesday] wensday night Davis & Ann & children, Mr Boggs & his too sons, Leland & Wille here.

[August 16, 1894-Thursday] thursday evening. Gim & Hatty Magill, Butler & Bessy, Mr Boggs was preachen abbout Qacies. I dont think no great things of him. I hope he will doo some good.

[August 19, 1894-Sunday] Sunday the 19 Ruff & Eliza came home with, gone back to preachen to night & then home.

[August 21, 1894-Tuesday] 21 oure meeting is still going on.

[August 23, 1894-Thursday] 23 this is the last night of our meeting. Mr Hay, Mr Boggs both came home with us & took dinner. All gone back for preachen. This is the last night. We have had preachen for twelve dayes & nights. Theire

has nineteen joined the Church. He is gone on to fishing creek church.

[August 26, 1894-Sunday] sunday evening 26 Mr Hay has preached to day on the duties of those that had joined the church. Theire was nineteen, five babtised.

[August 29, 1894-Wednesday] 29 I am going over to stay a week with Fanny & Cate.

[September 2, 1894-Sunday] Sept 2 I have been to sabbeth school to day. Gim Land is suppertendant, has a perty good school. They dont all take a right interest in it.

[September 15, 1894-Saturday] 15 I have got home this morning, stayed too weeks with Cate. Bell was gone to see her sister.

[September 16, 1894-Sunday] sabbeth evening Mr Hay was preachen abbout Nicademous to day. Oure sunday school has been about him.

[September 20, 1894-Thursday] 20 Cate has been over this evening.

[September 23, 1894-Sunday] 23 I have been to preachen to day. Mr Hay was preachen about the Samaritine woman.

[September 25, 1894-Tuesday] 25 this is the day that the members of the church has made a star for the mishanary quilt to rais money for the mishanary. Theire was a good many theire, had a nice dinner & had a fine time. Got it put to gether, lacked some stars, made some more & got it most done. Theire was not the half of the members that made one. They got over thirty dollars. The members that was most abble to help took no part in it, Bell Allison, Sue Coldwell, Mrs Dr Coldwell, Mrs Neel, Lissy Walker and lots more. Fanny Land, too stars, had five dollars & a half, Mag Hall three stars, three dollars, Cate one star, one dollar, Bell one star, one dollar & twenety cenets, Fanny Brown one star, one dollar, Minny Brown one star, one dollar & a half, Mary D Brown, one star, one dollar, Nanny & Bessy Thomison too stars, three dollars. Mrs Cain is dooing some work on it.

[September 27, 1894-Thursday] Sept 27 we have the equinoctial gale on us, wind & rain & cold. All well & at home. A cold, bad day.

[September 28, 1894-Friday] 28 Fanny & the children has been over to day helping on the quilt. Min & Fanny is most done it.

[November 1, 1894-Thursday] Nov 1 1894 Mr Hay preached to day, no more till the 2 of Dec.

[November 20, 1894-Tuesday] 20 I have been over with Fanny helping her with her web. Cate has been over to warp it & help her put it in. Ed Land & wife is back from Arcancis.

[November 24, 1894-Saturday] 24 I have been down with Sallie for a week. Joe has brought me home this evenning.

[November 28, 1894-Thursday] 28 theire is a singing over home to night.

[November 30, 1894-Friday] 30 Gim & Wille has been to Gastonia to mill, got back this evenning.

[December 9, 1894-Sunday] Dec 9 1894 Mr Hay has preached to day & organized a ladies aid socity with fifteen members.

[December 17, 1894-Monday] 17 Wille is halling his cotten till John Smith gin. Min & Mary is gone over to Fannies.

[December 19, 1894-Wednesday] 19 Wille has killed too fine hogs to day.

[December 21, 1894-Friday] Wille & Min has been to york to day fixen for Christmass.

[December 23, 1894-Sunday] 23 Mr Hay preached a great sermon to day abbout the King of Peace. Came home with us & took dinner. He was sick with the cold.

[December 25, 1894-Tuesday] 25 christmass evening Wille & Min & the children & I have spent this day with Cate, Gim, Fanny too. Gim & Fanny & the children, Cate & her children has all been her to day, cold & wet.

[December 27, 1894-Thursday] 27 Wille & Min has all been up to Mr Prices to day & Cate came home with me.

[December 28, 1894-Friday] 28 this is a dreadfull cold, snowing & freesing.

[December 30, 1894-Sunday] 30 Wille & Min & Cate is all gone to sunday school, the last sabbeth in 1894, one more year nearly gone.

**Years
1895, 1896, 1897, 1898
Missing**

1899

[June 11, 1899-Sunday] A sabbeth evening have all been to preachen to day. Joe came up this morning to preachen. Joe & Sallie went on home from the church. Joe had got better. Fanny was out. Some of the children is sick. Meek Burns wife is bad off now.

[June 15, 1899-Thursday] 15 Wille & Min has been to york to day.

[June 16, 1899-Friday] 16 I have been up to see John & Carry to day, ould Dave is bad off now.

[June 22, 1899-Thursday] 22 Mrs Carroll & Ela has spent to day with us & Gimmy Cain is bad off.

[June 23, 1899-Friday] 23 Gimmy Brown & Ola has come down to day & Jonny & Loury is both home now.

[June 25, 1899-Sunday] 25 Mr Hay done good preachen to day. He was

preaching about king Ahab wanting Naboth vinyard. Mr Hay went home with Lawson. The children was all at home.

[June 27, 1899-Tuesday] 27 Bell, Mary & Sallie Whitesides is all over this evening. Mary D Brown

[June 28, 1899-Wednesday] 28 I have been over with Lawson & Mag & all the children was home. Ola & the too little girls, Stella & Bessy. They are counting on starting home in the morning up in North Carolina, abbout sixty miles.

[June 30, 1899-Friday] 30 Wille is gone up with Vance to Meek Burns for a load of corn.

[July 8, 1899-Saturday] July 8 I have been a week with Cate & Fanny. Went to Fannies last satterday, over to Fannies staid with her till thursday, went over to Cates till this morning. Vance has brought me home. Lowry, Matty & Clanton was all at cates a thursday.

[July 9, 1899-Sunday] 9 I did not go to preachen to day, staid with the children.

[July 18, 1899-Tuesday] 18 Eliza, Mary & I went down to see Mrs Castel & Alice. They are not verry well & Wille Castle is not well. Gim & Hattie was all over one day. The thre ouldest is all going to school.

[July 22, 1899-Saturday] 22 I have been up with Eliza & the Children for near too weeks, found them all well. Brown is going to school. Eddy is knocking around, Eliza & I went & spent one day with Hatty Magill. Had a fine dinner. Found them all well, then we all went to Piedmont springs. Their was a good manny their, gone & coming all the time satterday. Joe & Sallie came up, took dinner with Eliza then went on to Hatties, staid awhile with them then all went to the spring. Joe & Sallie cam back to Elizas. Eddy, Mary & Brown all went to a picknick at Antock. Mag Magill is staying at the spring. Eliza sent for her a sunday morning to come & go to preachen. Newman & Tommy came up that morning. We all went to preachen but had none, had prayer meeting & sabbeth school. [Duplicate] July 22 I have come home this morning. Eddy, Mary & Brown all came. Theire was a big picknick at the mineral spring to day. Mary staid all night, went home with aunt Cate then Vance & Mary went with her over to

aunt Fannies, came here & we all went to preachen. Lowry Brown went home with Mary & Mr Hay & his Brother in law came home with us & took dinner, then went home.

[July 31, 1899-Monday] 31 I have been over to see Gims new house. They will have a good house soon & have been to Cates. Vance brought me home this morning.

[August 4, 1899-Friday] 4 this is the day that Wille has covered his new barn & has got allong with it fine.

[August 7, 1899-Monday] Aug 7 this is the day that Gim Land covered his new house. Lawson & Wille is gone to help him. Has got it all covered, gitting along fine.

[August 9, 1899-Wednesday] Aug 9 William & Min is gone over to Psalm Smiths to day. They was all to meet their to see what they would doo about selling the ould Price place & Cate & Mary & her cousin, Mary Whitesides from Noth Caroling was with them. Mary & her brother, Wille came down last week to Cates on a visit & they have spent this day with us.

[August 10, 1899-Thursday] 10 Mrs Hay & Mrs Cain has spent this day with us.

[August 11, 1899-Friday] 11 Min is gone on a visit to Mr Caroels to day & Edy Price has been here for dinner. We are all well. The children is at school. Min took Paul with her.

[August 15, 1899-Tuesday] 15 all as well as comin. I am not feeling well. Wille is going to york with a load of wattermellins.

[August 19, 1899-Saturday] I have been over with Fanny. She has got mooved in her new dining room & in one bed room. The boyes all sleeps in the new room. Mr _____ was to be their this week to build his chimneyes. They had to quit to pull fodder.

[August 20, 1899-Sunday] 20 ould Mrs Caroline Whitesides died August 20, a tusday morning.

[August 22, 1899-Tuesday] 22 busy pulling fodder & Wille went to Bob Whitesides this morning & got too sheep from him. Paid him five dollars for them, 1 buck & one yew. I have not been feeling well but have got better. I have been over with Fanny for near too weeks. Gim has bought me home this morning. Helpt her moove in her new house. Have not got it finished yet, have the setting room & the little room & dining room done. They will have a good house when they git it done. Was over with Cate one day & night. Gim & Jessy went to presbatary at Bethesda, started tusday evening & got back a thursday night. Had a fine turnout of preachers & Elders. Adjourend thursday evening.

[August 23, 1899-Wednesday] 23 we have had some rain & it has turned cold & cloudy. Jonny Brown spent the day yesterday with us. He has a month to rest till he will have to start back to colage, is not verry well. He is now attend oure sabbeth school. He does fine.

[August 27, 1899-Sunday] Sabbeth evening Aug 27 Joe & Sallie came yesterday, had a fine visit, all went to preachen to day. Mr Hay preached a fine sermon in Psalms 3 first six verses. It was stormy & some rain last evening. Joe & Sallies gone on home.

[September 8, 1899-Friday] Sept 8 1899 Wille has been down to Ruff Alisons & then went over & took dinner with Sallie & Joe. They are having their house painted & yard fence. They will look quite fine.

[September 9, 1899-Saturday] 9 Wille has been down to the ould Smyth place this morning, bought foure pigs & a calf for a beef.

[September 23, 1899-Saturday] 23 Jonny & Lowry spent this day to day, too nice & good young men.

[September 24, 1899-Sunday] 24 Mr Hefner preached for Mr Hay to day. I did not feel well, did not git out. Theire was a good congragation out & had a good sermon.

[September 25, 1899-Monday] 25 monday evening Jonny & Lowry is gone back to Clinton, started this evening. They are both studdying for the ministery. I pray that God will bless them & give them health & streanth for the labbores that is before them. Gimmy is down now seeing abbout a school over at Union church. Eddy Price has been down & took dinner with us to day &

the children is not well, Mary & Ester.

[September 28, 1899-Thursday] 28 Wille & Min & the children is gone up to Ed Prices to day on a visit. I, Mary, Cordy & Ester is at home.

[September 30, 1899-Sunday] Sabbeth morning Mary & Mart was with us last night, gone home. No Sabbeth school to day.

[October 2, 1899-Monday] Oct 2 cold & blowing & some frost & verry dry.

[October 5, 1899-Thursday] 5 Wille is gone to the flower mill up near Bethany, come back without it.

[October 6, 1899-Friday] 6 Cate & Fanny has both been over to day, all well.

[October 7, 1899-Saturday] 7 Wille is gone back for his flower & it is a wet & stormy evening.

[October 8, 1899-Sunday] 8 I have been to preachen to day. It has been sorty rainny & a bad day for preachen. Mr Hay preached us a good sermon. He was preaching how good oure Heavenly Farther was to us.

[October 13, 1899- Friday] 13 Gimmy Brown & family has mooved down yesterday. He is going to teach over at Union, going to live in John Quinns house. Wille wants to git done hauling up his corn to day. It is tolerabble good. Cate & Fanny has both been over, all tolerabble well, busy trying to git their cotten out & corn gathered & git to sowing wheat.

[October 20, 1899-Friday] Oct 20 1899 this is the commencement of our fall comunion. Wille & the children & I have been to preachen to day. Mr Hefner preached a good sermon. His tex was in John 1 41 v. These are the words, "He first findeth his own Brother Simmon." He preached a great sermmon. Mr & Mrs Hay, Mr & Mrs Hefner all went to Fannies for dinner. Mrs Hefner seems to be a nice, plain woman. Mr & Mrs Hefner went to Goods.

[October 21, 1899-Saturday] satterday evening no company at all. Joe & Sallie was up. They went home with Fanny. Mr Hefner done the preachen, his tex was in Luke the 9 c 23 verse. He preached a great sermon. The preachers all went home with Mrs Caroll for dinner & we have no company atall & I am

not feeling well, have preachen everry night.

[October 22, 1899-Sunday] Sabbeth evening Oct 22 1899 I did not go to day. I am affraid of Wille mules. They had fine preachen & Joe & Sallie came by a while & all gone home. So much good preachen & so soon forgot by us but it is not forgotten by him that knows all things, that the time is coming when we will have to give an acount of these great sermons & these great privilages. So many great sermons.

[October 24, 1899-Tuesday] 24 Wille is busy sowing wheat, all up.

[October 30, 1899-Monday] Oct 30 I have been over with Fanny for a few dayes & one day with Cate. They are all well. Fanny is fixed up nice in her new house.

[November 4, 1899-Saturday] Nov 4 I have had a visit down to see Joe & Sallie. Mary & I & Mary & Min had a fine time, enjoyed it fine Joe has brought us home this evening. Mary & I came in the buggy, Joe rode a mule, tied it to the other mule going back.

[November 9, 1899-Thursday] Nov 9 all well as comin. My leg is a little better. I am not feeling good.

[November 15, 1899-Wednesday] I was not preachen a Sunday. My leg is hurting me, can hardly get up off the chair. The rest was all theire but Esther & Paul & me. Mr Hay, Joe & Sallie came home with them, took dinner & all gone. Sixty years to day sence I came home here to live. It has been a long time. Many has been the ups & downs I have seen in that time but God has been good to me in that long years since I eat my first big dinner that day. Had a big crowd. How many more dayes God has for me in this world of sin & sorow I am resined to his will & try to be reddy when the summens comes, "Go ye out to meet him." I have a sore leg what it will do I dont know.

[November 18, 1899-Saturday] 18 Cate & Fanny has sent for me to go to Cates to help her make Vance a coat.

[November 20, 1899-Monday] Eliza came down to see me a monday the 20 & I was over at Fannies. She came on their. Eddy went on to york. Fanny & I went over to see Mag Hall, all at school but Myrtal. She was at home with her Mother.

[*November 22, 1899-Wednesday*] 22 Gim & Fanny went to york to day.

[*November 23, 1899-Thursday*] 23 I have come over to stay with Cate.

[*November 25, 1899-Saturday*] 25 Vance has brought me home this evening, all well.

[*December 6, 1899-Wednesday*] John Carrol & Iva Houge was married Dec 6 1899 by Mr Hay at six in the evening, came on up to Mr Carrols for supper & that is the last I heard of them.

[*December 15, 1899-Friday*] 15 Min & the children is gone visiting down to see Mrs Cain. Wille has been up to the Price place after some corn & Ed Price has come home with him sick.

[*December 23, 1899-Saturday*] Dec 23 I have been over with Cate & Fanny for a week. Got home this evening. wensday evening We have had a big croud to day, Fanny & all hers, Cate & all of hers, Joe & Sallie for dinner. The children had a christmas tree & all gone home. Ed Land & his wife & son, Gim Navel was here.

[*December 25, 1899-Monday*] 25 Willie went & took the four boyes & Ester to see Joe & Sallie, had a nice trip. Gimmy & Ola & too little girls was with us last night & Jonny & Lowry Brown was here.

[*December 30, 1899-Saturday*] 30 Jonny & Lowry was at aunt Fannies last night & Cates to day.

[*December 31, 1899-Sunday*] 31 the last day of 1899 is near at hand. This is sunday, the last day of 1899. Mr Hay preached to day, was bad & I did not go.

1900

[January 1, 1900-Monday] a new years morning 1900 I am here on the land of the living yet my God has spared me here a long time beffore I can be made meet for my Heavenly home. The dross to consume, the gold to reffin, but God has some work for me to doo & I will have to wait till his appointed time & try to be reddy when the sumons comes. I don't feel that it will be much longer. Jonny & Loury has bid us good by, gone back to Clinten Colage. Quilla Hall is gone back to Clemsen Colge. Thre of my grand sones in Colage. I pray God that he will take care of them & that they may make great & good soone fore the glory of God & the good of soules & Gimmy Brown is gone bck to his school. He is teachen at Union Church. Has a fine school.

[January 6, 1900-Saturday] Jan 6 I have been over with Fanny for a week. Gimmy has brought me home & Min has not been well this week.

[January 7, 1900-Sunday] Sabbeth evening Jan 7 I have been to preachen to day. Gimmy came over & took me to preachen. I have got scared out with Willes mules. Mr Hay preached us good sermon. His tex was in Malchi 3 chapt & 14 verse. Joe & Sallie was their. They came by a while, got some dinner & then went home, was at Fannies satterday night.

[January 15, 1900-Monday] monday evening 15 I feel sorty low spirits & not verry well. This is a perty day, calm & warm.

[January 25, 1900-Thursday] 25 we are most all sick with the cold. Bobby & his Paw is both perty bad off.

[January 26, 1900-Friday] 26 Wille has killed his hog this morn. It is fine. Fanny & the children is a over to day.

[January 28, 1900-Sunday] 28 Wille, Rob & I staid at home to day, was not abble to go to church. Joe, Sallie & Mary Whitesides cam by. Mary is down to stay a week with aunt Sallie.

[January 31, 1900-Wednesday] Jan 31 1900 I am all allone to day. Min & the children is gone over to Fannies, Wille to Cates, the children to school. Mr Brautus has missed too day. He has had this bad cold, is gone back this morning. It is a cold, windy day. It was a perty morning but has blowed cold. I said I am all allone. I am not allone, my God is verry near & dear too me. I have had a pleasant day reading & trying to be prepared for that long eternity that I am soon to pass into. I have oil in my lamp, have it trimed & brightly burning when Lord calls me home from this wourld of pain, sourer & sin. Theire will be no more pain ore sower their but home, home to spend a long eternity in Gods presence. Mary D Brown Jan 31 1900.

[February 2, 1900-Friday] Feb 2 this is a cold & winday day.

[February 4, 1900-Sunday] 4 Fanny has sent for me this morning. I am going to stay with her a while.

[February 17, 1900-Saturday] 17 James has brought me home this morning. Fanny had a pound party last night. I staid for it. They had a nice supper, cake & candies, chicken & every thing nice. Fanny & Cate went to york one day. Fanny got Jessy a fine flanen dress & Mary a blew wolen dress. Cate was over & helped to cut out Maries. Aunt Lawre was going to help Jessy.

[February 18, 1900-Sunday] 18 Gim Land has come this morning to help him to hall stock to the sawmill. He is talking of building. Ted Black has mooved his mill up to Lennies. Their holling them over their.

[February 21, 1900-Wednesday] 21 Gim has come back but it has rained so that they had to quit. Janey is over here.

[February 23, 1900-Friday] 23 Min & Harriet is washing to day. Wille & Ike is holling a way. I am setting in the corner, not well. Feb 23 MDBrown

[March 1, 1900-Thursday] March 1 had another bad night, cold, win & rain.

[March 10, 1900-Saturday] 10 Jessy has a calf. She is oneley too years & 3 month.

[March 11, 1900-Sunday] 11 Min & the children is gone to church. Wille would not go. Joe & Sallie came by with them & gone home. Fanny & Psalmy has been over to day.

[March 17, 1900-Saturday] 17 Fanny & haskel has been over this evening. I have not been well.

[March 19, 1900-Monday] 19 Jessy has come over to help Min to fix for the big birthday dinner. I am feeling bad, my back & leg & feel bad everry way.

[March 21, 1900-Wednesday] March 21 1900 this is my birthd day. I am seventy eight years ould to day & the children is going to have a birth day dinner to day.

well, the big day is over & it is near sundown & all gone but Jane Furgison. She staid all night with us & we have had a big day, a fine big crowd. My Children was all here & most of the grand children. Mart & Eb was not here. Mr & Mrs Hay, Mr & Mrs Smyth, Mrs Cains family, Mr Lesley Burns & wife, had a fine dinner & plenty on the tabble to feed them again, turkey, ham, & chickens & cacke in abundance. Jonny & Loury Brown did not git up. They are at Clinton at school, sent them a box, sent one big hole cacke, turkey & chicken & everything good. Mr Shob was out & took the pictures of the family, all that was here. Eb & Mart was not here & then they set the tabble & took the tabble & all the croud. We have had a beautiful day. How humble & thankful we all ought to be. I have felt so bad that it has not been much enjoyment to me, onley to see the rest enjoying themselves so well & never expect to have another one. My God & Farther who is in Heaven, I doo humbly thank the this night fore the great kindness thou hast blessed us with this day, a day that will be long rememberd by some that was here & o that though give every one that was here a heart to love & serve the in spirit & truth & to be reddy when the summons come to meet the in peace. Mr Hay red Samuel the 7 chapter & then talked some on it & sung the too hunderd & twentie__235 hymn & had prayer & they all left. "How firm a foundation ye saints of the Lord, Is laid for your faith in his excelent word."

[March 25, 1900-Sunday] March 25 1900 this has been a verry cold & wett day & Jane Furgison has come back to night.

[March 26, 1900-Monday] 26 Min & Jane is gone over to see Cate to day.

[March 27, 1900-Tuesday] 27 Gim Land has come for me to go over & stay with them a while.

[March 28, 1900-Wednesday] 28 Vance is gone to take his aunt Bell to york to meet Mrs Simeral. She is gone back to stay with her.

[April 6, 1900-Friday] Aprile 6 I have got home from Fannies & Cates Vance has brought me home this morning, have been with them near too weeks.

[April 7, 1900-Saturday] Aprile 7 this is a perty day, all well & busy plowing.

[April 10, 1900-Tuesday] 10 all well & busy as a bee in a tar bucket.

[April 14, 1900-Saturday] 14 Gim & Fanny & the children has been over to day & Fred Black.

[April 15, 1900-Sunday] 15 sunday has started, it has been a perty day.

[April 18, 1900-Wednesday] 18 Lawson has been over & took dinner with us & their has been a big rain.

[April 23, 1900-Monday] 23 Mins brother, Edward & Joe has been here to day. Joe is pedling stoves & it is still raining & wet. Wille is hawling wood to york. Looks like we will make no crop, cant git it planted.

[April 25, 1900-Wednesday] 25 Mart has been here for dinner to day. It has been a good while sence he took dinner with us. Fanny has been over this eve-

ning. Wile has been to york & I am feeling a little better.

[April 27, 1900-Friday] Aprile 27 to day is the commence of our communion seasen. Mr Robert Miller was to help Hay. He came down to Mr Hayes a thursday, took sick that night & had to go back. He lives in North Caroliny. We was all disapointed but Mr Hay preached a good sermon. His tex was in Mark the thirteenth chapt, thirty seventh verse. He came home with us, staid awhile then went to Fannies a while, then went to Lawsons & stayed all night.

[April 28, 1900-Saturday] 28 William & Min went to day, did not want to stop the plows. It has rained so much that he has not got done planting. We have no company.

[April 29, 1900-Sunday] Sabbeth evening Mr Hay tex was in _____. Joe & Sally came home with us & I am going home with them to stay a while. We have no company. Had good preachen & a nice time for it. I am feeling weak & bad.

[May 14, 1900-Monday] May 14 1900 I have got home. Joe & Sallie came home with me yesterday morning. They went on to preachin. I was not abble to go, had been dooing fine, had a pleasent visit with Joe & Sally till friday night. Had a bad spell with my kidneys, have got better. Wille & Min & Children all well.

[May 23, 1900-Wednesday] 23 have got home this evening, have been gone for a week with Fanny & Cate. Gim has had a bad spell with the grip, has got better & gone to work. Cate & Vance & I all went over to Marts, staid all day & then home. Mag was not verry well & Mammy was not well. Cate has had a bad spell with her feet. It must be rumatism. Little Caty Bell has been bad of with a bile on her. They took her to the Dr a monday.

[May 24, 1900-Thursday] thursday morning Dr Walker was over at Lennies, he called & opened it, it run a heap.

[May 26, 1900-Saturday] 26 Caty Bells bile is better now. Mary & Sallie Whitesides was over last night & we have had good rains now.

[May 28, 1900-Monday] May 28 Wille & Rob & Mary all went down to aunt Sallies last satterday night. We have preachen at home to day. I was not feeling like going. The rest came back for preachen. This is the time of their comunion at the grove.

[May 31, 1900-Thursday] May 31 Wille has went down to york & got him a reaper & a binder to day. It cost one henderd & thirty dollars, a perty big price.

[June 10, 1900-Sunday] June 10 I have been to preachen to day. Joe & Sallie came by & I went in the buggy with Joe & Sallie walked. Mr _____ preached a good sermon. His tex was in 2 Coronicals, seventeenth chapter, 6 verse. These are the words, "& his heart was lifted up in the wase of the Lord." Joe & Sallie would not stay for dinner, they was affraid it would rain.

Cary Brown is sick this morning, took sick yesterday while John was at church, sent for Mrs Cain & Min both this morning.

[June 13, 1900-Wednesday] June 13 Cary is a little better. Wille is cutting Lawsons wheat this evening, is done his own. It cuts fine whene the ground is smooth. I am not feeling well.

[June 15, 1900-Friday] 15 I have been up with Carry for too dayes. She is no better. Mr Horace Peters was burried to day. Mr Hay preached his funeral & then come on to Johns & I came home with him.

[June 24, 1900-Sunday] 24 I have been over with Fanny for a week. She has not been well, had the Dr to see her yesterday. Her head & stomic. I have been sick most all week, been having big rains. Gim brought me home this morning & gone on to preachen. I am not abble to go. Mr Hay came home with them & is gone on to see Mrs Smyth & Fanny & then going on to Mrs Blacks.

[June 26, 1900-Tuesday] 26 Jonny & Fanny hs been over to day.

[June 28, 1900-Thursday] 28 I have been feeling bad to day with my brest hurting me & Wille & Rob is gone to york & Wille has brought me a bottle of medicine. I hope it will help me.

[June 29, 1900-Friday] 29 Carry is some better & I am feeling better. All verry busy. The grass is abbout to take them & the wheat is growing in the field. Cant git it dry enough to hall to the barn.

[July 8, 1900-Sunday] 8 this is the first sabbeth they have been to sunday school & we have had a rain this evening & a storm of lightning that killed our yard pig, Jonny B, the children called him. Min put him in the pen before the rain. After the rain was over the Children was at the pen & said that Jonny would not git up when they called him. Wille & Min went to the pen & he was dead. We thought the lightning had struck something but did not think it was so close as that. I have lived here for over sixty years & it is the first thing that has been killed by lightning sence I have been on the place. Gods will be done, it might have been some one of us but that is the way the Lord tackes care of us weak, sinful creatures. Eliza Ann & Eddy was down last night.

[July 14, 1900-Saturday] July 14 Mr Mimagin Smytt died at Blacks July 13, & was burried at Bershaba to day. Joe & Wille is gone to the burrien.

[July 21, 1900-Saturday] 21 I have been over with Fanny & Cate for a week. Vance brought me home this morning. This is the day of the picknick at Cains spring & Mary & Brown is with us to night.

[July 22, 1900-Sunday] 22 sunday morning Brown is not well this morning. I am not gone to preachen, dont feel abble to go. Mary & Brown is gone to preachen, then home.

[July 24, 1900-Tuesday] 24 Cordy has a bealen on him. Dr Bratten came out & lanced it, had to put him under the influence of cloral, it was a bad one, run lots of blood & matter but he is dooing fine.

[July 26, 1900-Thursday] 26 Wille & Min has been up to see Davis Brown & Ann to day, had a stormy evening to come home.

[July 27, 1900-Friday] 27 Gim & Fanny has been over to day & spent the day with us.

[July 29, 1900-Sunday] 29 I have been to preachen to day. Mr Hay preached a good sermon. Mr Hay went home with Gim Land this evening. Gim Land has tacken bad sick this evening, have sent for Lawson & Wille both.

[July 30, 1900-Monday] 30 I am going over to see Gim this eve.

[August 5, 1900-Sunday] Augst 5 I have been over with Gim for a week. He

is mendind now, has had a bad spell. They sayes it is billinious fever, has sufferd bad for a week. He seems like he will git better now. Fanny was not well.

[August 6, 1900-Monday] 6 Eddy Whitesides was here this morning, gone on to york. They are tolerabble well.

[August 11, 1900-Saturday] 11 Wille, Mary, Robby & William is all gone over to the Chapple to preachen & to see Mart & Mag to day.

[August 13, 1900-Monday] 13 Wille & Min is gone up to Wille Neels on a visit & I am here by myself.

[August 27, 1900-Monday] 27 I have been up a few days with Cate & Fanny. Vance brought me home this evening.

[August 29, 1900-Wednesday] 29 this is the day the ladyes mishionry Society meets down at the minieral spring & Fanny came up for me & we had not much more than got their when Joe Whitesides came up for me to go & stay a while with them. I hated to leave the company but went on with him. Had a hot ride, got along fine, stayed near too weeks.

[September 11, 1900-Tuesday] Sept 11 Joe has brought me home this morning, Sept 11 & is gone back home. Had a nice time, did not visit eney, did feel so bad.

[September 12, 1900-Wednesday] 12 Fanny was over this evening & the children all has the hooping coughf. Fannys four, Cates four & oure five all has it perty bad.

[September 16, 1900-Sunday] 16 Vance has brought me home this morning. They are all coughfing. Cordy is the worst.

[September 17, 1900-Monday] 17 Joe & Sallie has been up to day, gone home. Wille & the children is all busy picken cotten. It ant much acount. They are all picken for John Brown to day, 20.

[September 28, 1900-Friday] Sept Wille & Min is gone on to Eds to day & to see Sally. Fanny has been sick & I have been over with her for a week, sick at the stomic & feeles so weak & bad. All got the coughf. Sept 28

[October 11, 1900-Thursday] Oct 11 I have got home from Fannies, helped Min to iron & bake some cackes. I have been to preachen to day. Mr & Mrs Dixon from Sharon was their. Mrs & Mr Hay was their. Mr Dixon tex was in Isah, these are the words, "Ye are my witness." He preached a good sermon. Bessy Thomison & Ella Brown came home with us satterday morning. I am gone to stay with the children to day. Sartdy night Joe & Sally & Nanny Thomison came home with them.

[October 14, 1900-Sunday] Sabbeth evening Mr & Mrs Hay came home with us & they are gone home. We have had fine preachen. Mr & Mrs Dixen went to Mr Hogues for dinner, then home. Oh that we would make the right improvement of so much good preachen, so much solem warnings we have heard, so much solem warning to be reddy for that great day of the Lord for it will come soon for me.

[October 27, 1900-Saturday] Oct 27 Satterday evening I have been a week with Fanny & Cate. Fanny is a little better. She went with me over to Cates yesterday & Vance has brought me home this eve.

[October 28, 1900-Sunday] 28 Sabbeth evening I have been to preachen to day. Mr Hayes tex was in Luke the 15 chapt 5 6 7 verses. He came home with us & went over to see Lesly Burns. He is sick with the cold.

[October 30, 1900-Tuesday] 30 Fanny Brown has been over to help Min to make Mary a new dress to day.

[November 5, 1900-Monday] Nov 5 Min & the children is gone over to spend the day with Fanny. Will has Ed Prices grain drill putting in his wheat. Jessy has brought Min home.

[November 11, 1900-Sunday] 11 The methidst preacher preached for Mr Hay to day. Min was sick. I did not go.

[November 12, 1900-Monday] 12 the children is gone to school, Robby, Mary, William & Cordy to Miss Cate Ratchford, a new teacher for us. MDBrown

[November 24, 1900-Saturday] Nov 24 I have been over with Fanny for a week. Gimmy has brought me home this morning. Fanny & I went over to see Mart & Mag yesterday. Mag has the pains in her feet, most past going.

[November 25, 1900-Sunday] 25 Fanny came by & took me to preachen. Mr Hay preached a fine sermon. He was preachen abbout the rich man & Lasaras.

[November 29, 1900-Thursday] 29 this is thanksgiven day & Ed Price & his new wife has been here to day, their first visit, also Cate Whitesides, Mary & Sally. Lawson is going to leave us, has rented his place & is going to Gastonia.

[December 1, 1900-Saturday] Dec 1 Lawson man has backed out & he will have to give out his big trip.

[December 3, 1900-Monday] monday this is sales day & he is gone to york & I am feeling bad with my breast and back.

[December 4, 1900-Tuesday] 4 Fanny & Jane & Bratten & I went with Eliza & Ginny over to Lawsons & spent the day. Mrs Castle, she has been with Mag this week.

[December 5, 1900-Wednesday] 5 I am feeling some better & Joe Whitesides has come up this morning to se how I was & we had too strangers with us to night, Cousin Eliza Brown & Cousin Ginny Deal from Blacks Burg, Cousin Eliza from Atlanta, Georgia.

[December 27, 1900-Thursday] 27 I have got home this morning. Fanny & all the family came home with me this morning. Mag Brown & Jonny & Lowry & children was all here for Dinner, all gone home.

[December 28, 1900-Friday] 28 Wille, Robby, Mary & Cordy is all gone up to Ed Prices.

1901

A newyers day of 1901

[January 1, 1901-Tuesday] A new year morning My God has spared me to see the light of a nother new morning. I have arrisen in usal health this morning, the monument of thy love & mercy. I will be sevenety nine the 21 of next March, if I live to see it. Time looks long to look to spend nine years but to look back it dont seem so long. But long enough to prepare for that glourious home that is beffore us. I soon expect to enter washed in the blood of the lamb, clothed with his bright robe of his richedness which he gives all that love & serve him, to spend eternity, a long eternity.

Jonny & Loury is both gone back this evening, back to clinton till June when they will be through colage.

[January 2, 1901-Wednesday] wensday morning I have had it in my head to go & stay with Fanny, that is to live with her, but Wille & Min all apose it. I have concluded to subbmit to them, set down in the corner.

[January 18, 1901-Friday] January 18 1901 I am going down to stay with Sally a while.

[February 8, 1901-Friday] Feb 8 I have got home from Sallies, had a fine visit. Joe has brought me home. Have been over a few dayes with Fanny, all porly & grunting.

[February 10, 1901-Sunday] sunday evening Feb 10 have been to preachen to day.

[February 19, 1901-Tuesday] Mins _____ was born Feb the 19, a tusday morning. Dr Bratten here. She was bad of that evening. Cate, Sally Bury & ould Sue, a darcky was here. The children is not well. Sally is gone home & Cate & Vance is here to night gitting along fine. We have ould aunt Nancy, Ben Bryans wife to cook for us. She does fine.

[February 24, 1901-Sunday] 24 This has been preachen to day. Wille is all that went. The children has stayed home on the acount of measels. Mr Hay went home with Mrs Cain, came up a while this evening to see the boy, a fine & big boy.

[February 25, 1901-Monday] 25 all dooing perty well. Min mends slow.

[March 1, 1901-Friday] March 1 March has come in like a lamb. A butifull day, have planted the irish potatoes & a little of most every thing in the garden. Jessy & Mary Land, Mary & Sally Berry is all here to day.

[March 6, 1901-Wednesday] 6 the children is sick, some of them most all the time. The babe is badly stopped up with the cold.

[March 8, 1901-Friday] 8 ould aunt Nancy is with us yet. It is verry dry & windy, great danger of fire.

[March 10, 1901-Sunday] March 10 I have been to preachen to day. Mr Hay preached a good sermon. His tex was, "As for me & my house, we will serve the Lord." Had a big rain. Mr Hay came home with us, gone home this evening. MDBrown

[March 21, 1901-Thursday] March 21 I have been staying with Fanny & Cate

for a week. Cates all well. Fanny has not been verry well but better, the rest all well. Mr Locart has been bad with the pneumonia, is a little better. Ould Mrs Locart died March 21 1901. Vance brought me home this evening. Cate had a big dinner. It was my birthday, was seventy nine years ould to day & feeling perty well, have better health now than I have been having. I thank thee O my God for all thy loving kindness & tender mercies through a long wilderness journey, through many dangers seen & unseen thou hast preserved me. I have no fears but thou will preserve me to the end. Ould Mr Locart died March 21 1901. Mr Gim Locart died March 24 1901, died in less than a week of each other. That was his Mother.

[March 26, 1901-Tuesday] March 26 we have had a big dayes rain. The creek is higher than it ever has been, land badly washed, Bridges & fences gone. Fanny is sick. Wille is busy on the creek fixin fences & water gaps.

[March 28, 1901-Thursday] 28 Sally Whitesides & Mag Magill has been up to see us to day & Cate Whitesides & Cate has come for me to go & stay with Fanny a while. She has been sick & I am going.

[April 3, 1901-Wednesday] Aprile 3 Gimmy has brought me home this morning. We have had another big rain. Fanny is some better. Wille has taken Min & the children up & left them to stay till the next day.

[April 4, 1901-Thursday] 4 Min has got home, had a nice visit.

[April 5, 1901-Friday] 5 Cary has been down this evening.

[April 8, 1901-Monday] 8 Minny, Mary, Paul & Ester is all gone over to see Fanny to day. It has been whil sence she spent a day with her. She is right porly. I am going over to stay withe her for a while.

[April 14, 1901-Sunday] Aprile 14 I have been to preachen to day. Mr Hay preached a good sermon. His tex was in luke 24 c 8 verse. Mrs Hay was down.

[April 15, 1901-Monday] 15 i have come over to Fannies to day to stay a while with her.

[April 18, 1901-Thursday] 18 Mrs Cain & Cate has both been over to day.

[April 20, 1901-Saturday] 20 Jessy & I have both been over to see Cate to day.

[April 23, 1901-Tuesday] 23 Wille & Cordy took dinner with Cate & here this evening, all well.

[April 24, 1901-Wednesday] 24 Cate & Mary, Jessy & Mary & Gim was all at york to day.

[April 25, 1901-Thursday] 25 Jessy & Mary & Haskal all gone over to their aunt Mags Hall to git Mammy too help them to make their new dresses. They got Jessyes done & Jessy & Haskal came home & left Mary to finish hers.

[April 28, 1901-Sunday] Sabbeth morning Mag has come & brought Mary home, is porly with the pains, was not abble to go to preachen. This is our preachen day. I did not go. Lib Jackson was at preachen, her & Mary & came by & stayed a while, all gone home.

[May 1, 1901-Wednesday] May 1 Mrs Anna Jones Cate & Mary & Sally has all been here this evening.

[May 12, 1901-Sunday] Sunday 12 Mr Hay preached to day, went home with Wille & Min. Gim nor I did not go to day. I have been with Fanny for foure weeks & don't know when I will git home.

[May 13, 1901-Monday] 13 Mag Hall & Murtel has been over to day. Mag is right smart better with her pains.

[May 14, 1901-Tuesday] 14 Min has been over this evening. Wille brought her & then went back.

[May 15, 1901-Wednesday] 15 Cate has been over this morning. Theire is a paicle going to Kings mountian with cotten this morning.

[May 21, 1901-Tuesday] May 21 Fanny gave birth to a fine son this morning at too oclock, a tusday morning. Dr Bratten was gone to Columbia. She had Dr Deloch. I thought he done fine. Fanny did not like him, her nor Cate.

[May 25, 1901-Saturday] 25 Fanny had a light chill last night, sent for Dr

Mcdowell. He came out but it was not bad one.

[May 28, 1901-Tuesday] 28 Dr Bratten has got home, has been out to see her. He thinks she is dooing verry well. The babe is right fretfull at night. Joe & Sally has been up one day. Cate has been here most everry night. Min has been over one night.

[May 31, 1901-Friday] 31 Gim is gone over to Filbert to a meeting their & I am with Fanny. Gimmy Land, that is junier, brought me home this morning.

[June 1, 1901-Saturday] June 1 I have stayed hear too months with Fanny. I think her & the babe is both dooing fine, the longest stay that I have ever tacken from home. Have got home this morning, a good stay for near too months but I got allong fine. They was all so good to wait on me & doo for me, one & all. My God will reward them all for what they have done & they seemed to be dooing fine while I was gone.

[June 2, 1901-Sunday] 2 Wille, Rob, Mary & little Wille is all gone to sab-beth school.

[June 7, 1901-Friday] June 7 this is the day oure comunion comenced. Wille, Robby, Mary, Wille & I all went. Mr Hefner preached for us. His tex was, "Blessed is the people whoes God is the Lord." He preached a good sermon. He is with us to night. Mr & Mrs Hay, at Mr Carolls.

[June 8, 1901-Saturday] 8 I staid at home with the Children, I did not feel abble to go everry day, no company to night.

[June 9, 1901-Sunday] June 9 sabbeth evening Min got ould Sue to come & stay with the children & we all went. Mr Heftner done the preachen. He done fine. He is a great preacher too. Theire was a large congration & good behavior. Their was seven joined the church, too of Mr Carols daughters, Vance Wh-itesides, Mary Whitesides, that is Cates too ouldest ones, Fanny Good, Robby Smyth, Gim Smyth son.

[June 15, 1901-Saturday] 15 I have had a sick day, something like grip. Fan-ny is sick again, had the Dr & Cate for several dayes. I was sick too & Mag Hall has been sick to with the flux. She is some better now.

[June 18, 1901-Tuesday] 18 I am feeling some better. Mag & Fanny is better. Cate was over & she said her Sally was sick, did not stay.

[June 19, 1901-Wednesday] 19 Mag & Lowry was here to day & Mrs Cain, Cate & Mary Land & Jane. All gone.

[June 21, 1901-Friday] 21 Wille is gone down to Sallies to the mill, him & Corda with twelve bushels of wheat. Mets calved June 10, male calf is dooing fine. MDBrown

[June 25, 1901-Tuesday] June 25 Eliza & Mary has been down a day & night, gone home. It is such a busy time.

[July 1, 1901-Monday] July 1 Gim & Fanny has been over to day, the first time in a long time, took dinner & then went home.

[July 13, 1901-Saturday] July 13 Wille is cleaning out the well this morning, plenty of toads in it.

[July 22, 1901-Monday] July 22 Eddy Whitesides came down for me & I am going home with him to stay a week.

[August 1, 1901-Thursday] Aug 1 I have got home to day, Augst 1. Joe & Sally came home with me, stait till we got our dinners. Sally & I went to see Cate. Lawson, Joe & Wille all went to see Butler. He is not rite. They are going to take him to Columbia to the Assylun to night. Joe, Sally & I all went & stayed with Gim & Fanny all night. Joe & Sally gone home & Jessy with them to stay a few dayes & I stayed till satterday evening & Gim brought me home.

[August 11, 1901-Sunday] Sunday 11 I did not go to preachen to day.

[August 12, 1901-Monday] 12 this is the day that Wille comenced his new house, building it up in the curch road. Gim Land & Mr Carrol is the workman.

[August 15, 1901-Thursday] 15 Bell Whitesides has been here to day.

[August 16, 1901-Friday] 16 Sally Berry & her too girls was here to day.

[August 19, 1901-Monday] 19 Wille has Gim Land, Mr Carol, Dave Clark &

Jessy Hogue all at work & him.

[August 22, 1901-Thursday] 22 An other big day. Fanny & Jessy & the children, Ed Price & his wife & a good many hands covering the house.

[August 23, 1901-Friday] 23 all the hands & Wille Land working, big rain this morning & when they got their dinners they all went home.

[August 24, 1901-Saturday] 24 have had a big dayes work done, have got the house covered & some of the porch. Had a good many hands & Cate came over & helped to git dinner, brought peaches, cabbitch & corn, a nice dinner, & good.

[August 26, 1901-Monday] 26 Wille has started to pull fodder this morning. We are all up.

[August 29, 1901-Thursday] 29 Cate has come for me this morning to go & stay a week with her & Fanny.

[September 4, 1901-Wednesday] September 4 Gim Land has brought me home this morning. They are all well. Ester has the araciplas on her leg. It is hurting her perty bad. I thought I had better come home & see what she was dooing. This is the day that Mr Caroll & Mr Hogue has started to finish the house.

[September 5, 1901-Thursday] 5 Wille is busy halling his flour & sealing, has it dressed at york, is gone after a load to day. They are to finish it. Mary D Brown

[September 7, 1901-Saturday] Sept 7 1901 this is the day that Mr Carroll & Mr Hogue has commenced to Finish Wille house for him.

[September 9, 1901-Monday] monday the 9 Mirtle Hall, Mary Whitesides & Matty Brown & Mr John Coldwell was all here last night.

[September 12, 1901-Thursday] Mr Clark came this morn to build the stack chimney the 12.

[September 14, 1901-Saturday] 14 Wille thinks Mr Clark will finish his chimney to day.

[September 18, 1901-Wednesday] 18 We are having the equinatall storm this morning, raining & blowing cold. They are still at work at the house. They have hard work to git the lumber sawed. Cant git the brick for the chimneyes, have put up a stack chiney.

[September 22, 1901-Sunday] Sept 22 I have been to curch to day. Mr Hay preached a good sermon. His tex was in Genesus 12 c four verses.

[September 23, 1901-Monday] 23 Joe & Sally as been up to day, all well. Gone by to see Lawson awhile. Wille has been for another load of lumber & most sick.

[September 24, 1901-Tuesday] 24 gone to york again, will soon be done.

[September 26, 1901-Thursday] 26 Mrs Smyth & Fanny has come over for me & I am going home with them.

[October 12, 1901-Saturday] Oct 12 Vance has brough me home this morn. Mag Hall was over to see Cate & Fanny. She is bad off with the _____most all over her. Did not think she could stand to ride over these hills. Vance took her home & then brought me home.

[October 13, 1901-Sunday] 13 I have been to preachen to day. Joe & Sallie came up to preachen & I went in the buggy with Sally. Mr Hay came with us. Eliza & Eddy Whitesides came home with us. Brown & Mary went home with Eims, Eliza & Eddy went home. Mary & Brown came back here & stayed all night & Jessy.

[October 14, 1901-Monday] 14 the children is gone home & Cate came over to see them.

[October 16, 1901-Wednesday] 16 Wille had a little shucking to night. Lawson & Mag & all the children is over.

[October 23, 1901-Wednesday] 23 all well & as busy as if they thought this wourld would never end, but that may come sooner than many is thinking. It will certainly come soon ore latter, yes it will.

[October 25, 1901-Friday] Oct 25 this is the commencement of oure comunion. I have not been well, was not to go every day. Mr Adkins is helping Mr Hay. Ann Brown & Ireen came home with them to night, friday evenning eve.

[October 26, 1901-Saturday] Satterday 26 I feel some better & have been abble to go to the house of God once more. Mr Ateins preached a fine sermon to day. His tex was in Mathew the eleventh chapter 28 verse. Cousin Molly Fewel & Nanny Thomison, Joe & Sally & Mr Atcions all came home with us. Joe & Sally, Nanny & Molly is all gone over to see Gim & Fanny this evening. Joe & Sally is going to stay with Cate to night. Molly & Nanny has come back here & Mr Hay to spend the night. Mr Atcions is a nice man, is a married man & has five children.

[October 27, 1901-Sunday] Sabbeth evening Oct 29 another comunion, have had a nice time & pleasent weather.

[November 6, 1901-Wednesday] Nov 6 Gim Land has brought me home this evening. I have had a right bad spell with my back & kidneys, have got better now.

[November 8, 1901-Friday] 8 I am still feeling better, the rest is all well. Mr Hudson & Mr Rose is taring down Wille crib to day to moove it up to the new house. evening- have got it all down & mooved up to the other house.

IN CONCLUSION
Rebecca T. Chambers

The last entry in Mary Davis Brown's diary was November 8, 1901 when she was almost 80 years old. We don't know why she stopped writing so abruptly. Her son, Willie and his wife, Minnie were preparing to move to their recently completed two-story home just up on the highway. It was still on the family property and was in sight of Mary's home. Willie and Minnie had lived with Mary since their marriage and were now insisting she come live with them. Mary's once durable, comfortable, two-story log home, now covered in weather boarding, had become in a state of disrepair. She, who all her adult life, had been a strong influence and support in the home and community, was now in declining health. Her eyesight was failing and she was in constant pain from cancer. Surely there was a sense of melancholy as reality set in that she could no longer manage the home alone and would soon, herself, need constant care. Mary must have been reluctant to leave the house she came to as a bride. More than likely she spent many days wandering through the house, picking up and fingering items that brought back memories. She probably held some of them close to her heart as she thought of her now deceased husband and children. As the sun was setting she may have wandered out onto the porch, lifting her large white apron around her arms to protect them from the chill of the coming winter. Looking to the east, out over the hill to the fields and pastures and down the steep hill to the bottom lands and the creek, she would have recalled the many times she and R. J. worked along side the help, trying to plant and gather the crops. The remembered sounds of the children running and playing in the yard echoed in her ears, "Look, Mama, look at me." A smile crossing her face, she would have gone back into the silent house. Sitting down in her favorite chair by the large open fireplace, memories would have flooded her mind. This was the home where the family had celebrated special occasions, where they had shared meals with friends, ministers and neighbors, where her children had made their entrance into the world and where three had died. It was here her beloved husband suddenly went to meet his maker sitting in that chair now pulled close by. Laying her hand on the arm of R. J.'s. chair, a tear must have slid down her check as she said, "R. J., what should I do? This is our home. It protected us during the terrifying earthquake back in 1886, bad storms, the War Between the States and the struggle and trials of the Reconstruction years." Brushing the tears away and rising slowly, she would have tended the fire for the night and headed to bed. Memories would have flooded her mind as she lay awake in the dark with only the crackling and flickering flames in the fireplace. What must she do? Minnie and Willie must have consoled her repeatedly, reminding her she would be moving just up the road and could come back down to the old home anytime she desired. Then this lady, who had all her life given her time and help to others, submitted to the times and situation and agreed to move with them. Yes, she would tell them tomorrow. This was true to her nature. We are sure she said as she had so often done, "Lord, not my will but thine be done."

It is also conceivable her diary was mislaid during the move and was not recovered until after her death. In all probability she was in constant pain, suffering from failing eyesight, or simply did not feel like pursuing her daily writings.

At least two of her daughters, Sally and Fannie, kept their own diaries for a short period. We have gathered from their entries that even though Mary made her home with Willie and Minnie, when able to travel she continued to visit among her children for weeks at a time. Fannie relates that her mother had cancer of the breast and that the site of the cancer was dreadful. Her health had deteriorated to the point of pain and agony and it was hard for her to get around or travel. She suffered constantly with pain in her head, eyes, back, legs and breast. Possibly she had glaucoma, cataracts, or her cancer had metastasized. At the time of her death she was almost totally blind. She unceasingly longed to go to her Father in Heaven and to eternal rest. Both Fannie and Sally spoke of their mother in loving terms, as did the other children. The family did all that loving children could do to make her happy and comfortable. Her children spoke of her tenderly and felt blessed when her health permitted her to visit.

On Tuesday morning, December 8, 1903 at 15 minutes after eight, 82 year old Mary Davis Brown's life came to an end. She went to her Heavenly home to be with her Lord as she had so often longed and prayed for. She was now reaping her rewards for being a true and faithful servant and was being reunited with the family and friends she had held dear. Rev. Hay, her friend and minister, preached her funeral, reading the 90th Psalm and took his text from Job 5:26. The two songs sung were her favorites, "I Would Not Live Always, I Ask Not to Stay" and "How Firm a Foundation."

Fannie stated in her diary: "It was a sad day, dear mother laid in her cold and silent grave and a day long to be remembered by her baby child. Oh how dear Mother did long to go home and to be with her Heavenly Father and be at rest. She bore her pains, which were many, with patience. It was cold, wet and snowing the day she was laid in her grave."

Sally documented in her diary: "Today we met at the grave, stood in a circle holding hands and cried." Their mother who spent her life helping and caring for family, friends, and neighbors was no more for this earth. She had taught her children well. She often prompted them to trust in the Lord and to continue to read and study His word. She instilled in them to live wholesome lives and to always do what was best.

What an influence this lady had on her family and community both then and now, over one hundred and fifty years later. She did not live in vain but left footprints in the sands of time.

Rebecca T. Chambers,
Gr. Gr. Granddaughter of
Mary Davis Brown

JOURNALS OF MARY DAVIS BROWN

List of Individuals Mentioned in the
JOURNALS OF MARY DAVIS BROWN

Compiled by Catherine Brown Michael

Following is an alphabetical listing of individuals mentioned by Mary in her diary. The list is not exhaustive. Included are family members, friends and neighbors and ministers mentioned in the entries dated 1854 to 1874. As her life story becomes established through her writing, the day to day activities of her children, grandchildren, nieces and nephews become the primary focus of her diary entries. The other story she tells is the history of Beersheba Presbyterian Church with its many ministers.

The family members and neighbors in Mary's life in the beginning of the diary can be quite confusing. When Mary married her first cousin, R. J. Brown, cousins became in-laws. Nieces and nephews became cousins. Mary's father was married twice, first to Mary Davis and second to Tabitha Floyd, Mary's mother. Mary considered her five half brothers and sisters simply brother and sister. As her children grew, she alternatively called a brother or sister or in-law "aunt" or "uncle". This list attempts to describe the relationship with Mary.

Much of the biographical information comes from the Joseph Hart Collection which is located at the York Historical Center. Other information was gathered from family histories and online family trees. Every effort has been made to verify the accuracy of the information listed here. For Mary's extended family, living descendants contributed data as it was passed on to them. Much of the information for other individuals came from a combination of the resources at McCelvey Center and other researchers posting data online. As to the other researchers, I do not know to what extent it reflects the information to be found in primary sources.

Adams, Mr. (Reverend)
James McEwen Hall Adams b: 25 Dec 1810 d: 1862. Son of James Samuel and Erixene McEwen Adams. Married Eliza Agatha Burton, daughter of Robert Henderson and Mary Fullenwider Burton. Was minister at First Presbyterian Church in Yorkville, 1851-1862. Rev. Adams niece married Mary's cousin.

Alexander, John James
John James Alexander b: 07 Aug 1859. Son of Robert and Margaret Elizabeth Allison Alexander. Mary's nephew.

Alexander, William
William B. Alexander b: 1858. Son of Robert B. And Margaret Elizabeth Allison Alexander. Mary's first cousin.

Alexander, John
John Randolph Alexander b: 16 Mar 1829 d: 10 Oct 1880. Son of William Rooker and Emily Eliza Brown Alexander Married 19 Jan 1859 Mary Jane Sutton, daughter of Jonathan Leroy and Jane Ross Sutton. John was Mary's cousin/nephew.

Alexander, John
John Barry Alexander b: 29 Oct. 1830 d: 21 Jan 1906, Alabama. Son of Eli Oliver and Mary Martha Barry Alexander. Married Margaret Jane Watson, daughter of William and Margaret Parks Watson.

Alexander, Jane
Jane Amanda Alexander b: 11 Feb 1836 d: 20 Jul 1913. Daughter of William Rooker and Emily Eliza Brown Alexander. Married James Young Ferguson, son of James C. and Nancy Emily Quinn Ferguson. Jane was Mary's cousin/niece.

Alexander, Jaily

Jaily Eliza Alexander b: 1834. Daughter of William Rooker and Emily Eliza Brown Alexander. Married John B. Massabeau, son of William Augustus and Elizabeth Massabeau. Jaily was Mary's cousin/niece.

Alexander, Hannah

Hannah Alexander b: 1838 d: 14 Jan 1863. Daughter of William Rooker and Emily Eliza Brown Alexander. Mary's cousin/niece. Never married.

Alexander, Hasting

Stephen Hastings Jennings Alexander b: 1811 d: 04 Mar 1894. Son of Herman A. and Catherine Alexander. Married Isabella Carson.

Alexander, Mary Jane

Mary Jane Brown Alexander b: 09 Mar 1838 d: 09 Apr 1855 Beersheba. Daughter of John Given and Sarah Simpson Good Brown. Married her first cousin Robert B. Alexander, son of William Rooker and Emily Eliza Brown Alexander. Her parents died when she was eleven years old. Mary's niece. She was raised by RJ and Mary Davis Brown.

Alexander, Robert

Robert Brown Alexander b: 1831. Son of William Rooker and Emily Eliza Brown Alexander. Married first, Mary Jane Brown, his first cousin. Married second, Margaret Elizabeth Allison. Married third, Rosilla Watson. Married fourth, Nancy Hambright. Mary's cousin/nephew.

Alexander, Anny

Ann D. Alexander b: 19 May 1867 d: 9 Jan 1868. Daughter of John Randolph and Mary Jane Sutton Alexander. Mary's first cousin.

Alexander, Robert

William Robert Alexander b: Apr 1860 d: 9 Jun 1861. Son of John Randolph and Mary Jane Sutton Alexander. Mary's first cousin.

Alison, Sarah (Allison)

Sarah Selina Allison b: 10 Sep 1821 d: 08 Feb 1862 Beersheba. Daughter of Hugh and Violet Barry Allison. Married William Davison, son of John B. and Elizabeth Barber Davison.

Allen, Mr. (Shot by Tom Bell)

Allison, Gim
James Breadner Allison b: 6 Jan 1834 d: 19 May 1911 Rose Hill Cemetery. Son of Robert Turner and Martha Burnett Allison. Married Susan Baldwin Meek, daughter of William Baldwin and Mary Moore McCorkle Meek.

Allison, Margaret
Margaret Elizabeth Alexander b: 21 Mar 1827. Daughter of Hugh and Violet Barry Allison. Married Robert Brown Alexander, son of William Rooker and Emily Eliza Brown Alexander.

Allison, Rasmus
Robert Erasmus Allison, b: 29 Jan 1830 d: 01 Sep 1906, Lancaster County, SC. Son of Robert Turner and Martha Burnett Clinton Allison. Married Mary Ann Chambers daughter of Edmund Rutter and Pamela Smith Chambers.

Allison, Dr.
Robert Turner Allison b: 17 Aug 1798 d: 21 Oct 1882. Son of Robert Eugene and Sarah Turner Allison. Married Martha Burnett Clinton, daughter of Joseph and Mary Burnett Clinton. He also married Mary Elvira Henry, daughter of James and Mary Neely Henry.

Alonzo Brown
John Alonzo Brown b: 12 Apr 1809 d: 20 Oct 1876 Bethesda. Son of John and Elizabeth Gordon Brown. Married Margaret (Mary) Little, daugther of William and Elizabeth Little. Alonzo was Mary's first cousin.

Anterson, Monroe (Reverend)
John Monroe Anderson b: 1821 d: 1879. First President and professor in the Yorkville Female Collegiate Institute. Was a chaplain in the Confederate army.

Baird, John

Baron, Dr. (Barron)
Archibald Ingram Barron b: 4 Jul 1807. Married Mary Adams Pressly, daughter of William and Eliza Elanor Adams Pressly. Physician.

Beard, Mr. (Old) Preacher

Beaty, William (Beattie)
William C. Beattie b: 14 March 1836. Married Mary Frances Burns January 21, 1858.

Bell, Joe
Elwood Fisher Bell b: 04 Sep 1850 d: 11 Jul 1910 Laurelwood Cemetery. Son of Thomas Jefferson and Martha Jane Brian Bell. Married Elizabeth Jane Jackson, daughter of Archibald M. And Sarah Wallace Jackson.

Bell, Susan E.
Susan Emma Bell b: 23 May 1853 d: 04 Dec 1901 Rose Hill Cemetery, York, SC. Daughter of Thomas Jefferson and Martha Jane Brian Bell. Married Rufus Edward Knox, son of Matthew and Lucinda Hopkins Knox.

Bell, Tom
Thomas Jefferson Bell b: 21 Mar 1821 d: 22 Aug 1883. Rose Hill Cemetery. Son of Christopher and Unk Bell. Married Martha Jane Brian, daughter of James and Susannah Collins Brian. Mary's daughter married Tom Bell's nephew.

Billy, Uncle
William Rooker Alexander b: 18 Jan 1802 d: 24 May 1858. Son of John Alexander and Anne Rooker. Married Emily Eliza Brown, Mary's cousin/sister-in-law. The Alexanders lived on the farm next door to Mary Brown.

Black, Mat
Black, Martha H. b: 1842 d: 1878 Beersheba. Daughter of William and Missini Ross McLain Black. Married Edward Peyton Wilkerson.

Bolles, Rev.
Reverend John Bolls

Bratton, John

Bratton, Dr.
Samuel Edward Bratton b: 1820 d: 1893. Son of John Simpson and Harriet Rainey Bratton. Practiced medicine in southern York County.

Brown, Addy
Sophie Adelaid Brown b: 04 May 1847 d: 24 May 1879 Beersheba. Daughter

of Samuel Gordon and Mary Margaret Byers Brown. Mary's cousin.

Brown, Laurey
Laura Iantha Medora Brown b: 24 Mar 1851 d: 22 Jun 1893 Bullocks Creek. Daughter of Samuel Gordon and Mary Margaret Byers Brown. Married John Morrison Russell, son of John Morrison and Sarah M. Burris Russell. Mary's cousin.

Brown, Margaret (Samuel's wife)
Mary Margaret Byers Brown b: 14 Nov 1812 d: 20 Jul 1867. Daughter of Edward and Mary Smith Byers. Married Samuel Gordon Brown, son of John and Mary Margaret Byers Brown. Samuel was Mary's first cousin.

Brown, Samuel Gordon
Samuel Gordon Brown b: 07 Feb 1814 d: 07 Jun 1888 Blacksburg Cemetery. Son of John and Elizabeth Gordon Brown. Married Mary Margaret Byers, daughter of Edward and Mary Smith Byers. Samuel was Mary's first cousin.

Brown, Mary S.
Mary Serena Brown b: 30 Nov 1837 d: May 1919. Daughter of John and Mary McElwee Caldwell Brown. Married first, William Quinn, son of John and Mary Ann Ferguson Quinn. Married second, Joseph Tilghman Ramsey.

Brown, Emily (Aunt Emily)
Emily Eliza Brown b: 1804 d: 20 Dec 1882 Beersheba. Daughter of Robert and Mary Given Brown. Married 01 May 1828 William Rooker Alexander. Sister of RJ. Mary's first cousin/sister-in-law.

Brown, Emily (Daughter)
Emily Jane Brown b: 17 May 1842 d: 27 Oct 1883 Beersheba. Daughter of RJ and Mary Davis Brown. Married 22 Mar 1864 Ebenzer Pressley Castles, son of Henry and Margaret Sterling Castles.

Brown, Eliza Ann (Daughter)
Eliza Ann Brown b: 23 Sep 1840 d: 16 Jan 1905 Smyrna. Daughter of RJ and Mary Davis Brown. Married 11 Aug 1859 Rufus Grier Whitesides, son of Thomas and Margaret Whitesides.

Brown, Jaly Catharine (Daughter)
Jaily Catherine Brown. b: 03 Mar 1855 d: 03 Jul 1942 Beersheba. Daughter of RJ and Mary Davis Brown. Married first 30 Jan 1883 Samuel Sylvanus White-sides, son of Thomas and Margaret Berry Whitesides. Married second 06 May 1915 Leonides Lowry Smith son of Samuel and Elizabeth Vaughn Smith. Was called Kate in her adult life.

Brown, Mag (Daughter)
Margaret Hannah Brown b: 23 Jan 1853 d: 15 May 1929 Beersheba. Daughter of RJ and Mary Davis Brown. Married 01 May 1873 Daniel Martin Hall son of Daniel Franklin and Mary Brian Hall.

Brown, Rachel (Niece)
Rachel Jane Brown b: 30 Nov 1844. Daughter of John and Mary M. McElwee Caldwell Brown. Married John W. Gamble. Mary's niece.

Brown, Robert (Nephew)
Robert Gilbreath Brown b: 25 Nov 1839 d: 23 Jul 1939 St. John's Lutheran Church, Gaston County. Son of John and Mary M. McElwee Caldwell Brown. Married Susan Froneberger. Mary's nephew.

Brown, Robert Jackson (Husband)
Robert Jackson Brown b: 13 Sep 1815 d: 20 Feb 1887 Beersheba. Husband of Mary Davis Brown. Son of Robert and Mary Given Brown.

Brown, William Davis
William Davis Brown b: 01 Jun 1850 d: 01 Sep 1912 Beersheba. Son of William Lawson and Jane Jackson Brown. Married 20 Mar 1873, Ann Gillie Scoggins, daughter of David and Jane Howell Scoggins. Mary's nephew.

Brown, William Given (Son)
William Given Brown b:14 Jun 1846 d: 06 Oct 1854 at the age of 8. Mary's son. It is possible that his death prompted her to take up her pen and begin the lifelong habit of keeping a diary.

Brown, Bob (little)
Robert Leander Brown b: 22 Dec 1859 d: 05 Dec 1891 Beersheba. Son of William Lawson and Jane Jackson Brown. Married Margaret Beatty Jackson, daughter of William Beaty and Margaret Isabella Lynn Jackson. Mary's nephew.

Brown, Eugenia
Margaret Eugenia Brown b: 05 Jun 1845 d: 22 Nov 1919 Blacksburg, SC. Daughter of Samuel Gordon and Mary Margaret Byers Brown. Married 07 Oct 1873 Jacob Augustus Deal, son of Jacob and Sarah Kinard Deal. Mary's first cousin.

Brown, John Franklin
John Franklin Brown b: 25 May 1857 d: 25 May 1862 at age 5. Son of William Lawson and Jane Jackson Brown. Mary's nephew.

Brown, Mary J.
Mary Jane Brown b: 09 Mar 1838 d: 09 Apr 1855 at age 17 only six months after her marriage to Robert Brown Alexander, her first cousin. Daughter of John Given and Sarah Simpson Good Brown. Her parents died when she was 9 years old and she was raised by RJ and Mary Davis Brown.

Brown, Frances
Frances (Fanny) Louise Brown b: 11 Nov 1845 d: 22 Mar 1881. Daughter of John Given and Sarah Simpson Good Brown. Her parents died when she was four years old. She was raised by her aunt Emily Brown Alexander. Married Thomas Marion Dobson, son of Leander and Cynthia Parrish Dobson. Mary's niece.

Brown, Cathern (Caty)
Katherine Cain Gibson Brown b: 31 Aug 1809 d: 09 Nov 1885. Daughter of Hugh Cain and Martha Turner Allison Cain. Married first, Thomas Gibson, who died. Married second, William C. Brown who was Mary Brown's cousin/brother in law. They had one child, John Given Brown. They lived on a farm next to Mary and RJ.

Brown, Chambers
James Chambers Brown b: 08 Mar 1849 d: 21 July 1921 Texas. Son of Samuel Gordon and Mary Margaret Byers Brown. Married first, Catherine Lawson. Married second, Mary A. Cameron.

Brown, Lawson (son)
Robert Lawson Brown b: 17 Oct 1848 d: 13 Feb 1922, Beersheba. Son of RJ and Mary Davis Brown. Married 17 Nov 1870 Margaret (Maggie) I. Castles, daughter of Rev. James Robinson and Martha Watt Castles.

Brown, Lawson (brother)

William Lawson Brown b: 09 Nov 1814 d: 08 Mar 1873, Beersheba. Son of William and Mary Davis Brown. Mary's half-brother. Married 17 Dec 1846 Jane Jackson, daugther of David, Jr. and Jane Venable Jackson.

Brown, Jane (Lawson's wife)

Jane Jackson, b: 18 Nov 1829 d: 27 Dec 1893, Beersheba. Daugther of David, Jr. and Jane Venable Jackson. Mary's sister-in-law.

Brown, Sally or Sallie (daughter)

Sarah Dorcas Brown b: 28 Nov 1850 d: 15 May 1929 Beersheba. Son of RJ and Mary Davis Brown. Married Joseph M. Whitesides, son of Thomas and Margaret Whitesides. Joe was the brother of Rufus Grier Whitesides who married Sallie's sister, Eliza.

Brown, John

John Brown, b: 24 Feb 1809 d: 02 Apr 1888 in Gaston County, NC. Son of William and Mary Davis Brown. Mary's half-brother. Married 10 Dec 1835 Mary Magdallen McElwee Caldwell, daughter of Galbraith and Jane McElwee Caldwell.

Brown, Johnny Rufus (son)

John Rufus Brown, b: 13 Feb 1862 d: 3 Aug 1866. Mary's son, her second young son to die.

Brown, Wille (son)

William Given Brown b: 21 Oct 1857 d: 16 Oct. 1932, Beersheba. Son of RJ and Mary Davis Brown. Married 02 Feb 1887 Mary R. (Minnie) Price, daughter of Joab and Mary Parker Price.

Brown, Harriet (daughter)

Mary Harriet Brown b: 11 Feb 1844 d: 25 Nov 1862 of typhoid fever, Beersheba. Daughter of RJ and Mary Davis Brown.

Burns, Lesley

Samuel L. Burns b: 12 Nov 1821 d: 12 Nov 1903 Beersheba. Son of Samuel and Elizabeth Wilkerson Burns. Married Rachel McElhenney.

Burns, Eliza

Eliza Amelia Enloe b: 1811 d: 11 May 1889 Beersheba. Daughter of Gilbert and Minerva (Minnie) Gordon Enloe. Married Amos Burns, son of Samuel and Mary Lesley Burns. Mary's second cousin.

Burns, Polly

Samuel Burns b: 17 Sep 1754 d: 20 April 1857 Beersheba. Married Mary Lesley. Mary states in her diary that "Aould Aunt Polly Burns died April 20, 1857." She probably was referring to the death of Aunt Polly's husband, Samuel Burns, who died April 18 1857.

Burns, Amos

Amos Burns b: 27 Oct 1802 d: 06 Aug 1882 Beersheba. Son of Samuel and Mary Lesley Burns. Married Eliza Amelia Enloe, daughter of Gilbert and Minerva Gordon Enloe. Mary's second cousin.

Burns, William

William Albertus Burns b: 5 Aug 1838 d: 2 Jul 1928 Beersheba. Son of Jediah and Erixina Ewing Burns. Married Margaret J. Robinson.

Butler

James Butler Thomasson b: 21 Oct 1849 d: 1913. Married 24 Nov 1870 Nancy Elizabeth Brian, daughter of Jerome and Mary Hunter Brian. Mary's nephew.

Byers, Old Aunt Polly

Mary (Polly) Gordon Byers b: 25 Dec 1779 d: 19 Jul 1867 Beersheba. Daughter of Henry and Mary Johnston Gordon. Married David Byers, son of William and Elizabeth Walton Byers. Mary's first cousin.

Cain, Betsy

Elizabeth M. Gibson Cain b: 22 Jun 1824 d: 09 Jun 1881. Daughter of Thomas and Pamela Carson Gibson. Married James M. M. Cain, son of Hugh and Martha Turner Allison Cain. Sister to Caty Brown, Mary's sister-in-law.

Cain, Nanny

Nancy Catherine Cain b: 16 Feb 1851 d: June 1855. Daughter of James M. M. and Elizabeth Gibson Cain.

Cain, Rachel

Cain, Old Mrs. (Old Ammy Cain)

Martha Turner Allison Cain b: 23 Feb 1782 d: 29 Jun 1860 Beersheba. Daughter of Robert E. And Sarah S. Turner Allison. Married Hugh M. M. Cain, son of Samuel and Agnes McDow Cain.

Cain, John

John A. Cain b: 29 Oct 1800 d: Alabama. Son of Hugh M. M. and Martha Turner Allison Cain. Married Jane Druscilla Allison, daughter of Hugh and Violet Barry Allison. Brother to Caty Brown, Mary's sister-in-law.

Cain, Thomas Gibson

Thomas Gibson Cain b: 1858 d: 11 May 1859. Son of James M. M. and Elizabeth Gibson Cain.

Cain, Sally

Sarah Z. Cain b: 20 July 1860 d: 7 May 1861 Beersheba. Daughter of James M. M. And Elizabeth M. Gibson Cain.

Cain, Franklin

William Franklin Cain b: 23 Jun 1818 d: 20 May 1862 Jasper County, MS. Son of Hugh M. M. and Martha Turner Allison Cain. Married Naomi Louisa Gibson.

Cain, Louisa

Louisa Cain b: 07 May 1854 d: 01 Sep 1854. Daughter of James M. M. and Elizabeth Gibson Cain.

Caldwell, Breathy

Caldwell, Galbraith

b: 10 Aug 1785 County Antrim, Ireland d: 20 July 1873 Beersheba. Son of William and Nancy Agnes McPhilemy Caldwell. Married Rachel McElwee, daughter of William and Rachel Newman McElwee.

Caldwell, James

James Caldwell b: Feb. 1787 County Antrim, Ireland d: 25 Nov 1871 Beersheba. Son of William and Nancy Agnes McPhilemy Caldwell. Married Sarah Turner Cain, daughter of Hugh M. M. and Martha Turner Allison Cain.

Caldwell, Mary

Caldwell, Margaret Ann

Caldwell, Son
Benjamin Franklin Caldwell b: 26 Feb 1857 d: 02 Mar 1915. Bethany Presbyterian Churchyard. Son of William and Mary Catherine McGill Caldwell.

Caldwell, Robert
Robert Caldwell b: 04 Apr 1844 d: 07 Dec 1903. Bullocks Creek Presbyterian Churchyard. Son of James Meek and Unknown Caldwell. Married Mary C.

Caldwell, Roben (Old Uncle Roben)
Robert Caldwell b: 1781 d: April 9 1858 Beersheba. Son of William and Agnes Nancy McPhilemy Caldwell. Married Elizabeth Love, daughter of John and Margaret Love. His brother was Galbraith Caldwell, father of Mary Caldwell Brown, Mary's sister-in-law.

Caldwell, John
John Caldwell b: 08 Jul 1844 d: 15 Oct 1910 Sharon. Son of William and Mary Catherine McGill Caldwell. Married Frances Jenkins, daughter of Lawson and Elizabeth Catherine Plaxco Jenkins. Mary's distant nephew.

Caldwell, William
William McGill Caldwell b: 1836 d: bef 1866. Son of William and Mary Catherine McGill Caldwell. Married Susan Emeline Ferguson, daughter of George Franklin and Hannah Brown Ferguson. Mary's second cousin.

Caldwell, John
Married Widow Good.

Caldwell, Martha
Martha Elizabeth Caldwell b: 1831 d: 08 Feb 1856. Daughter of Galbraith and Jane McElwee Caldwell. Martha was the sister of Mary Magdallen McElwee Caldwell Brown, Mary's sister in law.

Caldwell, Lorena
Maria Lorena Caldwell b: 1836 d: 21 April 1886. Daughter of Galbraith and Jane McElwee Caldwell.

Caldwell, Rachel
Rachel Caldwell b: 1821. Daugther of Galbraith and Jane McElwee Caldwell.

Caldwell, Docia
Docia Caldwell b: 29 Mar 1846 d: 12 Mar 1910 Smyrna. Daughter of James Meek Caldwell. Never married.

Caneda, Mrs.
Possibly Kennedy, Caroline Smith b: 1802 d: 1880 Beersheba. Daughter of Robert and Ann McCaw Smith. Married Nathaniel Porter Kennedy.

Castle, Eb or E. P.
Ebenezer Pressley Castles b: 18 Jun 1842 d: 14 December 1913 Smyrna. Son of Henry and Margaret Sterling Castles. Married Emily Jane Brown. Mary's son-in-law. Married second Alice Whisonant, daughter of Thomas and Mary Hambright Whisonant.

Castles, Mary Eliza
Mary Eliza Castles b: 29 Oct 1867 d: 27 Apr 1964. Daughter of Ebenezer P. and Emily Brown Castles. Married William Preston Whisonant. Mary Brown's granddaughter.

Castles, Dr.
Henry Carson Castles b: 01 Mar 1829 d: 13 Feb 1869 Fairfield County. Son of Henry and Margaret Sterling Castles. Brother of E. P. Castles, Mary's son-in-law.

Castles, Rev. James Robinson
James Robinson Castles b: 6 Jun 1829 d: 28 Nov 1878. Son of Henry and Margaret Sterling Castles. Married Martha Watt, daughter of James and Martha Bell Watt.

Caty's Rachel Amy
b: 18 Oct. 1863. Slave.

Caty's Coldwell
b: 25 May 1866.

Cauthern, Mr.

Cauthern, Rachel

Chambers, Mary Ann
Mary Ann Chambers b: 29 May 1834 d: 18 Sep 1909 Lancaster County, SC. Married Robert Erasmus Allison, son of Robert Turner and Robert Burnett Clinton Allison.

Chambers, Eddy
Edmund Ritter Chambers b: 28 Mar 1799 d: 7 Nov 1864. Married Pamela Smith. Their daughter, Mary Ann Chambers, married Robert Erasmus Allison.

Craig, Jane
Jane Campbell Craig b: 30 Aug 1843 d: 25 Mar 1918 Tennesee. Married James H. C. Duff, son of Henry Craig and Eliza Brown Duff. Wife of Mary's nephew.

Crenshaw, Sally
Sarah E. Crenshaw b: 1846 d: 08 Feb 1872. Daughter of E. A. and Margaret E. Adams Crenshaw. Sally is niece of Eliza Adams Davies.

Crenshaw, Lilly
Lilla M. Crenshaw b: 26 Jan 1843 d: 17 Mar 1920 Rose Hill Cemetery. Daughter of E. A. and Margaret E. Adams Crenshaw. Lilly is niece of Eliza Adams Davies.

Davis, Mrs. (Davies)
Eliza Adams Davies b: 22 Aug 1802 d: 26 June 1883 Beersheba. Daughter of Rev. James S. Adams. Married William B. Davies. My theory is that William B. Davies' grandfather's sister was Mary Davies, William Brown's first wife and for whom Mary Brown is named.

Davis, Mary
Mary E. Davis b:1826. Daughter of Rev. William B. and Eliza Adams Davis. Never married.

Davis, Susan (Davies)
Susan L. Davies b: 1835 d: Bef. 1910. Daughter of Rev. William B. and Eliza Adams Davis. Married John Alonzo Brown, son of Samuel Gordon and Margaret Byers Brown. Alonzo was Mary's first cousin.

Davis, Billy

William R. Davis b: 1837. Son of Rev. William B. And Eliza Adams Davis. Mary Elizabeth Ann Brown, daugther of Samuel Gordon and Margaret Byers Brown. Mary Elizabeth Ann was first cousin of Mary Brown.

Davis, William B. (Reverend) (Davies)

William Buford Davies b: 11 Dec 1801 d: 25 Mar 1855 Beersheba. Son of John Baird and Mary Buford Davies. Married Eliza Jane Adams, daughter of James Samuel and Erixene McEwen Adams. Was installed as minister at Beersheba in 1835 and served until his death in 1855.

Davis, William Buford (Davies)

William Buford Davies b:23 Aug 1867. Son of William R. and Mary Elizabeth Ann Brown Davies. Husband of first cousin of Mary Brown.

Davis, William A.

William A. Davis b: 31 Jan 1867. Son of John Leroy and Mary T. Black Davis.

Davis, Leroy (Reverend) (Davies)

John LeRoy Davies b: 03 Nov 1799 d: 16 June 1860 Beersheba. Son of John Baird and Mary Buford Davies. Married Mary Isabella Hemphill, daugther of James Andrew and Mary Nixon Hemphill.

Davison, William

William B. Davison b: 19 May 1827 d: 03 Oct 1902. Son of John B. and Elizbabeth Barber Davison. Married Sarah Selina Allison, daughter of Hugh and Violet Barry Allison.

Dawson, Jeremiah

Jeremiah Dawson b: 1780 d: 11 Apr 1856 Beersheba. Married Margaret Burns, daughter of Samuel and Mary Lesley Burns.

Derer, B. (Derrer)

Bernhardt Derer b: 14 Aug 1829 d: 16 Mar 1858. Married Sarintha Howell, daughter of Isom and Mary Kendrick Howell. Sister of Jane Elizabeth (Precious) Howell Scoggins.

Dickey, Old Mrs.

Margaret Wilson Dickey b: 2 Aug 1768 d: 15 April 1857. Married James Dickey.

Dickey, Jane
Margaret Jane Dickey b: 28 Dec 1835 d: 28 Nov 1854. Daughter of Hugh Wilson and Margaret M. Craig Dickey.

Dickson, Tom

Douglass, James H. (Reverend) (Douglas)
James Henry Douglas b: 15 Feb 1837 d: 13 Feb 1903 Bethany Presbyterian. Son of Joseph and Narcissa Kendrick Douglass. Married first, unknown. Married second, Harriet Enloe. Was minister at Beersheba spring of 1870 until 1874.

Dow, Reverend
John R. Dow, Presbyterian Clergyman.

Duff, James
James H. C. Duff b: 27 Jan 1838 d: 19 Aug 1902 Lincoln Co. TN. Son of Henry C. and Eliza Brown Duff. Married 06 Nov 1866 Jane Campbell Craig. Nephew of Mary Brown.

Duff, Henry
Henry Craig Duff b: 28 Aug 1808 d: 08 May 1894 Lincoln Co. TN. Son of James and Mary Craig Duff. Married 06 Apr 1837 Eliza Brown, sister of Mary Brown.

Duff, Eliza
Eliza Brown Duff b: 10 Dec 1810 d: 24 Oct 1868 Lincoln Co. TN. Daughter of William and Mary Davis Brown. Sister of Mary Brown. Married 06 Apr 1837 Henry Craig Duff.

Enloe, Asel
Asahel Enloe b: 1817 d: 1904. Son of Gilbert and Minerva Gordon Enloe. Cousin of Mary. Presbyterian Minister.

Enloe, Catherine
Catherine Jackson Allison b: 30 Sep 1833 d: 21 Apr 1856 Beersheba. Daughter of Hugh and Violet Barry Allison. Married John Gilbert Enloe, son of Gilbert and Minerva Gordan Enloe. Wife of Mary's second cousin.

Enloe, Eliza
Eliza E. Enloe b: 7 Nov 1864 d: 03 Jul 1903 Clover Woodside. Daughter of John Gilbert and Mary Ann Alexander Enloe. Married Caleb Thaddeus Thomas, son of Joseph and Margaret Hemphill Thomas. First cousin of Mary Brown.

Enloe, Isaac
Isaac Enloe b: 1807. Son of Gilbert and Minerva (Minnie) Gordon Enloe. Second cousin of Mary Brown.

Enloe, Isabella
Isabella Wilson Enloe d: 9 April 1863. Married Benjamin Enloe.

Enloe, John
John Gilbert Enloe b: 1814 d: 12 Aug 1875. Son of Gilbert and Minerva Gordan Enloe. Married Catherine Jackson Allison, Mary's second cousin. Married second Mary Ann Alexander, daughter of William Rooker and Emily Brown Alexander. She too was Mary's cousin.

Enloe, Mary Ann
Mary Ann Alexander Enloe b: 1832 d: 26 Oct 1867. Daughter of William Rooker and Emily Eliza Brown Alexander. Married John Gilbert Enloe. First cousin of Mary Brown.

Ould, Mr. Enloe
Gilbert Enloe b: 1776 d: 10 May 1861. Son of Isaac and Violet Porter Enloe. Married Minerva Gordan, Mary's cousin.

Falls, Martha
Martha Cain Allison Falls b: 23 Sep 1825 d: 15 Jul 1908. Daughter of Hugh and Violet Barry Allison. Married Eli Warren Falls.

Ferguson, Nancy Emily
Emily Nancy Ferguson b: May 1859 d: 21 Aug 1881. Daughter of James Young and Jane Amanda Alexander Ferguson. Mary's first cousin.

Ferguson, Mary Jane
Mary Jane Ferguson b: 16 Aug 1857 d: 03 Oct 1888. Daughter of James Young and Jane Amanda Alexander Ferguson. Mary's first cousin.

Ferguson, Susan

Susan Emeline Ferguson b: 27 Jul 1843 d: 13 Feb 1897. Bethel Presbyterian. Daughter of George Franklin and Hannah Brown Ferguson. Married first 16 Feb 1860 William McGill Caldwell. Married second 21 Dec 1869 Henry Franklin Glenn, her second cousin. Susan was first cousin of Mary Brown.

Ferguson, Franklin

George Franklin Ferguson b: 1811 d: 21 Jun 1865 Beersheba. Son of William and Elizabeth Carroll Ferguson. Married Hannah B. Brown, daughter of Robert and Mary Given Brown. Hannah was cousin/sister-in-law of Mary Brown.

Ferguson, Ann

Sarah Ann Ferguson b: 11 July 1846 d: 13 July 1885 Sharon A.R.P. Daughter of James C. And Nancy Emily Quinn Ferguson. Married Julius Amzi Hope, son of James Madison and Lucinda Powell Hope.

Ferguson, Young

James Young Ferguson b: 10 Feb 1836. Son of James C. and Nancy Emily Quinn Ferguson. Married 02 Oct 1856 Jane Amanda Alexander, daughter of William Rooker and Emily Eliza Brown Alexander.

Ferguson, Mary Jane

Mary Eliza Jane Ferguson b: 1841 d: 21 Jun 1865 Beersheba. Daughter of George Franklin and Hannah B. Brown Ferguson. First cousin of Mary Brown.

Floyd, Andrew

Andrew Gordon Floyd b: 24 Dec 1832 d: 11 Jun 1909 Spartanburg, SC. Son of John and Margaret Edmunds Brown Floyd. Married 08 Mar 1866 Susan Elizabeth Hall. Nephew of Mary Brown.

Floyd, Clementine

Nancy Clementine Floyd b: 27 Sep 1829 d: 11 Jun 1909 Rose Hill. Daughter of John and Margaret Edmunds Brown Floyd. Married John Edmund Jefferys, son of James J. and Elizabeth Hicks Smith Jefferys. Niece of Mary Brown.

Floyd, Billy

William Brown Floyd b: 1827 d: 12 Apr 1857 Bethel Presbyterian. Son of John and Margaret Edmunds Brown Floyd. Married Mary Margaret Johnston, daughter of David and Mary Glenn Johnston. Nephew of Mary Brown.

Floyd, Margaret

Margaret Edmunds Brown Floyd b: 15 Jan 1807 d: 11 Mar 1874 Beersheba. Daughter of William and Dorcas Tabitha Floyd Brown. Mary's half-sister. Married John Floyd, son of Andrew and Anne Nancy Gordon Floyd.

Floyd, Chambers

This is possibly a son of Mary's uncle, Robert Floyd. Robert and his wife, Elizabeth Baird, had four sons born 1805-1830, all untraced.

Floyd, Sally

Sarah Mendenhall Floyd b: Jul 1774 d: 23 Jan 1872 Clover Woodside. Daughter of Nathan and Rebecca Duckworth Mendenhall. Married James Floyd, son of Andrew and Nancy Gordon Floyd. Aunt of Mary Brown.

Floyd, Amanda

Amanda Dorcas Floyd b: 1836 d: in Gaston County. Daughter of John and Margaret Edmunds Brown Floyd. Married 12 Aug 1856 James Green Gullick. Niece of Mary Brown.

Glenn, Jane

Jane Brown Glenn b: 05 Dec 1812 d: 16 Aug 1857, Bethel. Daughter of William and Mary Davis Brown. Married Henry Glenn, son of James and Martha Craig Glenn. Mary's sister.

Gimison, Wesley (Jamieson)

John Wesley Jamieson b: 1833. Son of William and Jane Brown Jamieson. Mary's cousin/nephew.

Gimison, Billy (Jameson)

William Jameson b: 6 Oct 1794 d: 18 Oct 1862 in Tippah County, MS. Son of Joseph and Elizabeth Ann Rowe Jamieson. Married 1823 Jane Brown, daughter of Robert and Mary Given Brown, cousin/sister-in-law of Mary Brown.

Gladden, Andrew

Glenn, Henry

Henry Glenn b: 17 Jun 1797 d: 07 Apr 1872 Bethel Presbyterian. Son of James and Martha Craig Glenn. Married Jane Brown, daughter of William and Mary Davis Brown. Mary's sister.

Good, Widow
Married John Caldwell November 5, 1857.

Good, Dr.
William Jackson Good b: 1822 d: 4 July 1862. Dr. Good's sister was Sarah Simpson Good who married John Given Brown. Dr. Good was the brother of Mary Brown's cousin's wife. Sarah and John died in the same year, leaving three small children.

Good, Mrs., Sarah Ann
Sara Ann Smith Good b: 3 Jan 1813 d: 11 Jan 1864 Beersheba. Daughter of Robert and Ann McCaw Smith. Married William Jackson Good, son of James B. and Jane Plaxco Good. Her relationship to Mary is through marriage. Mrs. Good's sister-in-law (husband's sister) married Mary's cousin/brother-in-law, John Given Brown.

Grady Mr. (Reverend)

Gullick, Green
James Green Gullick b: 1833. Married Amanda Dorcas Floyd, daughter of John and Margaret Edmunds Brown Floyd, Mary's neice.

Gunnings, Harvey

Hall, Thomas preached at Centre

Hope, Lonnie
Julius Amzi Hope b: 18 Jun 1848 d: 09 Aug 1914 Sharon. Son of James Madison and Lucinda Powell Hope. Married Sarah Ann Ferguson, daughter of James C. and Nancy Emily Quinn Ferguson

Howell, Sarintha
Sarintha Howell b: 4 Nov 1839 d: 03 Oct 1887. Rose Hill Cemetery. Daughter of Isom and Mary Kendrick Howell. Married Bernhardt Derrer.

Hudson, Mrs.
Mary Hopkins b: 1798. Married Joshua Hudson.

Hudson, Emi
Emma F. L. Hudson b: 1841. Daughter of Joshua and Mary Hopkins Hudson. Married Hugh Nichols.

Hudson, Henrietta

Ida Sharlit
Ida Charlotte Thomasson b: 28 Dec 1858 d: 15 Apr 1885 Beersheba. Daughter of Hiram and Harriet Brown Thomasson. Married H. Crowell Warlick. Niece of Mary Brown.

Jackson, Hatty

Jackson, Ema
Emma Louisa Jackson b: 29 Nov 1847 d: 16 Jan 1896. Daughter of Archibald and Sarah Wallace Jackson. Married Joseph W. Neil, son of William and Mary Erwin Sutton Neil.

Jackson, Jane
Elizabeth Jane Jackson b. 1 Oct 1852 d: 14 Feb 1930 Laurelwood Cemetery. Daughter of Archibald and Sarah Wallace Jackson. Married Elwood Fisher Bell, son of Thomas Jefferson and Martha Jane Brian Bell.

Janes, Catherine
Catherine Janes d: in Arkansas. Daughter of John and Margaret Floyd Janes.

Janes, Peggy
Margaret Floyd Janes b:1776 d: in Arkansas. Daughter of Andrew and Anne Nancy Gordon Floyd. Married John Janes. Aunt of Mary Brown.

Janes, John
John Janes. Son of Thomas and Mary Gordon Janes. Married Margaret Floyd. First cousin of Mary Brown. When he married Margaret Floyd, he became Uncle John Janes.

Janes, James
James Janes b: Abt. 1834 d: Dec 1860 Perry County, Arkansas. Son of John and Margaret Floyd Janes. Married Mary C.

Janes, Robert
Robert B. Janes b: 20 April 1828 d: 30 April 1897 Stoney Point, Arkansas. Son of John and Margaret B. Floyd Janes. Married Mary Jane. Mary Brown's first cousin.

Jenkins, Fanny
Frances Jenkins b: 23 Jan 1846 d: 24 Jul 1897 Sharon. Daughter of Lawson and Elizabeth Catherine Plaxco Jenkins. Married John Caldwell, son of William and Mary Catherine McGill Caldwell.

Johnson, Willey, Wille
William Johnson. Son of Richard H. And Jane Davies Johnston.

Johnson, Cyrus (Reverend)
Cyrus Johnson. Ordained and installed as minister at Beersheba on November 6, 1824. He served Beersheba as well as its mission church in Yorkville until September 1833. He died 25 Jan 1855.

Johnson, Mrs. (Johnston)
Jane Davies Johnston b: 1827. Daughter of William B. and Eliza Adams Davies. Married Richard H. Johnson. Richard Johnson died 28 June 1853 leaving widow Jane and son William (Wille).

Knox, Mary (Miss)
Mary Emma Knox b: 22 Feb 1876 d:14 Nov 1955. Daugther of John and Eliza Ann Jackson Knox. Married John J. Jackson.

Knox, Jane (Miss)
Jane Lavinia Knox b: 28 Feb 1880 d: 19 Oct 1955. Daughter of John and Eliza Ann Jackson Knox. Married Robert D. Dorsett.

Kurkendall, Mr.
Died 28 April 1856.

Kurkendall, Sally
Sarah Kuykendall b: 1801 d: 1881 Beersheba.

Kurkendall, Old Mrs.

Land, Mrs.
Jane Olivia Davison Land b: 23 Mar 1833 d: 1876. Daughter of James Black and Sarah Latimer Davison. Married James Edward Land, son of James and Charlotte Coleman Land. Mrs. Land was the mother of Mary Brown's son-in-law.

Liles, Martha
d: 9 Nov 1864

Linn, Mrs. (Lynn)
Probably Hannah Neely Lynn b: abt 1770 d: 15 April 1857 Beersheba. Daughter of Thomas Neely and Hannah Star. Married Richard Lynn.

Love, Isabella

Love, Hugh
Hugh Love b: 24 Oct 1795 d: 17 Nov 1885 Smyrna. Married 13 Mar 1833 Mary Martha Brown, daughter of Robert and Mary Given Brown, cousin/sister-in-law of Mary Brown.

Love, Martha
Possibly Martha E. Love b: Feb 1839 d: 1918. Daughter of William and Sarah Martin Love.

Love, Mary

Love, Margaret E.

Massebeau, William Augustus
William Augustus Massebeau b: 13 July 1866. Son of John B. And Jaily E. Alexander Massebeau. Married Rosa Olivia Carson. Mary's first cousin.

Massebeau, Mr.
John B. Massebeau b: 1836 d: 1870 Spartanburg, SC. Son of William Augustus and Elizabeth Massebeau. Married Jaily E. Alexander, daughter of William Rooker and Emily Eliza Brown Alexander. Husband of Mary's first cousin.

Mathis, Mr.
Matthews

McAphee, Harriet Miss (McAfee)

Harriet Jane McAfee b 20 Jun 1849 d: 24 May 1888 Union Churchyard, York SC. Daughter of William Pickney and Minerva Ferguson McAfee. Married Thomas Nelson Thomasson.

McAphee, Mrs. (McAfee)

Minerva Ferguson McAfee b: 21 Nov 1818 d: 16 Sep 1884 Beersheba. Daughter of William and Elizabeth Carroll Ferguson. Married William Pickney McAfee. Minerva was the sister of Franklin Ferguson. Franklin and Hannah Brown Ferguson were Mary's brother and sister-in-law/cousin.

McCarter, Ginny

Mr. McCarter

William Meek McCarter b: 1845 d: 20 Dec 1866. Son of Robert Clinton and Elizabeth Jane Jackson McCarter. Married Adelia M. Packard.

McCaw, Robert G.

Robert Gadsden McCaw b. 28 Dec 1821 d. 24 Nov 1870 Rose Hill Cemetery. Son of Robert and Agnes Bratton McCaw. Married Belle Means Bratton, daugther of William and Isabella Means Bratton. Lt. Governor of South Carolina 1864-1865.

McCelhany, Miss (McElhenney)

Rachel McElhenney b: 30 Jun 1838 d: 09 Jun 1916 Beersheba. Married Samuel L. Burns.

McCorkle, Capt.

McElwee, Newman

Jonathan Newman McElwee b: 08 Mar 1795 d: 28 Mar 1882. Son of William and Rachel Newman McElwee. Married first Elizabeth Bonner McGill. Married second Mrs. Crawford.

McElwee, John Meek

John Meek McElwee b: 28 Apr 1833 d: 27 Aug 1861. Son of Jonathan Newman and Elizabeth Bonner McGill McElwee. Married Margaret Ann Caldwell, daughter of James and Sarah Turner Cain Caldwell. Distant nephew.

McElwee, Sally
Sarah McElwee b: 28 Oct 1860. Daughter of John Meek and Margaret Ann Caldwell McElwee. Married William Meek Faulkner. Distant niece of Mary Brown.

McElwee, Mr.
d: 14 May 1867.

McElwee, Meek
William Meek McElwee b: 01 Apr 1802 d: 01 Jun 1860. Son of William and Rachel Newman McElwee.

McFadden, Mary Jane
Mary Jane Amelia McFadden b: 06 Jun 1836 d: 22 Feb 1912. Daugther of William and Amelia Davies McFadden. Married John Josiah Smith son of Milas and Rebecca Patrick Smith.

Meek, Martha
Martha Catherine Caldwell Meek b: 25 Mar 1833 d: 09 Jul 1884. Daughter of James and Sarah Turner Cain Caldwell. Married as his second wife, John Rufus Starr Meek.

Meek, James Eli
James Eli Meek b:30 Jul 1857 d: 29 Nov 1888. Son of John Rufus Starr and Martha Catherine Caldwell Meek. Married Ida Elizabeth Kennedy.

Neely, Ann
Eliza Ann Neely b: 1841. Daughter of Hance and Isabella Neely.

Moore, Star
John Starr Moore b: 1784 d: 21 Sep 1859 Beersheba. Son of Samuel and Mary Starr Moore. Married Margaret Susan Meek, daughter of Adam and Nancy Ann Agnes Byers Meek.

More, Psalm (Moore)
Samuel Rufus Moore b: 21 Nov 1819 d: 18 Nov 1899 Rose Hill Cemetery. Son of John Starr and Margaret Susan Meek Moore. Married Floride Patterson, daughter of Wyatt and Mary B. Cunningham Patterson.

Mrs. Hill and sister Mority (Unity) Whisonant
Barbara Whisonant Hill b: 25 Nov 1836 d: 2 Dec 1913. Daughter of Joseph R. and Unity Harden Whisonant. Married Lawson Alexander Hill, son of John and Cynthia Hill.

Mullinax, James

Mullinax, Felix

Neel, Joe (Neil)
Joseph W. Neil b: 10 Feb 1840 d: 30 Mar 1897. Son of William and Mary Erwin Sutton Neil. Married Emma Louisa Jackson, daughter of Archibald and Sarah Wallace Jackson. Joseph is first cousin of RJ Brown.

Nichols, Hugh
Hugh Joshua Nichols b: 1836 d: 11 August 1866 Beersheba. Married Emma Hudson.

Nichols, Hugh Joshua
Hugh Joshua Nichols. Son of Hugh and Emma Hudson Nichols.

Pagin, Tom (Pagan)
Thomas Sumpter Pagan b: 1811 d: 25 Sep 1862 Arkansas. Son of Alexander and Mary Gill Mills Pagan. Married Elizabeth Emmaline Gill, daughter of John Gaston and Nancy Ann Rebecca King Gill.

Palmer, Dick
Dick Palmer b: 1837 d: 1862. Son of Thomas and Eleanor Smith Palmer. Dick Palmer was a waiter at his cousin, Jane Alexander's wedding.

Patrick, Mary
Mary Glenn Patrick b: 4 Feb 1835 d: 21 Jan 1916 Bethel. Daughter of Henry and Jane Brown Glenn. Married George Anderson Patrick. Mary's niece.

Patrick, George
George Anderson Patrick b: 6 Jul 1831 d: 25 May 1902 Bethel. Married Mary Glenn, daughter of Henry and Jane Brown Glenn. Husband of Mary's niece.

Patterson, Marg

Patterson, Perry

Polly, Aunt
Mary Jane Floyd b: 1789 d: 13 Jul 1861. Daughter of Andrew and Anne Nancy Gordon Floyd. Never married. Aunt of Mary Brown.

Porter, Mr. (Rev.)

Price, Mrs.
Mary Parker Price b: 02 Dec 1835 d: 18 Feb 1874 Union Baptist Cemetery. Daughter of Cortes Alamedo and Jane Childers Parker. Married Joab Price. The mother of Mary Brown's daughter in law.

Pursley, Susan (Pursely)
Susan Pursely b: 29 Dec 1818 d: 1920. Daughter of James and Sarah Quarrell Pursley.

Quinn, Emiline
Amelia Emeline Quinn b: 03 Dec. 1840 d: 1908. Daughter of John and Mary Ann Ferguson Quinn. Married John Miller Thomasson.

Quinn, William
William Quinn b: 1836 d: 1864. Son of John and Mary Ann Ferguson Quinn. Married 17 Aug 1856 Mary Serena Brown, daughter of John and Mary Magdalene Caldwell Brown, Mary's niece.

Quinn, Andrew
Andrew P. Quinn b: 13 May 1832 d: 10 Jul 1860. Son of John and Mary Ann Ferguson Quinn. Married 17 Aug. 1856 Jane Elizabeth Stua ⁻homasson, daughter of James and Jane Stuart Miller Thomasson.

Quinn, Warren
John Warren Quinn b: 22 Jun 1830 d: 18 Oct 1861. Son of Ferguson Quinn.

Richardson, Rev.

Ridel, Jane (Riddle)
Riddle, John b. 1783 d: 26 Jul 1871. Son of George and Margaret Riddle. Married Clarissa Duff, sister of Henry Duff, Mary's brother-in-law.

Robinson, Margaret
Margaret Jane Robinson b: 4 Mar 1843 d: 16 May 1909 Beersheba. Daughter of Andrew Egger and Nancy Meek Robinson. Married William Albertus Burns.

Scoggins, Newman McElwee
b: 10 June 1868. Son of David and Precious Scoggins.

Scogings, David (Scoggins)
David Buford Scoggins b: 15 Aug 1822 d: 16 Jan 1873. Son of Francis and (unknown) Scoggins. Married Jane Elizabeth Precious Howell, daughter of Isham and Mary Kendrick Howell.

Shephard, Marg (Schumpert)
Margaret M. Schumpert b: 12 Jan 1840 d: 9 July 1929. Married Robert Washington Whitesides, the first cousin of Rufus G. Whitesides, Mary's son-in-law.

Smith, John
John Josiah Smith b: 08 Feb 1836 d: 02 Jul 1910. Son of Milas and Rebecca Patrick Smith. Married Mary Amelia Jane McFadden.

Smith, Molly
Mary Amelia Smith b: 1862. Daughter of John and Mary McFadden Smith.

Stephenson, Cousin Rixeny
Erixene Floyd Stephenson b: 16 Sept 1819 d: 6 Aug 1866 Beersheba. Daughter of James and Sarah Floyd. Married first, James Lawson Jackson, son of David and Elizabeth Gordon Jackson. Married second Joseph G. Stephenson. Mary's cousin.

Strong, Cristy Rev.

Sutton, Mary
Jane Sutton b: 23 Mar 1840 d: 04 Oct 1880. Daugther of Jonathan Leroy

and Jane Ross Sutton. Married 19 Jan 1859 John Randolph Alexander, son of William Rooker and Emily Eliza Brown Alexander, Mary's first cousin.

Thomasson, Hiram
Hiram Cazort Thomasson b: 22 Jan 1811 d: 07 Feb 1882. Son of James C. and Charlotte Cazort Thomasson. Married Harriet Amanda Brown, Mary's sister.

Thomasson, Lafayette
Gilbert Lafayette Thomasson b: 04 Feb 1823. Son of James C. and Charlotte Cazort Thomasson Married Martha Boggs.

Thomasson, Dorcas Emily
Emily Dorcas Thomasson b: 28 June 1861 d: 21 Aug 1919 Bethshilo. Daughter of Hiram and Harriet Brown Thomasson. Married first cousin, John T. Quinn, son of William and Mary Serena Brown Quinn. Niece of Mary Brown.

Thomasson, Dr.
Doctor Alfred Thomasson b: 1816 d: 28 Nov 1850. Son of James C. and Charlotte Cazort Thomasson. Married Mary Whitaker. Brother of Hiram Thomasson, Mary's brother-in-law.

Thomasson, Eliza
Elizabeth Ann Brown Thomasson b: 20 Nov 1817 Pansy, AR. Daughter of John and Elizabeth Gordon Brown. Married William Pleasant Thomasson, son of James and Charlotte Cazort Thomasson. Eliza was Mary's first cousin.

Thomasson, Boliver
Simon Boliver Thomasson b: 19 May 1825 d: 17 Feb 1896 Drew County, AR. Married first Isabelle Elizabeth Floyd, daughter of John and Margaret Edmunds Brown Floyd. Married second 06 Oct 1845 Mary Adelaide Cooper.

Thomasson, Alvis
Passins Alvis Thomasson b: 08 Jan 1815 d: 1899 Conway County, AR. Son of James C. and Charlotte Cazort Thomasson. Married Elizabeth Gordon Jackson, daugther of David and Elizabeth Gordon Jackson, Mary Brown's first cousin.

Thomasson, Jane
Jane Elizabeth Stuart Thomasson b: 21 Dec 1838 d: 29 Jan 1918. Married James C. Thomasson, Jr., son of James C. And Charlotte Cazort Thomasson.

Thomasson, Harriet
Harriet Amanda Brown Thomasson b: 09 Feb 1826 d: 14 Sep 1896 Beersheba. Daughter of William and Dorcas Tabitha Floyd Brown. Married Hiram Cazort Thomasson, son of James C. and Charlotte Cazort Thomasson. Mary Brown's sister.

Turner, Andrew
Robert Andrew Turner b: unk d: 1871. Son of Christopher and Mary Patrick Turner.

Turner, Samuel
Samuel Turner b: 1760 Maryland d: 18 Mar 1857 Beersheba. Son of Thomas and Martha Turner. Father of Sarah Turner. Uncle Psalmy Turner to Mary Brown.

Turner, Sally
Sarah Turner b: 1784 d: 21 Mar 1857 Beersheba. Daughter of Samuel and Margaret Turner. Never married.

Vickers, Newton

Vickers, James

Wallace, Ould Mr.
d: May 30, 1859.

Walker, Franklin (ordained deacon in 1860)

Watson, Samuel (Reverend)
Samuel Lytle Watson b: 05 Feb 1798 d: 13 Nov 1882 Bethel Presbyterian Churchyard. Son of David and Margaret Adams Watson. Married Nancy Hannah Neil.

Watson, Mrs. (Old)
d: 24 Feb 1864.

Watson, Margaret
Margaret Watson. First wife of John Randolph Alexander, son of William Rooker and Emily Eliza Brown Alexander.

Whitesides, Jacky
Rufus Jackson Whitesides b: 16 Jun 1866 d: 14 Nov 1866. Son of Rufus G. and Eliza Brown Whitesides. Mary's grandson.

Whitesides, Rufus
Rufus Grier Whitesides b: 19 Mar 1835 d: 07 Feb 1897 Smyrna. Son of Thomas and Margaret Whitesides. Married Eliza Ann Brown, daugther of RJ and Mary Brown. Mary's son-in-law.

Whitesides, Robert
Robert Washington Whitesides b: 29 Jul 1835 d 4 April 1915 Smyrna. Son of Robert and Mary Brown Whitesides. Married Margaret Shumpert.

Whitesides, Hatty Lee
Harriet Lee Whitesides b: 19 May 1864 d: 04 Feb 1947 Smyrna. Daughter of Rufus G. and Eliza Ann Brown Whitesides. Married James Calvin McGill, son of John and Rachel Newman McElwee McGill. Mary's granddaughter.

Wilkason, Nancy Jane (Wilkerson)
Nancy Jane Wilkerson b: 2 Jul 1846 d: 15 Jul 1898 Beersheba. Daughter of E. P. and M. H.

Wilson, Jane
Mary Jane Floyd Wilson b:1834. Son of John and Margaret Edmunds Brown Floyd. Married William A. H. Wilson. Niece of Mary Brown.

Wilson, William (has school)

Wilson, Joe
Gazaway Joseph Wilson b: 13 Jun 1841. Son of Joseph and Mary Watkins Wilson. Married Jane Eliza Ferguson, daughter of George Franklin and Hannah Brown Ferguson. Jane is Mary's cousin. In 1870, Joe and Eliza Wilson were living in Lincoln County, TN with one child. Untraced after 1870.

Witherspoon, J. D.
Isaac Donnom Witherspoon b: 1803 d: 1858. Son of James Hervery and Ruth Donom Witherspoon. Elected Lt. Governor of South Carolina in 1842.

Genealogical Research and Compilation by Catherine Brown Michael

ENDNOTES

[1] According to James Lyles Strain's Reminiscences of Western York County by Jerry West, we learn that at the fall term of court for York District, James Vickers and his brother Newton Vickers were tried and convicted for the murder of William Dobson at a barroom in Rock Hill. Robert J. Brown was on the Jury. The sentence of death was given to both men by Judge O'Neal. It was learned at the trial that both men were orphans and raised in ignorance. Newton was later pardoned by the governor but remained in jail for another year. On the day of the hanging, the streets and side walks were crowded with horses, wagons, buggies and people. Col. Sadler marched the guard to the old jail where the prisoner, James Vickers was confined. The crowd gathered around. A wagon was backed up to the door of the jail, the jail door opened, and the prisoner, with a firm step, stepped into the wagon. Sheriff S. C. Youngblood was next to enter the wagon. He was a kind-hearted man and did not want to carry out the painful task of hanging this man. In fact, earlier that day he had visited the Vickers brothers in their cell and asked what they wanted for breakfast. Newton said he didn't want anything, but James said, "Bring me a good breakfast. I want to swing heavy today." After the sheriff entered the wagon, others that would be helping carry out the sentence and the officiat-

ing minister took their seats in the wagon. Col. Sadler commanded his guards to "forward-march," and the wagon drove off with the guard forming a square around it. A short ride and a turn toward the east led to the gallows. As far as the eye could see, the streets were crowded with people. The road was ankle deep in mud, but the guard marched through it. The prisoner remained seated and only occasionally looked to the front. Col. Sadler was in front of the guard and, with his saber waving right and left, opened the way for the guard to march to and around the gallows. The wagon was driven under the beam and stopped. The crowd swayed back and forth. Some were heartsick at the scene about to happen while others rushed to get a better view. The minister made a few remarks and gave out the hymn, "WHEN I CAN READ MY TITLE CLEAR." P. B. Darwin sang the hymn while many of the assembled people took part. Prayer was then offered by the minister. The prisoner and those in the wagon kneeled, while the guards and most of the assembly stood with hats off. The fatal trap was then adjusted. The prisoner arose from his seat and dropped his cloak on the chair, disclosing the snow white shroud in which he was dressed. With firm steps he walked to the end of the wagon from where he stepped upon "the drop." He was a fine looking young man about 22 years of age. He said nothing. The rope was put through a hole in the beam and brought down and fastened to a pin in the upright post on the prisoner's left, leaving a fall of about three feet. His hands and feet were pinioned, and the cap was drawn down over his face. The sheriff descended and with a hatchet cut the rope upon which the drop was suspended. At the first blow he missed the rope; at the second he cut it and James Vickers was launched into eternity. It was 5 minutes past 12 noon when the drop fell. The taunt rope was wrenched as the culprit whirled back and forth in the air. A writhing shroud fluttering in the wind added nausea to the sickening spectacle. After hanging 45 minutes he was pronounced dead, taken down, and placed in the coffin. As the corpse was being lowered, a rush was made by the people to get a glimpse. The guard ordered the people to stand back. Thus justice was done.

[2] Rev. William Buford Davies was installed as minister at Beersheba Church in 1835. During his term, a third place of worship was built which lasted until 1918. He married Eliza Adams, daughter of Bethel Presbyterian's minister, James Samuel Adams. During their marriage, he suffered from consumption and had answered the call of Beersheba because its location in the country provided much needed fresh air for sickly lungs. Their large plantation was near Mary and RJ's farm, and there were frequent visits between the two. Mary was

the impressionable age of 12 when she first started hearing the sermons of W. B. Davies. He performed the marriage and was her pastor for 20 years. After his death, she continued her friendship with his widow, Eliza Davies, and with the children. Mary's cousin, Eliza Ann Brown married William R. Davies, and the bonds of friendship became familial.

[3] Day of the great wind and fire:
James Lyles Strain wrote in the Yorkville Enquirer that March 9, 1855 was called "Windy Friday" and was a day of terror over much of the United States where entire towns were burned to the ground. Destructive fires could be found in every part of South Carolina. Several towns in South Carolina were reduced to ashes. Strain related it to the Day of Judgment. The wind was reported to have blown like a tornado all day toppling houses and spreading flames from hill top to hill top from around 9:00 a. m. until after sundown. By 3:00 p. m. that day the sun was scarcely visible. The air from the smoke was both blinding and stifling. Above King's Creek thousands and thousands of acres of land were burned and scarcely a house or cord of wood left. Women and children screaming in terror carried as many possessions as possible and fled to the fields where they huddled out of the reach of flames and falling trees. They watched as their homes were left to the mercy of the fires. Nearby Hopewell church was burned. Almost all plantations in the Broad River section of western York County had fires to contend with. Flames from houses were raised high into the air, and the strong winds spread them over the land. Men rode for miles to help their neighbors protect their families and property. Strain reported "as night fell the winds died down, and for miles and miles in every direction the landscape was aglow, as with ten thousand camp fires, and weary men fell down for needed rest."

[4] Mary Jane Brown Alexander was RJ and Mary Davis Brown's niece. Her father, John Given Brown, and mother, Sarah Simpson Good Brown, died in 1849, leaving Mary Jane and two younger siblings. The younger children were taken in by aunts and uncles. Mary Jane was raised by RJ and Mary and married her first cousin, Robert B. Alexander, at the age of 16.

[5] About four miles north of Yorkville a church was established to fill the needs of a growing community. Located approximately in the center point of dis-

tance from Bethel, Bethany and Beersheba Churches, the New Centre Church thrived for a time. Later, as commerce followed the railroad and a depot was established three miles to the west, the town of Clover came into being. The old New Centre Church moved to town and became Clover Presbyterian Church.

[6] Communion, also called the Lord's Supper, Holy Communion or the Eucharist is described in the Book of Confessions of the Presbyterian Church (U.S.A.) as "A sacrament, wherein by giving and receiving bread and wine, according to Christ's appointment, his death is showed forth; and the worthy receivers are, not after a corporal and carnal manner, but by faith made partakers of his body and blood, with all his benefits, to their spiritual nourishment and growth in grace."

[7] In the 1850's, stories of abundant and uncrowded lands, better hunting, and more opportunity enticed many York County residents to join the migration movement. Many, like Henry and Jane Duff, Mary's sister and brother-in-law, traveled to Tennessee. They settled in Lincoln County which is about ninety miles south of Nashville. Arkansas, Mississippi and Alabama were open territories for ambitious pioneers, and after the war, Texas and lands farther west enticed those anxious to make a new start in an untested territory.

[8] The Battle of Kings Mountain was fought on 7 October 1780 and was thought to be the turning point of the American Revolution in the South. On October 4, 1855, a grand 75th anniversary celebration was planned. The Wednesday morning edition of The Yorkville Enquirer was full of articles and poems in honor of the celebration. The Kings Mountain Ball was to be given at the Rose Hotel. The invitation to attend the celebration at Kings Mountain was extended to The Major Generals and Brigadier Generals of the several divisions with their respective staffers as well as the volunteer, uniform and Cavalry companies of the state. Also invited were the surviving soldiers of the Seminole and Mexican wars, the members of the Senate and House of Representatives as well as the Clergy, Masons, Odd Fellows and Temperance Lodges and the members of the press. There was also a notice requesting that the ladies attend. Mary's grandfather, Andrew Floyd, was a veteran of the Battle of Kings Mountain. Many of Mary and RJ's friends and relatives had ties to the great battle, and the celebration was a huge event for the community.

⁹ This three story handsome brick building with bell tower was located on a two acre lot located where the present McCelvey Center now stands. Prior to the building of this school the lot was used as a gathering place for important events and was known as the "Oak Grove." The school was organized in 1853 for young ladies. Though sponsored by the Presbyterians, much of the support came from the community. The school had a faculty of highly educated Christian ministers. Young ladies from the best families over the state and surrounding states attended the Yorkville Female College. The school operated until after the Civil War when public schools were opened.

¹⁰ In Jerry West's book, *Reminiscences of Western York County*, James Strain relates, "The winter of 1855-1856 was remarkable for its snow. On Saturday 21st of December, 1855, snow fell and for five consecutive weeks continued to fall on Saturday. The result was that on Monday, March 10, 1856, snow was still lying on the north hillsides. Snow lay on the ground for two months and 21 days continuously."

¹¹ Amusement to Mary's Beersheba community was simple and wholesome. Her home was often the lively spot for the day or night's singing. Shape Note, or Sacred Harp singing is a form of communal singing developed in the American south in the early 1800s. Although the music is religious, it was never sung as part of a service. Instead, sings were special occasions and often all day affairs. The participants were the only audience. There was a leader, called a "clerk" or "clark" who was often a traveling music teacher. There were no musical instruments. The clerk kept time and selected the music, usually from Rouses version of the psalms or selections from Watts Hymns. He would stand in front of the singers and "raise a tune," sometimes not knowing what tune he might be striking. But after a few bars, sounds in the proper key would emerge and slowly the entire room of singers would join in, creating a mighty volume of sound, variety and spontaneity. The emphasis of Shape note singing is on enjoyment of the singer, not quality of music, so participants are not turned away for having poor voices.

¹² According to the July 10, 1856 issue of The Yorkville Enquirer, the attendance at the commencement of the new female college far exceeded that of any other occasion. The Hall was filled almost to its capacity, and the hotels in

town were booked. There is no evidence that Mary's daughters attended The Yorkville Female Institute, but later their cousin, Frances (Fannie) Brown was a student.

[13] Cain's Springs was located near the York and Cherokee County line, and was the frequent gathering place for those in the Beersheba community and beyond to come and take the cure, experiencing the healing water of the springs. Often picnics were held there, and a visit to the springs was an all day affair.

[14] Weddings were joyous occasions, requiring all the good food, fellowship and ritual that modern day weddings include. It was rare that a young man in the agrarian community of York County went outside his neighborhood for a wife. After he had called on the young woman an appropriate number of times, the day of the marriage was fixed, almost always on Tuesday or Thursday. The bride to be and her mother had been preparing for the wedding day for years, accumulating linens, woolens and furnishings for her home. The bride's father often contributed a good cow or horse as part of her dowry.

The marriage was usually celebrated at the home of the bride, and after the ceremony, there would be feasting and merry making. The home of the bride would be where they would spend their first night together. The next day, the bridal party went to the groom's home for the "infare." There, relatives and friends of the groom celebrated. The following Sunday, the couple made their appearance at church. The bride and groom, along with their special attendants, arrayed in their wedding finery, would arrive at church and enter after everyone was seated. The couple would proceed, arm in arm down the aisle to their pew, thereby announcing to the rest of the community that they were husband and wife. Mary's niece, Amanda Floyd, is married on a Tuesday. On Thursday, two more nieces marry Quinn brothers to cap off a week of joyous wedding activities.

[15] The September 4, 1856 issue of The Yorkville Enquirer reported a "very heavy rain, accompanied by a severe North Easter, fell in many portions of our district, doing much damage to the corn crops, especially those on bottom lands. The impression seemed to be general that not more than one half an average crop would be made." The damage from the heavy rain, coupled with the summer's drought, had jeopardized the corn harvest for 1856.

[16] FENCED THE TABLE: This expression was used when observing Communion. Only those deemed worthy to partake of communion were invited to the table. The term fencing is administering a warning towards those who have gathered at the communion service. A fence separates in order to restrain, on the one hand, and to gather and to protect on the other hand. When the table of the Lord is fenced, those involved in scandalous, unrepentant sin are to be restrained, while repentant sinners are invited to come and partake of the sacred meal. During the 1800s tokens were given to the people in the church who were considered worthy to partake of the elements. The Communion tokens were returned to the church at the time of the communion.

[17] John Janes' mill was located on Henry's Knob in the western portion of York County near the SC/NC boundary line.

[18] In early 1857, a prediction was made in England that a comet would strike the earth on 13 June, 1857. Many were alarmed and end-of-world prophecies abounded. Others were merely amused.

[19] The flux was an abnormal discharge from the bowels, often called dysentary. It was sometimes diagnosed as cholera.

[20] G. L. Thomasson's brother Hiram bought his land, but not before Lafayette had advertised in the Yorkville Enquirer. His property, on the Kings Mountain Road and about 3 miles north of Yorkville, contained 260 acres, a good dwelling house, a gold mine, good bottom land and a "first rate meadow."

[21] Thomas Jefferson Bell, a Yorkville attorney, was put on trial for the shooting of Mr. Allen. The trial lasted three days with the Jury rendering a verdict of manslaughter. The sentence of the Court was imprisonment for one year and a fine of one thousand dollars.

[22] Mary is permitted to go to church again two and a half months after the birth of her son, William Given Brown.

[23] Thomas H. Dickson, co-owner with his brother of a tailor shop in Yorkville, was put on trial for the murder of his cousin, Bernhard Derer. The Yorkville Enquirer reported that most in the community regarded Dickson's offense as one of "excusable homicide." Dickson was convicted of manslaughter, with a recommendation to mercy. He was sentenced to two months imprisonment and a fine of two hundred dollars. A petition for clemency was immediately circulated among the community and was signed by many and sent to the Governor.

[24] The Grange movement began during Reconstruction all across the South. It was the first segment in a long chain of organizations that expressed the discontentment of farmers and ultimately lead to the revolt headed by the populist party in the 1890's. For more information on The Grange see West, Robert Jerald L. *"The Grange" Patrons of Husbandry in York County, South Carolina*, Broad River Basin Historical Society, Hickory Grove, South Carolina, June 1998.